HANDBOOK OF MILITARY TERMS AND DEFINITIONS

HANDBOOK OF MILITARY TERMS AND DEFINITIONS

By

K. K SINGH

M. Sc. (Mathematics),
PGDBM (HR/Marketing)
C.A.- IIB, an Ex-Serviceman, Banker and HR/ Administration/Facilities/IR -Professional.

Neha Publishers & Distributors

4832/24, Prahlad Lane, S-207 Ansari Raod, Daryaganj, New Delhi-110002

Published by
Neha Publishers & Distributors
4832/24, Prahlad Lane, S-207 Ansari Raod, Daryaganj,
New Delhi-110002
Tel.: 011-43570976, 23278261
Email-nehapubdistributors@gmail.com

First Edition : 2013

ISBN : 978-93-80318-48-6

Price : 1695/-

Laser Typesetting by : Vinod Bhardwaj

Printed at: VIKAS COMPUTERS,Delhi

PRINTED IN INDIA

Published by Neha Publishers & Distributors, New Delhi-110002

PREFACE

This book has been designed to meet the requirements of all the People of India or abroad who are interested in History , Geography, Psychology and effects of Science and Technologies on the Indo-China War and Indo-China Relations in past and effects of that war in the present and future. Students who are preparing for different Competitions with regard to Army Navy and Air Force and for the onward studies of Courses at different Arny Colleges and Scools or taking lessons at the august Universities of India or abroad. It would be helpful for all who are appearing at graduation or post graduation in the Army, Navy and Air Force in the the Indian Universities. This type of knowledge must be known to ALL.

This book is not only limited to Battle Field but also have numerous amount of knowledgeable informations and rational activities. Every educated person has write to know the all round knowledge of the world.

The present book is a novel attempt to cover a wide range of the problems of societies. This book faces very busy ideological preparedness in my life. I have written about different knowledgeable matters though it is not our area of professional work., it is in the context of all round subjects that we have studied partially , but in this book it has by no means unlimited to that context.

The problem is not a lack of knowledge or resources. The real problem is that they simply do not read those things. They spend their time spinning their wheels, attending meetings and responding to every little query and problem.

And to so many others who have been left unnamed. We are also grateful to the United States of America and United Kingdom of England for their great help from Educational Associations of Literature Studies, which provided a literature, without that nothing was possible. I am also thankful to community of colleagues whose help and advice improved the quality of our thinking and portrayal of this book.

What I have described in this book are as follows:

- Film and Craft,
- Health and Wellness,
- Mental Development and Wonderful thoughts,
- History and Government,
- Science and Technology
- Law and Order- Policing,
- Internet and computer

(Total 108 topics)

This book seeks to serve as a reliable guide and companion to all students and educated people of this world, and all those who are involved directly or indirectly with the Education of different groups. Although efforts are required for a drastic change in the English Literature studies in India or in abroad, yet it will still take quite some time to get those proposals translated into reality.

In this context I would like to enunciate that the Capitalism or hoarding of resources at the center point it will not do the society's problems to be resolved in the near future. Resources are meant for all not for counted people in the segment of studies or with some Temple Estates, so called Gurus and so many types of property hoarders which are becoming gorgeously richer and richer and our poverty stricken people are in dearth of even two loaves of bread a day.

At one place, abundance of lavishness and aristocracy is prevailed and at another, there is nothing to be pulled on their life. This ingratitude must be worn out from the society of India. Now days, few people are busy with the hoarding of the cash and kind from all means. They don't have any thinking behind it that how the rest of the population will survive even with appropriate needs of the survival.

That is why the need to know the rudimentary rules and rubrics of law for all, as these is necessary. Much has been changing in general laws but nothing we find in shape of progress and prosperity. The basic tenet and underpinning philosophy of general laws is to protect the interests of the people by saving them from exploitation and harassment on one hand and providing enough leverage and stick of good governance to the Government so as to have conducive art of living culture on the other hand. The cordial and congenial relationship can be had only when both the limbs of society have better understanding in the light of the limits of their rights, responsibilities and duties.

As stated ibid, they are something serious rather than contextual but everything is fair in LOVE and WAR. Here love is for the public of India and war is against the cruel people of society who are behaving like blackcaps of India.

Most of the Indian professionals are unable to forget work while on a holiday, working up to three hours instead of enjoying the free time with family and friends. Developments in technology mean that students are always connected and the temptation to check emails and complete any tasks that follow on from them is easy to succumb to.

It does not matter that only a few in each generation will grasp and achieve the full reality of man's proper stature—and that the rest will betray it. It is those few that move the world and give life its meaning—and it is these few that we have always sought to address. The rest are no concern of mine; it is not me or all others that they will betray: it is their own souls.

Now, it is, I am hoping in very compassionate way that this book will be proved in positive manner, boon for the readers.

Faridabad
2013

Krishna Kumar Singh

SECTION ONE

MILITARY TERMS AND DEFINITIONS

This Chapter contains a comprehensive list of military terms and definitions.

Abort: 1. To terminate a mission for any reason other than enemy action. It may occur at any point after the beginning of the mission and prior to its completion. 2. To discontinue aircraft take-off or missile launch.

Absolute altimeter: A type of altimeter which measures vertical distance to the surface below, using radio, radar, sonic, laser, or capacitive technology.

Absolute dud: A nuclear weapon which, when launched at or emplaced on a target, fails to explode.

Absolute filter: A filter capable of cutting off 100% by weight of solid particles greater than a stated micron size.

Absolute height: The height of an aircraft directly above the surface or terrain over which it is flying.

Acceptability: The joint operation plan review criterion for assessing whether the contemplated course of action is proportional and worth the cost in personnel, equipment, materiel, time involved, or position; is consistent with the law of war; and is militarily and politically supportable.

Access to classified information: The ability and opportunity to obtain knowledge of classified information. Persons have access to classified information if they are permitted to gain knowledge of the information or if they are in a place where they would be expected to gain such knowledge. Persons do not have access to classified information by being in a place where classified information is kept if security measures prevent them from gaining knowledge of the information.

Accidental attack: An unintended attack which occurs without deliberate national design as a direct result of a random event, such as a mechanical failure, a simple human error, or an unauthorized action by a subordinate.

Accompanying supplies: Unit supplies that deploy with forces.

Accountability: The obligation imposed by law or lawful order or regulation on an officer or other person for keeping accurate record of property, documents, or funds. The person having this obligation may or may not have actual possession of the property, documents, or funds. Accountability is concerned primarily with records, while responsibility is concerned primarily with custody, care, and safekeeping.

Accounting line designator: A five-character code, consisting of the target desired ground zero designator and the striking command suffix, to indicate a specific nuclear strike by a specified weapon delivery system on a target objective to the operation plan.

Accuracy of fire: The precision of fire expressed by the closeness of a grouping of shots at and around the center of the target.

Acoustical surveillance: Employment of electronic devices, including sound-recording,-receiving, or -transmitting equipment, for the collection of information.

Acoustic circuit: A mine circuit which responds to the acoustic field of a target.

Acoustic intelligence: Intelligence derived from the collection and processing of acoustic phenomena.

Acoustic jamming: -The deliberate radiation or irradiation of mechanical or electroacoustic signals with the objectives of obliterating or obscuring signals that the enemy is attempting to receive and of disrupting enemy weapons systems. Barrage jamming; electronic warfare; jamming; spot jamming.

Acoustic mine: A mine with an acoustic circuit which responds to the acoustic field of a ship or sweep.

Acoustic mine hunting: The use of a sonar to detect mines or mine-like objects which may be on or protruding from the seabed, or buried.

Acoustic warfare: Action involving the use of underwater acoustic energy to determine, exploit, reduce, or prevent hostile use of the underwater acoustic spectrum and actions which retain friendly use of the underwater acoustic spectrum. There are three divisions within acoustic warfare. acoustic warfare support measures. That aspect of acoustic warfare involving actions to search for, intercept, locate, record, and analyze radiated acoustic energy in water for the purpose of exploiting such radiations. The use of acoustic warfare support measures involves no intentional underwater acoustic emission and is generally not detectable by the enemy. Acoustic warfare countermeasures. That aspect of acoustic warfare involving actions taken to prevent or reduce an enemy's effective use of the underwater acoustic spectrum. Acoustic warfare countermeasures involve intentional underwater acoustic emissions for deception and jamming. acoustic warfare counter-countermeasures. That aspect of acoustic warfare involving actions taken to ensure friendly effective use of the underwater acoustic spectrum despite the enemy's use of underwater acoustic warfare. Acoustic warfare counter-countermeasures involve anti-acoustic warfare support measures and anti acoustic warfare countermeasures, and may not involve underwater acoustic emissions.

Acquire — 1. When applied to acquisition radars, the process of detecting the presence and location of a target in sufficient detail to permit identification. 2. When applied to tracking radars, the process of positioning a radar beam so that a target is in that beam to permit the effective employment of weapons.

Acquisition and cross-servicing agreement: Agreements negotiated on a bilateral basis with US allies or coalition partners that allow US forces to exchange most common types of support, including food, fuel, transportation, ammunition, and equipment. Authority to negotiate these agreements is usually delegated to the combatant commander by the Secretary of Defense. Authority to execute these agreements lies with the Secretary of Defense, and may or may not be delegated. Governed by legal guidelines, these agreements are used for contingencies, peacekeeping operations, unforeseen emergencies, or exercises to correct logistic deficiencies that cannot be adequately corrected by national means. The support received or given is reimbursed under the conditions of the acquisition and cross-servicing agreement.

Action agent: In intelligence usage, one who has access to, and performs actions against, the target.

Action deferred: Tactical action on a specific track is being withheld for better tactical advantage. Weapons are available and commitment is pending.

Action information center: Air defense control center; combat information center.

Action phase: In an amphibious operation, the period of time between the arrival of the landing forces of the amphibious force in the operational area and the accomplishment of their mission. Amphibious force; amphibious operation; landing force; mission.

Activation: Order to active duty in the federal service.

Activation detector: A device used to determine neutron flux or density by virtue of the radioactivity induced in it as a result of neutron capture.

Active air defence: Direct defensive action taken to destroy, nullify, or reduce the effectiveness of hostile air and missile threats against friendly forces and assets. It includes the use of aircraft, air defense weapons, electronic warfare, and other available weapons.

Active defence: The employment of limited offensive action and counterattacks to deny a contested area or position to the enemy. Passive defense.

Active duty: Full-time duty in the active military service of the United States. This includes members of the Reserve Components serving on active duty or full-time training duty, but does not include full-time National Guard duty. Active duty for training; inactive duty training.

Active Guard and Reserve: National Guard and Reserve members who are on voluntary active duty providing full-time support to National Guard, Reserve, and Active Component organizations for the purpose of organizing, administering, recruiting, instructing, or training the Reserve Components.

Active homing guidance: A system of homing guidance wherein both the source for illuminating the target and the receiver for detecting the energy reflected from the target as the result of the illumination are carried within the missile.

Active mine: A mine actuated by the reflection from a target of a signal emitted by the mine.

Active sealift forces: Military Sealift Command active, common-user sealift and the afloat pre-positioning force, including the required cargo handling and delivery systems as well as necessary operating personnel. Afloat pre-positioning force; common-user sealift; Military Sealift Command.

Active status: Status of all Reserves except those on an inactive status list or in the Retired Reserve. Reservists in an active status may train for points and/

or pay and may be considered for promotion.

Activity: 1. A unit, organization, or installation performing a function or mission, e.g., reception center, redistribution center, naval station, naval shipyard. 2. A function, mission, action, or collection of actions.

Act of mercy: In personnel recovery, assistance rendered to evaders by an individual or elements of the local population who sympathize or empathize with the evaders' cause or plight. Evader; evasion; recovery; recovery operations.

Actual ground zero: The point on the surface of the Earth at, or vertically below or above, the center of an actual nuclear detonation.

Actuate: To operate a mine-firing mechanism by an influence or a series of influences in such a way that all the requirements of the mechanism for firing, or for registering a target count, are met.

Acute care services: Medical services provided for patients with conditions that generally have a rapid onset and follow a short course or require immediate attention. Most battlefield care rendered after wounding, illness, or injury onset is acute care service. Acute care service is delivered after the onset of symptoms, which differentiates it from preventive care that is delivered before symptoms appear.

Acute radiation dose: Total ionizing radiation dose received at one time and over a period so short that biological recovery cannot occur.

Acute radiation syndrome: An acute illness caused by irradiation of the body by a high dose of penetrating radiation in a very short period of time.

Adequacy: The joint operation plan review criterion for assessing whether the scope and concept of planned operations can accomplish the assigned mission and comply with the planning guidance provided. Acceptability; feasibility.

Adjust: An order to the observer or spotter to initiate an adjustment on a designated target.

Administrative airlift service: The airlift service normally provided by specifically identifiable aircraft assigned to organizations or commands for internal administration.

Administrative escort: A warship or merchant ship under naval control, carrying a convoy commodore and staff, and serving as a platform for simultaneous communication with an operational control authority and a coastal convoy.

Administrative landing: An unopposed landing involving debarkation from vessels that have been administratively loaded. Administrative loading; administrative movement; logistics over-the-shore operations.

Administrative loading: A loading system which gives primary consideration to achieving maximum utilization of troop and cargo space without regard to tactical considerations. Equipment and supplies must be unloaded and sorted before they can be used. Commercial loading.

Administrative movement: A movement in which troops and vehicles are arranged to expedite their movement and conserve time and energy when no enemy interference, except by air, is anticipated.

Administrative order: An order covering traffic, supplies, maintenance, evacuation, personnel, and other administrative details.

Administrative shipping: Support shipping that is capable of transporting troops and cargo from origin to destination, but that cannot be loaded or unloaded without non As organic personnel and/or equipment. Administrative loading; administrative movement.

Advanced base: A base located in or near an operational area whose primary mission is to support military operations.

Advanced geospatial intelligence: Refers to the technical, geospatial, and intelligence information derived through interpretation or analysis using advanced processing of all data collected by imagery or imagery-related collection systems. Also known as imagery-derived measurement and signature intelligence.

Advanced operations base: In special operations, a small temporary base established near or within a joint special operations area to command, control, and/or support training or tactical operations. Facilities are normally austere. The base may be ashore or afloat. If ashore, it may include an airfield or unimproved airstrip, a pier, or an anchorage. An advanced operations base is normally controlled and/or supported by a main operations base or a forward operations base. Forward operations base; main operations base.

Advance force: A temporary organization within the amphibious task force which precedes the main body to the objective area. Its function is to participate in preparing the objective for the main assault by conducting such operations as reconnaissance, seizure of supporting positions, mines weeping, preliminary bombardment, underwater demolitions, and air support.

Advance guard: Detachment sent ahead of the main force to ensure its uninterrupted advance; to protect the main body against surprise; to facilitate the advance by removing obstacles and repairing roads and bridges; and to cover the deployment of the main body if it is committed to action.

Advance guard reserve: Second of the two main parts of an advance guard, the other being the advance guard support. It protects the main force and is itself protected by the advance guard support. Small advance guards do not have reserves.

Advance guard support: First of the two main parts of an advance guard, the other being the advance guard reserve. It is made up of three smaller elements, in order from front to rear, the advance guard point, the advance party, and the support proper. The advance guard support protects the advance guard reserve.

Adversary: A party acknowledged as potentially hostile to a friendly party and against which the use of force may be envisaged.

Advisory area: A designated area within a flight information region where air traffic advisory service is available.

Aerial port: An airfield that has been designated for the sustained air movement of personnel and materiel as well as an authorized port for entrance into or departure from the country where located. Port of debarkation; port of embarkation.

Aerial port control center: The agency responsible for the management and control of all aerial port resources and for the receipt and dissemination of all airlift requirements received from the airlift control team as the joint force commander's agent. Aerial port; airlift control team.

Aerial port squadron: An Air Force organization that operates and provides the functions assigned to aerial ports, including processing personnel and cargo, rigging for airdrop, packing parachutes, loading equipment, preparing air cargo and load plans, loading and securing aircraft, ejecting cargo for in-flight delivery, and supervising units engaged in aircraft loading and unloading operations.

Aerodynamic missile: A missile which uses aerodynamic forces to maintain its flight path. Ballistic missile; guided missile.

Aero medical evacuation: The movement of patients under medical supervision to and between medical treatment facilities by air transportation.

Aero medical evacuation control officer: An officer of the air transport force or air command controlling the flow of patients by air.

Aero medical evacuation control team: A cell within the air operations center and one of the core teams in the air mobility division. Provides command and control for theater Aero medical evacuation elements. It is responsible to the director of mobility forces for current Aero medical evacuation operational planning and mission execution. The Aero medical evacuation control team analyzes patient movement requirements; coordinates airlift to meet Aero medical evacuation requirements; tasks the appropriate Aero medical evacuation elements including special medical requirements, when necessary; and passes mission information to the patient movement requirement center. Aero medical evacuation; Aero medical evacuation cell; air mobility division.

Aero medical evacuation system: A system that provides: a. control of patient movement by air transport; b. specialized medical aircrew, medical crew augmentees, and specialty medical attendants and equipment for in flight medical care; c. facilities on or in the vicinity of air strips and air bases for the limited medical care of in transit patients entering, en route via, or leaving the system; and d. communication with originating, destination, and en route medical facilities concerning patient transportation. Aero medical evacuation.

Aero medical evacuation unit: An operational medical organization concerned primarily with the management and control of patients being transported via an Aero medical evacuation system or system echelon.

Aeronautical chart: A specialized representation of mapped features of the Earth, or some part of it, produced to show selected terrain, cultural and hydrographic features, and supplemental information required for air navigation, pilot age, or for planning air operations.

Aeronautical information overprint: Additional information which is printed or stamped on a map or chart for the specific purpose of air navigation.

Aeronautical plotting chart: A chart designed for the graphical processes of navigation.

Aerospace: Of, or pertaining to, Earth's envelope of atmosphere and the space above it; two separate entities considered as a single realm for activity in launching, guidance, and control of vehicles that will travel in both entities.

Aerospace defence: 1. All defensive measures designed to destroy or nullify attacking enemy aircraft and missiles and also negate hostile space systems. 2. An inclusive term encompassing air defense, ballistic missile defense, and space defense.

Afloat pre-positioning operations: Pre-positioning of ships, preloaded with equipment and supplies (including ammunition and petroleum) that provides for an alternative to land-based programs. This concept provides for ships and onboard force support equipment and supplies positioned near potential crisis areas that can be delivered rapidly to joint airlifted forces in the operational area. Afloat pre-positioning in forward areas enhances a force's capability to respond to a crisis, resulting in faster reaction time.

Afloat pre-positioning ships: Forward deployed merchant ships loaded with tactical equipment and supplies to support the initial deployment of military forces. Merchant ship.

Air alert: Airborne alert; air defense warning conditions; ground alert.

Air and space expeditionary task force: A deployed numbered air force (NAF) or command echelon immediately subordinate to a NAF provided as the US Air Force component command committed to a joint operation. Air expeditionary force; air expeditionary wing.

Air assault: The movement of friendly assault forces by rotary-wing aircraft to engage and destroy enemy forces or to seize and hold key terrain.

Air assault force: A force composed primarily of ground and rotary-wing air units organized, equipped, and trained for air assault operations.

Air assault operation: An operation in which assault forces (combat, combat support, and combat service support), using the mobility of rotary-wing assets and the total integration of available firepower, maneuver under the control of a ground or air maneuver commander to engage enemy forces or to seize and hold key terrain.

Air attack: 1. **coordinated** — A combination of two or more types of air attack (dive, glide, low-level) in one strike, using one or more types of aircraft. 2. **deferred** – A procedure in which attack groups rendezvous as a single unit. It is used when attack groups are launched from more than one station with their departure on the mission being delayed pending further orders. 3. **divided** - A method of delivering a coordinated air attack which consists of holding the units in close tactical concentration up to a point, then splitting them to attack an objective from different directions.

Airborne: 1. In relation to personnel, troops especially trained to effect, following transport by air, an assault debarkation, either by parachuting or touchdown. 2. In relation to equipment, pieces of equipment that have been especially designed for use by airborne troops during or after an assault debarkation. It also designates some aeronautical equipment used to accomplish a particular mission. 3. When applied to materiel, items that form an integral part of the aircraft. 4. The state of an aircraft, from the instant it becomes entirely sustained by air until it ceases to be so sustained. A lighter-than-air aircraft is not considered to be airborne when it is attached to the ground, except that moored balloons are airborne whenever sent aloft. Air transportable unit.

Airborne alert: A state of aircraft readiness wherein combat-equipped aircraft are airborne and ready for immediate action. Fighter cover. It is designed to reduce reaction time and to increase survivability. combat air patrol; fighter cover; ground alert.

Airborne assault weapon: An unarmored, mobile, full-tracked gun providing a mobile antitank capability for airborne troops.

Airborne command post: A suitably equipped aircraft used by the commander for the control of his or her forces.

Airborne early warning: The detection of enemy air or surface units by radar or other equipment carried in an airborne vehicle, and the transmitting of a warning to friendly units.

Airborne early warning and control: Air surveillance and control provided by airborne early warning aircraft which are equipped with search and height-finding radar and communications equipment for controlling weapon systems.

Airborne force: A force composed primarily of ground and air units organized, equipped, and trained for airborne operations.

Airborne interception equipment: A fire control system, including radar equipment, installed in interceptor aircraft used to effect air interception.

Airborne lift: The total capacities expressed in terms of personnel and cargo that are, or can be, carried by available aircraft in one trip.

Airborne operation: An operation involving the air movement into an objective area of combat forces and their logistic support for execution of a tactical, operational, or strategic mission. The means employed may be any combination of airborne units, air transportable units, and types of transport aircraft, depending on the mission and the overall situation. Assault; assault phase.

Airborne order: A command and authorization for flight when a predetermined time greater than five minutes is established for aircraft to become airborne.

Airborne radio relay:-Airborne equipment used to relay radio transmission from selected originating transmitters.

Airborne sensor operator: An individual trained to operate sensor equipment aboard aircraft and to perform limited interpretations of collected information produced in flight.

Airborne troops: Those ground units whose primary mission is to make assault landings from the air.

Air-breathing missile: -A missile with an engine requiring the intake of air for combustion of its fuel, as in a ramjet or turbojet. To be contrasted with the rocket missile, which carries its own oxidizer and can operate beyond the atmosphere.

Airburst: An explosion of a bomb or projectile above the surface as distinguished from an explosion on contact with the surface or after penetration.

Air cargo: Stores, equipment or vehicles, which do not form part of the aircraft, and are either part or all of its payload.

Air cartographic camera: A camera having the accuracy and other characteristics essential for air survey or cartographic photography.

Air cartographic photography: The taking and processing of air photographs for mapping and charting purposes.

Air component coordination element: An Air Force component element that interfaces and provides liaison with the joint force land component commander, or commander Army forces. The air component coordination element is the senior Air Force element assisting the joint force land component commander, or commander Army forces in planning air component supporting and supported requirements. The air component coordination element is responsible to the joint force air component commander and coordinates with the joint force land component commander's staff, representing the joint force air component commander's needs in either a supporting or supported role.

Air corridor: A restricted air route of travel specified for use by friendly aircraft and established for the purpose of preventing friendly aircraft from being fired on by friendly forces.

Aircraft: Inactive aircraft inventory; program aircraft; reserve aircraft; supporting aircraft; unit aircraft.

Aircraft arresting barrier: A device, not dependent on an aircraft arresting hook, used to stop an aircraft by absorbing its forward momentum in an emergency landing or an aborted takeoff. Also called barricade; emergency barrier.

Aircraft arresting cable: That portion of an aircraft arresting system which spans the runway surface or flight deck landing area and is engaged by the aircraft arresting hook. Aircraft arresting wire.

Aircraft arresting gear: A device used to engage hook-equipped aircraft to absorb the forward momentum of a routine or emergency landing or aborted takeoff.

Aircraft arresting hook: A device fitted to an aircraft to engage arresting gear. Tail hook. Aircraft arresting system.

Aircraft arresting system: A series of components used to stop an aircraft by absorbing its momentum in a routine or emergency landing or aborted takeoff. Aircraft arresting barrier; aircraft arresting gear; aircraft arresting hook.

Aircraft arresting wire: Aircraft arresting cable. Aircraft arresting system.

Aircraft arrestment: -Controlled stopping of an aircraft by external means.

Aircraft block speed: True airspeed in knots under zero wind conditions adjusted in relation to length of sortie to compensate for takeoff, climb out, letdown, instrument approach, and landing.

Aircraft carrier: A warship designed to support and operate aircraft, engage in attacks on targets afloat or ashore, and engage in sustained operations in support of other forces. Designated as CV or CVN. CVN is nuclear powered.

Aircraft commander: The aircrew member designated by competent authority as being in command of an aircraft and responsible for its safe operation and accomplishment of the assigned mission.

Aircraft control and warning system: A system established to control and report the movement of aircraft. It consists of observation facilities, control center, and necessary communications.

Aircraft loading table: A data sheet used by the airlift commander containinginformation as to the load that actually goes into each aircraft.

Aircraft mission equipment: Equipment that must be fitted to an aircraft to enable it to fulfill a particular mission or task.

Aircraft modification: A change in the physical characteristics of aircraft, accomplished either by a change in production specifications or by alteration of items already produced.

Aircraft monitoring and control: That equipment installed in aircraft to permitmonitoring and control of staffing, arming, and fuzing functions of nuclear weapons or nuclear weapon systems.

Aircraft scrambling: Directing the immediate takeoff of aircraft from a ground alert condition of readiness.

Aircraft store: Any device intended for internal or external carriage and mounted on aircraft suspension and release equipment, whether or not the item is intended to be separated in flight from the aircraft. Aircraft stores are classified in two categories as follows. a. expendable store – An aircraft store normally separated from the aircraft in flight such as a missile, rocket, bomb, nuclear weapon, mine, torpedo, pyrotechnic device, sono buoy, signal underwater sound device, or other similar items. b. nonexpendable store – An aircraft store which is not normally separated from the aircraft in flight such as a tank (fuel and spray), line-source disseminator, pod, multiple rack, target, cargo drop container, drone, or other similar items.

Aircraft tie down: Securing aircraft when parked in the open to restrain movement due to the weather or condition of the parking area.

Aircraft transient servicing: Services performed on an aircraft by an organization other than that to which the aircraft is assigned and for which there may be a financial charge. This activity is separate from the established aircraft cross-servicing program and requires that the transient aircrew supervise the correct application of ground crew procedures.

Aircraft utilization: Average numbers of hours during each 24-hour period that an aircraft is actually in flight.

Aircraft vectoring: The directional control of in-flight aircraft through transmission of azimuth headings.

Air cushion vehicle: A vehicle capable of being operated so that its weight, including its payload, is wholly or significantly supported on a continuously generated cushion or "bubble" of air at higher than ambient pressure.

Air defence: Defensive measures designed to destroy attacking enemy aircraft or missiles in the atmosphere, or to nullify or reduce the effectiveness of such attack. Active air defence; aerospace defence; passive air defence.

Air defence area: -1. overseas – A specifically defined airspace for which air defence must be planned and provided. 2. United States – Airspace of defined dimensions designated by the appropriate agency within which the ready control of airborne vehicles is required in the interest of national security during an air defense emergency.

Air defence artillery: Weapons and equipment for actively combating air targets from the ground.

Air defence control center: The principal information, communications, andoperations center from which all aircraft, antiaircraft operations, air defense artillery, guided missiles, and air warning functions of a specific area of air defense responsibility are supervised and coordinated. Air defence operations center.

Air defence direction center – An installation having the capability of performing air surveillance, interception, control, and direction of allocated air defense weapons within an assigned sector of responsibility. It may also have an identification capability.

Air defence emergency: An emergency condition, declared by the Commander in Chief, North American Air Defense Command, that exists when attack upon the continental United States, Alaska, Canada, or United States installations in Greenland by hostile aircraft or missiles is considered probable, is imminent, or is taking place.

Air defence ground environment: The network of ground radar sites and command and control centers within a specific theater of operations which are used for the tactical control of air defence operations.

Air defence identification zone: Airspace of defined dimensions within which the ready identification, location, and control of airborne vehicles are required.

Air defence operations team: A team of United States Air Force ground environment personnel assigned to certain allied air defense control and warning units/elements.

Air defence readiness: An operational status requiring air defense forces to maintain higher than ordinary preparedness for a short period of time.

Air defence region: A geographical subdivision of an air defence area. **Air defence sector:** A geographical subdivision of an air defence region.

Air defence warning conditions: A degree of air raid probability according to the following code. The term air defence region/sector referred to herein may include forces and units afloat and/or deployed to forward areas, as applicable. Air defense warning yellow – attack by hostile aircraft and/or missiles is probable. This means that hostile aircraft and/or missiles are en route toward an air defence region/sector, or unknown aircraft and/or missiles suspected to be hostile are en route toward or are within an air defence region/sector. Air defence warning red – attack by hostile aircraft and/or missiles is imminent or is in progress. This means that hostile aircraft and/or missiles are within an air defence region/sector or are in the immediate vicinity of an air defence region/sector with high probability of entering the region/sector. **Warning white:** attack by hostile aircraft and/or missiles is improbable. May be called either before or after air defence warning yellow or red. The initial declaration of air defence emergency will automatically establish a condition of air defense warning other than white for purposes of security control of air traffic. Warning white /warning yellow

Air delivery container: A sling, bag, or roll, usually of canvas or webbing, designed to hold supplies and equipment for air delivery. **Air delivery equipment:** Special items of equipment used in air delivery of personnel, supplies, and equipment.

Air direct delivery: The inter theater air movement of cargo or personnel from an airlift point of embarkation to a point as close as practicable to the user's specified final destination, thereby minimizing transshipment requirements. Air direct delivery eliminates the traditional Air Force two step inter theater and intra theater airlift transshipment mission mix.

Airdrop: The unloading of personnel or materiel from aircraft in flight. Airdrop platform; air movement; free drop; free fall; high velocity drop; low velocity drop.

Airdrop platform: A base upon which vehicles, cargo, or equipment are loaded for airdrop.

Air employment/allocation plan: The means by which subordinate commanders advise the joint force commander of planned employment/allocation of organic or assigned assets, of any expected excess sorties, or of any additional air support requirements.

Air expeditionary force: Deployed US Air Force wings, groups, and squadronscommitted to a joint operation.

Air expeditionary wing: A wing or wing slice placed under the administrative control of an air and space expeditionary task force or air and space task force by Department of the Air Force orders for a joint operation.

Air facility: An installation from which air operations may be or are being conducted.

Airfield: An area prepared for the accommodation (including any buildings, installations, and equipment), landing, and takeoff of aircraft. See also alternate airfield; departure airfield; landing area; landing point; landing site; main airfield; redeployment airfield.

Airfield traffic: All traffic on the maneuvering area of an airfield and all aircraftflying in the vicinity of an airfield.**Air Force air and space operations center:** The senior agency of the Air Forcecomponent commander that provides command and control of Air Force air and space operations and coordinates with other components and Services.

Air Force Component Headquarters: The field headquarters facility of the Air Force commander charged with the overall conduct of Air Force operations. It is composed of the command section and appropriate staff elements.

Air Force special operations base: A base, airstrip, or other appropriate facility that provides physical support to Air Force special operations forces (AFSOF). The facility may be used solely to support AFSOF or may be a portion of a larger base supporting other operations. As a supporting facility, it is distinct from the forces operating from or being supported by it.

Air Force special operations component: The Air Force component of a joint force special operations component. Army special operations component; Navy special operations component.

Air Force special operations detachment: A squadron-size headquarters that could be a composite organization composed of different Air Force special operations assets. The detachment is normally subordinate to an Air Force special operations component, joint special operations task force, or joint task force, depending upon size and duration of the operation.

Air Force special operations element: An element-size Air Force special operations headquarters. It is normally subordinate to an Air Force special operations component or detachment, depending upon size and duration of the operation.

Air Force special operations forces: Those Active and Reserve Component Air Force forces designated by the Secretary of Defense that are specifically organized, trained, and equipped to conduct and support special operations.

Airhead: 1. A designated area in a hostile or potentially hostile operational area that, when seized and held, ensures the continuous air landing of troops and materiel and provides the maneuver space necessary for projected operations. Normally it is the area seized in the assault phase of an airborne operation. 2. A designated location in an operational area used as a base for supply and evacuation by air.

Airhead line: A line denoting the limits of the objective area for an airborne assault. The airhead line is bounded by assault objectives that are operationally located to ensure that enemy fires cannot be brought to bear on the main objective and for friendly forces to conduct defensive operations in depth.

Air intercept control common: A tactical air-to-ground radio frequency, monitored by all air intercept control facilities within an area, that is used as a backup for other discrete tactical control frequencies.

Air interception: To effect visual or electronic contact by a friendly aircraft with another aircraft. Normally, the air intercept is conducted in the following five phases: a. climb phase – Airborne to cruising altitude.

b. maneuver phase — Receipt of initial vector to target until beginning transition to attack speed and altitude. c. transition phase — Increase or decrease of speed and altitude required for the attack. d. attack phase — Turn to attack heading, acquire target, complete attack, and turn to breakaway heading. e. recovery phase — Breakaway to landing.

Air interdiction: Air operations conducted to divert, disrupt, delay, or destroy the enemy's military potential before it can be brought to bear effectively against friendly forces, or to otherwise achieve objectives. Air interdiction is conducted at such distance from friendly forces that detailed integration of each air mission with the fire and movement of friendly forces is not required.

Air landed: Moved by air and disembarked, or unloaded, after the aircraft has landed or while a helicopter is hovering.

Air landed operation: An operation involving movement by air with a designated destination for further ground deployment of units and personnel and/or further ground distribution of supplies. Air landed.

Air-launched ballistic missile: A ballistic missile launched from an airborne vehicle.

Air liaison officer: The senior tactical air control party member attached to a ground unit who functions as the primary advisor to the ground commander on air power. An air liaison officer is usually an aeronautically rated officer. ALO.

Airlift capability: The total capacity expressed in terms of number of passengers and/or weight/cubic displacement of cargo that can be carried at any one time to a given destination by available airlift.

Airlift control team: A cell within the air operations center and one of the core teams in the air mobility division. The airlift control team brings intra theater airlift functional expertise from the theater organizations to plan, coordinate, manage, and execute intra theater airlift operations in the area of responsibility and joint operations area for the joint force air component commander. US Transportation Command and Air Mobility Command may augment the airlift control team with intra theater airlift expertise. These two sources of airlift expertise integrate into a single airlift control team within the air mobility division.

Airlift coordination cell: A cell within the air operations center which plans, coordinates, manages, and executes theater airlift operations in the area of responsibility or joint operations area. Normally consists of an airlift plans branch, an airlift operations branch, and an airlift support branch. ALCC. Air Force air and space operations center; area of responsibility; joint operations area.

Airlift mission commander: A commander designated when airlift aircraft are participating in airlift operations specified in the implementing directive. The airlift mission commander is usually designated by the commander of the deployed airlift unit, but may be selected by the Air Force component commander or joint force air component commander depending on the nature of the mission. Joint force air component commander.

Airlift requirement: The total number of passengers and/or weight/cubic displacement of cargo required to be carried by air for a specific task. Airlift capability.

Airlift service: The performance or procurement of air transportation and services incident thereto required for the movement of persons, cargo, mail, or other goods.

Air logistic support: Support by air landing or airdrop, including air supply, movement of personnel, evacuation of casualties and enemy prisoners of war, and recovery of equipment and vehicles.

Air logistic support operation: An air operation, excluding an airborne operation, conducted within a theater to distribute and recover personnel, equipment, and supplies.

Air mission intelligence report: A detailed report of the results of an air mission, including a complete intelligence account of the mission.

Airmobile forces: The ground combat, supporting, and air vehicle units required to conduct an airmobile operation.

Airmobile operation: An operation in which combat forces and their equipmentmove about the battlefield by aircraft to engage in ground combat.

Air mobility: The rapid movement of personnel, materiel and forces to and from or within a theater by air. This includes both airlift and air refueling. Air refueling.

Air Mobility Command: The Air Force component command of the US Transportation Command.

Air mobility control team: A cell within the air operations center and one of the core teams in the air mobility division. The air mobility control team is the centralized source of air mobility command, control, and communications for the director of mobility forces during mission execution. The director of mobility forces uses the air mobility control team to direct (or redirect as required) air mobility forces in concert with other air and space forces to respond to requirement changes, higher priorities, or immediate execution limitations. The air mobility control team deconflicts all air mobility operations into, out of, and within the area of responsibility or joint operations area. The air mobility control team maintains execution process and communications connectivity for tasking, coordination, and flight with the air operations center's combat operations division, subordinate air mobility units, and mission forces. Air Force air and space operations center; air mobility; air mobility division.

Air mobility division: Located in the joint air operations center to plan, coordinate, task, and execute the air mobility mission. Consists of the air mobility control team, airlift control team, aerial refueling control team, Aero medical evacuation control team, and the air mobility element. Coordinates with the joint force commander's movement requirements and control authority, the theater air mobility operations control center, if established, and the Air Mobility Command's tanker/airlift control center, as required.

Air mobility express: An express airlift system that is activated when Department of Defence requirements dictate. It is comprised of express carrier aircraft and related continental United States infrastructure, Air Mobility Command airlift, and an in theater rapid distribution system. Air mobility; Air Mobility Command.

Air mobility liaison officer: An officer specially trained to implement the theater air control system and to advise on control of airlift assets. They are highly qualified, rated airlift officers with airdrop airlift experience, and assigned duties supporting US Army units. Air mobility liaison officers provide expertise on the efficient use of air mobility assets.

Air movement: Air transport of units, personnel, supplies, and equipment including airdrops and air landings. Airdrop; air landed.

Air movement column: In airborne operations, the lead formation and the serials following, proceeding over the same flight path at the same altitude.

Air movement table: A table prepared by a ground force commander in coordination with an air force commander. This form, issued as an annex to the operation order: a. indicates the allocation of aircraft space to elements of the ground units to be airlifted; b. designates the number and type of aircraft in each serial; c. specifies the departure area, time of loading, and takeoff.

Air observer: An individual whose primary mission is to observe or take photographs from an aircraft in order to adjust artillery fire or obtain military information.

Air observer adjustment: The correcting of gunfire from an aircraft.

Air offensive: Sustained operations by strategic and/or tactical air weapon systems against hostile air forces or surface targets.

Air photographic reconnaissance: The obtaining of information by air photography, divided into three types: a. Strategic photographic reconnaissance; b. Tactical photographic reconnaissance; and c. Survey/cartographic photography-air photography taken for survey/cartographical purposes and to survey/cartographic standards of accuracy. It may be strategic or tactical.

Air picket: An airborne early warning aircraft positioned primarily to detect, report, and track approaching enemy aircraft or missiles and to control intercepts. Also called aerial picket. See also airborne early warning and control.

Air plot: 1. A continuous plot used in air navigation of a graphic representation oftrue headings steered and air distances flown. 2. A continuous plot of the position of an airborne object represented graphically to show true headings steered and air distances flown. 3. Within ships, a display that shows the positions and movements of an airborne object relative to the plotting ship.

Air portable: Denotes materiel which is suitable for transport by an aircraft loaded internally or externally, with no more than minor dismantling and reassembling within the capabilities of user units. This term must be qualified to show the extent of air portability.

Airport surface detection equipment: Short-range radar displaying the airport surface. Aircraft and vehicular traffic operating on runways, taxiways, and ramps, moving or stationary, may be observed with a high degree of resolution.

Airport surveillance radar: Radar displaying range and azimuth that is normallyemployed in a terminal area as an aid to approach- and departure-control.

Airport traffic area — Unless otherwise specifically designated, that airspace within a horizontal radius of five statute miles from the geographic center of any airport at which a control tower is operating, extending from the surface up to, but not including, an altitude of 3,000 feet above the elevation of the airport.

Air position: The calculated position of an aircraft assuming no wind effect.

Air priorities committee: A committee set up to determine the priorities of passengers and cargo.

Air raid reporting control ship: A ship to which the air defense ship has delegated the duties of controlling air warning radar and air raid reporting.

Air reconnaissance: The acquisition of information by employing visual observation and/or sensors in air vehicles.

Air reconnaissance liaison officer: An Army officer especially trained in airreconnaissance and imagery interpretation matters who is attached to a tactical air reconnaissance unit. This officer assists and advises the air commander and staff on matters concerning ground operations and informs the supported ground commander on the status of air reconnaissance requests.

Air refueling: The capability to refuel aircraft in flight, which extends presence, increases range, and serves as a force multiplier.

Air refueling control point: During refueling operations, the geographic point where the receiver arrives in the observation or pre contact position with respect to the tanker.

Air refueling control team: A cell within the air operations center and one of the core teams in the air mobility division. Part of the air operations center that coordinates aerial refueling planning, tasking, and scheduling to support combat air operations or to support a strategic air bridge within the area of responsibility or joint area of operations. Air Force air and space operations center; air mobility division; air refueling.

Air refueling control time: During refueling operations, the time the receiver and tanker arrive at the air refueling control point.

Air refueling initiation point: During refueling operations, a point located upstream from the air refueling control point (inbound to the air refueling control point) where the receiver aircraft initiates the rendezvous.

Air request net: A high frequency, single sideband, non secure net monitored by all tactical air control parties (TACPs) and the air support operations center (ASOC) that allows immediate requests to be transmitted from a TACP at any Army echelon directly to the ASOC for rapid response.

Air route: The navigable airspace between two points, identified to the extentnecessary for the application of flight rules.

Air route traffic control center: The principal facility exercising en route control of aircraft operating under instrument flight rules within its area of jurisdiction.Approximately 26 such centers cover the United States and its possessions. Each has a communication capability to adjacent centers.

Air smuggling event: In counterdrug operations, the departure of a suspected drug smuggling aircraft, an airdrop of drugs, or the arrival of a suspected drug smuggling aircraft.

Air sovereignty: A nation's inherent right to exercise absolute control and authority over the airspace above its territory. See also air sovereignty mission.

Air sovereignty mission: The integrated tasks of surveillance and control, the execution of which enforces a nation's authority over its territorial airspace.

Airspace control: Airspace control in the combat zone.

Airspace control area: Airspace that is laterally defined by the boundaries of the operational area, and may be subdivided into airspace control sectors.

Airspace control boundary: The lateral limits of an airspace control area, airspace control sector, high density airspace control zone, or airspace restricted area.

Airspace control center: The airspace control authority's primary airspace control facility, including assigned Service component, host-nation, and/or multinational personnel and equipment.

Airspace control facility: Any of the several Service component, host nation, ormultinational facilities that provide airspace control in the combat zone.

Airspace control in the combat zone: A process used to increase combat effectiveness by promoting the safe, efficient, and flexible use of airspace. Airspace control is provided in order to reduce the risk of friendly fire, enhance air defense operations, and permit greater flexibility of operations. Airspace control does not infringe on the authority vested in commanders to approve, disapprove, or deny combat operations. Airspace control; combat airspace control.

Airspace control order: An order implementing the airspace control plan that provides the details of the approved requests for airspace coordinating measures. It is published either as part of the air tasking order or as a separate document.

Airspace control plan: The document approved by the joint force commander that provides specific planning guidance and procedures for the airspace control system for the joint force operational area. Airspace control system; joint force commander.

Airspace control procedures: Rules, mechanisms, and directions that facilitate the control and use of airspace of specified dimensions. Airspace control authority; airspace control in a combat zone; airspace control order; airspace control plan.

Airspace control sector: A sub element of the airspace control area, established to facilitate the control of the overall area. Airspace control sector boundaries normally coincide with air defense organization subdivision boundaries. Airspace control sectors are designated in accordance with procedures and guidance contained in the airspace control plan in consideration of Service component, host nation, and multinational airspace control capabilities and requirements. Airspace control area.

Airspace control system: An arrangement of those organizations, personnel, policies, procedures, and facilities required to perform airspace control functions.

Airspace coordinating measures: Measures employed to facilitate the efficient use of airspace to accomplish missions and simultaneously provide safeguards for friendly forces. Airspace control area; airspace control boundary; airspace control sector; airspace coordination area; high-density airspace control zone; weapons engagement zone.

Airspace management: The coordination, integration, and regulation of the use of airspace of defined dimensions.

Airspace reservation: The airspace located above an area on the surface of the land or water, designated and set apart by Executive Order of the President or by a state, commonwealth, or territory, over which the flight of aircraft is prohibited or restricted for the purpose of national defense or for other governmental purposes.

Airspace restrictions: Special restrictive measures applied to segments of airspace of defined dimensions.

Airspeed : The speed of an aircraft relative to its surrounding air mass. The unqualified term "airspeed" can mean any one of the following. a. calibrated airspeed – Indicated airspeed corrected for instrument installation error. b. equivalent airspeed – Calibrated airspeed corrected for compressibility error. d. indicated airspeed – The airspeed shown by an airspeed indicator. e. true airspeed – Equivalent airspeed corrected for error due to air density.

Airspeed indicator: An instrument which displays the indicated airspeed of the aircraft derived from inputs of pilot and static pressures.

Air staging unit: A unit situated at an airfield and concerned with reception, handling, servicing, and preparation for departure of aircraft and control of personnel and cargo.

Air station: In photogrammetric, the point in space occupied by the camera lens at the moment of exposure.

Air strike: An attack on specific objectives by fighter, bomber, or attack aircraft on an offensive mission. May consist of several air organizations under a single command in the air.

Air strike coordinator: The air representative of the force commander in a target area, who is responsible for directing all aircraft in the target area and coordinating their efforts to achieve the most effective use of air striking power.

Air strip: An unimproved surface which has been adapted for takeoff or landing of aircraft, usually having minimum facilities.

Air superiority: That degree of dominance in the air battle of one force over another that permits the conduct of operations by the former and its related land, sea, and air forces at a given time and place without prohibitive interference by the opposing force.

Air supply: The delivery of cargo by airdrop or air landing.

Air support: All forms of support given by air forces on land or sea. Close air support; immediate air support; preplanned air support; tactical air support.

Air support operations center: The principal air control agency of the theater air control system responsible for the direction and control of air operations directly supporting the ground combat element. It processes and coordinates requests for immediate air support and coordinates air missions requiring integration with other supporting arms and ground forces. It normally collocates with the Army tactical headquarters senior fire support coordination center within the ground combat element.

Air support request: A means to request preplanned and immediate close air support, air interdiction, air reconnaissance, surveillance, escort, helicopter airlift, and other aircraft missions. AIRSUPREQ.

Air supremacy: That degree of air superiority wherein the opposing air force is incapable of effective interference.

Air surface zone: A restricted area established for the purpose of preventing friendly surface vessels and aircraft from being fired upon by friendly forces and for permitting antisubmarine operations, unrestricted by the operation of friendly submarines.

Air surveillance: The systematic observation of airspace by electronic, visual or other means, primarily for the purpose of identifying and determining the movements of aircraft and missiles, friendly and enemy, in the airspace under observation. Satellite and missile surveillance; surveillance.

Air surveillance officer: An individual responsible for coordinating and maintaining an accurate, current picture of the air situation within an assigned airspace area.

Air survey photography: -Air cartographic photography.

Air target chart: A display of pertinent air target intelligence on a specialized graphic base. It is designed primarily to support operations against designated air targets by various weapon systems.

Air Target Materials Program: A Department of Defense program under themanagement control of the National Imagery and Mapping Agency established for and limited to the production of medium- and large-scale map, chart, and geodetic products, that supports worldwide targeting requirements of the unified and specified commands, the Military Departments, and allied participants. It encompasses the determination of production and coverage requirements, standardization of products, establishment of production priorities and schedules, and the production, distribution, storage, and release/exchange of products included under it.

Air target mosaic: A large-scale mosaic providing photographic coverage of an area and permitting comprehensive portrayal of pertinent target detail. These mosaics are used for intelligence study and in planning and briefing for air operations.

Air tasking order: A method used to task and disseminate to components, subordinate units, and command and control agencies projected sorties, capabilities and/or forces to targets and specific missions. Normally provides specific instructions to include call signs, targets, controlling agencies, etc., as well as general instructions.

Air tasking order/confirmation: A message used to task joint force components; to inform the requesting command and the tasking authority of the action being taken; and/or to provide additional information about the mission. The message is used only for preplanned missions and is transmitted on a daily basis, normally 12 hours prior to the start of the air tasking day or in accordance with established operation plans for the operational area. ATOCONF.

Air terminal: A facility on an airfield that functions as an air transportation hub and accommodates the loading and unloading of airlift aircraft and the in transit processing of traffic. The airfield may or may not be designated an aerial port.

Air-to-air guided missile: An air-launched guided missile for use against air targets. Guided missile.

Air-to-surface guided missile: An air-launched guided missile for use against surface targets.

Air traffic control and landing system: Department of Defense facilities, personnel, and equipment (fixed, mobile, and seaborne) with associated avionics to provide safe, orderly, and expeditious aerospace vehicle movements worldwide.

Air traffic control center: A unit combining the functions of an area control center and a flight information center.

Air traffic control clearance: Authorization by an air traffic control authority for an aircraft to proceed under specified conditions.

Air traffic control facility: Any of the component airspace control facilities primarily responsible for providing air traffic control services and, as required, limited tactical control services.

Air traffic controller: An air controller especially trained for and assigned to the duty of airspace management and traffic control of airborne objects.

Air traffic control service: A service provided for the purpose of: a. preventing collisions: (1) between aircraft; and (2) on the maneuvering area between aircraft and obstructions; and b. expediting and maintaining an orderly flow of air traffic.

Air traffic identification: The use of electronic devices, operational procedures, visual observation, and/or flight plan correlation for the purpose of identifying and locating aircraft flying within the airspace control area.

Air traffic section: The link between the staging post and the local air priority committee. It is the key to the efficient handling of passengers and cargo at a staging post. It must include load control (including Customs and Immigrations facilities), freight, and mail sections.

Air transportable unit: A unit, other than airborne, whose equipment is adapted for air movement. Airborne; airborne operation.

Air transported operations: The movement by aircraft of troops and their equipment for an operation.

Air transport group: A task organization of transport aircraft units that provides air transport for landing force elements or provides logistic support.

Airways station: A ground communication installation established, manned, and equipped to communicate with aircraft in flight, as well as with other designated airways installations, for the purpose of expeditious and safe movements of aircraft. These stations may or may not be located on designated airways.

Air weapons controller: An individual especially trained for and assigned to the duty of employing and controlling air weapon systems against airborne and surface objects.

Alert force: Specified forces maintained in a special degree of readiness.

Alerting service: A service provided to notify appropriate organizations regarding aircraft in need of search and rescue aid, and assist such organizations as required.

All appropriate action: Action taken in self-defense that is reasonable in intensity, duration, and magnitude, based on all the facts known to the commander at the time.

Alliance — The relationship that results from a formal agreement between two or more nations for broad, long-term objectives that further the common interests of the members.

Allocation: In a general sense, distribution for employment of limited forces and resources among competing requirements. Specific allocations are described as allocation of air sorties, nuclear weapons, etc. Allocation (air); allocation (nuclear); allocation (transportation); apportionment.

Allocation (air): The translation of the air apportionment decision into total numbers of sorties by aircraft type available for each operation or task. Allocation.

Allocation (nuclear): The apportionment of specific numbers and types of nuclear weapons to a commander for a stated time period as a planning factor for use in the development of war plans.

Allocation request: A message used to provide an estimate of the total air effort, to identify any excess and joint force general support aircraft sorties, and to identify unfilled air requirements. This message is used only for preplanned missions and is transmitted on a daily basis, normally 24 hours prior to the start of the next air tasking day.

Allocation (transportation): Distribution by designated authority of available transport capability to users. Allocation.

Allotment: The temporary change of assignment of tactical air forces between subordinate commands. The authority to allot is vested in the commander having combatant command. Combatant command.

Allowable cabin load: The maximum payload that can be carried on an individual sortie.

Allowable load: The total load that an aircraft can transport over a given distance, taking into account weight and volume. Airlift capability; airlift requirement; load; payload.

Allowable stacking weight: The amount of weight that can be stacked on corner posts of a container when subjected to 1.8 times the force of gravity.

All-weather air defense fighter: A fighter aircraft with equipment and weapons which enable it to engage airborne targets in all weather conditions, day and night.

Alongside replenishment: The transfer at sea of personnel and/or supplies by rigs between two or more ships proceeding side by side.

Alternate airfield: An airfield specified in the flight plan to which a flight may proceed when it becomes inadvisable to land at the airfield of intended landing. An alternate airfield may be the airfield of departure.

Alternate command authority: One or more pre designated officers empowered by the commander through pre delegation of authority to act under stipulated emergency conditions in the accomplishment of previously defined functions.

Alternate command post: Any location designated by a commander to assume command post functions in the event the command post becomes inoperative. It may be partially or fully equipped and manned or it may be the command post of a subordinate unit.

Alternate headquarters: An existing headquarters of a component or subordinate command that is pre designated to assume the responsibilities and functions of another headquarters under prescribed emergency conditions.

Altitude: The vertical distance of a level, a point or an object considered as a point, measured from mean sea level. Drop altitude; elevation; minimum safe altitude; transition altitude; true altitude.

Altitude acclimatization: A slow physiological adaptation resulting from prolonged exposure to significantly reduced atmospheric pressure.

Altitude delay: Synchronization delay introduced between the time of transmission of the radar pulse and the start of the trace on the indicator, for the purpose of eliminating the altitude hole on the plan position indicator-type display.

Altitude hole: The blank area at the origin of a radial display, on a radar tube

presentation, the center of the periphery of which represents the point on the ground immediately below the aircraft. In side-looking airborne radar, this is known as the altitude slot.

Ambulance exchange point: A location where a patient is transferred from one ambulance to another en route to a medical treatment facility. This may be an established point in an ambulance shuttle or it may be designated independently. Medical treatment facility.

Ammunition and toxic material open space: An area especially prepared for storage of explosive ammunition and toxic material. For reporting purposes, it does not include the surrounding area restricted for storage because of safety distance factors. It includes barricades and improvised coverings.

Ammunition controlled supply rate: In Army usage, the amount of ammunition estimated to be available to sustain operations of a designated force for a specified time if expenditures are controlled at that rate. It is expressed in terms of rounds per weapon per day for ammunition items fired by weapons, and in terms of units of measure per organization per day for bulk allotment ammunition items. Tactical commanders use this rate to control expenditures of ammunition during tactical operations at planned intervals. It is issued through command channels at each level. It is determined based on consideration of the required supply rates submitted by subordinate commanders and ammunition assets available.

Ammunition lot: A quantity of homogeneous ammunition, identified by a unique lot number, which is manufactured, assembled, or renovated by one producer under uniform conditions and which is expected to function in a uniform manner.

Amphibian: A small craft, propelled by propellers and wheels or by air cushions for the purpose of moving on both land and water.

Amphibious assault: The principal type of amphibious operation that involves establishing a force on a hostile or potentially hostile shore. Assault; assault phase.

Amphibious assault ship (dock): A naval ship designed to embark, deploy, and land elements of a landing force in an assault by helicopters, landing craft, amphibious vehicles, and by combinations of these methods. LHD

Amphibious assault ship (general purpose): A naval ship designed to embark, deploy, and land elements of a landing force in an assault by helicopters, landing craft, amphibious vehicles, and by combinations of these methods. LHA.

Amphibious aviation assault ship: An amphibious assault ship, landing platform helicopter; general purpose amphibious assault ship; or general purpose amphibious assault ship.

Amphibious bulk liquid transfer system: Hose reel system providing capability to deliver fuel and/or water from ship to shore. System includes 10,000 feet of 6" buoyant hose for fuel, and 10,000 ft of 4" buoyant hose for water. System are deployed on Maritime Pre-positioning Squadrons, and are normally used in direct support of maritime pre-positioning force operations. ABLTS.

Amphibious chart: A special naval chart designed to meet special requirements for landing operations and passive coastal defense, at a scale of 1:25,000 or larger, and showing foreshore and coastal information in greater detail than a combat chart.

Amphibious command ship: A naval ship from which a commander exercises control in amphibious operations. Designated as LCC.

Amphibious construction battalion: A permanently commissioned naval unit, subordinate to the Commander, Naval Beach Group, designed to provide an administrative unit from which personnel and equipment are formed in tactical elements and made available to appropriate commanders to operate pontoon causeways, transfer barges, warping tugs, and assault bulk fuel systems, and to meet salvage requirements of the naval beach party. PHIBCB.

Amphibious control group: Personnel, ships, and craft designated to control the waterborne ship-to-shore movement in an amphibious operation.

Amphibious demonstration: A type of amphibious operation conducted for the purpose of deceiving the enemy by a show of force with the expectation of deluding the enemy into a course of action unfavorable to him.

Amphibious force: An amphibious task force and a landing force together with other forces that are trained, organized, and equipped for amphibious operations. AF. Amphibious operation; amphibious task force; landing force.

Amphibious group: A command within the amphibious force, consisting of the commander and staff, designed to exercise operational control of assigned units in executing all phases of a division-size amphibious operation.

Amphibious lift: The total capacity of assault shipping utilized in an amphibious operation, expressed in terms of personnel, vehicles, and measurement or weight tons of supplies.

Amphibious objective area: A geographical area (delineated for command and control purposes in the order initiating the amphibious operation) within which is located the objective(s) to be secured by the amphibious force. This area must be of sufficient size to ensure accomplishment of the amphibious force's mission and must provide sufficient area for conducting necessary sea, air, and land operations. AOA.

Amphibious objective study: A study designed to provide basic intelligence data of a permanent or semi permanent nature required for planning amphibious operations. Each study deals with a specific area, the selection of which is based on strategic location, susceptibility to seizure by amphibious means, and other considerations.

Amphibious operation: A military operation launched from the sea by an amphibious force, embarked in ships or craft with the primary purpose of introducing a landing force ashore to accomplish the assigned mission.

Amphibious planning: The process of planning for an amphibious operation, distinguished by the necessity for concurrent, parallel, and detailed planning by all participating forces. The planning pattern is cyclical in nature, composed of a series of analyses and judgments of operational situations, each stemming from those that have preceded.

Amphibious raid: A type of amphibious operation involving swift incursion into or temporary occupation of an objective followed by a planned withdrawal.

Amphibious reconnaissance: An amphibious landing conducted by minor elements, normally involving stealth rather than force of arms, for the purpose of securing information, and usually followed by a planned withdrawal.

Amphibious reconnaissance unit: A unit organized, equipped, and trained to conduct and support amphibious reconnaissance missions. An amphibious reconnaissance unit is made up of a number of amphibious reconnaissance teams.

Amphibious shipping: Organic Navy ships specifically designed to transport, land, and support landing forces in amphibious assault operations and capable of being loaded or unloaded by naval personnel without external assistance in the amphibious objective area.

Amphibious squadron: A tactical and administrative organization composed of amphibious assault shipping to transport troops and their equipment for an amphibious assault operation. PHIBRON.

Amphibious striking forces: Forces capable of projecting military power from the sea upon adjacent land areas for initiating and/or conducting operations in the face of enemy opposition.

Amphibious task force: A Navy task organization formed to conduct amphibious operations. The amphibious task force, together with the landing force and other forces, constitutes the amphibious force. Also called ATF.

Amphibious transport dock: A ship designed to transport and land troops, equipment, and supplies by means of embarked landing craft, amphibious vehicles, and helicopters. Designated as LPD.

Amphibious transport group: A subdivision of an amphibious task force composed primarily of transport ships. The size of the transport group will depend upon the scope of the operation. Ships of the transport group will be combat-loaded to support the landing force scheme of maneuver ashore. A transport unit will usually be formed to embark troops and equipment to be landed over a designated beach or to embark all helicopter-borne troops and equipment.

Amphibious vehicle: A wheeled or tracked vehicle capable of operating on both land and water. Landing craft.

Amphibious vehicle availability table: A tabulation of the type and number of amphibious vehicles available primarily for assault landings and for support of other elements of the operation.

Amphibious vehicle employment plan: A plan showing in tabular form the planned employment of amphibious vehicles in landing operations, including their employment after the initial movement to the beach.

Amphibious vehicle launching area: An area, in the vicinity of and to seaward of the line of departure, to which landing ships proceed and launch amphibious vehicles.

Amphibious withdrawal: A type of amphibious operation involving the extraction of forces by sea in ships or craft from a hostile or potentially hostile shore. Amphibious operation.

Analysis and production: In intelligence usage, the conversion of processed information into intelligence through the integration, evaluation, analysis, and interpretation of all source data and the preparation of intelligence products in support of known or anticipated user requirements. Intelligence process.

Anchorage: A specified location for anchoring or mooring a vessel in-stream or offshore.

Anchor cable: In air transport, a cable in an aircraft to which the parachute static lines or strops are attached.

Anchor line extension kit: A device fitted to an aircraft equipped with removable clamshell doors to enable paratroopers to exit from the rear.

Annex: A document appended to an operation order or other document to make it clearer or to give further details.

Annotated print: A photograph on which interpretation details are indicated by words or symbols.

Annotation: A marking placed on imagery or drawings for explanatory purposes or to indicate items or areas of special importance.

Annual screening: One day of active duty for training required each year for Individual Ready Reserve members so the Services can keep current on each member's physical condition, dependency status, military qualifications, civilian occupational skills, availability for service, and other information.

Annual training: The minimal period of training reserve members must perform each year to satisfy the training requirements associated with their Reserve Component assignment. AT.

Ante mortem identification media: Records, samples, and photographs taken prior to death. These include (but are not limited to) fingerprints, dental x-rays, body tissue samples, photographs of tattoos, or other identifying marks. These "predeath" records would be compared against records completed after death to help establish a positive identification of human remains. Mortuary affairs.

Antenna mine: In naval mine warfare, a contact mine fitted with antennae which, when touched by a steel ship, sets up galvanic action to fire the mine.

Ant armor helicopter: A helicopter armed primarily for use in the destruction of armored targets. Antitank helicopter.

Anti countermining device: A device fitted in an influence mine designed to prevent its actuation by shock.

Anti deficiency violations: The incurring of obligations or the making of expenditure (outlays) in violation of appropriation law as to purpose, time, and amounts as specified in the defense appropriation or appropriations of funds.

Anti-G suit: A device worn by aircrew to counteract the effects on the human body of positive acceleration.

Anti lift device: A device arranged to detonate the mine to which it is attached, or to detonate another mine or charge nearby, if the mine is disturbed.

Anti materiel agent: A living organism or chemical used to cause deterioration of, or damage to, selected materiel.

Anti materiel operation: The employment of anti materiel weapons or agents in military operations.

Antipersonnel mine (land mine warfare): A mine designed to cause casualties to personnel.

Anti radiation missile: A missile which homes passively on a radiation source. ARM. Guided missile.

Anti recovery device: In naval mine warfare, any device in a mine designed to prevent an enemy discovering details of the working of the mine mechanism.

Antisubmarine action: An operation by one or more antisubmarine-capable ships, submarines, or aircraft (or a combination thereof) against a particular enemy submarine.

Antisubmarine air distant support: Antisubmarine air support at a distance from, but directly related to, specific convoys or forces.

Antisubmarine air search attack unit: The designation given to one or more aircraft separately organized as a tactical unit to search for and destroy submarines.

Antisubmarine barrier: The line formed by a series of static devices or mobile units arranged for the purpose of detecting, denying passage to, or destroying hostile submarines. Antisubmarine patrol.

Antisubmarine close air support: Air operations for the antisubmarine warfare protection of a supported force.

Antisubmarine operation: Operation contributing to the conduct of antisubmarine warfare.

Antisubmarine patrol: The systematic and continuing investigation of an area or along a line to detect or hamper submarines, used when the direction of submarine movement can be established. Antisubmarine barrier.

Antisubmarine screen: An arrangement of ships and/or aircraft for the protection of a screened unit against attack by a submarine.

Antisubmarine search: Systematic investigation of a particular area for the purpose of locating a submarine known or suspected to be somewhere in the area. Some types of search are also used in locating the position of a distress incident.

Antisubmarine support operation: An operation conducted by an antisubmarine force in the area around a force or convoy, in areas through which the force or convoy is passing, or in defense of geographic areas. Support operations may be completely coordinated with those of the force or convoy, or they may be independent operations coordinated only to the extent of providing operational intelligence and information.

Antisubmarine warfare: Operations conducted with the intention of denying the enemy the effective use of submarines. ASW.

Antisubmarine warfare forces: Forces organized primarily for antisubmarine action. May be composed of surface ships, aircraft, submarines, or any combination of these, and their supporting systems.

Anti surface air operation: An air operation conducted in an air/sea environment against enemy surface forces.

Anti sweep device: Any device incorporated in the mooring of a mine or obstructer, or in the mine circuits to make the sweeping of the mine more difficult.

Anti sweeper mine: A mine which is laid or whose mechanism is designed or adjusted with the specific object of damaging mine countermeasures vessels.

Antitank mine: A mine designed to immobilize or destroy a tank.

Anti watching device: A device fitted in a moored mine which causes it to sink should it show on the surface, so as to prevent the position of the mine or minefield being disclosed. See also watching mine.

Any Service member mail: Mail sent by the general public to an unspecified Service member deployed on a contingency operation, as an expression of patriotic support.

Apogee : The point at which a missile trajectory or a satellite orbit is farthest from the center of the gravitational field of the controlling body or bodies.

Apparent horizon: The visible line of demarcation between land/sea and sky.

Apparent precession: The apparent deflection of the gyro axis, relative to the Earth, due to the rotating effect of the Earth and not due to any applied force.

Appendix: A document appended to an annex of an operation order, operation plan, or other document to clarify or to give further details.

Applicable materiel assets: That portion of the total acceptable materiel assets that meets the military or other characteristics as defined by the responsible Military Service and that is in the right condition and location to satisfy a specific military requirement.

Application: 1. The system or problem to which a computer is applied. Reference is often made to an application as being either of the computational type or of the data processing type. 2. In the intelligence context, the direct extraction and tailoring of information from an existing foundation of intelligence and near real time reporting. It is focused on and meets specific, narrow requirements, normally on demand.

Apportionment: In the general sense, distribution for planning of limited resources among competing requirements. Specific apportionments (e.g., air sorties and forces for planning) are described as apportionment of air sorties and forces for planning, etc.

Apportionment (air): The determination and assignment of the total expected effort by percentage and/or by priority that should be devoted to the various air operations for a given period of time.

Approach clearance: Authorization for a pilot conducting flight in accordance with instrument flight rules to commence an approach to an airport.

Approach end of runway: That end of the runway nearest to the direction from which the final approach is made.

Approach lane: An extension of a boat lane from the line of departure toward the transport area.

Approach march: Advance of a combat unit when direct contact with the enemy is imminent. Troops are fully or partially deployed. The approach march ends when ground contact with the enemy is made or when the attack position is occupied.

Approach schedule: The schedule that indicates, for each scheduled wave, the time of departure from the rendezvous area, from the line of departure, and from other control points and the time of arrival at the beach.

Approach sequence: The order in which two or more aircraft are cleared for an approach.

Approach time: The time at which an aircraft is expected to commence approach procedure.

Approval authority: A representative (person or organization) of the Commandant, US Coast Guard, authorized to approve containers within terms of the International Conference for Safe Containers. International Convention for Safe Containers.

Apron: A defined area on an airfield intended to accommodate aircraft for purposes of loading or unloading passengers or cargo, refueling, parking, or maintenance.

Archipelagic sea lanes passage: The nonsuspendable right of continuous and expeditious transit through archipelagic waters in the normal mode through and over routes normally used for navigation and over flight.

Architecture: A framework or structure that portrays relationships among all the elements of the subject force, system, or activity.

Area air defense commander: Within a unified command, subordinate unified command, or joint task force, the commander will assign overall responsibility for air defense to a single commander. Normally, this will be the component commander with the preponderance of air defense capability and the command, control, and communications capability to plan and execute integrated air defense operations. Representation from the other components involved will be provided, as appropriate, to the area air defense commander's headquarters. AADC.

Area bombing: Bombing of a target which is in effect a general area rather than a small or pinpoint target.

Area command: A command which is composed of those organized elements of one or more of the Armed Services, designated to operate in a specific geographical area, which are placed under a single commander.

Area control center: A unit established to provide air traffic control service to controlled flights in control areas under its jurisdiction. See also air traffic control center; flight information region.

Area damage control: Measures taken before, during, or after hostile action or natural or manmade disasters, to reduce the probability of damage and minimize its effects. ADC.

Area of influence: A geographical area wherein a commander is directly capable of influencing operations by maneuver or fire support systems normally under the commander's command or control.

Area of interest: That area of concern to the commander, including the area of influence, areas adjacent thereto, and extending into enemy territory to the objectives of current or planned operations. This area also includes areas occupied by enemy forces who could jeopardize the accomplishment of the mission. AOI.

Area of limitation – A defined area where specific limitations apply to the strength and fortifications of disputing or belligerent forces. Normally, upper limits are established for the number and type of formations, tanks, antiaircraft weapons, artillery, and other weapons systems in the area of limitation. AOL.

Area of militarily significant fallout: Area in which radioactive fallout affects the ability of military units to carry out their normal mission.

Area of northern operations: A region of variable width in the Northern Hemisphere that lies north of the 50 degrees isotherm — a line along which the average temperature of the warmest 4-month period of the year does not exceed 50 degrees Fahrenheit. Mountain regions located outside of this area are included in this category of operations provided these same temperature conditions exist.

Area of operations — An operational area defined by the joint force commander for land and maritime forces. Areas of operation do not typically encompass the entire operational area of the joint force commander, but should be large enough for component commanders to accomplish their missions and protect their forces. AO.

Area of responsibility: The geographical area associated with a combatant command within which a geographic combatant commander has authority to plan and conduct operations. AOR.

Area operations: In maritime usage, operations conducted in a geographical area and not related to the protection of a specific force.

Area oriented: Personnel or units whose organizations, mission, training, and equipping are based on projected operational deployment to a specific geographic or demographic area.

Area radar prediction analysis: Radar target intelligence study designed to provide radar-significant data for use in the preparation of radar target predictions.

Area search: Visual reconnaissance of limited or defined areas.

Area target: A target consisting of an area rather than a single point.

Armament delivery recording: Motion picture, still photography, and video recordings showing the delivery and impact of ordnance. This differs from reconnaissance imagery in that it records the act of delivery and impact and normally is done by the weapon system delivering the ordnance. Armament delivery recording is used primarily for evaluating strike effectiveness and for combat crew training. It is also one of the principal sources of over-the-target documentation in force employments, and may be used for public affairs purposes. ADR.

Armed forces: The military forces of a nation or a group of nations.

Armed forces censorship: The examination and control of personal communications to or from persons in the Armed Forces of the United States and persons accompanying or serving with the Armed Forces of the United States.

Armed forces courier: An officer or enlisted member in the grade of E-7 or above, of the US Armed Forces, assigned to perform Armed Forces Courier Service duties and identified by possession of an Armed Forces Courier Service Identification Card (ARFCOS Form 9).

Armed Forces Courier Service: A joint service of the Departments of the Army, the Navy, and the Air Force, with the Chief of Staff, US Army, as Executive Agent. The courier service provides one of the available methods for the secure and expeditious transmission of material requiring protected handling by military courier.

Armed forces courier station: An Army, Navy, or Air Force activity, approved by the respective military department and officially designated by Headquarters, Armed Forces Courier Service, for the acceptance, processing, and dispatching of Armed Forces Courier Service material.

Armed Forces of the United States: A term used to denote collectively all components of the Army, Navy, Air Force, Marine Corps, and Coast Guard. United States Armed Forces.

Armed Forces Radio and Television Service: A worldwide radio and television broadcasting organization that provides US military commanders overseas and at sea with sufficient electronic media resources to effectively communicate theater, local, Department of Defense, and Service-unique command information to their personnel and family members. AFRTS.

Armed mine: A mine from which all safety devices have been withdrawn and, after laying, all automatic safety features and/or arming delay devices have operated. Such a mine is ready to be actuated after receipt of a target signal, influence, or contact.

Armed reconnaissance: A mission with the primary purpose of locating and attacking targets of opportunity, i.e., enemy materiel, personnel, and facilities, in assigned general areas or along assigned ground communications routes, and not for the purpose of attacking specific briefed targets.

Armed sweep: A sweep fitted with cutters or other devices to increase its ability to cut mine moorings.

Arming: As applied to explosives, weapons, and ammunition, the changing from a safe condition to a state of readiness for initiation.

Arming delay device: A device fitted in a mine to prevent it being actuated for a preset time after laying.

Arming pin: A safety device inserted in a munitions, which until its removal, prevents the unintentional action of the arming cycle. Also called safety pin.

Arming system: That portion of a weapon that serves to ready (arm), safe, or re-safe (disarm) the firing system and fuzing system and that may actuate devices in the nuclear system.

Armistice: In international law, a suspension or temporary cessation of hostilities by agreement between belligerent powers.

Armistice demarcation line: A geographically defined line from which disputing or belligerent forces disengage and withdraw to their respective sides following a truce or cease fire agreement. Cease fire line in some United Nations operations. ADL.

Arm or de-arm: Applies to those procedures in the arming or de-arming section of the applicable aircraft loading manual or checklist that places the ordnance or explosive device in a ready or safe condition i.e., rocket launchers, guided missi es, guns – internal and pods, para flares. Arming; de-arming; ordnance.

Armored personnel carrier: A lightly armored, highly mobile, full-tracked vehicle, amphibious and air-droppable, used primarily for transporting personnel and their individual equipment during tactical operations. Production modifications or application of special kits permit use as a mortar carrier, command post, flame thrower, antiaircraft artillery chassis, or limited recovery vehicle: APC.

Arms control agreement: The written or unwritten embodiment of the acceptance of one or more arms control measures by two or more nations.

Arms control agreement verification: A concept that entails the collection, processing, and reporting of data indicating testing or employment of proscribed weapon systems, including country of origin and location, weapon and payload identification, and event type.

Arms control measure: Any specific arms control course of action.

Army Air Defense Command Post: The tactical headquarters of an Army air defense commander.

Army air-ground system: The Army system which provides for interface between Army and tactical air support agencies of other Services in the planning, evaluating, processing, and coordinating of air support requirements and operations. It is composed of appropriate staff members, including G-2 air and G-3 air personnel, and necessary communication equipment. AAGS.

Army base: A base or group of installations for which a local commander is responsible, consisting of facilities necessary for support of Army activities including security, internal lines of communications, utilities, plants and systems, and real property for which the Army has operating responsibility.

Army corps: A tactical unit larger than a division and smaller than a field army. A corps usually consists of two or more divisions together with auxiliary arms and services.

Army service area: The territory between the corps rear boundary and the combat zone rear boundary. Most of the Army administrative establishment and service troops are usually located in this area. Rear area.

Army Service component command: Command responsible for recommendations to the joint force commander on the allocation and employment of Army forces within a combatant command. ASCC.

Army space support team: A team of space operations experts provided by the Commander, US Army Forces Strategic Command upon request of an Army component commander or a geographic combatant commander to assist the supported commander in integrating space power into the terrestrial operation or campaign. ARSST.

Army special operations component: The Army component of a joint force special operations component. ARSOC. Air Force special operations component; Navy special operations component.

Army special operations forces: Those Active and Reserve Component Army forces designated by the Secretary of Defense that are specifically organized, trained, and equipped to conduct and support special operations. ARSOF.

Arrival zone: In counterdrug operations, the area in or adjacent to the United States where smuggling concludes and domestic distribution begins.

Artillery fire plan table: A presentation of planned targets giving data for engagement. Scheduled targets are fired in a definite time sequence. The starting time may be on call, at a prearranged time, or at the occurrence of a specific event.

Artillery survey control point: A point at which the coordinates and the altitude are known and from which the bearings/azimuths to a number of reference objects are also known.

Assault: 1. The climax of an attack, closing with the enemy in hand-to-hand fighting. 2. In an amphibious operation, the period of time between the arrival of the major assault forces of the amphibious task force in the objective area and the accomplishment of the amphibious task force mission. 3. To make a short, violent, but well-ordered attack against a local objective, such as a gun emplacement, a fort, or a machine gun nest. 4. A phase of an airborne operation beginning with delivery by air of the assault echelon of the force into the objective area and extending through attack of assault objectives and consolidation of the initial airhead.

Assault aircraft: A powered aircraft that moves assault troops and/or cargo into an objective area.

Assault area: In amphibious operations, that area that includes the beach area, the boat lanes, the lines of departure, the landing ship areas, the transport areas, and the fire support areas in the immediate vicinity of the boat lanes.

Assault area diagram: A graphic means of showing, for amphibious operations, the beach designations, boat lanes, organization of the line of departure, scheduled waves, landing ship area, transport areas, and the fire support areas in the immediate vicinity of the boat lanes.

Assault craft: A landing craft or amphibious vehicle primarily employed for landing troops and equipment in the assault waves of an amphibious operation.

Assault craft unit: A permanently commissioned naval organization, subordinate to the commander, naval beach group, that contains landing craft and crews necessary to provide lighter age required in an amphibious operation. ACU.

Assault echelon: In amphibious operations, the element of a force comprised of tailored units and aircraft assigned to conduct the initial assault on the operational area. AE.

Assault fire: 1. That fire delivered by attacking troops as they close with the enemy. 2. In artillery, extremely accurate, short-range destruction fire at point targets.

Assault follow-on echelon: In amphibious operations, that echelon of the assault troops, vehicles, aircraft, equipment, and supplies that, though not needed to initiate the assault, is required to support and sustain the assault. In order to accomplish its purpose, it is normally required in the objective area no later than five days after commencement of the assault landing. AFOE.

Assault phase: 1. In an amphibious operation, the period of time between the arrival of the major assault forces of the amphibious task force in the objective area and the accomplishment of their mission. 2. In an airborne operation, a phase beginning with delivery by air of the assault echelon of the force into the objective area and extending through attack of assault objectives and consolidation of the initial airhead.

Assault shipping: Shipping assigned to the amphibious task force and utilized for transporting assault troops, vehicles, equipment, and supplies to the objective area.

Assembly: - In logistics, an item forming a portion of an equipment, that can be provisioned and replaced as an entity and which normally incorporates replaceable parts or groups of parts. Component; subassembly.

Assembly anchorage: An anchorage intended for the assembly and onward routing of ships.

Assembly area: 1. An area in which a command is assembled preparatory to further action. 2. In a supply installation, the gross area used for collecting and combining components into complete units, kits, or assemblies.

Assessment: 1. A continuous process that measures the overall effectiveness of employing joint force capabilities during military operations. 2. Determination of the progress toward accomplishing a task, creating an effect, or achieving an objective. 3. Analysis of the security, effectiveness, and potential of an existing or planned intelligence activity. 4. Judgment of the motives, qualifications, and characteristics of present or prospective employees or "agents."

Assessment agent: The organization responsible for conducting an assessment of an approved joint publication. The assessment agent is assigned by the Director, J-7, Joint Staff; normally US Joint Forces Command. AA.

Asset (intelligence): Any resource — person, group, relationship, instrument, installation, or supply — at the disposition of an intelligence organization for use in an operational or support role. Often used with a qualifying term such as agent asset or propaganda asset.

Asset visibility: Provides users with information on the location, movement, status, and identity of units, personnel, equipment, and supplies. It facilitates the capability to act upon that information to improve overall performance of the Department of Defense's logistics practices. AV.

Assign: 1. To place units or personnel in an organization where such placement is relatively permanent, and/or where such organization controls and administers the units or personnel for the primary function, or greater portion of the functions, of the unit or personnel. 2. To detail individuals to specific duties or functions where such duties or functions are primary and/or relatively permanent.

Assistance in kind: The provision of material and services for a logistic exchange of materials and services of equal value between the governments of eligible countries. AIK.

Assumed azimuth: The assumption of azimuth origins as a field expedient until the required data are available.

Assumed grid: A grid constructed using an arbitrary scale superimposed on a map, chart, or photograph for use in point designation without regard to actual geographic location.

Assumption: A supposition on the current situation or a presupposition on the future course of events, either or both assumed to be true in the absence of positive proof, necessary to enable the commander in the process of planning to complete an estimate of the situation and make a decision on the course of action.

Astern fueling: The transfer of fuel at sea during which the receiving ship(s) keep(s) station astern of the delivering ship.

Asymmetrical sweep: A sweep whose swept path under conditions of no wind or cross-tide is not equally spaced either side of the sweeper's track.

Atmospheric environment: The envelope of air surrounding the Earth, including its interfaces and interactions with the Earth's solid or liquid surface.

At my command: In artillery and naval gunfire support, the command used when it is desired to control the exact time of delivery of fire.

Atomic demolition munitions: A nuclear device designed to be detonated on or below the ground surface, or under water as a demolition munitions against material-type targets to block, deny, and/or canalize the enemy.

At priority call: A precedence applied to the task of an artillery unit to provide fire to a formation/unit on a guaranteed basis. Normally observer, communications, and liaison are not provided. An artillery unit in "direct support" or "in support" may simultaneously be placed "at priority call" to another unit or agency for a particular task and/or for a specific period of time.

At sea: Includes the following maritime areas: foreign internal waters, archipelagic waters, and territorial seas; foreign contiguous zones; foreign exclusive economic zones; the high seas; and US-exclusive economic zone, territorial sea, and internal waters.

Attach: 1. The placement of units or personnel in an organization where such placement is relatively temporary. 2. The detailing of individuals to specific functions where such functions are secondary or relatively temporary, e.g., attached for quarters and rations; attached for flying duty.

Attack assessment: An evaluation of information to determine the potential or actual nature and objectives of an attack for the purpose of providing information for timely decisions. Damage estimation.

Attack cargo ship: A naval ship designed or converted to transport combat-loaded cargo in an assault landing. Capabilities as to carrying landing craft, speed of ship, armament, and size of hatches and booms are greater than those of comparable cargo ship types. Designated as LKA.

Attack group: A subordinate task organization of the navy forces of an amphibious task force. It is composed of assault shipping and supporting naval units designated to transport, protect, land, and initially support a landing group.

Attack heading: 1. The interceptor heading during the attack phase that will achieve the desired track-crossing angle. 2. The assigned magnetic compass heading to be flown by aircraft during the delivery phase of an air strike.

Attack origin: 1. The location or source from which an attack was initiated. 2. The nation initiating an attack. See also attack assessment.

Attack pattern: The type and distribution of targets under attack. Target pattern. Attack assessment.

Attack position: The last position occupied by the assault echelon before crossing the line of departure.

Attack timing: The predicted or actual time of bursts, impacts, or arrival of weapons at their intended targets.

Attenuation: -1. Decrease in intensity of a signal, beam, or wave as a result of

absorption of energy and of scattering out of the path of a detector, but not including the reduction due to geometric spreading, i.e., the inverse square of distance effect. 2. In mine warfare, the reduction in intensity of an influence as distance from the source increases. 3. In camouflage and concealment, the process of making an object or surface less conspicuous by reducing its contrast to the surroundings and/or background. Tone down.

Attenuation factor: The ratio of the incident radiation dose or dose rate to the radiation dose or dose rate transmitted through a shielding material. This is the reciprocal of the transmission factor.

Attitude: The position of a body as determined by the inclination of the axes to some frame of reference. If not otherwise specified, this frame of reference is fixed to the Earth.

Attitude indicator: An instrument which displays the attitude of the aircraft by reference to sources of information which may be contained within the instrument or be external to it. When the sources of information are self-contained, the instrument may be referred to as an artificial horizon.

Attrition: -The reduction of the effectiveness of a force caused by loss of personnel and materiel.

Attrition minefield: In naval mine warfare, a field intended primarily to cause damage to enemy ships. Minefield.

Attrition rate: A factor, normally expressed as a percentage, reflecting the degree of losses of personnel or materiel due to various causes within a specified period of time.

Attrition reserve aircraft: Aircraft procured for the specific purpose of replacing the anticipated losses of aircraft because of peacetime and/or wartime attrition.

Attrition sweeping: The continuous sweeping of minefields to keep the risk of mines to all ships as low as possible.

Augmentation forces: Forces to be transferred from a supporting combatant commander to the combatant command or operational control of a supported combatant commander during the execution of an operation order approved by the President and Secretary of Defense.

Authenticate: A challenge given by voice or electrical means to attest to the authenticity of a message or transmission.

Authentication: 1. A security measure designed to protect a communications system against acceptance of a fraudulent transmission or simulation by establishing the validity of a transmission, message, or originator. 2. A means of identifying individuals and verifying their eligibility to receive specific categories of information. 3. Evidence by proper signature or seal that a document is genuine and official. 4. In personnel recovery missions, the process whereby the identity of an isolated person is confirmed. Evader; evasion; recovery operations; security.

Authenticator: A symbol or group of symbols, or a series of bits, selected or derived in a prearranged manner and usually inserted at a predetermined point within a message or transmission for the purpose of attesting to the validity of the message or transmission.

Authorized departure: A procedure, short of ordered departure, by which mission employees or dependents or both, are permitted to leave post in advance of normal rotation when the national interests or imminent threat to life require it.

Auto code format — An abbreviated and formatted message header used in conjunction with the mobile crypto logic support facility (MCSF) to energize the automatic communications relay functions of the MCSF, providing rapid exchange of data through the system.

Automated identification technology: A suite of tools for facilitating total asset visibility source data capture and transfer. Automated identification technology includes a variety of devices, such as bar codes, magnetic strips, optical memory cards, and radio frequency tags for marking or "tagging" individual items, multi-packs, equipment, air pallets, or containers, along with the hardware and software required to create the devices, read the information on them, and integrate that information with other logistic information. AIT.

Automated Repatriation Reporting System: The Defense Manpower Data Center uses this system to track the status of noncombatant evacuees after they have arrived in an initial safe haven in the US.

Automatic approach and landing: A control mode in which the aircraft's speed and flight path are automatically controlled for approach, flare-out, and landing. ground-controlled approach procedure.

Automatic data handling: A generalization of automatic data processing to include the aspect of data transfer.

Automatic data processing: 1. Data processing largely performed by automatic means. 2. That branch of science and technology concerned with methods and techniques relating to data processing largely performed by automatic means.

Automatic flight control system: A system which includes all equipment to control automatically the flight of an aircraft or missile to a path or attitude described by references internal or external to the aircraft or missile. AFCS.

Automatic message processing system: Any organized assembly of resources and methods used to collect, process, and distribute messages largely by automatic means.

Automatic resupply: A resupply mission fully planned before insertion of a special operations team into the operations area that occurs at a prearranged time and location, unless changed by the operating team after insertion. Emergency resupply; on-call resupply.

Automatic search jammer: An intercept receiver and jamming transmitter system which searches for and jams signals automatically which have specific radiation characteristics.

Automatic supply: A system by which certain supply requirements are automatically shipped or issued for a predetermined period of time without requisition by the using unit. It is based upon estimated or experience-usage factors.

Automation network: The automation network combines all of the information collection devices, automatic identification technologies, and the automated information systems that either support or facilitate the joint reception, staging, onward movement, and integration process. Automated identification technology; joint reception, staging, onward movement, and integration.

Autonomous operation: In air defense, the mode of operation assumed by a unit after it has lost all communications with higher echelons. The unit commander assumes full responsibility for control of weapons and engagement of hostile targets.

Availability date: The date after notification of mobilization by which forces will be marshaled at their home station or mobilization station and available for deployment. Home station; mobilization; mobilization station.

Available payload: The passenger and/or cargo capacity expressed in weight and/or space available to the user.

Available-to-load date: A date specified for each unit in a time-phased force and deployment data indicating when that unit will be ready to load at the point of embarkation. ALD.

Avenue of approach — An air or ground route of an attacking force of a given size leading to its objective or to key terrain in its path. AA.

Average speed: The average distance traveled per hour, calculated over the whole journey, excluding specifically ordered halts.

Aviation medicine: The special field of medicine which is related to the biological and psychological problems of flight.

Aviation ship: An aircraft carrier. Air-capable ship; aircraft; amphibious aviation assault ship.

Axial route: A route running through the rear area and into the forward area. Route.

Axis of advance: A line of advance assigned for purposes of control; often a road or a group of roads, or a designated series of locations, extending in the direction of the enemy.

Azimuth: Quantities may be expressed in positive quantities increasing in a clockwise direction, or in X, Y coordinates where south and west are negative. They may be referenced to true north or magnetic north depending on the particular weapon system used.

Azimuth angle: An angle measured clockwise in the horizontal plane between a reference direction and any other line.

Azimuth guidance: Information which will enable the pilot or autopilot of an aircraft to follow the required track.

Azimuth resolution: The ability of radar equipment to separate two reflectors at similar ranges but different bearings from a reference point. Normally the minimum separation distance between the reflectors is quoted and expressed as the angle subtended by the reflectors at the reference point.

B

Backfill: Reserve Component units and individuals recalled to replace deploying active units and/or individuals in the continental United States and outside the continental United States. Reserve Components.

Background count: The evidence or effect on a detector of radiation caused by background radiation. In connection with health protection, the background count includes but is not limited to radiations produced by naturally occurring radioactivity and cosmic rays.

Background radiation: Nuclear radiations arising from within the body and from the surroundings to which individuals are always exposed.

Back-haul airlift: The rearward movement of personnel and materiel from an air terminal in forward deployed areas back to a staging base after the normal forward delivery.

Backscatter: Refers to a portion of the laser energy that is scattered back in the direction of the seeker by an obscurant.

Back-scattering: Radio wave propagation in which the direction of the incident and scattered waves, resolved along a reference direction (usually horizontal), are oppositely directed. A signal received by back-scattering is often referred to as "backscatter."

Backshore: The area of a beach extending from the limit of high water foam lines to dunes or extreme inland limit of the beach.

Back tell: The transfer of information from a higher to a lower echelon of command.

Back-up: In cartography, an image printed on the reverse side of a map sheet already printed on one side.

Backwash: An even layer of water that moves along the sea floor from the beach through the surf zone and caused by the pile-up of water on the beach from incoming breakers.

Balance: A concept as applied to an arms control measure that connotes: a. adjustments of armed forces and armaments in such a manner that one state does not obtain military advantage over other states agreeing to the measure; and b. internal adjustments by one state of its forces in such manner as to enable it to cope with all aspects of remaining threats to its security in a post arms control agreement era.

Balanced stock(s):- 1. That condition of supply when availability and requirements are in equilibrium for specific items. 2. An accumulation of supplies in quantities determined necessary to meet requirements for a fixed period.

Bale cubic capacity: The space available for cargo measured in cubic feet to the inside of the cargo battens, on the frames, and to the underside of the beams. In a general cargo of mixed commodities, the bale cubic applies. The stowage of the mixed cargo comes in contact with the cargo battens and as a general rule does not extend to the skin of the ship.

Bali sage: The marking of a route by a system of dim beacon lights enabling vehicles to be driven at near day-time speed, under blackout conditions.

Ballistic missile: Any missile which does not rely upon aerodynamic surfaces to produce lift and consequently follows a ballistic trajectory when thrust is terminated.

Ballistic missile early warning system: An electronic system for providing detection and early warning of attack by enemy intercontinental ballistic missiles. BMEWS.

Ballistics: The science or art that deals with the motion, behavior, appearance, or modification of missiles or other vehicles acted upon by propellants, wind, gravity, temperature, or any other modifying substance, condition, or force.

Ballistic trajectory: The trajectory traced after the propulsive force is terminated and the body is acted upon only by gravity and aerodynamic drag.

Ballistic wind: That constant wind that would have the same effect upon the trajectory of a bomb or projectile as the wind encountered in flight.

Balloon reflector: In electronic warfare, a balloon-supported confusion reflector to produce fraudulent radar echoes.

Bandwidth: The difference between the limiting frequencies of a continuous frequency band expressed in hertz. The term bandwidth is also loosely used to refer to the rate at which data can be transmitted over a given communications circuit. In the latter usage, bandwidth is usually expressed in either kilobits per second or megabits per second.

Bank angle: The angle between the aircraft's normal axis and the Earth's vertical plane containing the aircraft's longitudinal axis.

Bar: A submerged or emerged embankment of sand, gravel, or mud created on the sea floor in shallow water by waves and currents. A bar may be composed of mollusk shells.

Bare base: A base having minimum essential facilities to house, sustain, and support operations to include, if required, a stabilized runway, taxiways, and aircraft parking areas. A bare base must have a source of water that can be made potable. Other requirements to operate under bare base conditions form a necessary part of the force package deployed to the bare base.

Barge: A flat-bed, shallow-draft vessel with no superstructure that is used for the transport of cargo and ships' stores or for general utility purposes. Watercraft.

Barometric altitude: The altitude determined by a barometric altimeter by reference to a pressure level and calculated according to the standard atmosphere laws.

Barrage: 1. A prearranged barrier of fires, except that delivered by small arms, designed to protect friendly troops and installations by impeding enemy movements across defensive lines or areas. 2. A protective screen of balloons that is moored to the ground and kept at given heights to prevent or hinder operations by enemy aircraft. This meaning also called balloon barrage. 3. A type of electronic attack intended for simultaneous jamming over a wide area of frequency spectrum.

Barrage fire: Fire which is designed to fill a volume of space or area rather than aimed specifically at a given target.

Barrage jamming: Simultaneous electromagnetic jamming over a broad band of frequencies. Jamming.

Barrier: A coordinated series of obstacles designed or employed to channel, direct, restrict, delay, or stop the movement of an opposing force and to impose additional losses in personnel, time, and equipment on the opposing force. Barriers can exist naturally, be man-made, or a combination of both.

Barrier forces: Air, surface, and submarine units and their supporting systems positioned across the likely courses of expected enemy transit for early detection and providing rapid warning, blocking, and destruction of the enemy.

Barrier, obstacle, and mine warfare plan: A comprehensive, coordinated plan that includes responsibilities; general location of unspecified and specific barriers, obstacles, and minefields; special instructions; limitations; coordination; and completion times. The plan may designate locations of obstacle zones or belts. It is normally prepared as an annex to a campaign plan, operation plan, or operation order.

Base: 1. A locality from which operations are projected or supported. 2. An area or locality containing installations which provide logistic or other support. Establishment. 3. (DOD only) Home airfield or home carrier.

Base boundary: A line that delineates the surface area of a base for the purpose of facilitating coordination and deconfliction of operations between adjacent units, formations, or areas.

Base cluster: In base defense operations, a collection of bases, geographically grouped for mutual protection and ease of command and control.

Base cluster commander: In base defense operations, a senior base commander designated by the joint force commander responsible for coordinating the defense of bases within the base cluster and for integrating defense plans of bases into a base cluster defense plan.

Base cluster operations center: A command and control facility that serves as the base cluster commander's focal point for defense and security of the base cluster. BCOC.

Base commander: In base defense operations, the officer assigned to command a base.

Base complex: Army base; installation complex; Marine base; naval base; naval or Marine (air) base.

Base defence: -The local military measures, both normal and emergency, required to nullify or reduce the effectiveness of enemy attacks on, or sabotage of, a base, to ensure that the maximum capacity of its facilities is available to US forces.

Base defense forces: Troops assigned or attached to a base for the primary purpose of base defense and security as well as augmentees and selectively armed personnel available to the base commander for base defense from units performing primary missions other than base defense.

Base defense operations center: A command and control facility, with responsibilities similar to a base cluster operations center, established by the base commander to serve as the focal point for base security and defense. It plans, directs, integrates, coordinates, and controls all base defense efforts. BDOC.

Base Development Zone: -An air defense zone established around an air base and limited to the engagement envelope of short-range air defense weapons systems defending that base. Base defense zones have specific entry, exit, and identification, friend or foe procedures established. BDZ.

Base development (less force bed down): The acquisition, development, expansion, improvement, and construction and/or replacement of the facilities and resources of an area or location to support forces employed in military operations or deployed in accordance with strategic plans.

Base development plan: A plan for the facilities, installations, and bases required to support military operations.

Base line: 1. (**surveying**) A surveyed line established with more than usual care, to which surveys are referred for coordination and correlation. 2. (**photogrammetry**) The line between the principal points of two consecutive vertical air photographs. It is usually measured on one photograph after the principal point of the other has been transferred. 3. (**radio navigation systems**) The shorter arc of the great circle joining two radio transmitting stations of a navigation system. 4. (**triangulation**) The side of one of a series of coordinated triangles the length of which is measured with prescribed accuracy and precision and from which lengths of the other triangle sides are obtained by computation.

Baseline costs: The continuing annual costs of military operations funded by the operations and maintenance and military personnel appropriations.

Base map: A map or chart showing certain fundamental information, used as a base upon which additional data of specialized nature are compiled or overprinted. Also, a map containing all the information from which maps showing specialized information can be prepared.

Base of operations: An area or facility from which a military force begins its offensive operations, to which it falls back in case of reverse, and in which supply facilities are organized.

Base period: That period of time for which factors were determined for use in current planning and programming.

Base plan: In the context of joint operation planning level 2 planning detail, a type of operation plan that describes the concept of operations, major forces, sustainment concept, and anticipated timelines for completing the mission. It normally does not include annexes or a time-phased force and deployment data.

Base section: An area within the communications zone in an operational area organized to provide logistic support to forward areas.

Base support installation: A Department of Defense Service or agency installation within the United States and its possessions and territories tasked to serve as a base for military forces engaged in either homeland defense or civil support operations. BSI.

Base surge: A cloud which rolls out from the bottom of the column produced by a subsurface burst of a nuclear weapon. For underwater bursts the surge is, in effect, a cloud of liquid droplets which has the property of flowing almost as if it were a homogeneous fluid. For subsurface land bursts the surge is made up of small solid particles but still behaves like a fluid.

Base unit: Unit of organization in a tactical operation around which a movement or maneuver is planned and performed.

Basic cover: Coverage of any installation or area of a permanent nature with which later coverage can be compared to discover any changes that have taken place.

Basic encyclopedia: A compilation of identified installations and physical areas of potential significance as objectives for attack. BE.

Basic intelligence: Fundamental intelligence concerning the general situation, resources, capabilities, and vulnerabilities of foreign countries or areas which may be used as reference material in the planning of operations at any level and in evaluating subsequent information relating to the same subject.

Basic load: The quantity of supplies required to be on hand within, and which can be moved by, a unit or formation. It is expressed according to the wartime organization of the unit or formation and maintained at the prescribed levels.

Basic military route network: Axial, lateral, and connecting routes designated in peacetime by the host nation to meet the anticipated military movements and transport requirements, both Allied and national.

Basic research: Research directed toward the increase of knowledge, the primary aim being a greater knowledge or understanding of the subject under study.

Basic stocks: Stocks to support the execution of approved operational plans for an initial predetermined period. Sustaining stocks.

Basic stopping power: The probability, expressed as a percentage, of a single vehicle being stopped by mines while attempting to cross a minefield.

Basic tactical organization: The conventional organization of landing force units for combat, involving combinations of infantry, supporting ground arms, and aviation for accomplishment of missions ashore. This organizational form is employed as soon as possible following the landing of the various assault components of the landing force.

Basic undertakings: The essential things, expressed in broad terms, that must be done in order to implement the commander's concept successfully. These may include military, diplomatic, economic, informational, and other measures.

Basis of issue: Authority that prescribes the number of items to be issued to an individual, a unit, a military organization, or for a unit piece of equipment.

Battalion landing team: In an amphibious operation, an infantry battalion normally reinforced by necessary combat and service elements; the basic unit for planning an assault landing. BLT.

Battery: 1. Tactical and administrative artillery unit or subunit corresponding to a company or similar unit in other branches of the Army. 2. All guns, torpedo tubes, searchlights, or missile launchers of the same size or caliber or used for the same purpose, either installed in one ship or otherwise operating as an entity.

Battery center: A point on the ground, the coordinates of which are used as a reference indicating the location of the battery in the production of firing data.

Battery (troop) left (right): A method of fire in which weapons are discharged from the left (right), one after the other, at five second intervals.

Battle damage assessment: The estimate of damage resulting from the application of lethal or nonlethal military force. Battle damage assessment is composed of physical damage assessment, functional damage assessment, and target system assessment. BDA.

Battle damage repair: Essential repair, which may be improvised, carried out rapidly in a battle environment in order to return damaged or disabled equipment to temporary service. BDR.

Battlefield coordination detachment: An Army liaison that provides selected operational functions between the Army forces and the air component commander. Battlefield coordination detachment located in the air operations center interface includes exchanging current intelligence and operational data, support requirements, coordinating the integration of Army forces requirements for airspace coordinating measures, fire support coordination measures, and theater airlift. BCD.

Battlefield illumination: The lighting of the battle area by artificial light, either visible or invisible to the naked eye.

Battlefield surveillance: Systematic observation of the battle area for the purpose of providing timely information and combat intelligence.

Battle force: A standing operational naval task force organization of carriers, surface combatants, and submarines assigned to numbered fleets. A battle force is subdivided into battle groups.

Battle injury: Damage or harm sustained by personnel during or as a result of battle conditions. BI.

Battle management: The management of activities within the operational environment based on the commands, direction, and guidance given by appropriate authority. BM.

Battle reserves: Reserve supplies accumulated by an army, detached corps, or detached division in the vicinity of the battlefield, in addition to unit and individual reserves.

Battle rhythm: A deliberate daily cycle of command, staff, and unit activities intended to synchronize current and future operations.

Battle space — The environment, factors, and conditions that must be understood to successfully apply combat power, protect the force, or complete the mission. This includes the air, land, sea, space, and the included enemy and friendly forces; facilities; weather; terrain; the electromagnetic spectrum; and the information environment within the operational areas and areas of interest. Electromagnetic spectrum; information environment; joint intelligence preparation of the battle space.

Battle space awareness: Knowledge and understanding of the operational area's environment, factors, and conditions, to include the status of friendly and adversary forces, neutrals and noncombatants, weather and terrain, that enables timely, relevant, comprehensive, and accurate assessments, in order to successfully apply combat power, protect the force, and/or complete the mission.

Beach: 1. The area extending from the shoreline inland to a marked change in physiographic form or material, or to the line of permanent vegetation (coastline). 2. In amphibious operations, that portion of the shoreline designated for landing of a tactical organization.

Beach capacity: An estimate, expressed in terms of measurement tons, or weight tons, of cargo that may be unloaded over a designated strip of shore per day. Clearance capacity; port capacity.

Beachhead: A designated area on a hostile or potentially hostile shore that, when seized and held, ensures the continuous landing of troops and materiel, and provides maneuver space requisite for subsequent projected operations ashore.

Beach landing site: A geographic location selected for across-the-beach infiltration, Exfiltration, or resupply operations. BLS.

Beach marker: A sign or device used to identify a beach or certain activities thereon for incoming waterborne traffic. Markers may be panels, lights, buoys, or electronic devices.

Beach master — The naval officer in command of the beach master unit of the naval beach group. BM.

Beach master unit: A commissioned naval unit of the naval beach group designed to provide to the shore party a Navy component known as a beach party, which is capable of supporting the amphibious landing of one division (reinforced). BMU.

Beach minefield: A minefield in the shallow water approaches to a possible amphibious landing beach. Minefield.

Beach organization: In an amphibious operation, the planned arrangement of personnel and facilities to effect movement, supply, and evacuation across beaches and in the beach area for support of a landing force.

Beach party: The naval component of the shore party. Beach master unit; shore party.

Beach party commander: The naval officer in command of the naval component of the shore party.

Beach photography: Vertical, oblique, ground, and periscope coverage at varying scales to provide information of offshore, shore, and inland areas. It covers terrain that provides observation of the beaches and is primarily concerned with the geological and tactical aspects of the beach.

Beach reserves: In an amphibious operation, an accumulation of supplies of all classes established in dumps in beachhead areas.

Beach support area: In amphibious operations, the area to the rear of a landing force or elements thereof, established and operated by shore party units, which contains the facilities for the unloading of troops and materiel and the support of the forces ashore; it includes facilities for the evacuation of wounded, enemy prisoners of war, and captured materiel. BSA.

Beach survey: The collection of data describing the physical characteristics of a beach; that is, an area whose boundaries are a shoreline, a coastline, and two natural or arbitrary assigned flanks.

Beach width: The horizontal dimensions of the beach measured at right angles to the shoreline from the line of extreme low water inland to the landward limit of the beach.

Beam rider: A missile guided by an electronic beam.

Beam width: The angle between the directions, on either side of the axis, at which the intensity of the radio frequency field drops to one-half the value it has on the axis.

Bearing: The horizontal angle at a given point measured clockwise from a specific datum point to a second point.

Beaten zone: The area on the ground upon which the cone of fire falls.

Begin morning civil twilight: The period of time at which the sun is halfway between beginning morning and nautical twilight and sunrise, when there is enough light to see objects clearly with the unaided eye. At this time, light intensification devices are no longer effective, and the sun is six degrees below the eastern horizon. BMCT.

Begin morning nautical twilight: The start of that period where, in good conditions and in the absence of other illumination, enough light is available to identify the general outlines of ground objects and conduct limited military operations. Light intensification devices are still effective and may have enhanced capabilities. At this time, the sun is 12 degrees below the eastern horizon. BMNT.

Bermnatural: The nearly horizontal portion of a beach or backshore having an abrupt fall and formed by deposition of material by wave action. A berm marks the limit of ordinary high tide. For air cushion vehicles, berms are required to protect materials handling equipment operations.

Bight: A bend in a coast forming an open bay or an open bay formed by such a bend.

Bilateral infrastructure: Infrastructure which concerns only two NATO members and is financed by mutual agreement between them.

Bill: A ship's publication listing operational or administrative procedures.

Billet: 1. Shelter for troops. 2. To quarter troops. 3. A personnel position or assignment that may be filled by one person.

Binding: The fastening or securing of items to a movable platform called a pallet. Palletized unit load.

Bin storage: Storage of items of supplies and equipment in an individual compartment or subdivision of a storage unit in less than bulk quantities.

Biographical intelligence: That component of intelligence that deals with individual foreign personalities of actual or potential importance.

Biological agent: A microorganism that causes disease in personnel, plants, or animals or causes the deterioration of materiel.

Biological hazard: An organism, or substance derived from an organism, that poses a threat to human or animal health. This can include medical waste, samples of a microorganism, virus, or toxin that can impact human health.

Biological warfare: Employment of biological agents to produce casualties in personnel or animals, or damage to plants or materiel; or defense against such employment.

Biological weapon: An item of materiel which projects, disperses, or disseminates a biological agent including arthropod vectors.

Biometric: Measurable physical characteristic or personal behavior trait used to recognize the identity or verify the claimed identity of an individual.

Biometrics: The process of recognizing an individual based on measurable anatomical, physiological, and behavioral characteristics.

Black: In intelligence handling, a term used in certain phrases to indicate reliance on illegal concealment rather than on cover.

Black list: An official counter-intelligence listing of actual or potential enemy collaborators, sympathizers, intelligence suspects, and other persons whose presence menaces the security of friendly forces.

Black propaganda: Propaganda that purports to emanate from a source other than the true one. Propaganda.

Blast effect: Destruction of or damage to structures and personnel by the force of an explosion on or above the surface of the ground. Blast effect may be contrasted with the crate ring and ground-shock effects of a projectile or charge that goes off beneath the surface.

Blast line: A horizontal radial line on the surface of the Earth originating at ground zero on which measurements of blast from an explosion are taken.

Blast wave: A sharply defined wave of increased pressure rapidly propagated through a surrounding medium from a center of detonation or similar disturbance.

Blast wave diffraction: The passage around and envelopment of a structure by the nuclear blast wave.

Bleeding edge: That edge of a map or chart on which cartographic detail is extended to the edge of the sheet.

Blind transmission: Any transmission of information that is made without expectation of acknowledgement.

Blister agent: A chemical agent which injures the eyes and lungs, and burns or blisters the skin. Vesicant agent.

Blocking and chocking: The use of wedges or chocks to prevent the inadvertent shifting of cargo in transit.

Blocking position: A defensive position so sited as to deny the enemy access to a given area or to prevent the enemy's advance in a given direction.

Block shipment: A method of shipment of supplies to overseas areas to provide balanced stocks or an arbitrary balanced force for a specific number of days, e.g., shipment of 30 days' supply for an average force of 10,000 individuals.

Block stowage loading: A method of loading whereby all cargo for a specific destination is stowed together. The purpose is to facilitate rapid off-loading at the destination, with the least possible disturbance of cargo intended for other points.

Blood agent: A chemical compound, including the cyanide group, that affects bodily functions by preventing the normal utilization of oxygen by body tissues.

Blood chit: A small sheet of material depicting an American flag and a statement in several languages to the effect that anyone assisting the bearer to safety will be rewarded.

Blue Bark: US military personnel, US citizen civilian employees of the Department of Defence, and the dependents of both categories who travel in connection with the death of an immediate family member. It also applies to designated escorts for dependents of deceased military members. Furthermore, the term is used to designate the personal property shipment of a deceased member.

Blue force tracking: Employment of techniques to actively or passively identify or track US, allied, or coalition forces for the purpose of providing the combatant commander enhanced situational awareness and reducing fratricide. BFT.

Board: An organized group of individuals within a joint force commander's headquarters, appointed by the commander (or other authority) that meets with the purpose of gaining guidance or decision. Its responsibilities and authority are governed by the authority which established the board.

Boat diagram: In the assault phase of an amphibious operation, a diagram showing the positions of individuals and equipment in each boat.

Boat group: The basic organization of landing craft. One boat group is organized for each battalion landing team to be landed in the first trip of landing craft or amphibious vehicles.

Boat lane: A lane for amphibious assault landing craft, which extends seaward from the landing beaches to the line of departure. The width of a boat lane is determined by the length of the corresponding beach.

Boat space: The space and weight factor used to determine the capacity of boats, landing craft, and amphibious vehicles. With respect to landing craft and amphibious vehicles, it is based on the requirements of one person with individual equipment. The person is assumed to weigh 224 pounds and to occupy 13.5 cubic feet of space.

Boat tail: The conical section of a ballistic body that progressively decreases in diameter toward the tail to reduce overall aerodynamic drag.

Bomber: -Intermediate-range bomber aircraft; long-range bomber aircraft; medium-range bomber aircraft.

Bomb impact plot: A graphic representation of the target area, usually a pre-strike air photograph, on which prominent dots are plotted to mark the impact or detonation points of bombs dropped on a specific bombing attack.

Bombing angle: The angle between the vertical and a line joining the aircraft to what would be the point of impact of a bomb released from it at that instant.

Bombing run: In air bombing, that part of the flight that begins, normally from an initial point, with the approach to the target, includes target acquisition, and ends normally at the weapon release point.

Bomb release line: An imaginary line around a defended area or objective over which an aircraft should release its bomb in order to obtain a hit or hits on an area or objective.

Bomb release point: The point in space at which bombs must be released to reach the desired point of detonation.

Bona fides: Good faith. In personnel recovery, the use of verbal or visual communication by individuals who are unknown to one another, to establish their authenticity, sincerity, honesty, and truthfulness. Evasion; recovery; recovery operations.

Booby trap: An explosive or non explosive device or other material, deliberately placed to cause casualties when an apparently harmless object is disturbed or a normally safe act is performed.

Booster: 1. A high-explosive element sufficiently sensitive so as to be actuated by small explosive elements in a fuze or primer and powerful enough to cause detonation of the main explosive filling. 2. An auxiliary or initial propulsion system which travels with a missile or aircraft and which may or may not separate from the parent craft when its impulse has been delivered. A booster system may contain, or consist of, one or more units.

Boost phase: That portion of the flight of a ballistic missile or space vehicle during which the booster and sustainer engines operate.

Border: In cartography, the area of a map or chart lying between the neat line and the surrounding framework.

Border break: A cartographic technique used when it is required to extend a portion of the cartographic detail of a map or chart beyond the sheet lines into the margin.

Border crosser: An individual, living close to a frontier, who normally has to cross the frontier frequently for legitimate purposes.

Bore safe fuze: Type of fuze having an interrupter in the explosive train that prevents a projectile from exploding until after it has cleared the muzzle of a weapon.

Bottom Line: A mine with negative buoyancy which remains on the seabed. Ground mine.

Bound: 1. In land warfare, a single movement, usually from cover to cover, made by troops often under enemy fire. 2. Distance covered in one movement by a unit that is advancing by bounds.

Boundary: A line that delineates surface areas for the purpose of facilitating coordination and deconfliction of operations between adjacent units, formations, or areas. Airspace control boundary.

Bouquet mine: In naval mine warfare, a mine in which a number of buoyant mine cases are attached to the same sinker, so that when the mooring of one mine case is cut, another mine rises from the sinker to its set depth.

Bracketing: A method of adjusting fire in which a bracket is established by obtaining an over and a short along the spotting line, and then successively splitting the bracket in half until a target hit or desired bracket is obtained.

Branch: 1. A subdivision of any organization. 2. A geographically separate unit of an activity, which performs all or part of the primary functions of the parent activity on a smaller scale. Unlike an annex, a branch is not merely an overflow addition. 3. An arm or service of the Army. 4. The contingency options built into the base plan. A branch is used for changing the mission, orientation, or direction of movement of a force to aid success of the operation based on anticipated events, opportunities, or disruptions caused by enemy actions and reactions.

Breakaway: 1. The onset of a condition in which the shock front moves away from the exterior of the expanding fireball produced by the explosion of a nuclear weapon. 2. After completion of attack, turn to heading as directed.

Break bulk cargo: Any commodity that, because of its weight, dimensions, or incompatibility with other cargo, must be shipped by mode other than military van or SEAVAN.

Break bulk ship: A ship with conventional holds for stowage of break bulk cargo, below or above deck, and equipped with cargo-handling gear. Ships also may be capable of carrying a limited number of containers, above or below deck.

Breaker: A wave in the process of losing energy where offshore energy loss is caused by wind action and near shore energy loss is caused by the impact of the sea floor as the wave enters shallow (shoaling) water. Breakers either plunge, spill, or surge.

Breaker angle: The angle a breaker makes with the beach. Breaker.

Break off position: The position at which a leaver or leaver section breaks off from the main convoy to proceed to a different destination.

Break-up: 1. In detection by radar, the separation of one solid return into a number of individual returns which correspond to the various objects or structure groupings. This separation is contingent upon a number of factors including range, beam width, gain setting, object size and distance between objects. 2. In imagery interpretation, the result of magnification or enlargement which causes the imaged item to lose its identity and the resultant presentation to become a random series of tonal impressions.

Brevity code: A code which provides no security but which has as its sole purpose the shortening of messages rather than the concealment of their content.

Bridgehead: An area of ground held or to be gained on the enemy's side of an obstacle. Airhead; beachhead.

Bridgehead line: -The limit of the objective area in the development of the bridgehead. Objective area.

Briefing: The act of giving in advance specific instructions or information.

Brigade: A unit usually smaller than a division to which are attached groups and/or battalions and smaller units tailored to meet anticipated requirements. BDE.

Broach: When a water craft is thrown broadside to the wind and waves, against a bar, or against the shoreline.

Buddy-aid: Acute medical care (first aid) provided by a non-medical Service member to another person.

Buffer distance: In nuclear warfare: 1. The horizontal distance which, when added to the radius of safety, will give the desired assurance that the specified degree of risk will not be exceeded. The buffer distance is normally expressed quantitatively in multiples of the delivery error. 2. The vertical distance which is added to the fallout safe-height of burst in order to determine a desired height of burst which will provide the desired assurance that militarily significant fallout will not occur. It is normally expressed quantitatively in multiples of the vertical error.

Bug: 1. A concealed microphone or listening device or other audio surveillance device. 2.To install means for audio surveillance.

Bugged: Room or object that contains a concealed listening device.

Building systems: Structures assembled from manufactured components designed to provide specific building configurations.

Buildup: The process of attaining prescribed strength of units and prescribed levels of vehicles, equipment, stores, and supplies. Also may be applied to the means of accomplishing this process.

Bulk cargo: That which is generally shipped in volume where the transportation conveyance is the only external container; such as liquids, ore, or grain.

Bulk petroleum product: A liquid petroleum product transported by various means and stored in tanks or containers having an individual fill capacity greater than 250 liters.

Bulk storage: 1. Storage in a warehouse of supplies and equipment in large quantities, usually in original containers, as distinguished from bin storage. 2. Storage of liquids, such as petroleum products in tanks, as distinguished from drum or packaged storage.

Bulls eye: An established reference point from which the position of an object can be referenced.

Bureau: A long-standing functional organization, with a supporting staff designed to perform a specific function or activity within a joint force commander's headquarters.

Burn notice: An official statement by one intelligence agency to other agencies, domestic or foreign, that an individual or group is unreliable for any of a variety of reasons.

Burnout: The point in time or in the missile trajectory when combustion of fuels in the rocket engine is terminated by other than programmed cutoff.

Burn-through range: The distance at which a specific radar can discern targets through the external interference being received.

C

Cache: A source of subsistence and supplies, typically containing items such as food, water, medical items, and/or communications equipment, packaged to prevent damage from exposure and hidden in isolated locations by such methods as burial, concealment, and/or submersion, to support isolated personnel. Concealment; evader; evasion; recovery; recovery operations.

Calibrated focal length: An adjusted value of the equivalent focal length, so computed as to equalize the positive and negative values of distortion over the entire field used in a camera.

Call fire: Fire delivered on a specific target in response to a request from the supported unit.

Call for fire: A request for fire containing data necessary for obtaining the required fire on a target.

Call sign: Any combination of characters or pronounceable words, which identifies a communication facility, a command, an authority, an activity, or a unit; used primarily for establishing and maintaining communications. CS. Collective call sign; indefinite call sign; international call sign; net call sign; tactical call sign; visual call sign; voice call sign.

Camera axis: An imaginary line through the optical center of the lens perpendicular to the negative photo plane.

Camera axis direction: Direction on the horizontal plane of the optical axis of the camera at the time of exposure. This direction is defined by its azimuth expressed in degrees in relation to true/magnetic north.

Camera calibration: The determination of the calibrated focal length, the location of the principal point with respect to the fiducially marks and the lens distortion effective in the focal plane of the camera referred to the particular calibrated focal length.

Camera cycling rate: The frequency with which camera frames are exposed, expressed as cycles per second.

Camouflage: The use of natural or artificial material on personnel, objects, or tactical positions with the aim of confusing, misleading, or evading the enemy.

Camouflage detection photography: Photography utilizing a special type of film designed for the detection of camouflage.

Camouflet: The resulting cavity in a deep underground burst when there is no rupture of the surface.

Campaign: A series of related major operations aimed at

achieving strategic and operational objectives within a given time and space.

Campaign plan: A joint operation plan for a series of related major operations aimed at achieving strategic or operational objectives within a given time and space.

Candidate target list: A list of objects or entities submitted by component commanders, appropriate agencies, or the joint force commander's staff for further development and inclusion on the joint target list and/or restricted target list, or moved to the no-strike list. Also called CTL. Joint integrated prioritized target list; target, target nomination list.

Cannibalize: To remove serviceable parts from one item of equipment in order to install them on another item of equipment.

Cannot observe: A type of fire control which indicates that the observer or spotter will be unable to adjust fire, but believes a target exists at the given location and is of sufficient importance to justify firing upon it without adjustment or observation.

Cantilever lifting frame: Used to move Navy lighter age causeway systems on to and off of lighter aboard ship (LASH) vessels. This device is suspended from the Morgan LASH barge crane and can lift one causeway section at a time. It is designated to allow the long sections to clear the rear of the ship as they are lowered into the water. CLF.

Capability: The ability to execute a specified course of action.

Capacity load (Navy): The maximum quantity of all supplies which each vessel can carry in proportions prescribed by proper authority.

Capstone publications: The top joint doctrine publication in the hierarchy of joint publications. The capstone publication links joint doctrine to national strategy and the contributions of other government agencies, alliances, and coalitions, and reinforces policy for command and control. The Chairman of the Joint Chiefs of Staff signs this publication, and it is intended to be used by combatant commanders, sub unified commanders, joint task force commanders, Service Chiefs, and Joint Staff directors. Joint publication; keystone publications.

Capstone requirements document: A document that contains performance-based requirements to facilitate development of individual operational requirements documents by providing a common framework and operational concept to guide their development. CRD.

Capsule: 1. A sealed, pressurized cabin for extremely high altitude or space flight which provides an acceptable environment for man, animal, or equipment. 2. An ejectable sealed cabin having automatic devices for safe return of the occupants to the surface.

Captive firing: A firing test of short duration, conducted with the missile propulsion system operating while secured to a test stand.

Cardinal point effect: The increased intensity of a line or group of returns on the radarscope occurring when the radar beam is perpendicular to the rectangular surface of a line or group of similarly aligned features in the ground pattern.

Cargo classification (combat loading): The division of military cargo into categories for combat loading aboard ships.

Cargo increment number: A seven-character alphanumeric field that uniquely describes a non-unit-cargo entry (line) in the Joint Operation Planning and Execution System time-phased force and deployment data.

Cargo outturn message: A brief message report transmitted within 48 hours of completion of ship discharge to advise both the Military Sealift Command and the terminal of loading of the condition of the cargo, including any discrepancies in the form of overages, shortages, or damages between cargo as manifested and cargo as checked at time of discharge.

Cargo sling: A strap, chain, or other material used to hold cargo items securely which are to be hoisted, lowered, or suspended.

Cargo tie-down point: A point on military materiel designed for attachment of various means for securing the item for transport.

Cargo transporter: A reusable metal shipping container designed for worldwide surface and air movement of suitable military supplies and equipment through the cargo transporter service.

Carpet bombing: The progressive distribution of a mass bomb load upon an area defined by designated boundaries, in such manner as to inflict damage to all portions thereof.

Carrier air wing: Two or more aircraft squadrons formed under one commander for administrative and tactical control of operations from a carrier.

Carrier battle group: A standing naval task group consisting of a carrier, surface combatants, and submarines as assigned in direct support, operating in mutual support with the task of destroying hostile submarine, surface, and air forces within the group's assigned operational area and striking at targets along hostile shore lines or projecting fire power inland. CVBG.

Carrier striking force: A naval task force composed of aircraft carriers and supporting combatant ships capable of conducting strike operations.

Cartridge actuated device: Small explosive devices used to eject stores from launched devices, actuate other explosive systems, or provide initiation for aircrew escape devices. CAD.

Carver: A special operations forces acronym used throughout the targeting and mission planning cycle to assess mission validity and requirements. The acronym stands for criticality, accessibility, recuperability, vulnerability, effect, and recognizability.

Case: 1. An intelligence operation in its entirety. 2. Record of the development of an intelligence operation, including personnel, modus operandi, and objectives.

Casualty category: A term used to specifically classify a casualty for reporting purposes based upon the casualty type and the casualty status. Casualty categories include killed in action, died of wounds received in action, and wounded in action.

Casualty evacuation: The unregulated movement of casualties that can include movement both to and between medical treatment facilities. CASEVAC.

Casualty receiving and treatment ship: In amphibious operations, a ship designated to receive, provide treatment for, and transfer casualties.

Casualty status — A term used to classify a casualty for reporting purposes. There are seven casualty statuses: (1) deceased; (2) duty status - whereabouts unknown; (3) missing; (4) very seriously ill or injured; (5) seriously ill or injured; (6) incapacitating illness or injury; and (7) not seriously injured. Casualty; casualty category; casualty type; deceased; duty status - whereabouts unknown; incapacitating illness or injury; missing; not seriously injured; seriously ill or injured; very seriously ill or injured.

Casualty type: A term used to identify a casualty for reporting purposes as either a hostile casualty or a non hostile casualty. Casualty; casualty category; casualty status; hostile casualty; non hostile casualty.

Catalytic attack: An attack designed to bring about a war between major powers through the disguised machinations of a third power.

Catapult: A structure which provides an auxiliary source of thrust to a missile or aircraft; must combine the functions of directing and accelerating the missile during its travel on the catapult; serves the same functions for a missile as does a gun tube for a shell.

Catastrophic event: Any natural or man-made incident, including terrorism, which results in extraordinary levels of mass casualties, damage, or disruption severely affecting the population, infrastructure, environment, economy, national morale, and/or government functions.

Categories of data: In the context of perception management and its constituent approaches, data obtained by adversary individuals, groups, intelligence systems, and officials. Such data fall in two categories: a. information — A compilation of data provided by protected or open sources that would provide a substantially complete picture of friendly intentions, capabilities, or activities. b. indicators — Data derived from open sources or from detectable actions that adversaries can piece together or interpret to reach personal conclusions or official estimates concerning friendly intentions, capabilities, or activities.

Causeway: A craft similar in design to a barge, but longer and narrower, designed to assist in the discharge and transport of cargo from vessels. barge; watercraft.

Causeway launching area: An area located near the line of departure but clear of the approach lanes, where ships can launch pontoon causeways.

Caveat: A designator used with a classification to further limit the dissemination of restricted information.

Cease fire: 1. A command given to any unit or individual firing any weapon to stop engaging the target. See also call for fire; fire mission. 2. A command given to air defense artillery units to refrain from firing on, but to continue to track, an airborne object. Missiles already in flight will be permitted to continue to intercept.

Cease fire line: Armistice demarcation line.

Ceiling: The height above the Earth's surface of the lowest layer of clouds or obscuration phenomena that is reported as "broken," "overcast," or "obscured" and not classified as "thin" or "partial."

Celestial guidance: The guidance of a missile or other vehicle by reference to celestial bodies.

Celestial sphere: An imaginary sphere of infinite radius concentric with the Earth, on which all celestial bodies except the Earth are imagined to be projected.

Cell: A subordinate organization formed around a specific process, capability, or activity within a designated larger organization of a joint force commander's headquarters. A cell usually is part of both a functional and traditional staff structures.

Censorship: Armed forces censorship; civil censorship; field press censorship; national censorship; primary censorship; prisoner of war censorship; secondary censorship.

Center: An enduring functional organization, with a supporting staff, designed to perform a joint function within a joint force commander's headquarters.

Center of gravity: The source of power that provides moral or physical strength, freedom of action, or will to act. COG. decisive point.

Centigray: A unit of absorbed dose of radiation.

Central control officer: The officer designated by the amphibious task force commander for the overall coordination of the waterborne ship-to-shore movement. The central control officer is embarked in the central control ship. CCO.

Centralized control: 1. In air defense, the control mode whereby a higher echelon makes direct target assignments to fire units. 2. In joint air operations, placing within one commander the responsibility and authority for planning, directing, and coordinating a military operation or group/category of operations. decentralized control.

Centrally managed item: An item of materiel subject to inventory control point management.

Central procurement: The procurement of materiel, supplies, or services by an officially designated command or agency with funds specifically provided for such procurement for the benefit and use of the entire component or, in the case of single managers, for the Military Departments as a whole.

Chaff: Radar confusion reflectors, consisting of thin, narrow metallic strips of various lengths and frequency responses, which are used to reflect echoes for confusion purposes. Causes enemy radar guided missiles to lock on to it instead of the real aircraft, ship, or other platform. deception; rope.

Chain of command: The succession of commanding officers from a superior to a subordinate through which command is exercised. command channel.

Chairman of the Joint Chiefs of Staff instruction: A replacement document for all types of correspondence containing Chairman of the Joint Chiefs of Staff policy and guidance that does not involve the employment of forces. An instruction is of indefinite duration and is applicable to external agencies, or both the Joint Staff and external agencies. It remains in effect until superseded, rescinded, or otherwise canceled. Chairman of the Joint Chiefs of Staff instructions, unlike joint publications, will not contain joint doctrine. Terminology used in these publications will be consistent with. CJCSI. Chairman of the Joint Chiefs of Staff manual.

Chairman of the Joint Chiefs of Staff manual: A document containing detailed procedures for performing specific tasks that do not involve the employment of forces. A manual is of indefinite duration and is applicable to external agencies or both the Joint Staff and external agencies. It may supplement a Chairman of the Joint Chiefs of Staff instruction or stand alone and remains in effect until superseded, rescinded, or otherwise canceled. Chairman of the Joint Chiefs of Staff manuals, unlike joint publications, will not contain joint doctrine. Terminology used in these publications will be consistent with JP 1-02. CJCSM. Chairman of the Joint Chiefs of Staff instruction.

Chairman of the Joint Chiefs of Staff memorandum of policy: A statement of policy approved by the Chairman of the Joint Chiefs of Staff and issued for the guidance of the Services, the combatant commands, and the Joint Staff.

Chairman's program assessment: Provides the Chairman of the Joint Chiefs of Staff's personal appraisal on alternative program recommendations and budget proposals to the Secretary of Defense for consideration in refining the defense program and budget in accordance with 10 United States Code. The Chairman's program assessment comments on the risk associated with the programmed allocation of Defense resources and evaluates the conformance of program objective memoranda to the priorities established in strategic plans and combatant commanders' priority requirements. CPA.

Chairman's program recommendations: Provides the Chairman of the Joint Chiefs of

Staff's personal recommendations to the Secretary of Defense for the programming and budgeting process before publishing the Defense Planning Guidance (DPG) in accordance with 10 United States Code. The Chairman's program recommendations articulates programs the Chairman deems critical for the Secretary of Defense to consider when identifying Department of Defense priorities and performance goals in the DPG and emphasizes specific recommendations that will enhance joint readiness, promote joint doctrine and training, improve joint War fighting capabilities, and satisfy joint War fighting requirements within DOD resource constraints and within acceptable risk levels. CPR.

Chalk commander: The commander of all troops embarked under one chalk number. chalk number; chalk troops.

Chalk number: The number given to a complete load and to the transporting carrier. chalk commander; chalk troops.

Chalk troops: A load of troops defined by a particular chalk number. chalk commander; chalk number.

Challenge: Any process carried out by one unit or person with the object of ascertaining the friendly or hostile character or identity of another. countersign; password.

Chancery: The building upon a diplomatic or consular compound which houses the offices of the chief of mission or principal officer.

Change detection: An image enhancement technique that compares two images of the same area from different time periods. Identical picture elements are eliminated, leaving signatures that have undergone change.

Characteristic actuation width: In naval mine warfare, the width of path over which mines can be actuated by a single run of the sweep gear.

Characteristic detection probability: In naval mine warfare, the ratio of the number of mines detected on a single run to the number of mines which could have been detected within the characteristic detection width.

Characteristic detection width: In naval mine warfare, the width of path over which mines can be detected on a single run.

Charged demolition target: A demolition target on which all charges have been placed and which is in the states of readiness, either state 1 – safe, or state 2 – armed. state of readiness –

state 1 – safe; state of readiness – state 2 – armed.

Chart base: A chart used as a primary source for compilation or as a framework on which new detail is printed. Topographic base.

Check firing: In artillery, mortar, and naval gunfire support, a command to cause a temporary halt in firing. cease fire; fire mission.

Checkout: A sequence of functional, operational, and calibrational tests to determine the condition and status of a weapon system or element thereof.

Checkpoint: 1. A predetermined point on the surface of the Earth used as a means of controlling movement, a registration target for fire adjustment, or reference for location. 2. Center of impact; a burst center. 3. Geographical location on land or water above which the position of an aircraft in flight may be determined by observation or by electrical means. 4. A place where military police check vehicular or pedestrian traffic in order to enforce circulation control measures and other laws, orders, and regulations.

Check sweeping: In naval mine warfare, sweeping to check that no moored mines are left after a previous clearing operation.

Chemical agent: A chemical substance which is intended for use in military operations to kill, seriously injure, or incapacitate mainly through its physiological effects. The term excludes riot control agents when used for law enforcement purposes, herbicides, smoke, and flames. Chemical dose; chemical warfare; riot control agent.

Chemical agent cumulative action: The building up, within the human body, of small ineffective doses of certain chemical agents to a point where eventual effect is similar to one large dose.

Chemical, biological, radiological, and nuclear defense: Measures taken to minimize or negate the vulnerabilities and/or effects of a chemical, biological, radiological, or nuclear incident. CBRN defense.

Chemical, biological, radiological, and nuclear environment: Conditions found in an area resulting from immediate or persisting effects of chemical, biological, radiological, or nuclear attacks or unintentional releases. CBRN environment.

Chemical, biological, radiological, and nuclear protection: Measures that are taken to keep chemical, biological, radiological, and nuclear threats and hazards from having an adverse effect on personnel, equipment, or critical assets and facilities. CBRN protection.

Chemical, biological, radiological, and nuclear sense: Activities that continually provide chemical, biological, radiological, and nuclear threat and hazard information and intelligence in a timely manner to support the common operational picture. CBRN sense.

Chemical, biological, radiological, and nuclear shape: The command and control activity that integrates the sense, shield, and sustain operational elements to characterize chemical, biological, radiological, and nuclear hazards and threats and employ necessary capabilities to counter their effects. CBRN shape.

Chemical, biological, radiological, and nuclear shield: Individual and collective protection measures essential to mitigating the effects of chemical, biological, radiological, and nuclear hazards. CBRN shield.

Chemical, biological, radiological, and nuclear sustain: The decontamination and medical activities to restore combat power and continue operations. CBRN sustain.

Chemical, biological, radiological, nuclear, and high-yield explosives consequence management: The consequence management activities for all deliberate and inadvertent releases of chemical, biological, radiological, nuclear, and high-yield explosives that are undertaken when directed or authorized by the President. CBRNE CM.

Chemical, biological, radiological, nuclear, or high-yield explosives incident : An emergency resulting from the deliberate or unintentional release of nuclear, biological, radiological, or toxic or poisonous chemical materials, or the detonation of a high-yield explosive. CBRNE incident.

Chemical, biological, radiological, or nuclear incident: Any occurrence, resulting from the use of chemical, biological, radiological and nuclear weapons and devices; the emergence of secondary hazards arising from counterforce targeting; or the release of toxic industrial materials into the environment, involving the emergence of chemical, biological, radiological and nuclear hazards.

Chemical, biological, radiological, or nuclear weapon: A fully engineered assembly designed for employment to cause the release of a chemical or biological agent or radiological material onto a chosen target or to generate a nuclear detonation. CBRN weapon.

Chemical dose: The amount of chemical agent, expressed in milligrams, that is taken or absorbed by the body.

Chemical hazard: Any chemical manufactured, used, transported, or stored which can cause death or other harm through toxic properties of those materials. This includes chemical agents and chemical weapons, as well as toxic industrial chemicals and toxic industrial materials.

Chemical horn: In naval mine warfare, a mine horn containing an electric battery, the electrolyte for which is in a glass tube protected by a thin metal sheet.

Chemical monitoring: The continued or periodic process of determining whether or not a chemical agent is present.

Chemical survey: The directed effort to determine the nature and degree of chemical hazard in an area and to delineate the perimeter of the hazard area.

Chemical weapon: Together or separately, (a) a toxic chemical and its precursors, except when intended for a purpose not prohibited under the Chemical Weapons Convention; (b) munitions or device, specifically designed to cause death or other harm through toxic properties of those chemicals specified in (a), above, which would be released as a result of the employment of such munitions' or device; (c) any equipment specifically designed for use directly in connection with the employment of munitions or devices specified in (b), above. Chemical agent; chemical dose; chemical warfare; riot control agent.

Chief Army, Navy, Air Force, or Marine Corps censor: An officer appointed by the commander of the Army, Navy, Air Force, or Marine Corps component of a unified command to supervise all censorship activities of that Service.

Chief of mission: The principal officer (the ambassador) in charge of a diplomatic facility of the United States, including any individual assigned to be temporarily in charge of such a facility. The chief of mission is the personal representative of the President to the country of accreditation. The chief of mission is responsible for the direction, coordination, and supervision of all US Government executive branch employees in that country (except those under the command of a US area military commander). The security of the diplomatic post is the chief of mission's direct responsibility. COM.

Chief of staff: The senior or principal member or head of a staff, or the principal assistant in a staff capacity to a person in a command capacity; the head or controlling member of a staff, for purposes of the coordination of its work; position that in itself is without inherent power of command by reason of assignment, except that which is invested in such a position by delegation to exercise command in another's name.

Chronic radiation dose: A dose of ionizing radiation received either continuously or intermittently over a prolonged period of time. A chronic radiation dose may be high enough to cause radiation sickness and death but, if received at a low dose rate, a significant portion of the acute cellular damage may be repaired. acute radiation dose; radiation dose; radiation dose rate.

Chuffing: The characteristic of some rockets to burn intermittently and with an irregular noise.

Cipher: Any cryptographic system in which arbitrary symbols (or groups of symbols) represent units of plain text of regular length, usually single letters; units of plain text are rearranged; or both, in accordance with certain predetermined rules.

Circular error probable: An indicator of the delivery accuracy of a weapon system, used as a factor in determining probable damage to a target. It is the radius of a circle within which half of a missile's projectiles are expected to fall. CEP.

Civil administration — An administration established by a foreign government in (1) friendly territory, under an agreement with the government of the area concerned, to exercise certain authority normally the function of the local government; or (2) hostile territory, occupied by United States forces, where a foreign government exercises executive, legislative, and judicial authority until an indigenous civil government can be established. CA.

Civil affairs: Designated Active and Reserve Component forces and units organized, trained, and equipped specifically to conduct civil affairs operations and to support civil-military operations. CA.

Civil affairs activities: Activities performed or supported by civil affairs that (1) enhance the relationship between military forces and civil authorities in areas where military forces are present; and (2) involve application of civil affairs functional specialty skills, in areas normally the responsibility of civil government, to enhance conduct of civil military operations. civil affairs; civil-military operations.

Civil affairs agreement: An agreement that governs the relationship between allied armed forces located in a friendly country and the civil authorities and people of that country.

Civil augmentation program: Standing, long-term external support contacts designed to augment Service logistic capabilities with contracted support in both preplanned and short notice contingencies. Examples include US Army Logistics Civil Augmentation Program, Air Force Contract Augmentation Program, and US Navy Global Contingency Capabilities Contracts. CAP.

Civil authorities: Those elected and appointed officers and employees who constitute the government of the United States, the governments of the 50 states, the District of Columbia, the Commonwealth of Puerto Rico, United States possessions and territories, and political subdivisions thereof.

Civil censorship: Censorship of civilian communications, such as messages, printed matter, and films entering, leaving, or circulating within areas or territories occupied or controlled by armed forces. Censorship.

Civil damage assessment: An appraisal of damage to a nation's population, industry, utilities, communications, transportation, food, water, and medical resources to support planning for national recovery.

Civil defence: All those activities and measures designed or undertaken to: a. minimize the effects upon the civilian population caused or which would be caused by an enemy attack on the United States; b. deal with the immediate emergency conditions that would be created by any such attack; and c. effectuate emergency repairs to, or the emergency restoration of, vital utilities and facilities destroyed or damaged by any such attack.

Civil disturbance: Group acts of violence and disorder prejudicial to public law and order. Domestic emergencies.

Civil disturbance readiness conditions: Required conditions of preparedness to be attained by military forces in preparation for deployment to an objective area in response to an actual or threatened civil disturbance.

Civil emergency: Any occasion or instance for which, in the determination of the President, federal assistance is needed to supplement state and local efforts and capabilities to save lives and to protect property and public health and safety, or to lessen or avert the threat of a catastrophe in any part of the United States.

Civilian internee: A civilian who is interned during armed conflict, occupation, or other military operation for security reasons, for protection, or because he or she committed an offense against the detaining power. CI.

Civilian internee camp: An installation established for the internment and administration of civilian internees.

Civil-military medicine: A discipline within operational medicine comprising public health and medical issues that involve a civil-military interface, including military medical support to civil authorities, medical engagement cooperation activities, and medical civil-military operations.

Civil-military operations: The activities of a commander that establish, maintain, influence, or exploit relations between military forces, governmental and nongovernmental civilian organizations and authorities, and the civilian populace in a friendly, neutral, or hostile operational area in order to facilitate military operations, to consolidate and achieve operational US objectives. Civil-military operations may include performance by military forces of activities and functions normally the responsibility of the local, regional, or national government. These activities may occur prior to, during, or subsequent to other military actions. They may also occur, if directed, in the absence of other military operations. Civil-military operations may be performed by designated civil affairs, by other military forces, or by a combination of civil affairs and other forces. CMO.

Civil-military operations center: An organization normally comprised of civil affairs, established to plan and facilitate coordination of activities of the Armed Forces of the United States with indigenous populations and institutions, the private sector, intergovernmental organizations, nongovernmental organizations, multinational forces, and other governmental agencies in support of the joint force commander. CMOC.

Civil nuclear power: A nation that has the potential to employ nuclear technology for development of nuclear weapons but has deliberately decided against doing so.

Civil requirements: The necessary production and distribution of all types of services, supplies, and equipment during periods of armed conflict or occupation to ensure the productive efficiency of the civilian economy and to provide to civilians the treatment and protection to which they are entitled under customary and conventional international law.

Civil support — Department of Defense support to US civil authorities for domestic emergencies, and for designated law enforcement and other activities. CS.

Civil transportation: The movement of persons, property, or mail by civil facilities, and the resources necessary to accomplish the movement.

Classes of supply: There are ten categories into which supplies are grouped in order to facilitate supply management and planning. I. Rations and gratuitous issue of health, morale, and welfare items. II. Clothing, individual equipment, tentage, tool sets, and administrative and housekeeping supplies and equipment. III. Petroleum, oils, and lubricants. IV. Construction materials. V. Ammunition. VI. Personal demand items. VII. Major end items, including tanks, helicopters, and radios. VIII. Medical. IX. Repair parts and components for equipment maintenance. X. Nonstandard items to support nonmilitary programs such as agriculture and economic development.

Classification: The determination that official information requires, in the interests of national security, a specific degree of protection against unauthorized disclosure, coupled with a designation signifying that such a determination has been made. security classification.

Classification of bridges and vehicles: military load classification.

Classified information: Official information that has been determined to require, in the interests of national security, protection against unauthorized disclosure and which has been so designated.

Classified matter: Official information or matter in any form or of any nature which requires protection in the interests of national security. Unclassified matter.

Clean aircraft: 1. An aircraft in flight configuration (versus landing configuration); i.e., landing gear and flaps retracted, etc. 2. An aircraft that does not have external stores.

Clear: 1. To approve or authorize, or to obtain approval or authorization for: a. a person or persons with regard to their actions, movements, duties, etc.; b. an object or group of objects, as equipment or supplies, with regard to quality, quantity, purpose, movement, disposition, etc.; and c. a request, with regard to correctness of form, validity, etc. 2. To give one or more aircraft a clearance. 3. To give a person a security clearance. 4.To fly over an obstacle without touching it. 5. To pass a designated point, line, or object. The end of a column must pass the designated feature before the latter is cleared. 6. a. To operate a gun so as to unload it or make certain no ammunition remains; and b. to free a gun of stoppages. 7. To clear an engine; to open the throttle of an idling engine to free it from carbon. 8. To clear the air to gain either temporary or permanent air superiority or control in a given sector.

Clearance capacity: An estimate expressed in terms of measurement or weight tons per day of the cargo that may be transported inland from a beach or port over the available means of inland communication, including roads, railroads, and inland waterways. The estimate is based on an evaluation of the physical characteristics of the transportation facilities in the area. Beach capacity; port capacity.

Clearance decontamination: The final level of decontamination that provides the decontamination of equipment and personnel to a level that allows unrestricted transportation, maintenance, employment, and disposal.

Clearance rate: The area which would be cleared per unit time with a stated minimum percentage clearance, using specific mine hunting and/or minesweeping procedures.

Clearing operation: An operation designed to clear or neutralize all mines and obstacles from a route or area.

Clock code position: The position of a target in relation to an aircraft or ship with dead-ahead position considered as 12 o'clock.

Close air support: Air action by fixed- and rotary-wing aircraft against hostile targets that are in close proximity to friendly forces and that require detailed integration of each air mission with the fire and movement of those forces. CAS.

Close-controlled air interception: An interception in which the interceptor is continuously controlled to a position from which the target is within visual range or radar contact. Air interception.

Closed area: A designated area in or over which passage of any kind is prohibited. Prohibited area.

Close support: That action of the supporting force against targets or objectives which are sufficiently near the supported force as to require detailed integration or coordination of the supporting action with the fire, movement, or other actions of the supported force.

Close support area: Those parts of the ocean operating areas nearest to, but not necessarily in, the objective area. They are assigned to naval support carrier battle groups, surface action groups, surface action units, and certain logistic combat service support elements.

Closure minefield: In naval mine warfare, a minefield which is planned to present such a threat that waterborne shipping is prevented from moving.

Closure shortfall: The specified movement requirement or portion thereof that did not meet scheduling criteria and/or movement dates.

Cloud amount: The proportion of sky obscured by cloud, expressed as a fraction of sky covered.

Cloud top height: The maximal altitude to which a nuclear mushroom cloud rises.

Cluster bomb unit: -An aircraft store composed of a dispenser and sub munitions. CBU.

Clutter: Permanent echoes, cloud, or other atmospheric echo on radar scope; as contact has entered scope clutter.

Coalition: An ad hoc arrangement between two or more nations for common action.

Coalition action: Multinational action outside the bounds of established alliances, usually for single occasions or longer cooperation in a narrow sector of common interest.

Coarse mine: In naval mine warfare, a relatively insensitive influence mine.

Co assembly: With respect to exports, a cooperative arrangement by which finished parts, components, assemblies, or subassemblies are provided to an eligible foreign government, international organization, or commercial producer for the assembly of an end-item or system. This is normally accomplished under the provisions of a manufacturing license agreement per the US International Traffic in Arms Regulation and could involve the implementation of a government-to- government memorandum of understanding.

Coastal convoy: A convoy whose voyage lies in general on the continental shelf and in coastal waters.

Coastal frontier: A geographic division of a coastal area, established for organization and command purposes in order to ensure the effective coordination of military forces employed in military operations within the coastal frontier area.

Coastal refraction: The change of the direction of travel of a radio ground wave as it passes from land to sea or from sea to land. Land effect or shoreline effect.

Coastal sea control: The employment of forces to ensure the unimpeded use of an offshore coastal area by friendly forces and, as appropriate, to deny the use of the area to enemy forces.

Code: 1. Any system of communication in which arbitrary groups of symbols represent units of plain text of varying length. Codes may be used for brevity or for security. 2. A cryptosystem in which the cryptographic equivalents, typically consisting of letters or digits in otherwise meaningless combinations, are substituted for plain text elements which are primarily words, phrases, or sentences. Cryptosystem.

Code word: 1. A word that has been assigned a classification and a classified meaning to safeguard intentions and information regarding a classified plan or operation. 2. A cryptonym used to identify sensitive intelligence data.

Cold war: A state of international tension wherein political, economic, technological, sociological, psychological, paramilitary, and military measures short of overt armed conflict involving regular military forces are employed to achieve national objectives.

Collaborative purchase: A method of purchase whereby, in buying similar commodities, buyers for two or more departments exchange information concerning planned purchases in order to minimize competition between them for commodities in the same market.

Collapse depth: The design depth, referenced to the axis of the pressure hull, beyond which the hull structure or hull penetrations are presumed to suffer catastrophic failure to the point of total collapse.

Collate: 1. The grouping together of related items to provide a record of events and facilitate further processing. 2. To compare critically two or more items or documents concerning the same general subject; normally accomplished in the processing and exploitation portion of the intelligence process. Intelligence process.

Collateral damage: Unintentional or incidental injury or damage to persons or objects that would not be lawful military targets in the circumstances ruling at the time. Such damage is not unlawful so long as it is not excessive in light of the overall military advantage anticipated from the attack.

Collection: In intelligence usage, the acquisition of information and the provision of this information to processing elements. Intelligence process.

Collection (acquisition): The obtaining of information in any manner, including direct observation, liaison with official agencies, or solicitation from official, unofficial, or public sources.

Collection agency: Any individual, organization, or unit that has access to sources of information and the capability of collecting information from them. See also agency.

Collection asset: A collection system, platform, or capability that is supporting, assigned, or attached to a particular commander. See also capability; collection.

Collection management: In intelligence usage, the process of converting intelligence requirements into collection requirements, establishing priorities, tasking or coordinating with appropriate collection sources or agencies, monitoring results, and retasking, as required. See also collection; collection requirement; collection requirements management; intelligence; intelligence process.

Collection management authority: Within the Department of Defense, collection management authority constitutes the authority to establish, prioritize, and validate theater collection requirements, establish sensor tasking guidance, and develop theater wide collection policies. CMA. Collection manager; collection plan; collection requirement.

Collection manager: An individual with responsibility for the timely and efficient tasking of organic collection resources and the development of requirements for theater and national assets that could satisfy specific information needs in support of the mission. CM. Collection; collection management authority.

Collection operations management: The authoritative direction, scheduling, and control of specific collection operations and associated processing, exploitation, and reporting resources. COM. Collection management; collection requirements management.

Collection plan: A plan for collecting information from all available sources to meet intelligence requirements and for transforming those requirements into orders and requests to appropriate agencies. See also information; information requirements; intelligence process.

Collection planning: A continuous process that coordinates and integrates the efforts of all collection units and agencies. Collection.

Collection point: A point designated for the assembly of personnel casualties, stragglers, disabled materiel, salvage, etc., for further movement to collecting stations or rear installations.

Collection requirements management: The authoritative development and control of collection, processing, exploitation, and/or reporting requirements that normally result in either the direct tasking of assets over which the collection manager has authority, or the generation of tasking requests to collection management authorities at a higher, lower, or lateral echelon to accomplish the collection mission. CRM. Collection; collection management; collection operations management.

Collection resource: A collection system, platform, or capability that is not assigned or attached to a specific unit or echelon which must be requested and coordinated through the chain of command. Collection management.

Collective call sign: Any call sign which represents two or more facilities, commands, authorities, or units. The collective call sign for any of these includes the commander thereof and all subordinate commanders therein. Call sign.

Collective protection: The protection provided to a group of individuals which permits relaxation of individual chemical, biological, radiological, and nuclear protection. COLPRO.

Collective self-defense: Collective self-defense is the act of defending other designated non-US forces. Only the President or Secretary of Defense may authorize US forces to exercise the right of collective self-defense.

Collocation: The physical placement of two or more detachments, units, organizations, or facilities at a specifically defined location.

Colored beach: That portion of usable coastline sufficient for the assault landing of a regimental landing team or similar sized unit. In the event that the landing force consists of a single battalion landing team, a colored beach will be used and no further subdivision of the beach is required. Numbered beach.

Column formation: A formation in which elements are placed one behind the other.

Column gap: The space between two consecutive elements proceeding on the same route. It can be calculated in units of length or in units of time measured from the rear of one element to the front of the following element.

Column length: The length of the roadway occupied by a column or a convoy in movement. Road space.

Combat air patrol: An aircraft patrol provided over an objective area, the force protected, the critical area of a combat zone, or in an air defense area, for the purpose of intercepting and destroying hostile aircraft before they reach their targets. CAP. Airborne alert; barrier combat air patrol; patrol; rescue combat air patrol.

Combat airspace control: -Airspace control in the combat zone.

Combat and operational stress: The expected and predictable emotional, intellectual, physical, and/or behavioral reactions of Service members who have been exposed to stressful events in war or military operations other than war. Combat stress reactions vary in quality and severity as a function of operational conditions, such as intensity, duration, rules of engagement, leadership, effective communication, unit morale, unit cohesion, and perceived importance of the mission.

Combat and operational stress control: Programs developed and actions taken by military leadership to prevent, identify, and manage adverse combat and operational stress reactions in units; optimize mission performance; conserve fighting strength; prevent or minimize adverse effects of combat and operational stress on members' physical, psychological, intellectual and social health; and to return the unit or Service member to duty expeditiously.

Combatant command: A unified or specified command with a broad continuing mission under a single commander established and so designated by the President, through the Secretary of Defense and with the advice and assistance of the Chairman of the Joint Chiefs of Staff. Combatant commands typically have geographic or functional responsibilities. Specified command; unified command.

Combatant commander logistic procurement support board: A combatant commander-level joint board established to ensure that contracting support and other sources of support are properly synchronized across the entire area of responsibility. CLPSB. Joint acquisition review board; joint contracting support board.

Combatant commander's required date: The original date relative to C-day, specified by the combatant commander for arrival of forces or cargo at the destination; shown in the time-phased force and deployment data to assess the impact of later arrival. CRD.

Combat area: A restricted area (air, land, or sea) that is established to prevent or minimize mutual interference between friendly forces engaged in combat operations. Combat zone.

Combat assessment: The determination of the overall effectiveness of force employment during military operations. Combat assessment is composed of three major components: (a) battle damage assessment; (b) munitions effectiveness assessment; and (c) reattack recommendation. CA. Battle damage assessment; munitions effectiveness assessment; reattack recommendation.

Combat camera: The acquisition and utilization of still and motion imagery in support of combat, information, humanitarian, special force, intelligence, reconnaissance, engineering, legal, public affairs, and other operations involving the Military Services. CMCAM. Visual information; visual information documentation.

Combat cargo officer: An embarkation officer assigned to major amphibious ships or naval staffs, functioning primarily as an adviser to and representative of the naval commander in matters pertaining to embarkation and debarkation of troops and their supplies and equipment. CCO. Embarkation officer.

Combat chart: A special naval chart, at a scale of 1:50,000, designed for naval surface fire support and close air support during coastal or amphibious operations and showing detailed hydrography and topography in the coastal belt. Amphibious chart.

Combat control team: A small task organized team of Air Force parachute and combat diver qualified personnel trained and equipped to rapidly establish and control drop, landing, and extraction zone air traffic in austere or hostile conditions. They survey and establish terminal airheads as well as provide guidance to aircraft for airlift operations. They provide command and control, and conduct reconnaissance, surveillance, and survey assessments of potential objective airfields or assault zones. They also can perform limited weather observations and removal of obstacles or unexploded ordinance with demolitions. CCT.

Combat engineering: Those engineering capabilities and activities that support the maneuver of land combat forces and that require close support to those forces. Combat engineering consists of three types of capabilities and activities: mobility, counter mobility, and survivability.

Combat forces: Those forces whose primary missions are to participate in combat. Operating forces.

Combat identification: The process of attaining an accurate characterization of detected objects in the operational environment sufficient to support an engagement decision. CID.

Combat information center: The agency in a ship or aircraft manned and equipped to collect, display, evaluate, and disseminate tactical information for the use of the embarked flag officer, commanding officer, and certain control agencies. CIC.

Combat intelligence: That knowledge of the enemy, weather, and geographical features required by a commander in the planning and conduct of combat operations.

Combat loading: The arrangement of personnel and the stowage of equipment and supplies in a manner designed to conform to the anticipated tactical operation of the organization embarked. Each individual item is stowed so that it can be unloaded at the required time. Loading.

Combat power: The total means of destructive and/or disruptive force which a military unit/formation can apply against the opponent at a given time.

Combat readiness: Synonymous with operational readiness, with respect to missions or functions performed in combat.

Combat search and rescue: The tactics, techniques, and procedures performed by forces to effect the recovery of isolated personnel during combat. CSAR. Search and rescue.

Combat search and rescue task force: All forces committed to a specific combat search and rescue operation to locate, identify, support, and recover isolated personnel during combat. This includes those elements assigned to provide command and control and to protect the recovery vehicle(s) from attack. CSARTF. Combat search and rescue; search; search and rescue.

Combat service support: The essential capabilities, functions, activities, and tasks necessary to sustain all elements of operating forces in theater at all levels of war. Within the national and theater logistic systems, it includes but is not limited to that support rendered by service forces in ensuring the aspects of supply, maintenance, transportation, health services, and other services required by aviation and ground combat troops to permit those units to accomplish their missions in combat. Combat service support encompasses those activities at all levels of war that produce sustainment to all operating forces on the battlefield. CSS. Combat support.

Combat service support area: An area ashore that is organized to contain the necessary supplies, equipment, installations, and elements to provide the landing force with combat service support throughout the operation. CSSA.

Combat service support elements: Those elements whose primary missions are to provide service support to combat forces and which are a part, or prepared to become a part, of a theater, command, or task force formed for combat operations. Operating forces; service troops; troops.

Combat support: Fire support and operational assistance provided to combat elements. CS. Combat service support.

Combat support agency: A Department of Defense agency so designated by Congress or the Secretary of Defense that supports military combat operations. CSA

Combat support elements: Those elements whose primary missions are to provide combat support to the combat forces and which are a part, or prepared to become a part, of a theater, command, or task force formed for combat operations. See also operating forces.

Combat support troops: Those units or organizations whose primary mission is to furnish operational assistance for the combat elements. Troops.

Combat surveillance: A continuous, all-weather, day-and-night, systematic watch over the battle area in order to provide timely information for tactical combat operations.

Combat surveillance radar: Radar with the normal function of maintaining continuous watch over a combat area.

Combat survival: Those measures to be taken by Service personnel when

involuntarily separated from friendly forces in combat, including procedures relating to individual survival, evasion, escape, and conduct after capture.

Combat vehicle: A vehicle, with or without armor, designed for a specific fighting function. Armor protection or armament mounted as supplemental equipment on noncombat vehicles will not change the classification of such vehicles to combat vehicles.

Combat visual information support center: A visual information support facility established at a base of operations during war or military operations other than war to provide limited visual information support to the base and its supported elements. CVISC.

Combat zone: 1. That area required by combat forces for the conduct of operations. 2. The territory forward of the Army rear area boundary. Combat area; communications zone.

Combination influence mine: A mine designed to actuate only when two or more different influences are received either simultaneously or in a predetermined order. Combined influence mine.

Combination mission/level of effort-oriented items: Items for which requirement computations are based on the criteria used for both level of effort-oriented and mission-oriented items.

Combined: Between two or more forces or agencies of two or more allies. (When all allies or services are not involved, the participating nations and services shall be identified, e.g., combined navies.) Joint.

Combined airspeed indicator: An instrument which displays both indicated airspeed and mach number.

Combined arms team: The full integration and application of two or more arms or elements of one Military Service into an operation.

Combined force: A military force composed of elements of two or more allied nations. Force(s).

Combined joint special operations task force: A task force composed of special operations units from one or more foreign countries and more than one US Military Department formed to carry out a specific special operation or prosecute special operations in support of a theater campaign or other operations. The combined joint special operations task force may have conventional non special operations units assigned or attached to support the conduct of specific missions. CJSOTF. Joint special operations task force; special operations; task force.

Combined operation: An operation conducted by forces of two or more Allied nations acting together for the accomplishment of a single mission.

Combustor: A name generally assigned to the combination of flame holder or

stabilizer, igniter, combustion chamber, and injection system of a ramjet or gas turbine.

Command: 1. The authority that a commander in the armed forces lawfully exercises over subordinates by virtue of rank or assignment. Command includes the authority and responsibility for effectively using available resources and for planning the employment of, organizing, directing, coordinating, and controlling military forces for the accomplishment of assigned missions. It also includes responsibility for health, welfare, morale, and discipline of assigned personnel. 2. An order given by a commander; that is, the will of the commander expressed for the purpose of bringing about a particular action. 3. A unit or units, an organization, or an area under the command of one individual. CMD. Area command; combatant command; combatant command (command authority).

Command and control: The exercise of authority and direction by a properly designated commander over assigned and attached forces in the accomplishment of the mission. Command and control functions are performed through an arrangement of personnel, equipment, communications, facilities, and procedures employed by a commander in planning, directing, coordinating, and controlling forces and operations in the accomplishment of the mission. C2.

Command and control system: The facilities, equipment, communications, procedures, and personnel essential to a commander for planning, directing, and controlling operations of assigned and attached forces pursuant to the missions assigned.

Command assessment element: The small team of personnel sent by the United States Northern Command or United States Pacific Command to a chemical, biological, radiological, nuclear, or high-yield explosives incident site to conduct a consequence management assessment and make an evaluation of potential shortfalls in federal and state capabilities, which may become requests for Department of Defense assistance. CAE.

Command axis: A line along which a headquarters will move.

Command center: A facility from which a commander and his or her representatives direct operations and control forces. It is organized to gather, process, analyze, display, and disseminate planning and operational data and perform other related tasks. CC.

Command chaplain: The senior chaplain assigned to or designated by a commander of a staff, command, or unit. Combatant command chaplain; lay leader; religious support; religious support plan.

Command controlled stocks: Stocks which are placed at the disposal of a designated NATO commander in order to provide him with a flexibility with which to influence the battle logistically. "Placed at the disposal of" implies responsibility for storage, maintenance, accounting, rotation or turnover, physical security, and subsequent transportation to a particular battle area.

Command destruct signal: -A signal used to operate intentionally the destruction signal in a missile.

Command detonated mine: A mine detonated by remotely controlled means.

Command element: The core element of a Marine air-ground task force (MAGTF) that is the headquarters. The command element is composed of the commander, general or executive and special staff sections, headquarters section, and requisite communications support, intelligence, and reconnaissance forces necessary to accomplish the MAGTF mission. The command element provides command and control, intelligence, and other support essential for effective planning and execution of operations by the other elements of the MAGTF. The command element varies in size and composition. CE. Aviation combat element; combat service support element; ground combat element; Marine air-ground task force; Marine expeditionary force; Marine expeditionary force; Marine expeditionary unit; special purpose Marine air-ground task force; task force.

Commander, amphibious task force: The Navy officer designated in the order initiating the amphibious operation as the commander of the amphibious task force. CATF. Amphibious operation; amphibious task force; commander, landing force.

Commander, landing force: The officer designated in the order initiating the amphibious operation as the commander of the landing force for an amphibious operation. CLF. Amphibious operation; commander, amphibious task force; landing force.

Commander's critical information requirement: An information requirement identified by the commander as being critical to facilitating timely decision-making. The two key elements are friendly force information requirements and priority intelligence requirements. CCIR. Information; information requirements; intelligence; priority intelligence requirement.

Commander's estimate of the situation: A process of reasoning by which a commander considers all the circumstances affecting the military situation and arrives at a decision as to a course of action to be taken to accomplish the mission. A commander's estimate, which considers a military situation so far in the future as to require major assumptions, is called a commander's long-range estimate of the situation.

Commander's intent: A concise expression of the purpose of the operation and the desired end state. It may also include the commander's assessment of the adversary commander's intent and an assessment of where and how much risk is acceptable during the operation. Assessment; end state.

Command guidance: A guidance system wherein intelligence transmitted to the missile from an outside source causes the missile to traverse a directed flight path.

Command information: Communication by a military organization with Service members, civilian employees, retirees, and family members of the organization that creates an awareness of the organization's goals, informs them of significant developments affecting them and the organization, increases their effectiveness as ambassadors of the organization, and keeps them informed about what is going on in the organization. Internal information. Command; information; public affairs.

Commanding officer of troops: On a ship that has embarked units, a designated officer who is responsible for the administration, discipline, and training of all embarked units. COT.

Command net: A communications network which connects an echelon of command with some or all of its subordinate echelons for the purpose of command and control.

Command post: A unit's or subunit's headquarters where the commander and the staff perform their activities. In combat, a unit's or subunit's headquarters is often divided into echelons; the echelon in which the unit or subunit commander is located or from which such commander operates is called a command post. CP.

Command post exercise: An exercise in which the forces are simulated, involving the commander, the staff, and communications within and between headquarters. CPX. Exercise; maneuver.

Command relationships: The interrelated responsibilities between commanders, as well as the operational authority exercised by commanders in the chain of command; defined further as combatant command (command authority), operational control, tactical control, or support. See also chain of command; combatant command; command; operational control; support; tactical control.

Command-sponsored dependent: A dependent entitled to travel to overseas commands at Government expense and endorsed by the appropriate military commander to be present in a dependent's status.

Commercial items: Articles of supply readily available from established commercial distribution sources which the Department of Defense or inventory managers in the Military Services have designated to be obtained directly or indirectly from such sources.

Commercial vehicle: A vehicle that has evolved in the commercial market to meet civilian requirements and which is selected from existing production lines for military use.

Commission: -1. To put in or make ready for service or use, as to commission an aircraft or a ship. 2. A written order giving a person rank and authority as an officer in the armed forces. 3. The rank and the authority given by such an order. constitute.

Commit: The process of committing one or more air interceptors or surface-to-air missiles for interception against a target track.

Commodity manager: An individual within the organization of an inventory control point or other such organization assigned management responsibility for homogeneous grouping of materiel items.

Commonality: A quality that applies to materiel or systems: a. possessing like and interchangeable characteristics enabling each to be utilized, or operated and maintained, by personnel trained on the others without additional specialized training; b. having interchangeable repair parts and/or components; and c. applying to consumable items interchangeably equivalent without adjustment.

Common control (artillery): Horizontal and vertical map or chart location of points in the target area and position area, tied in with the horizontal and vertical control in use by two or more units. May be established by firing, survey, or combination of both, or by assumption. Control point; ground control.

Common infrastructure: Infrastructure essential to the training of NATO forces or to the implementation of NATO operational plans which, owing to its degree of common use or interest and its compliance with criteria laid down from time to time by the North Atlantic Council, is commonly financed by NATO members. Infrastructure.

Common item: 1. Any item of materiel that is required for use by more than one activity. 2. Sometimes loosely used to denote any consumable item except repair parts or other technical items. 3. Any item of materiel that is procured for, owned by, or used by any Military Department of the Department of Defense and is also required to be furnished to a recipient country under the grant-aid Military Assistance Program. 4. Readily available commercial items. 5. Items used by two or more Military Services of similar manufacture or fabrication that may vary between the Services as to color or shape. 6. Any part or component that is required in the assembly of two or more complete end-items.

Common servicing: That function performed by one Military Service in support of another Military Service for which reimbursement is not required from the Service receiving support. Servicing.

Common supplies: Those supplies common to two or more Services.

Common tactical picture: An accurate and complete display of relevant tactical data that integrates tactical information from the multi-tactical data link network, ground network, intelligence network, and sensor networks. CTP.

Common use: Services, materiel, or facilities provided by a Department of Defense agency or a Military Department on a common basis for two or more Department of Defense agencies, elements, or other organizations as directed.

Common use alternatives: Systems, subsystems, devices, components, and materials, already developed or under development, that could be used to reduce the cost of new systems acquisition and support by reducing duplication of research and development effort and by limiting the addition of support base.

Common-use container: Any Department of Defense-owned, -leased, or -controlled 20-or 40-foot International Organization for Standardization container managed by US Transportation Command as an element of the Department of Defense common-use container system. Component- owned container; Service-unique container.

Common-user airlift service: The airlift service provided on a common basis for all Department of Defense agencies and, as authorized, for other agencies of the US Government.

Common-user item: An item of an interchangeable nature which is in common use by two or more nations or Services of a nation.

Common-user logistics: Materiel or service support shared with or provided by two or more Services, Department of Defense (DOD) agencies, or multinational partners to another Service, DOD agency, non-DOD agency, and/or multinational partner in an operation. Common-user logistics is usually restricted to a particular type of supply and/or service and may be further restricted to specific unit(s) or types of units, specific times, missions, and/or geographic areas. CUL. Common use.

Common-user military land transportation: Point-to-point land transportation service operated by a single Service for common use by two or more Services.

Common-user network: A system of circuits or channels allocated to furnish communication paths between switching centers to provide communication service on a common basis to all connected stations or subscribers. It is sometimes described as a general purpose network.

Common-user ocean terminals: A military installation, part of a military installation, or a commercial facility operated under contract or arrangement by the Surface Deployment and Distribution Command which regularly provides for two or more Services terminal functions of receipt, transit storage or staging, processing, and loading and unloading of passengers or cargo aboard ships.

Common-user transportation : Transportation and transportation services provided on a common basis for two or more Department of Defense agencies and, as authorized, non-Department of Defense agencies. Common-user assets are under the combatant command (command authority) of Commander, United States Transportation Command, excluding Service-organic or theater-assigned transportation assets. Common use.

Communicate: To use any means or method to convey information of any kind from one person or place to another.

Communication deception: Use of devices, operations, and techniques with the intent of confusing or misleading the user of a communications link or a navigation system.

Communications intelligence; - Technical information and intelligence derived from foreign communications by other than the intended recipients. COMINT.

Communications intelligence database: The aggregate of technical information and intelligence derived from the interception and analysis of foreign communications (excluding press, propaganda, and public broadcast) used in the direction and redirection of communications intelligence intercept, analysis, and reporting activities.

Communications mark: An electronic indicator used for directing attention to a particular object or position of mutual interest within or between command and control systems.

Communications net: An organization of stations capable of direct communications on a common channel or frequency.

Communications network: An organization of stations capable of inter communications, but not necessarily on the same channel.

Communications satellite: An orbiting vehicle, which relays signals between communications stations. There are two types: a. active communications satellite — A satellite that receives, regenerates, and retransmits signals between stations; b. passive communications satellite — A satellite which reflects communications signals between stations. COMSAT.

Communications security: The protection resulting from all measures designed to deny unauthorized persons information of value that might be derived from the possession and study of telecommunications, or to mislead unauthorized persons in their interpretation of the results of such possession and study. COMSEC.

Communications security equipment: Equipment designed to provide security to telecommunications by converting information to a form unintelligible to an unauthorized interceptor and by reconverting such information to its original form for authorized recipients, as well as equipment designed specifically to aid in the conversion process. Communications security equipment is crypto equipment, crypto ancillary equipment, crypto production equipment, and authentication equipment.

Communications security material: All documents, devices, equipment, or apparatus, including crypto material, used in establishing or maintaining secure communications.

Communications security monitoring: The act of listening to, copying, or recording transmissions of one's own circuits (or when specially agreed, e.g., in allied exercises, those of friendly forces) to provide material for communications security analysis in order to determine the degree of security being provided to those transmissions. In particular, the purposes include providing a basis for advising commanders on the security risks resulting from their transmissions, improving the security of communications, and planning and conducting manipulative communications deception operations.

Communications system: Communications networks and information services that enable joint and multinational war fighting capabilities. Command and control.

Communications terminal: Terminus of a communications circuit at which data can be either entered or received; located with the originator or ultimate addressee. CT.

Communications zone: Rear part of a theater of war or theater of operations (behind but contiguous to the combat zone) which contains the lines of communications, establishments for supply and evacuation, and other agencies required for the immediate support and maintenance of the field forces.

COMMZ. Combat zone; line of communications; rear area; theater of operations; theater of war.

Community relations: 1. The relationship between military and civilian communities. 2. Those public affairs programs that address issues of interest to the general public, business, academia, veterans, Service organizations, military-related associations, and other non-news media entities. These programs are usually associated with the interaction between US military installations and their surrounding or nearby civilian communities. Interaction with overseas non-news media civilians in an operational area is handled by civil-military operations with public affairs support as required. Public affairs.

Community relations program: That command function that evaluates public attitudes, identifies the mission of a military organization with the public interest, and executes a program of action to earn public understanding and acceptance.

Comparative cover: Coverage of the same area or object taken at different times, to show any changes in details. Cover.

Compartmentation: 1. Establishment and management of an organization so that information about the personnel, internal organization, or activities of one component is made available to any other component only to the extent required for the performance of assigned duties. 2. Effects of relief and drainage upon avenues of approach so as to produce areas bounded on at least two sides by terrain features such as woods, ridges, or ravines that limit observation or observed fire into the area from points outside the area.

Compass rose: A graduated circle, usually marked in degrees, indicating directions and printed or inscribed on an appropriate medium.

Complaint-type investigation: A counterintelligence investigation in which sabotage, espionage, treason, sedition, subversive activity, or disaffection is suspected.

Completeness: The joint operation plan review criterion for assessing whether operation plans incorporate major operations and tasks to be accomplished and to what degree they include forces required, deployment concept, employment concept, sustainment concept, time estimates for achieving objectives, description of the end state, mission success criteria, and mission termination criteria.

Complete round: A term applied to an assemblage of explosive and non explosive components designed to perform a specific function at the time and under the conditions desired. Examples of complete rounds of ammunition are: a. separate loading, consisting of a primer, propelling charge and, except for blank ammunition, a projectile and a fuze; b. fixed or semifixed, consisting of a primer, propelling charge, cartridge case, a projectile and, except when solid projectiles are used, a fuze; c. bomb, consisting of all component parts required to drop and function the bomb once; d. missile, consisting of a complete warhead section and a missile body with its associated components and propellants; and e. rocket, consisting of all components necessary to function.

Complex contingency operations: Large-scale peace operations conducted by a combination of military forces and nonmilitary organizations that involve one or more of the elements of peace operations that include one or more elements of other types of operations such as foreign humanitarian assistance, nation assistance, support to insurgency, or support to counterinsurgency. CCOs. Operation; peace operations.

Component: 1. One of the subordinate organizations that constitute a joint force. Normally a joint force is organized with a combination of Service and functional components. 2. In logistics, a part or combination of parts having a specific function, which can be installed or replaced only as an entity. COMP. functional component command; Service component command.

Component (materiel): An assembly or any combination of parts, subassemblies, and assemblies mounted together in manufacture, assembly, maintenance, or rebuild.

Component-owned container: A 20- or 40-foot International Organization for Standardization container procured and owned by a single Department of Defense component. May be either on an individual unit property book or contained within a component pool. May be temporarily assigned to the Department of Defense common-use container system. Service-unique container. Common-use container.

Composite air photography: Air photographs made with a camera having one principal lens and two or more surrounding and oblique lenses. The several resulting photographs are corrected or transformed in printing to permit assembly as verticals with the same scale.

Composite warfare commander: The officer in tactical command is normally the composite warfare commander. However the composite warfare commander concept allows an officer in tactical command to delegate tactical command to the composite warfare commander. The composite warfare commander wages combat operations to counter threats to the force and to maintain tactical sea control with assets assigned; while the officer in tactical command retains close control of power projection and strategic sea control operations.

Composite wing: An Air Force wing that operates more than one type of weapon system. Some composite wings are built from the ground up and designed to put all resources required to meet a specific war fighting objective in a single wing under one commander at one location. Other composite wings need not be built from the ground up but combine different weapon systems operating at the same base into a single wing.

Compromise: The known or suspected exposure of clandestine personnel, installations, or other assets or of classified information or material, to an unauthorized person.

Compromised: A term applied to classified matter, knowledge of which has, in whole or in part, passed to an unauthorized person or persons, or which has been subject to risk of such passing. Classified matter.

Computed air release point: A computed air position where the first paratroop or cargo item is released to land on a specified impact point.

Computer intrusion: An incident of unauthorized access to data or an automated information system.

Computer intrusion detection: The process of identifying that a computer intrusion has been attempted, is occurring, or has occurred.

Computer modeling: -Configuration management; independent review; validation; verification.

Computer network attack: Actions taken through the use of computer networks to disrupt, deny, degrade, or destroy information resident in computers and computer networks, or the computers and networks themselves. CNA. Computer network defense; computer network exploitation; computer network operations.

Computer network defense: Actions taken to protect, monitor, analyze, detect, and respond to unauthorized activity within the Department of Defense information systems and computer networks. CND. Computer network attack; computer network exploitation; computer network operations.

Computer network exploitation: Enabling operations and intelligence collection

capabilities conducted through the use of computer networks to gather data from target or adversary automated information systems or networks. CNE. Computer network attack; computer network defense; computer network operation .

Computer network operations: Comprised of computer network attack, computer network defense, and related computer network exploitation enabling operations. CNO. Computer network attack; computer network defense; computer network exploitation.

Confusion agent: An individual who is dispatched by the sponsor for the primary purpose of confounding the intelligence or counterintelligence apparatus of another country rather than for the purpose of collecting and transmitting information.

Confusion reflector: A reflector of electromagnetic radiations used to create echoes for confusion purposes. Radar confusion reflectors include such devices as chaff, rope, and corner reflectors.

Connecting route: A route connecting axial and/or lateral routes. Route.

Consecutive voyage charter: A contract by which a commercial ship is chartered by the Military Sealift Command for a series of specified voyages.

Consequence management: Actions taken to maintain or restore essential services and manage and mitigate problems resulting from disasters and catastrophes, including natural, manmade, or terrorist incidents. CM.

Console: A grouping of controls, indicators, and similar electronic or mechanical

equipment, used to monitor readiness of, and/or control specific functions of, a system, such as missile checkout, countdown, or launch operations.

Consolidated vehicle table: A summary of all vehicles loaded on a ship, listed by types and showing the units to which they belong.

Consolidation: The combining or merging of elements to perform a common or related function.

Consolidation of position: Organizing and strengthening a newly captured position so that it can be used against the enemy.

Constellation: A number of like satellites that are part of a system. Satellites in a constellation generally have a similar orbit. For example, the Global Positioning System constellation consists of 24 satellites distributed in six orbital planes with similar eccentricities, altitudes, and inclinations. Global Positioning System.

Constitute: To provide the legal authority for the existence of a new unit of the Armed Services. The new unit is designated and listed, but it has no specific existence until it is activated. Commission.

Constraint: In the context of joint operation planning, a requirement placed on the command by a higher command that dictates an action, thus restricting freedom of action. Operational limitation; restraint.

Consumer: Person or agency that uses information or intelligence produced by either its own staff or other agencies.

Consumer logistics: That part of logistics concerning reception of the initial product, storage, inspection, distribution, transport, maintenance, and disposal of materiel as well as the provision of support and services. In consequence, consumer logistics includes materiel requirements determination, follow-on support, stock control, provision or construction of facilities, movement control, codification, reliability and defect reporting, storage, transport and handling safety standards, and related training.

Consumption rate: The average quantity of an item consumed or expended during a given time interval, expressed in quantities by the most appropriate unit of measurement per applicable stated basis.

Contact: 1. In air intercept, a term meaning, "Unit has an unevaluated target." 2. In health services, an unevaluated individual who is known to have been sufficiently near an infected individual to have been exposed to the transfer of infectious material.

Contact burst preclusion: A fuzing arrangement that prevents an unwanted surface burst in the event of failure of the air burst fuze.

Contact mine: A mine detonated by physical contact. Mine.

Contact point: 1. In land warfare, a point on the terrain, easily identifiable, where two or more units are required to make contact. 2. In air operations, the position at which a mission leader makes radio contact with an air control agency. 3. (DOD only) In personnel recovery, a location where isolated personnel can establish contact with recovery forces. CP. Checkpoint; control point; coordinating point.

Contact print: A print made from a negative or a dispositive in direct contact with sensitized material.

Contact procedure: Those pre designated actions taken by isolated personnel and recovery forces that permit link-up between the two parties in hostile territory and facilitate the return of isolated personnel to friendly control. Evader; hostile; recovery force.

Contact reconnaissance: Locating isolated units out of contact with the main force.

Contact report: A report indicating any detection of the enemy.

Contain: To stop, hold, or surround the forces of the enemy or to cause the enemy to center activity on a given front and to prevent the withdrawal of any part of the enemy's forces for use elsewhere.

Container: An article of transport equipment that meets American National Standards Institute/International Organization for Standardization standards that is designed to be transported by various modes of transportation. These containers are also designed to facilitate and optimize the carriage of goods by one or more modes of transportation without intermediate handling of the contents and equipped with features permitting ready handling and transfer from one mode to another. Containers may be fully enclosed with one or more doors, open top, refrigerated, tank, open rack, gondola, flat rack, and other designs. Containerization.

Container anchorage terminal: A sheltered anchorage with the appropriate facilities for the transshipment of containerized cargo from containerships to other vessels.

Container control officer: A designated official within a command, installation, or activity who is responsible for control, reporting, use, and maintenance of all Department of Defense-owned and controlled intermodal containers and equipment. This officer has custodial responsibility for containers from time received until dispatched.

Container-handling equipment: Items of materials-handling equipment required to specifically receive, maneuver, and dispatch International Organization for Standardization containers. CHE. Materials handling equipment.

Containerization: The use of containers to unitize cargo for transportation, supply, and storage. Containerization incorporates supply, transportation, packaging, storage, and security together with visibility of container and its contents into a distribution system from source to user. See also container.

Containership — A ship specially constructed and equipped to carry only containers without associated equipment, in all available cargo spaces, either below or above deck. Containerships are usually non-self-sustaining, do not have built-in capability to load or off-load containers, and require port crane service. A containership with shipboard-installed cranes capable of loading and off-loading containers without assistance of port crane service is considered self-sustaining. Non-self-sustaining containership; self-sustaining containership.

Contaminated remains: Remains of personnel which have absorbed or upon which have been deposited radioactive material, or biological or chemical agents. Mortuary affairs.

Contamination: 1. The deposit, absorption, or adsorption of radioactive material, or of biological or chemical agents on or by structures, areas, personnel, or objects. Induced radiation; residual radiation. 2. Food and/or water made unfit for consumption by humans or animals because of the presence of environmental chemicals, radioactive elements, bacteria or organisms, the byproduct of the growth of bacteria or organisms, the decomposing material, or waste in the food or water.

Contamination avoidance: Individual and/or unit measures taken to reduce the effects of chemical, biological, radiological, and nuclear hazards.

Contamination control: A combination of preparatory and responsive measures designed to limit the vulnerability of forces to chemical, biological, radiological, nuclear, and toxic industrial hazards and to avoid, contain, control exposure to, and, where possible, neutralize them. Biological agent; chemical agent; contamination.

Contiguous zone: 1. A maritime zone adjacent to the territorial sea that may not extend beyond 24 nautical miles (nms) from the baselines from which the breadth of the territorial sea is measured. Within the contiguous zone the coastal state may exercise the control necessary to prevent and punish infringement of its customs, fiscal, immigration, or sanitary laws and regulations within its territory or territorial sea. In all other respects the contiguous zone is an area subject to high seas freedom of navigation, over flight, and related freedoms, such as the conduct of military exercises. 2. The zone of the ocean extending 3-12 nms from the US coastline.

Continental United States: United States territory, including the adjacent territorial waters, located within North America between Canada and Mexico. CONUS.

Contingency: A situation requiring military operations in response to natural disasters, terrorists, subversives, or as otherwise directed by appropriate authority to protect US interests. Contingency contracting.

Contingency contracting: The process of obtaining goods, services, and construction via contracting means in support of contingency operations. contingency; contingency contract.

Contingency engineering management organization: An organization that may be formed by the combatant commander or subordinate joint force commander to augment the combatant command or subordinate joint force staffs to provide additional Service engineering expertise to support both contingency and crisis action planning and to provide construction management in contingency and wartime operations. Combat engineering; contingency; crisis action planning; geospatial engineering.

Contingency planning: The Joint Operation Planning and Execution System planning activities that occur in no crisis situations. The Joint Planning and Execution Community uses contingency planning to develop operation plans for a broad range of contingencies based on requirements identified in the Contingency Planning Guidance, Joint Strategic Capabilities Plan, or other planning directive. Contingency planning underpins and facilitates the transition to crisis action planning.

Contingency planning facilities list program: A joint Defense Intelligence Agency and unified and specified command program for the production and maintenance of current target documentation of all countries of contingency planning interest to US military planners.

Contingency Planning Guidance: The Contingency Planning Guidance (CPG) fulfills the statutory duty of the Secretary of Defense to furnish written policy guidance annually to the Chairman of the Joint Chiefs of Staff for contingency planning. The Secretary issues this guidance with the approval of the President after consultation with the Chairman of the Joint Chiefs of Staff. The CPG focuses the guidance given in the National Security Strategy and Defense Planning Guidance, and is the principal source document for the Joint Strategic Capabilities Plan. CPG.

Contingency response program: Fast reaction transportation procedures intended to provide for priority use of land transportation assets by Department of Defense when required. CORE.

Contingency retention stock: That portion of the quantity of an item excess to the approved force retention level for which there is no predictable demand or quantifiable requirement, and which normally would be allocated as potential DOD excess stock, except for a determination that the quantity will be retained for possible contingencies for United States forces.

Contingency ZIP Code: A ZIP Code assigned by Military Postal Service Agency to a contingency post office for the tactical use of the Armed Forces on a temporary basis. The number consists of a five-digit base with a four-digit add-on to assist in routing and sorting.

Contingent effects: The effects, both desirable and undesirable, that are in addition to the primary effects associated with a nuclear detonation.

Continuity of command: The degree or state of being continuous in the exercise of the authority vested in an individual of the Armed Forces for the direction, coordination, and control of military forces.

Continuity of operations: The degree or state of being continuous in the conduct of functions, tasks, or duties necessary to accomplish a military action or mission in carrying out the national military strategy. It includes the functions and duties of the commander, as well as the supporting functions and duties performed by the staff and others acting under the authority and direction of the commander. COOP.

Continuous fire: -1. Fire conducted at a normal rate without interruption for application of adjustment corrections or for other causes. 2. In field artillery and naval gunfire support, loading and firing at a specified rate or as rapidly as possible consistent with accuracy within the prescribed rate of fire for the weapon. Firing will continue until terminated by the command "end of mission" or temporarily suspended by the command "cease loading" or "check firing."

Continuous illumination fire: A type of fire in which illuminating projectiles are fired at specified time intervals to provide uninterrupted lighting on the target or specified area.

Continuous strip camera: A camera in which the film moves continuously past a slit in the focal plane, producing a photograph in one unbroken length by virtue of the continuous forward motion of the aircraft.

Continuous strip imagery: Imagery of a strip of terrain in which the image remains unbroken throughout its length, along the line of flight.

Contour interval: Difference in elevation between two adjacent contour lines.

Contour line: A line on a map or chart connecting points of equal elevation.

Contract administration: A subset of contracting that includes efforts to ensure that supplies, services, and construction are delivered in accordance with the terms and conditions of the contract.

Contracted logistic support: Support in which maintenance operations for a particular military system are performed exclusively by contract support personnel. CLS. Logistic support; support.

Contracting officer: The Service member or Department of Defense civilian with the legal authority to enter into, administer, modify, and/or terminate contracts.

Contracting officer representative: A Service member or Department of Defense civilian appointed in writing and trained by a contracting officer, responsible for monitoring contract performance and performing other duties specified by their appointment letter. COR.

Contractor management: The oversight and integration of contractor personnel and associated equipment providing support to the joint force in a designated operational area.

Contractors authorized to accompany the force: Contingency contractor employees and all tiers of subcontractor employees who are specifically authorized through their contract to accompany the force and have protected status in accordance with international conventions. CAAF.

Contractors not authorized to accompany the force: Contingency contractor employees and all tiers of subcontractor employees who are not authorized through their contract to accompany the force and do not have protected status in accordance with international conventions. Non-CAAF.

Contract support integration: The coordination and synchronization of contracted support executed in a designated operational area in support of the joint force.

Contract termination: Defense procurement: the cessation or cancellation, in whole or in part, of work under a prime contractor a subcontract there under for the convenience of, or at the option of, the government, or due to failure of the contractor to perform in accordance with the terms of the contract (default).

Control: 1. Authority that may be less than full command exercised by a commander over part of the activities of subordinate or other organizations. 2. In mapping, charting, and photogrammetry, a collective term for a system of marks or objects on the Earth or on a map or a photograph, whose positions or elevations (or both) have been or will be determined. 3. Physical or psychological pressures exerted with the intent to assure that an agent or group will respond as directed. 4. An indicator governing the distribution and use of documents, information, or material. Such indicators are the subject of intelligence community agreement and are specifically defined in appropriate regulations. Administrative control; operational control; tactical control.

Control area: A controlled airspace extending upwards from a specified limit above the Earth. Controlled airspace; control zone; terminal control area.

Control group: Personnel, ships, and craft designated to control the waterborne ship-to-shore movement.

Controllable mine: A mine which after laying can be controlled by the user, to the extent of making the mine safe or live, or to fire the mine. Mine.

Controlled airspace: An airspace of defined dimensions within which air traffic control service is provided to controlled flights.

Controlled dangerous air cargo: Cargo which is regarded as highly dangerous and which may only be carried by cargo aircraft operating within specific safety regulations.

Controlled effects nuclear weapons: Nuclear weapons designed to achieve variation in the intensity of specific effects other than normal blast effect.

Controlled exercise: An exercise characterized by the imposition of constraints on some or all of the participating units by planning authorities with the principal intention of provoking types of interaction. Free play exercise.

Controlled firing area: An area in which ordnance firing is conducted under controlled conditions so as to eliminate hazard to aircraft in flight. Restricted area.

Controlled forces: Military or paramilitary forces under effective and sustained political and military direction.

Controlled information: 1. Information conveyed to an adversary in a deception

operation to evoke desired appreciations. 2. Information and indicators deliberately conveyed or denied to foreign targets to evoke invalid official estimates that result in foreign official actions advantageous to US interests and objectives.

Controlled map: A map with precise horizontal and vertical ground control as a basis. Scale, azimuth, and elevation are accurate. Map.

Controlled mosaic: A mosaic corrected for scale, rectified and laid to ground control to provide an accurate representation of distances and direction. Mosaic; rectification.

Controlled port: A harbor or anchorage at which entry and departure, assignment of berths, and traffic within the harbor or anchorage are controlled by military authorities.

Controlled response: The selection from a wide variety of feasible options one of which will provide the specific military response most advantageous in the circumstances.

Controlled route: A route, the use of which is subject to traffic or movement restrictions which may be supervised. Route.

Controlled shipping: Shipping that is controlled by the Military Sealift Command. Included in this category are Military Sealift Command ships, government-owned ships operated under a general agency agreement, and commercial ships under charter to the Military Sealift Command. Military Sealift Command; United States Naval Ship.

Controlled substance: A drug or other substance, or immediate precursor included in Schedule I, II, III, IV, or V of the Controlled Substances Act.

Control of electromagnetic radiation: A national operation plan to minimize the use of electromagnetic radiation in the United States and its possessions and the Panama Canal Zone in the event of attack or imminent threat thereof, as an aid to the navigation of hostile aircraft, guided missiles, or other devices. Emission control orders.

Control point: 1. A position along a route of march at which men are stationed to give information and instructions for the regulation of supply or traffic. 2. A position marked by a buoy, boat, aircraft, electronic device, conspicuous terrain feature, or other identifiable object which is given a name or number and used as an aid to navigation or control of ships, boats, or aircraft. 3. In marking mosaics, a point located by ground survey with which a corresponding point on a photograph is matched as a check.

Control zone: A controlled airspace extending upwards from the surface of the Earth to a specified upper limit. Control area; controlled airspace; terminal control area.

Control operation: 1. Those forces capable of conducting operations using nonnuclear weapons. 2. Those forces other than designated special operations forces.

Conventional mines: Land mines, other than nuclear or chemical, that are not designed to self-destruct. They are designed to be emplaced by hand or mechanical means. Conventional mines can be buried or surface laid and are normally emplaced in a pattern to aid in recording. Mine.

Conventional weapon: A weapon which is neither nuclear, biological, nor chemical.

Converge: A request or command used in a call for fire to indicate that the observer or spotter desires a sheaf in which the planes of fire intersect at a point.

Converged sheaf: The lateral distribution of fire of two or more pieces so that the planes of fire intersect at a given point. Parallel sheaf.

Convergence: Convergence factor; grid convergence; grid convergence factor; map convergence; true convergence.

Convergence factor: The ratio of the angle between any two meridians on the chart to their actual change of longitude. Convergence.

Convergence zone: That region in the deep ocean where sound rays, refracted from the depths, return to the surface.

Conversion angle: The angle between a great circle bearing and a rhumb line bearing of a point, measured at a common origin.

Conversion scale: A scale indicating the relationship between two different units of measurement. Scale.

Convoy: 1. A number of merchant ships and/or naval auxiliaries usually escorted by warships and/or aircraft — or a single merchant ship or naval auxiliary under surface

Escort: assembled and organized for the purpose of passage together. 2. A group of vehicles organized for the purpose of control and orderly movement with or without escort protection that moves over the same route at the same time and under one commander. Coastal convoy; evacuation convoy; ocean convoy.

Convoy commodore: A naval officer, or master of one of the ships in a convoy, designated to command the convoy, subject to the orders of the officer in tactical command. If no surface escort is present, the convoy commodore takes entire command.

Convoy dispersal point: The position at sea where a convoy breaks up, each ship proceeding independently thereafter.

Convoy escort: 1. A naval ship(s) or aircraft in company with a convoy and responsible for its protection. 2. An escort to protect a convoy of vehicles from being scattered, destroyed, or captured. Escort.

Convoy loading: The loading of troop units with their equipment and supplies in

vessels of the same movement group, but not necessarily in the same vessel. Loading.

Convoy route: The specific route assigned to each convoy by the appropriate routing authority.

Convoy schedule: Planned convoy sailings showing the shipping lanes, assembly and terminal areas, scheduled speed, and sailing interval.

Convoy speed: For ships, the speed which the convoy commodore orders the guide of the convoy to make good through the water.

Convoy terminal area: A geographical area, designated by the name of a port or anchorage on which it is centered, at which convoys or sections of convoys arrive and from which they will be dispersed to coastal convoy systems or as independents to their final destination.

Convoy through escort: Those ships of the close escort which normally remain with the convoy from its port of assembly to its port of arrival.

Convoy title: A combination of letters and numbers that gives the port of departure and arrival, speed, and serial number of each convoy.

Cooperating agency: An agency that provides technical and resource support, at the request of the coordinating agency, to conduct operations using their own authorities, subject-matter experts, capabilities or resources. The Department of Defence is considered a cooperating agency for the majority of the National Response Plan support annexes.

Cooperative logistics: The logistic support provided a foreign government or agency through its participation in the US Department of Defense logistic system, with reimbursement to the United States for support provided.

Cooperative logistic support arrangements: The combining term for procedural arrangements and implementing procedures that together support, define, or implement cooperative logistic understandings between the United States and a friendly foreign government under peacetime conditions.

Cooperative security location: A facility located outside the United States and US territories with little or no permanent US presence, maintained with periodic Service, contractor, or host-nation support. Cooperative security locations provide contingency access, logistic support, and rotational use by operating forces and are a focal point for security cooperation activities. CSL. Forward operating site; main operating base.

Coordinated draft plan: A plan for which a draft plan has been coordinated with the nations involved. It may be used for future planning and exercises and may be implemented during an emergency. Draft plan; final plan; initial draft plan; operation plan.

Coordinated fire line: A line beyond which conventional and indirect surface fire support means may fire at any time within the boundaries of the establishing headquarters without additional coordination. The purpose of the coordinated fire line is to expedite the surface-to-surface attack of targets beyond the coordinated fire line without coordination with the ground commander in whose area the targets are located. CFL. Fire support.

Coordinated procurement assignee: The agency or Military Service assigned purchase responsibility for all Department of Defense requirements of a particular Federal Supply Group/class, commodity, or item.

Coordinates: Linear or angular quantities which designate the position that a point occupies in a given reference frame or system. Also used as a general term to designate the particular kind of reference frame or system such as plane rectangular coordinates or spherical coordinates. Geographic coordinates; georef; grid coordinates.

Coordinating agency: An agency that supports the incident management mission by providing the leadership, expertise, and authorities to implement critical and specific aspects of the response. Responsible for orchestrating a coordinated response, provides staff for operations functions, notifies and tasks cooperating agencies, manages tasks with cooperating agencies, works with private-sector organizations, communicates ongoing activities to organizational elements, plans for short- and long-term incident management and maintains trained personnel to execute their appropriate support responsibilities.

Coordinating altitude: A procedural airspace control method to separate fixed- and rotary-wing aircraft by determining an altitude below which fixed-wing aircraft will normally not fly and above which rotary-wing aircraft normally will not fly. The coordinating altitude is normally specified in the airspace control plan and may include a buffer zone for small altitude deviations.

Coordinating authority: A commander or individual assigned responsibility for coordinating specific functions or activities involving forces of two or more Military Departments, two or more joint force components, or two or more forces of the same Service. The commander or individual has the authority to require consultation between the agencies involved, but does not have the authority to compel agreement. In the event that essential agreement cannot be obtained, the matter shall be referred to the appointing authority. Coordinating authority is a consultation relationship, not an authority through which command may be exercised. Coordinating authority is more applicable to planning and similar activities than to operations.

Coordinating point: Designated point at which, in all types of combat, adjacent units/formations must make contact for purposes of control and coordination.

Coordinating review authority: An agency appointed by a Service or combatant command to coordinate with and assist the primary review authority in joint doctrine development and maintenance. Each Service or combatant command must assign a coordinating review authority. When authorized by the appointing Service or combatant command, coordinating review authority comments provided to designated primary review authorities will represent the position of the appointing Service or combatant command with regard to the publication under development. CRA. Joint doctrine; joint publication; lead agent; primary review authority.

Coproduction: 1. With respect to exports, a cooperative manufacturing arrangement providing for the transfer of production information that enables an eligible foreign government, international organization, or commercial producer to manufacture, in whole or in part, an item of US defense equipment. Such an arrangement would include the functions of production engineering, controlling, quality assurance, and determination of resource requirements. This is normally accomplished under the provisions of a manufacturing license agreement per the US International Traffic in Arms Regulation and could involve the implementation of a government-to- government memorandum of understanding. 2. A cooperative manufacturing arrangement providing for the transfer of production information which enables the receiving government, international organization, or commercial producer to manufacture, in whole or in part, an item of defense equipment. The receiving party could be an eligible foreign government, international organization, or foreign producer; or the US Government or a US producer, depending on which direction the information is to flow. A typical coproduction arrangement would include the functions of production engineering, controlling, quality assurance, and determining of resource requirements. It may or may not include design engineering information and critical materials production and design information.

Copy negative: A negative produced from an original not necessarily at the same scale.

Corner reflector: 1. A device, normally consisting of three metallic surfaces or screens perpendicular to one another, designed to act as a radar target or marker. 2. In radar interpretation, an object which, by means of multiple reflections from smooth surfaces, produces a radar return of greater magnitude than might be expected from the physical size of the object.

Corps support command: Provides corps logistic support and command and control of water supply battalions.

Corps troops: Troops assigned or attached to a corps, but not a part of one of the divisions that make up the corps.

Correlation factor: The ratio of a ground dose rate reading to a reading taken at

approximately the same time at survey height over the same point on the ground.

Cost-plus award fee contract: A type of contract that provides for a payment consisting of a base amount fixed at inception of the contract along with an award amount that is based upon a judgmental evaluation by the United States Government.

Cost-type contract: A contract that provides for payment to the contractor of allowable cost, to the extent prescribed in the contract, incurred in performance of the contract.

Counter air: A mission that integrates offensive and defensive operations to attain and maintain a desired degree of air superiority. Counter air missions are designed to destroy or negate enemy aircraft and missiles, both before and after launch. Air superiority; mission; offensive counter air.

Counterattack: Attack by part or all of a defending force against an enemy attacking force, for such specific purposes as regaining ground lost or cutting off or destroying enemy advance units, and with the general objective of denying to the enemy the attainment of the enemy's purpose in attacking. In sustained defensive operations, it is undertaken to restore the battle position and is directed at limited objectives. Countermove; counteroffensive.

Counter battery fire: Fire delivered for the purpose of destroying or neutralizing indirect fire weapon systems.

Counter deception: Efforts to negate, neutralize, diminish the effects of, or gain advantage from a foreign deception operation. Counter deception does not include the intelligence function of identifying foreign deception operations. Deception.

Counterdrug: Those active measures taken to detect, monitor, and counter the production, trafficking, and use of illegal drugs. CD and counter narcotics (CN).

Counterdrug activities: Those measures taken to detect, interdict, disrupt, or curtail any activity that is reasonably related to illicit drug trafficking. This includes, but is not limited to, measures taken to detect, interdict, disrupt, or curtail activities related to substances, materiel, weapons, or resources used to finance, support, secure, cultivate, process, or transport illegal drugs.

Counterdrug nonoperational support: Support provided to law enforcement agencies or host nations that includes loan or lease of equipment without operators, use of facilities, training conducted in formal schools, transfer of excess equipment, or other support provided by the Services from forces not assigned or made available to the combatant commanders. Counterdrug operational support; counter drug operations.

Counterdrug operational support: Support to host nations and drug law enforcement agencies involving military personnel and their associated equipment, provided by the geographic combatant commanders from forces assigned to them or made available to them by the Services for this purpose. Counterdrug nonoperational support; counterdrug operations.

Counterdrug operations: Civil or military actions taken to reduce or eliminate illicit drug trafficking. Counterdrug; counterdrug nonoperational support; counterdrug operational support.

Counterespionage: That aspect of counterintelligence designed to detect, destroy, neutralize, exploit, or prevent espionage activities through identification, penetration, manipulation, deception, and repression of individuals, groups, or organizations conducting or suspected of conducting espionage activities.

Counter fire: Fire intended to destroy or neutralize enemy weapons. Includes counter battery, counter bombardment, and counter mortar fire.

Counterforce: The employment of strategic air and missile forces in an effort to destroy, or render impotent, selected military capabilities of an enemy force under any of the circumstances by which hostilities may be initiated.

Counter guerrilla warfare: Operations and activities conducted by armed forces, paramilitary forces, or nonmilitary agencies against guerrillas.

Counterinsurgency: Those military, paramilitary, political, economic, psychological, and civic actions taken by a government to defeat insurgency. COIN.

Counterintelligence: Information gathered and activities conducted to protect against espionage, other intelligence activities, sabotage, or assassinations conducted by or on behalf of foreign governments or elements thereof, foreign organizations, or foreign persons, or international terrorist activities. CI. Counterespionage; counter sabotage; counter subversion; security; security intelligence.

Counterintelligence activities: One or more of the five functions of counterintelligence: operations, investigations, collection, analysis and production, and functional services. Analysis and production; collection; counterintelligence; operation.

Counterintelligence collection: The systematic acquisition of information (through investigations, operations, or liaison) concerning espionage, sabotage, terrorism, other intelligence activities or assassinations conducted by or on behalf of foreign governments or elements thereof, foreign organizations, or foreign persons that are directed against or threaten Department of Defense interests. Counterintelligence.

Counterintelligence investigation: An official, systematic search for facts to determine whether a person(s) is engaged in activities that may be injurious to US national security or advantageous to a foreign power. Counterintelligence.

Counterintelligence operational tasking authority: The levying of counterintelligence requirements specific to joint military activities and operations. Counterintelligence operational tasking authority is exercised through supporting components. CIOTA. Counterintelligence.

Counterintelligence operations: Proactive activities designed to identify, exploit, neutralize, or deter foreign intelligence collection and terrorist activities directed against the United States. Counterintelligence; operation.

Counterintelligence production: The process of analyzing all-source information concerning espionage or other multidiscipline intelligence collection threats, sabotage, terrorism, and other related threats to US military commanders, the Department of Defense, and the US Intelligence Community and developing it into a final product that is disseminated. Counterintelligence production is used in formulating security policy, plans, and operations. See also counterintelligence.

Counterintelligence support: Conducting counterintelligence activities to protect against espionage and other foreign intelligence activities, sabotage, international terrorist activities, or assassinations conducted for or on behalf of foreign powers, organizations, or persons. Counterintelligence.

Countermeasures: That form of military science that, by the employment of devices and/or techniques, has as its objective the impairment of the operational effectiveness of enemy activity. Electronic warfare.

Countermine: To explode the main charge in a mine by the shock of a nearby

explosion of another mine or independent explosive charge. The explosion of the main charge may be caused either by sympathetic detonation or through the explosive train and/or firing mechanism of the mine.

Countermine operation: In land mine warfare, an operation to reduce or eliminate the effects of mines or minefields. Counter mine; mine warfare.

Counter mobility operations: The construction of obstacles and emplacement of minefields to delay, disrupt, and destroy the enemy by reinforcement of the terrain. Minefield; operation; target acquisition.

Countermove: An operation undertaken in reaction to or in anticipation of a move by the enemy. See also counterattack.

Counteroffensive: A large scale offensive undertaken by a defending force to seize the initiative from the attacking force. Counterattack.

Counter preparation fire: Intensive prearranged fire delivered when the imminence of the enemy attack is discovered. It is designed to: break up enemy formations; disorganize the enemy's systems of command, communications, and observation; decrease the effectiveness of artillery preparation; and impair the enemy's offensive spirit.

Counter proliferation: Those actions taken to defeat the threat and/or use of weapons of mass destruction against the United States, our military forces, friends, and allies. CP. Nonproliferation.

Counterpropaganda operations: Those psychological operations activities that identify adversary propaganda, contribute to situational awareness, and serve to expose adversary attempts to influence friendly populations and military forces.

Counter reconnaissance: All measures taken to prevent hostile observation of a force, area, or place.

Counter sabotage: That aspect of counterintelligence designed to detect, destroy, neutralize, or prevent sabotage activities through identification, penetration, manipulation, deception, and repression of individuals, groups, or organizations conducting or suspected of conducting sabotage activities.

Countersign: A secret challenge and its reply. Challenge; password.

Counter surveillance: All measures, active or passive, taken to counteract hostile surveillance. Surveillance.

Counterterrorism: Operations that include the offensive measures taken to prevent, deter, preempt, and respond to terrorism. CT. Antiterrorism; combating terrorism; terrorism.

Country cover diagram: A small scale index, by country, depicting the existence of air photography for planning purposes only.

Country team: The senior, in-country, US coordinating and supervising body, headed by the chief of the US diplomatic mission, and composed of the senior member of each represented US department or agency, as desired by the chief of the US diplomatic mission.

Coup de main: An offensive operation that capitalizes on surprise and simultaneous execution of supporting operations to achieve success in one swift stroke.

Courier: A messenger responsible for the secure physical transmission and delivery of documents and material. Generally referred to as a command or local courier. Armed forces courier.

Course: The intended direction of movement in the horizontal plane.

Coverage: 1. The ground area represented on imagery, photomaps, mosaics, maps, and other geographical presentation systems. 2. Cover or protection, as the coverage of troops by supporting fire. 3. The extent to which intelligence information is available in respect to any specified area of interest. 4. The summation of the geographical areas and volumes of aerospace under surveillance. Comparative cover.

Covering fire: 1. Fire used to protect troops when they are within range of enemy small arms. 2. In amphibious usage, fire delivered prior to the landing to cover preparatory operations such as underwater demolition or minesweeping. Fire.

Covering force: 1. A force operating apart from the main force for the purpose of intercepting, engaging, delaying, disorganizing, and deceiving the enemy before the enemy can attack the force covered. 2. Anybody or detachment of troops which provides security for a larger force by observation, reconnaissance, attack, or defense, or by any combination of these methods. Force(s).

Covering force area: The area forward of the forward edge of the battle area out to the forward positions initially assigned to the covering forces. It is here that the covering forces execute assigned tasks.

Cover (military): Actions to conceal actual friendly intentions, capabilities, operations, and other activities by providing a plausible yet erroneous explanation of the observable.

Cover search: In air photographic reconnaissance, the process of selection of the most suitable existing cover for a specific requirement.

Covert operation: An operation that is so planned and executed as to conceal the identity of or permit plausible denial by the sponsor. A covert operation differs from a clandestine operation in that emphasis is placed on concealment of the identity of the sponsor rather than on concealment of the operation. Clandestine operation; overt operation.

Coxswain: A person in charge of a small craft (in the Army, a Class B or smaller craft) who often functions as the helmsman. For a causeway ferry, the pilot is in charge with the coxswain performing helmsman functions. Causeway.

Crash locator beacon: An automatic emergency radio locator beacon to help searching forces locate a crashed aircraft. Emergency locator beacon; personal locator beacon.

Crash rescue and fire suppression: Extraction of aircrew members from crashed or burning aircraft and the control and extinguishing of aircraft and structural fires.

Crater : The pit, depression, or cavity formed in the surface of the Earth by an explosion. It may range from saucer shaped to conical, depending largely on the depth of burst. In the case of a deep underground burst, no rupture of the surface may occur. The resulting cavity is termed a "Camouflet."

Crater depth: The maximum depth of the crater measured from the deepest point of the pit to the original ground level.

Cratering charge: A charge placed at an adequate depth to produce a crater.

Crater radius: The average radius of the crater measured at the level corresponding to the original surface of the ground.

Creeping barrage: A barrage in which the fire of all units participating remains in the same relative position throughout and which advances in steps of one line at a time.

Creeping mine: In naval mine warfare, a buoyant mine held below the surface by a weight, usually in the form of a chain, which is free to creep along the seabed under the influence of stream or current.

Crest: A terrain feature of such altitude that it restricts fire or observation in an area beyond, resulting in dead space, or limiting the minimum elevation, or both.

Crested: A report that indicates that engagement of a target or observation of an area is not possible because of an obstacle or intervening crest.

Crisis: An incident or situation involving a threat to a nation, its territories, citizens, military forces, possessions, or vital interests that develops rapidly and creates a condition of such diplomatic, economic, political, or military importance that commitment of military forces and resources is contemplated to achieve national objectives.

Crisis management: Measures to identify, acquire, and plan the use of resources needed to anticipate, prevent, and/or resolve a threat or an act of terrorism. It is predominantly a law enforcement response, normally executed under federal law. CrM.

Critical asset: A specific entity that is of such extraordinary importance that its

incapacitation or destruction would have a very serious, debilitating effect on the ability of a nation to continue to function effectively.

Critical asset list: A prioritized list of assets, normally identified by phase of the operation and approved by the joint force commander, that should be defended against air and missile threats. Also called the CAL.

Critical capability: A means that is considered a crucial enabler for a center of gravity to function as such and is essential to the accomplishment of the specified or assumed objective(s).

Critical information: Specific facts about friendly intentions, capabilities, and activities vitally needed by adversaries for them to plan and act effectively so as to guarantee failure or unacceptable consequences for friendly mission accomplishment.

Critical infrastructure protection: Actions taken to prevent, remediate, or mitigate the risks resulting from vulnerabilities of critical infrastructure assets. Depending on the risk, these actions could include: changes in tactics, techniques, or procedures; adding redundancy; selection of another asset; isolation or hardening; guarding, etc. CIP. Defense critical infrastructure; national critical infrastructure and key assets.

Critical intelligence: Intelligence that is crucial and requires the immediate attention of the commander. It is required to enable the commander to make decisions that will provide a timely and appropriate response to actions by the potential or actual enemy. It includes but is not limited to the following: a. strong indications of the imminent outbreak of hostilities of any type (warning of attack); b. aggression of any nature against a friendly country; c. indications or use of chemical, biological, radiological, nuclear, or high-yield explosives weapons; and d. significant events within adversary countries that may lead to modifications of nuclear strike plans.

Critical item: An essential item which is in short supply or expected to be in short supply for an extended period. Critical supplies and materiel; regulated item.

Critical item list: Prioritized list, compiled from a subordinate commander's composite critical item lists, identifying supply items and weapon systems that assist Service and Defense Logistics Agency's selection of supply items and systems for production surge planning. Also may be used in operational situations by the combatant commander and/or subordinate joint force commander to cross-level critical supply items between Service components. CIL. Critical item.

Criticality assessment: An assessment that identifies key assets and infrastructure that support Department of Defense missions, units, or activities and are deemed mission critical by military commanders or civilian agency managers. It addresses the impact of temporary or permanent loss of key assets or infrastructures to the installation or a unit's ability to perform its mission. It examines costs of recovery and reconstitution including time, dollars, capability, and infrastructure support.

Critical joint duty assignment billet: A joint duty assignment position for which, considering the duties and responsibilities of the position, it is highly important that the assigned officer be particularly trained in, and oriented toward, joint matters. Critical billets are selected by heads of joint organizations, approved by the Secretary of Defense and documented in the Joint Duty Assignment List.

Critical mass: The minimum amount of fissionable material capable of supporting a chain reaction under precisely specified conditions.

Critical node: An element, position, or command and control entity whose disruption or destruction immediately degrades the ability of a force to command, control, or effectively conduct combat operations. Target critical damage point.

Critical occupational specialty: A military occupational specialty selected from among the combat arms in the Army or equivalent military specialties in the Navy, Air Force, or Marine Corps. Equivalent military specialties are those engaged in operational art in order to attain strategic goals in an operational area through the design, organization, and conduct of campaigns and major operations. Critical occupational specialties are designated by the Secretary of Defense. COS.

Critical point: 1. A key geographical point or position important to the success of an operation. 2. In point of time, a crisis or a turning point in an operation. 3. A selected point along a line of march used for reference in giving instructions. 4. A point where there is a change of direction or change in slope in a ridge or stream. 5. Any point along a route of march where interference with a troop movement may occur.

Critical requirement: An essential condition, resource, and means for a critical capability to be fully operational.

Critical safety item: A part, assembly, installation, or production system with one or more essential characteristics that, if not conforming to the design data or quality requirements, would result in an unsafe condition that could cause loss or serious damage to the end item or major components, loss of control, or serious injury to personnel. CSI.

Critical speed: A speed or range of speeds which a ship cannot sustain due to vibration or other similar phenomena.

Critical supplies and materiel: -Those supplies vital to the support of operations, which owing to various causes are in short supply or are expected to be in short supply. Critical item; regulated item.

Critical sustainability item: Any item described at National Stock Number level of detail, by federal supply class, as part of the logistic factors file, that significantly affect the commander's ability to execute an operation plan. CSI.

Critical vulnerability: An aspect of a critical requirement which is deficient or vulnerable to direct or indirect attack that will create decisive or significant effects.

Crossing area: 1. A number of adjacent crossing sites under the control of one commander. 2. A controlled access area for a river crossing operation used to decrease traffic congestion at the river. It is normally a brigade-sized area defined by lateral boundaries and release lines 3 to 4 kilometers from each side of the river.

Cross-leveling: The authority and ability to shift materiel inventory from one owner to meet the requirement of another. At the theater strategic level and operational level, it is the process of diverting en route or in-theater materiel from one military element to meet the higher priority of another within the combatant commander's directive authority for logistics. Cross-leveling plans must include specific reimbursement procedures.

Cross-loading (personnel): The distribution of leaders, key weapons, personnel, and key equipment among the aircraft, vessels, or vehicles of a formation to preclude the total loss of command and control or unit effectiveness if an aircraft, vessel, or vehicle is lost. It is also an important factor in aiding rapid assembly of units at the drop zone or landing zone. Loading.

Cross-servicing: A subset of common-user logistics in which a function is performed by one Military Service in support of another Military Service and for which reimbursement is required from the Service receiving support. Acquisition and cross-servicing agreement; common-user logistics; servicing.

Cross-targeting (nuclear): The layering of weapons from different delivery platforms to increase the probability of target damage or destruction.

Cross tell: The transfer of information between facilities at the same operational level. Track telling.

Cruise missile: Guided missile, the major portion of whose flight path to its target is conducted at approximately constant velocity; depends on the dynamic reaction of air for lift and upon propulsion forces to balance drag.

Cruising altitude: A level determined by vertical measurement from mean sea level, maintained during a flight or portion thereof.

Cruising level: A level maintained during a significant portion of a flight. Altitude.

Cryogenic liquid: Liquefied gas at very low temperature, such as liquid oxygen, nitrogen, or argon.

Cryptanalysis: The steps and operations performed in converting encrypted messages into plain text without initial knowledge of the key employed in the encryption.

Cryptochannel: 1. A complete system of crypto-communications between two or more holders. 2. The basic unit for naval cryptographic communication. It includes: a. the cryptographic aids prescribed; b. the holders thereof; c. the indicators or other means of identification; d. the area or areas in which effective; e. the special purpose, if any, for which provided; and f. pertinent notes as to distribution, usage, etc. A cryptochannel is analogous to a radio circuit.

Cryptographic information: All information significantly descriptive of cryptographic techniques and processes or of cryptographic systems and equipment and all crypto material.

Cryptology: The science that deals with hidden, disguised, or encrypted communications. It includes communications security and communications intelligence.

Crypto security: The component of communications security that results from the provision of technically sound cryptosystems and their proper use. Communications security.

Crypto system: The associated items of crypto material that are used as a unit and provide a single means of encryption and decryption. Cipher; code; decrypt; encipher.

Culminating point: The point at which a force no longer has the capability to continue its form of operations, offense or defense. a. In the offense, the point at which effectively continuing the attack is no longer possible and the force must consider reverting to a defensive posture or attempting an operational pause. b. In the defense, the point at which effective counteroffensive action is no longer possible.

Cultivation: A deliberate and calculated association with a person for the purpose of recruitment, obtaining information, or gaining control for these or other purposes.

Culture: A feature of the terrain that has been constructed by man. Included are such items as roads, buildings, and canals; boundary lines; and, in a broad sense, all names and legends on a map.

Curb weight: Weight of a ground vehicle including fuel, lubricants, coolant, and on-vehicle materiel, excluding cargo and operating personnel.

Current: A body of water moving in a certain direction and caused by wind and density differences in water. The effects of a current are modified by water depth, underwater topography, basin shape, land masses, and deflection from the earth's rotation.

Current force: The force that exists today. The current force represents actual force structure and/or manning available to meet present contingencies. It is the basis for operations and contingency plans and orders. Force; Intermediate Force Planning Level; Programmed Forces.

Current intelligence: One of two categories of descriptive intelligence that is concerned with describing the existing situation.

Current, offshore: Deep water movements caused by tides or seasonal changes in ocean water level.

Current, rip: A water movement that flows from the beach through the surf zone in swiftly moving narrow channels. Surf zone.

Curve of pursuit: The curved path described by a fighter plane making an attack on a moving target while holding the proper aiming allowance.

Cusps: Ridges of beach material extending seaward from the beach face with intervening troughs.

Custodian of postal effects: Members of the US Armed Forces or Department of Defense civilian employees accountable for administration of the postal effects entrusted to them by the United States Postal Service. Civilian custodians of postal effects are supervised by the members of the US Armed Forces. COPE.

Customer wait time: The total elapsed time between issuance of a customer order and satisfaction of that order. CWT.

Customs Over-The-Horizon Enforcement Network: United States Customs Service long-range voice communications system. COTHEN.

Cut-off": The deliberate shutting off of a reaction engine.

Cutoff attack: An attack that provides a direct vector from the interceptor's position to an intercept point with the target track.

Cut-off velocity: The velocity attained by a missile at the point of cut-off.

Cutout: An intermediary or device used to obviate direct contact between members of a clandestine organization.

Cutter: 1. In naval mine warfare, a device fitted to a sweep wire to cut or part the moorings of mines or obstructers; it may also be fitted in the mooring of a mine or obstructor to part a sweep. 2. Coast Guard watercraft 65 feet long or larger. Mine warfare; watercraft.

Cutting charge: A charge which produces a cutting effect in line with its plane of symmetry.

Cyber counterintelligence: Measures to identify, penetrate, or neutralize foreign operations that use cyber means as the primary tradecraft methodology, as well as foreign intelligence service collection efforts that use traditional methods to gauge cyber capabilities and intentions. Counterintelligence.

Cyberspace: A global domain within the information environment consisting of the interdependent network of information technology infrastructures, including the Internet, telecommunications networks, computer systems, and embedded processors and controllers.

Cyberspace operations: The employment of cyber capabilities where the primary purpose is to achieve military objectives or effects in or through cyberspace. Such operations include computer network operations and activities to operate and defend the Global Information Grid.

D

Daily intelligence summary: A report prepared in message form at the joint force headquarters that provides higher, lateral, and subordinate headquarters with a summary of all significant intelligence produced during the previous 24-hour period. The "as of" time for information, content, and submission time for the report will be as specified by the joint force commander. DISUM.

Daily movement summary (shipping): A tabulation of departures and arrivals of all merchant shipping (including neutrals) arriving or departing ports during a 24-hour period.

Damage area: In naval mine warfare, the plan area around a minesweeper inside which a mine explosion is likely to interrupt operations.

Damage assessment: 1. The determination of the effect of attacks on targets. 2. A determination of the effect of a compromise of classified information on national security. Civil damage assessment; military damage assessment.

Damage control: In naval usage, measures necessary aboard ship to preserve and reestablish watertight integrity, stability, maneuverability, and offensive power; to control list and trim; to effect rapid repairs of materiel; to limit the spread of and provide adequate protection from fire; to limit the spread of, remove the contamination by, and provide adequate protection from chemical, biological, and radiological agents; and to provide for care of wounded personnel. Area damage control; disaster control.

Damage criteria: The critical levels of various effects, such as blast pressure and thermal radiation, required to achieve specified levels of damage.

Damage estimation: A preliminary appraisal of the potential effects of an attack. Attack assessment.

Damage expectancy (nuclear): The probability that a weapon will arrive, detonate, and achieve at least a specified level of damage (severe or moderate) against a given target. Damage expectancy is a function of both probability of arrival and probability of damage of a weapon.

Damage radius: In naval mine warfare, the average distance from a ship within which a mine containing a given weight and type of explosive must detonate if it is to inflict a specified amount of damage.

Damage threat: The probability that a target ship passing once through a minefield will explode one or more mines and sustain a specified amount of damage.

Danger area: 1. In air traffic control, an airspace of defined dimensions within which activities dangerous to the flight of aircraft may exist at specified times. 2. A specified area above, below, or within which there may be potential danger. Closed area; prohibited area; restricted area.

Danger close: In close air support, artillery, mortar, and naval gunfire support fires, it is the term included in the method of engagement segment of a call for fire which indicates that friendly forces are within close proximity of the target. The close proximity distance is determined by the weapon and munitions fired. Call for fire; final protective fire.

Dangerous cargo: Cargo which, because of its dangerous properties, is subject to special regulations for its transport.

Danger space: That space between the weapon and the target where the trajectory does not rise 1.8 meters (the average height of a standing human). This includes the area encompassed by the beaten zone. Beaten zone.

Data: Representation of facts, concepts, or instructions in a formalized manner suitable for communication, interpretation, or processing by humans or by automatic means. Any representations such as characters or analog quantities to which meaning is or might be assigned.

Database: Information that is normally structured and indexed for user access and review. Databases may exist in the form of physical files or formatted automated data processing system data files.

Data block: Information presented on air imagery relevant to the geographical position, altitude, attitude, and heading of the aircraft and, in certain cases, administrative information and information on the sensors employed.

Data code: A number, letter, character, or any combination thereof used to represent a data element or data item.

Data element: 1. A basic unit of information built on standard structures having a unique meaning and distinct units or values. 2. In electronic record keeping, a combination of characters or bytes referring to one separate item of information, such as name, address, or age.

Data item: A subunit of descriptive information or value classified under a data element. For example, the data element "military personnel grade" contains data items such as sergeant, captain, and colonel.

Data link: The means of connecting one location to another for the purpose of transmitting and receiving data. Tactical digital information link.

Data link coordination net: A voice coordination net of voice circuits used to coordinate technical operation of data terminal equipment. One voice circuit is required for each tactical digital information link (TADIL)-B pair, and one net is required for participants on each TADIL-A, TADIL-J, or interim Joint Tactical Information Distribution

System message specification net. The net is normally secure or covered. DCN.

Data mile: A standard unit of distance

Date-time group: The date and time, expressed in digits and time zone suffix, at which the message was prepared for transmission. DTG.

Datum: Any numerical or geometrical quantity or set of such quantities which may serve as reference or base for other quantities. Where the concept is geometric, the plural form is "datums" in contrast to the normal plural "data."

Datum (antisubmarine warfare): A datum is the last known position of a submarine, or suspected submarine, after contact has been lost.

Datum error (antisubmarine warfare): An estimate of the degree of accuracy in the reported position of datum.

Datum (geodetic): 1. A reference surface consisting of five quantities: the latitude and longitude of an initial point, the azimuth of a line from that point, and the parameters of the reference ellipsoid. 2. The mathematical model of the earth used to calculate the coordinates on any map. Different nations use different datums for printing coordinates on their maps. The datum is usually referenced in the marginal information of each map.

Datum level: A surface to which elevations, heights, or depths on a map or chart are related. Altitude.

Datum point: Any reference point of known or assumed coordinates from which

calculation or measurements may be taken. Pinpoint.

Datum time (antisubmarine warfare): The time when contact with the submarine, or suspected submarine, was lost.

Davit: A small crane on a vessel that is used to raise and lower small boats, such as lifeboats, side loadable warping tugs, or causeway sections.

Dazzle: Temporary loss of vision or a temporary reduction in visual acuity; may also be applied to effects on optics. Directed-energy warfare; flash blindness.

D-day consumption/production differential assets: As applied to the D-to-P concept, these assets are required to compensate for the inability of the production base to meet expenditure (consumption) requirements during the D-to-P period. D-to-P concept.

D-day materiel readiness gross capability: As applied to the D-to-P concept, this capability represents the sum of all assets on hand on D-day and the gross production capability (funded and unfunded) between D-day and P-day. When this capability equals the D-to-P materiel readiness gross requirement, requirements and capabilities are in balance. D-to-P concept.

D-day pipeline assets: As applied to the D-to-P concept, these assets represent the sum of continental United States and overseas operating and safety levels and in transit levels of supply. D-to-P concept.

Deadline: To remove a vehicle or piece of equipment from operation or use for one of the following reasons: a. is inoperative due to damage, malfunctioning, or necessary repairs; b. is unsafe; and c. would be damaged by further use.

Dead mine: A mine which has been neutralized, sterilized, or rendered safe. Mine.

Dead space: 1. An area within the maximum range of a weapon, radar, or observer, which cannot be covered by fire or observation from a particular position because of intervening obstacles, the nature of the ground, or the characteristics of the trajectory, or the limitations of the pointing capabilities of the weapon. 2. An area or zone which is within range of a radio transmitter, but in which a signal is not received. 3. The volume of space above and around a gun or guided missile system into which it cannot fire because of mechanical or electronic limitations.

De-arming: An operation in which a weapon is changed from a state of readiness for initiation to a safe condition. Safing. Arm or de-arm.

Debarkation: The unloading of troops, equipment, or supplies from a ship or aircraft.

Debarkation net: A specially prepared type of cargo net employed for the debarkation of troops over the side of a ship.

Debarkation schedule: A schedule that provides for the timely and orderly debarkation of troops and equipment and emergency supplies for the waterborne ship-to-shore movement.

Decentralized control: In air defense, the normal mode whereby a higher echelon monitors unit actions, making direct target assignments to units only when necessary to ensure proper fire distribution or to prevent engagement of friendly aircraft. Centralized control.

Decentralized execution: Delegation of execution authority to subordinate commanders.

Decentralized items: Those items of supply for which appropriate authority has prescribed local management and procurement.

Deception: Those measures designed to mislead the enemy by manipulation, distortion, or falsification of evidence to induce the enemy to react in a manner prejudicial to the enemy's interests. Counter deception; military deception.

Deception action: A collection of related deception events that form a major component of a deception operation.

Deception concept: The deception course of action forwarded to the Chairman of the Joint Chiefs of Staff for review as part of the combatant commander's strategic concept.

Deception course of action: A deception scheme developed during the estimate process in sufficient detail to permit decision making. At a minimum, a deception course of action will identify the deception objective, the deception target, the desired perception, the deception story, and tentative deception means.

Deception event: A deception means executed at a specific time and location in support of a deception operation.

Deception means: Methods, resources, and techniques that can be used to convey information to the deception target. There are three categories of deception means: a. physical means. Activities and resources used to convey or deny selected information to a foreign power. b. technical means. Military material resources and their associated operating techniques used to convey or deny selected information to a foreign power. c. administrative means. Resources, methods, and techniques to convey or deny oral, pictorial, documentary, or other physical evidence to a foreign power.

Deception objective: The desired result of a deception operation expressed in terms of what the adversary is to do or not to do at the critical time and/or location.

Deception story: A scenario that outlines the friendly actions that will be portrayed to cause the deception target to adopt the desired perception.

Deception target: The adversary decision maker with the authority to make the decision that will achieve the deception objective.

Decision: In an estimate of the situation, a clear and concise statement of the line of action intended to be followed by the commander as the one most favorable to the successful accomplishment of the assigned mission.

Decision point: A point in space and time when the commander or staff anticipates making a key decision concerning a specific course of action. Course of action; decision support template; target area of interest.

Decision support template: A graphic record of war gaming. The decision support template depicts decision points, timelines associated with movement of forces and the flow of the operation, and other key items of information required to execute a specific friendly course of action. Course of action; decision point.

Decisive point: A geographic place, specific key event, critical factor, or function that, when acted upon, allows commanders to gain a marked advantage over an adversary or contribute materially to achieving success. Center of gravity.

Deck status light: A three-colored light controlled from the primary.

Declared speed: The continuous speed which a master declares the ship can maintain on a forthcoming voyage under moderate weather conditions having due regard to the ship's present condition.

Declassification: The determination that, in the interests of national security, classified information no longer requires any degree of protection against unauthorized disclosure, coupled with removal or cancellation of the classification designation.

Declassify: To cancel the security classification of an item of classified matter. DECL. Downgrade.

Declination: The angular distance to a body on the celestial sphere measured north or south through 90 degrees from the celestial equator along the hour circle of the body. Comparable to latitude on the terrestrial sphere. See also magnetic declination; magnetic variation.

Decompression: In personnel recovery, the process of normalizing psychological and behavioral reactions that recovered isolated personnel experienced or are currently experiencing as a result of their isolation and recovery.

Decompression sickness: A syndrome, including bends, chokes, neurological disturbances, and collapse, resulting from exposure to reduced ambient pressure and caused by gas bubbles in the tissues, fluids, and blood vessels.

Decontamination: The process of making any person, object, or area safe by absorbing, destroying, neutralizing, making harmless, or removing chemical or biological agents, or by removing radioactive material clinging to or around it.

Decoy: An imitation in any sense of a person, object, or phenomenon which is intended to deceive enemy surveillance devices or mislead enemy evaluation. Dummy.

Decrypt: To convert encrypted text into its equivalent plain text by means of a cryptosystem. Cryptosystem.

Deep fording capability: The characteristic of a self-propelled gun or ground vehicle equipped with built-in waterproofing and/or a special waterproofing kit, to negotiate a water obstacle with its wheels or tracks in contact with the ground.

Deep minefield: An antisubmarine minefield which is safe for surface ships to cross. Minefield.

De facto boundary: An international or administrative boundary whose existence and legality is not recognized, but which is a practical division between separate national and provincial administering authorities.

Defended asset list: In defensive counter air operations, a listing of those assets from the critical asset list prioritized by the joint force commander to be defended with the resources available. DAL.

Defense area: For any particular command, the area extending from the forward edge of the battle area to its rear boundary. It is here that the decisive defensive battle is fought.

Defense Business Operations Fund: A revolving industrial fund concept for a large number of Defense support functions, including transportation. Utilizes business-like cost accounting to determine total cost of a business activity. Defense Business Operations Fund-Transportation is comprised of those Defense Business Operations Fund accounts assigned by the Office of the Secretary of Defense for Commander in Chief, United States Transportation Command control. DBOF.

Defense Communications System: Department of Defense long-haul voice, data, and record traffic system which includes the Defense Data Network, Defense Satellite Communications System, and Defense Switched Network. DCS. Defense Switched Network.

Defense coordinating element: A staff and military liaison officers who assist the defense coordinating officer in facilitating coordination and support to activated emergency support functions. DCE.

Defense coordinating officer: Department of Defense single point of contact for domestic emergencies. Assigned to a joint field office to process requirements for military support, forward mission assignments through proper channels to the appropriate military organizations, and assign military liaisons, as appropriate, to activated emergency support functions. DCO.

Defense critical infrastructure: Department of Defense and non-Department of Defense networked assets and essential to project, support, and sustain military forces and operations worldwide. DCI.

Defense emergency: An emergency condition that exists when: a. a major attack is made upon US forces overseas or on allied forces in any theater and is confirmed by either the commander of a command established by the Secretary of Defense or higher authority; or b. an overt attack of any type is made upon the United States and is confirmed either by the commander of a command established by the Secretary of Defense or higher authority.

Defense in depth: The siting of mutually supporting defense positions designed to absorb and progressively weaken attack, prevent initial observations of the whole position by the enemy, and to allow the commander to maneuver the reserve.

Defense industrial base: The Department of Defense, government, and private sector worldwide industrial complex with capabilities to perform research and development, design, produce, and maintain military weapon systems, subsystems, components, or parts to meet military requirements.

Defense information infrastructure: The shared or interconnected system of computers, communications, data applications, security, people, training, and other support structures serving Department of Defense local, national, and worldwide information needs. The defense information infrastructure connects DOD mission support, command and control, and intelligence computers through voice, telecommunications, imagery, video, and multimedia services. It provides information processing and services to subscribers over the Defense Information Systems Network and includes command and control, tactical, intelligence, and commercial communications systems used to transmit DOD information. DII. Global information infrastructure; information; infrastructure; national information infrastructure.

Defense Information Systems Network – Integrated network, centrally managed and configured to provide long-haul information transfer services for all Department of Defense activities. It is an information transfer utility designed to provide dedicated point-to-point, switched voice and data, imagery, and video teleconferencing services. DISN.

Defense message system: Consists of all hardware, software, procedures, standards, facilities, and personnel used to exchange messages electronically.

Defense Meteorological Satellite Program: Military weather satellite controlled by National Oceanic and Atmospheric Administration. DMSP.

Defense Planning Guidance: This document, issued by the Secretary of Defense, provides firm guidance in the form of goals, priorities, and objectives, including fiscal constraints, for the development of the Program Objective Memorandums by the Military Departments and Defense agencies. DPG.

Defense readiness condition: A uniform system of progressive alert postures for use between the Chairman of the Joint Chiefs of Staff and the commanders of unified and specified commands and for use by the Services. Defense readiness conditions are graduated to match situations of varying military severity (status of alert). Defense readiness conditions are identified by the short title DEFCON (5), (4), (3), (2), and (1), as appropriate.

Defense Satellite Communications System: Geosynchronous military communications satellites that provide high data rate communications for military forces, diplomatic corps, and the White House. The Defense Satellite Communications System provides long-haul super-high frequency 7/8 gigahertz voice and high data rate communications for fixed and transportable terminals, and extends mobile service to a limited number of ships and aircraft. DSCS.

Defense support of civil authorities: Civil support provided under the auspices of the National Response Plan. DSCA.

Defense Support Program: Satellites that provide early warning of missile launches; the first line of defense against missile attack against North America. DSP.

Defense support to public diplomacy: Those activities and measures taken by the Department of Defense components to support and facilitate public diplomacy efforts of the United States Government. DSPD.

Defense Switched Network: Component of the Defense Communications System that handles Department of Defense voice, data, and video communications. DSN. Defense Communications System.

Defense Transportation System: That portion of the Nation's transportation infrastructure that supports Department of Defense common-user transportation needs across the range of military operations. It consists of those common-user military and commercial assets, services, and systems organic to, contracted for, or controlled by the Department of Defense. DTS. common-user transportation; transportation system.

Defensive coastal area: A part of a coastal area and of the air, land, and water area adjacent to the coastline within which defense operations may involve land, sea, and air forces.

Defensive counter air: All defensive measures designed to detect, identify, intercept, and destroy or negate enemy forces attempting to penetrate or attack through friendly airspace. DCA. Counter air; offensive counter air.

Defensive minefield: 1. In naval mine warfare, a minefield laid in international waters or international straits with the declared intention of controlling shipping in defense of sea communications. 2. In land mine warfare, a minefield laid in accordance with an established plan to prevent a penetration between positions and to strengthen the defense of the positions themselves. Minefield.

Defensive sea area: A sea area, usually including the approaches to and the waters of important ports, harbors, bays, or sounds, for the control and protection of shipping; for the safeguarding of defense installations bordering on waters of the areas; and for provision of other security measures required within the specified areas. It does not extend seaward beyond the territorial waters. Maritime control area.

Defensive space control: Operations conducted to preserve the ability to exploit space capabilities via active and passive actions, while protecting friendly space capabilities from attack, interference, or unintentional hazards.

Defensive zone: A belt of terrain, generally parallel to the front, that includes two or more organized, or partially organized, battle positions.

Defilade: 1. Protection from hostile observation and fire provided by an obstacle such as a hill, ridge, or bank. 2. A vertical distance by which a position is concealed from enemy observation. 3. To shield from enemy fire or observation by using natural or artificial obstacles.

Definitive care: Care rendered to conclusively manage a patient's condition. It includes the full range of preventive, curative acute, convalescent, restorative, and rehabilitative medical care. This normally leads to rehabilitation, return to duty, or discharge from the Service.

Defoliant operation: The employment of defoliating agents on vegetated areas in support of military operations.

Defoliating agent: A chemical which causes trees, shrubs, and other plants to shed their leaves prematurely.

Degaussing: The process whereby a ship's magnetic field is reduced by the use of electromagnetic coils, permanent magnets, or other means.

Degree of risk: As specified by the commander, the risk to which friendly forces may be subjected from the effects of the detonation of a nuclear weapon used in the attack of a close-in enemy target; acceptable degrees of risk under differing tactical conditions are emergency, moderate, and negligible. Emergency risk (nuclear); negligible risk (nuclear).

De jure boundary: An international or administrative boundary whose existence and legality is recognized.

Delayed entry program: A program under which an individual may enlist in a Reserve Component of a military service and specify a future reporting date for entry on active duty that would coincide with availability of training spaces and with personal plans such as high school graduation. DEP. Active duty.

Delaying operation: An operation in which a force under pressure trades space for time by slowing down the enemy's momentum and inflicting maximum damage on the enemy without, in principle, becoming decisively engaged.

Delay release sinker: A sinker which holds a moored mine on the sea-bed for a predetermined time after laying.

Delegation of authority: The action by which a commander assigns part of his or her authority commensurate with the assigned task to a subordinate commander. While ultimate responsibility cannot be relinquished, delegation of authority carries with it the imposition of a measure of responsibility. The extent of the authority delegated must be clearly stated.

Deliberate breaching: The creation of a lane through a minefield or a clear route through a barrier or fortification, which is systematically planned and carried out.

Deliberate crossing: The crossing of an inland water obstacle that requires extensive planning and detailed preparations. Hasty crossing.

Deliberate defense: A defense normally organized when out of contact with the enemy or when contact with the enemy is not imminent and time for organization is available. It normally includes an extensive fortified zone incorporating pillboxes, forts, and communications systems. Hasty defense.

Delivering ship: The ship in a replenishment unit that delivers the rig(s).

Delivery error: The inaccuracy associated with a given weapon system resulting in a dispersion of shots about the aiming point. Circular error probable; deviation; dispersion; dispersion error; horizontal error.

Demilitarized zone: A defined area in which the stationing or concentrating of military forces, or the retention or establishment of military installations of any description, is prohibited.

Demobilization: The process of transitioning a conflict or wartime military establishment and defense-based civilian economy to a peacetime configuration while maintaining national security and economic vitality. See also mobilization.

Demolition belt: A selected land area sown with explosive charges, mines, and other available obstacles to deny use of the land to enemy operations, and as a protection to friendly troops. There are two types of demolition belts: a. primary. A continuous series of obstacles across the whole front, selected by the division or higher commander. The preparation of such a belt is normally a priority engineer task. b. subsidiary. A supplement to the primary belt to give depth in front or behind or to protect the flanks.

Demolition chamber: Space intentionally provided in a structure for the emplacement of explosive charges.

Demolition firing party: The party at the site that is technically responsible for the demolition and that actually initiates detonation or fires the demolitions. See also demolition guard; state of readiness.

Demolition guard: A local force positioned to ensure that a target is not captured by an enemy before orders are given for its demolition and before the demolition has been successfully fired. The commander of the demolition guard is responsible for the tactical control of all troops at the demolition site, including the demolition firing party. The commander of the demolition guard is responsible for transmitting the order to fire to the demolition firing party.

Demolition kit: The demolition tool kit complete with explosives. demolition tool kit.

Demolition target: A target of known military interest identified for possible future demolition. See also charged demolition target; preliminary demolition target; pre withdrawal demolition target; reserved demolition target; uncharged demolition target.

Demolition tool kit: The tools, materials and accessories of a non explosive nature necessary for preparing demolition charges. Demolition kit.

Demonstration: 1. An attack or show of force on a front where a decision is not

sought, made with the aim of deceiving the enemy. Amphibious demonstration; diversion; diversionary attack. 2. (DOD only) In military deception, a show of force in an area where a decision is not sought that is made to deceive an adversary. It is similar to a feint but no actual contact with the adversary is intended.

Denial measure: An action to hinder or deny the enemy the use of territory, personnel, or facilities. It may include destruction, removal, contamination, or erection of obstructions.

Denied area: An area under enemy or unfriendly control in which friendly forces cannot expect to operate successfully within existing operational constraints and force capabilities.

Departmental intelligence: Intelligence that any department or agency of the Federal Government requires to execute its own mission.

Department of Defense civilian: A Federal civilian employee of the Department of Defense directly hired and paid from appropriated or non appropriated funds, under permanent or temporary appointment. Specifically excluded are contractors and foreign host nationals as well as third country civilians.

Department of Defense components: The Office of the Secretary of Defense, the Military Departments, the Chairman of the Joint Chiefs of Staff, the combatant commands, the Office of the Inspector General of the Department of Defense, the Department of Defense agencies, field activities, and all other organizational entities in the Department of Defense.

Department of Defense construction agent: The Corps of Engineers, Naval Facilities Engineering Command, or other such approved Department of Defense activity, that is assigned design or execution responsibilities associated with military construction programs, facilities support, or civil engineering support to the combatant commanders in contingency operations. Contingency operation.

Department of Defense Intelligence Information System: The combination of Department of Defense personnel, procedures, equipment, computer programs, and supporting communications that support the timely and comprehensive preparation and presentation of intelligence and information to military commanders and national-level decision makers. DODIIS.

Department of Defense Intelligence Information System Enterprise: The global set of resources (people, facilities, hardware, software and processes) that provide information technology and information management services to the military intelligence community through a tightly-integrated, interconnected and geographically distributed regional service center architecture.

Department of Defense intelligence production: The integration, evaluation, analysis, and interpretation of information from single or multiple sources into finished intelligence for known or anticipated military and related national security consumer requirements.

Department of Defense internal audit organizations: The Army Audit Agency; Naval Audit Service; Air Force Audit Agency; and the Office of the Assistant Inspector General for Auditing, Office of the Inspector General, Department of Defense.

Department of Defense support to counterdrug operations: Support provided by the Department of Defense to law enforcement agencies to detect, monitor, and counter the production, trafficking, and use of illegal drugs. Counterdrug operations.

Department of the Air Force: The executive part of the Department of the Air Force at the seat of government and all field headquarters, forces, Reserve

Components, installations, activities, and functions under the control or supervision of the Secretary of the Air Force. DAF. Military Department.

Department of the Army: The executive part of the Department of the Army at the seat of government and all field headquarters, forces, Reserve Components, installations, activities, and functions under the control or supervision of the Secretary of the Army. DA. Military Department.

Department of the Navy – The executive part of the Department of the Navy at the seat of government; the headquarters, US Marine Corps; the entire operating forces of the United States Navy and of the US Marine Corps, including the Reserve Components of such forces; all field activities, headquarters, forces, bases, installations, activities, and functions under the control or supervision of the Secretary of the Navy; and the US Coast Guard when operating as a part of the Navy pursuant to law. DON. Military Department.

Departure airfield: An airfield on which troops and/or materiel are enplaned for flight. Airfield.

Departure area: The general area encompassing all base camps, bivouacs, and departure airfield facilities.

Departure end: That end of a runway nearest to the direction in which initial departure is made.

Departure point: 1. A navigational check point used by aircraft as a marker for

setting course. 2. In amphibious operations, an air control point at the seaward end of the helicopter approach lane system from which helicopter waves are dispatched along the selected helicopter approach lane to the initial point.

Dependents/immediate family: An employee's spouse; children who are unmarried and under age 21 years or who, regardless of age, are physically or mentally incapable of self-support; dependent parents, including step and legally adoptive parents of the employee's spouse; and dependent brothers and sisters, including step and legally adoptive brothers and sisters of the employee's spouse who are unmarried and under 21 years of age or who, regardless of age, are physically or mentally incapable of self support.

Deployable joint task force augmentation cell: A combatant commander asset composed of personnel from the combatant command and components' staffs. The members are a joint, multidiscipline group of planners and operators who operationally report to the combatant commander's operations directorate until deployed to a joint task force. DJTFAC.

Deployed nuclear weapons: 1. When used in connection with the transfer of weapons between the Department of Energy and the Department of Defense, this term describes those weapons transferred to and in the custody of the Department of Defense. 2. Those nuclear weapons specifically authorized by the Joint Chiefs of Staff to be transferred to the custody of the storage facilities or carrying or delivery units of the Armed Forces.

Deployment: 1. In naval usage, the change from a cruising approach or contact disposition to a disposition for battle. 2. The movement of forces within operational areas. 3. The positioning of forces into a formation for battle. 4. The relocation of forces and materiel to desired operational areas. Deployment encompasses all activities from origin or home station through destination, specifically including intra-continental United States, inter theater, and intratheater movement legs, staging, and holding areas. Deployment order; deployment planning; prepare to deploy order.

Deployment database: The Joint Operation Planning and Execution System database containing the necessary information on forces, materiel, and filler and replacement personnel movement requirements to support execution. The database reflects information contained in the refined time-phased force and deployment data from the contingency planning process or developed during the various phases of the crisis action planning process, and the movement schedules or tables developed by the transportation component commands to support the deployment of required forces, personnel, and materiel. Time-phased force and deployment data.

Deployment diagram: In the assault phase of an amphibious operation, a diagram showing the formation in which the boat group proceeds from the rendezvous area to the line of departure and the method of deployment into the landing formation.

Deployment health surveillance: The regular or repeated collection, analysis, archiving, interpretation, and distribution of health-related data used for monitoring the health of a population or of individuals, and for intervening in a timely manner to prevent, treat, or control the occurrence of disease or injury. It includes occupational and environmental health surveillance and medical surveillance subcomponents.

Deployment order: A planning directive from the Secretary of Defense, issued by the Chairman of the Joint Chiefs of Staff, that authorizes and directs the transfer of forces between combatant commands by reassignment or attachment. A deployment order normally specifies the authority that the gaining combatant commander will exercise over the transferred forces. DEPORD. Deployment; deployment planning; prepare to deploy order.

Deployment planning: Operational planning directed toward the movement of forces and sustainment resources from their original locations to a specific operational area for conducting the joint operations contemplated in a given plan. Encompasses all activities from origin or home station through destination, specifically including intra-continental United States, inter theater, and intratheater movement legs, staging areas, and holding areas. Deployment; deployment order; prepare to deploy order.

Depot: 1. supply — An activity for the receipt, classification, storage, accounting, issue, maintenance, procurement, manufacture, assembly, research, salvage, or disposal of material. 2. personnel — An activity for the reception, processing, training, assignment, and forwarding of personnel replacements.

Depot maintenance: That maintenance performed on materiel requiring major overhaul or a complete rebuild of parts, assemblies, subassemblies, and end-items, including the manufacture of parts, modifications, testing, and reclamation as required. Depot maintenance serves to support lower categories of maintenance by providing technical assistance and performing that maintenance beyond their responsibility. Depot maintenance provides stocks of serviceable equipment by using more extensive facilities for repair than are available in lower level maintenance activities.

Depth: In maritime/hydrographic use, the vertical distance from the plane of the hydrographic datum to the bed of the sea, lake, or river.

Depth contour: A line connecting points of equal depth below the hydrographic datum. Also called bathymetric contour or depth curve.

Descriptive name: Written indication on maps and charts, used to specify the nature of a feature (natural or artificial) shown by a general symbol.

Designated planning agent: The commander responsible for planning, coordinating, and executing military taskings in civil emergencies for a particular branch or agency of the Department of Defense.

Design basis threat: The threat against which an asset must be protected and upon which the protective system's design is based. It is the baseline type and size of threat that buildings or other structures are designed to withstand. The design basis threat includes the tactics aggressors will use against the asset and the tools, weapons, and explosives employed in these tactics. DBT.

Desired effects: The damage or casualties to the enemy or materiel that a commander desires to achieve from a nuclear weapon detonation. Damage effects on materiel are classified as light, moderate, or severe. Casualty effects on personnel may be immediate, prompt, or delayed.

Desired ground zero: The point on the surface of the Earth at, or vertically below or above, the center of a planned nuclear detonation. DGZ. Actual ground zero; ground zero.

Desired mean point of impact: A precise point, associated with a target, and assigned as the center for impact of multiple weapons or area munitions to create a desired effect. May be defined descriptively, by grid reference, or by geolocation. DMPI. Aim point; desired point of impact.

Desired perception: In military deception, what the deception target must believe for it to make the decision that will achieve the deception objective.

Desired point of impact: A precise point, associated with a target, and assigned as the impact point for a single unitary weapon to create a desired effect. May be defined descriptively, by grid preferences, or geolocation. DPI. Aim point; desired mean point of impact.

Destroyed: A condition of a target so damaged that it can neither function as intended nor be restored to a usable condition. In the case of a building, all vertical supports and spanning members are damaged to such an extent that nothing is salvageable. In the case of bridges, all spans must have dropped and all piers must require replacement.

Destruction: A type of adjustment for destroying a given target. destruction fire – Fire delivered for the sole purpose of destroying material objects.

Destruction fire mission: In artillery, fire delivered for the purpose of destroying a point target.

Destruction radius: In mine warfare, the maximum distance from an exploding charge of stated size and type at which a mine will be destroyed by sympathetic detonation of the main charge, with a stated probability of destruction, regardless of orientation.

Detachment: 1. A part of a unit separated from its main organization for duty elsewhere. 2. A temporary military or naval unit formed from other units or parts of units. DET.

Detailed photographic report: A comprehensive, analytical, intelligence report

written as a result of the interpretation of photography usually covering a single subject, a target, target complex, and of a detailed nature.

Detainee: A term used to refer to any person captured or otherwise detained by an armed force.

Detainee collecting point: A facility or other location where detainees are assembled for subsequent movement to a detainee processing station.

Detecting circuit: The part of a mine firing circuit which responds to the influence of a target.

Detection: 1. In tactical operations, the perception of an object of possible military interest but unconfirmed by recognition. 2. In surveillance, the determination and transmission by a surveillance system that an event has occurred. 3. In arms control, the first step in the process of ascertaining the occurrence of a violation of an arms control agreement. 4. In chemical, biological, radiological, and nuclear environments, the act of locating chemical, biological, radiological, and nuclear hazards by use of chemical, biological, radiological, and nuclear detectors or monitoring and/or survey teams. Hazard; monitoring.

Deterioration limit: A limit placed on a particular product characteristic to define the minimum acceptable quality requirement for the product to retain its NATO code number.

Deterrence: The prevention from action by fear of the consequences. Deterrence is a state of mind brought about by the existence of a credible threat of unacceptable counteraction.

Deterrent options: A course of action, developed on the best economic, diplomatic, political, and military judgment, designed to dissuade an adversary from a current course of action or contemplated operations.

Detonating cord: A waterproof, flexible fabric tube containing a high explosive designed to transmit the detonation wave.

Detonator: A device containing a sensitive explosive intended to produce a detonation wave.

Developmental assistance: US Agency for International Development function chartered under chapter one of the Foreign Assistance Act of 1961, primarily designed to promote economic growth and the equitable distribution of its benefits.

Deviation: 1. The distance by which a point of impact or burst misses the target. Circular error probable; delivery error; dispersion error; horizontal error. 2. The angular difference between magnetic and compass headings.

Diapositive: A positive photograph on a transparent medium.

Died of wounds received in action: A casualty category applicable to a hostile casualty, other than the victim of a terrorist activity, who dies of wounds or other injuries received in action after having reached a medical treatment facility. DWRIA. Casualty category.

Differential ballistic wind: In bombing, a hypothetical wind equal to the difference in velocity between the ballistic wind and the actual wind at a release altitude.

Diffraction loading: The total force which is exerted on the sides of a structure by the advancing shock front of a nuclear explosion.

Dip: In naval mine warfare, the amount by which a moored mine is carried beneath its set depth by a current or tidal stream acting on the mine casing and mooring.

Diplomatic authorization: Authority for over flight or landing obtained at government-to-government level through diplomatic channels.

Diplomatic and/or consular facility: Any Foreign Service establishment maintained by the US Department of State abroad. It may be designated a "mission" or "consular office," or given a special designation for particular purposes, such as "United States Liaison Office." A "mission" is designated as an embassy and is maintained in order to conduct normal continuing diplomatic relations between the US Government and other governments. A "consular office" is any consulate general or consulate that may participate in most foreign affairs activities, and varies in size and scope.

Dip needle circuit: In naval mine warfare, a mechanism which responds to a change in the magnitude of the vertical component of the total magnetic field.

Direct action: Short-duration strikes and other small-scale offensive actions conducted as a special operation in hostile, denied, or politically sensitive environments and which employ specialized military capabilities to seize, destroy, capture, exploit, recover, or damage designated targets. Direct action differs from conventional offensive actions in the level of physical and political risk, operational techniques, and the degree of discriminate and precise use of force to achieve specific objectives. DA. Special operations; special operations forces.

Direct action fuze: Impact action fuze; proximity fuze; self-destroying fuse; time fuze.

Direct air support center: The principal air control agency of the US Marine air command and control system responsible for the direction and control of air operations directly supporting the ground combat element. It processes and coordinates requests for immediate air support and coordinates air missions requiring integration with ground forces and other supporting arms. It normally collocates with the senior fire support coordination center within the ground combat element and is subordinate to the tactical air command center. DASC. Marine air command and control system; tactical air operations center.

Direct air support center (airborne): An airborne aircraft equipped with the necessary staff personnel, communications, and operations facilities to function as a direct air support center. DASC(A). Direct air support center.

Directed energy: An umbrella term covering technologies that relate to the production of a beam of concentrated electromagnetic energy or atomic or subatomic particles. DE. Directed-energy device; directed-energy weapon.

Directed-energy device: A system using directed energy primarily for a purpose other than as a weapon. Directed-energy devices may produce effects that could allow the device to be used as a weapon against certain threats; for example, laser rangefinders and designators used against sensors that are sensitive to light. Directed energy; directed-energy weapon.

Directed-energy protective measures: That division of directed-energy warfare involving actions taken to protect friendly equipment, facilities, and personnel to ensure friendly effective uses of the electromagnetic spectrum that are threatened by hostile directed-energy weapons and devices.

Directed-energy warfare: Military action involving the use of directed-energy weapons, devices, and countermeasures to either cause direct damage or destruction of enemy equipment, facilities, and personnel, or to determine, exploit, reduce, or prevent hostile use of the electromagnetic spectrum through damage, destruction, and disruption. It also includes actions taken to protect friendly equipment, facilities, and personnel and retain friendly use of the electromagnetic spectrum. DEW. Directed energy; directed-energy device; directed-energy weapon; electromagnetic spectrum; electronic warfare.

Directed-energy weapon: A system using directed energy primarily as a direct means to damage or destroy enemy equipment, facilities, and personnel. Directed energy; directed-energy device.

Direct exchange: A supply method of issuing serviceable materiel in exchange for unserviceable materiel on an item-for-item basis. DX.

Direct fire: Fire delivered on a target using the target itself as a point of aim for either the weapon or the director.

Direct illumination: Illumination provided by direct light from pyrotechnics or searchlights.

Direction: In artillery and naval gunfire support, a term used by a spotter and/or observer in a call for fire to indicate the bearing of the spotting line. Bearing; call for fire; naval gunfire support; spotter; spotting line.

Directional gyro indicator: An azimuth gyro with a direct display and means for setting the datum to a specified compass heading.

Direction finding: A procedure for obtaining bearings of radio frequency emitters by using a highly directional antenna and a display unit on an intercept receiver or ancillary equipment.

Direction of attack: A specific direction or route that the main attack or center of mass of the unit will follow. The unit is restricted, required to attack as indicated, and is not normally allowed to bypass the enemy. The direction of attack is used primarily in counterattacks or to ensure that supporting attacks make maximal contribution to the main attack.

Directive authority for logistics: Combatant commander authority to issue directives to subordinate commanders, including peacetime measures, necessary to ensure the effective execution of approved operation plans. Essential measures include the optimized use or reallocation of available resources and prevention or elimination of redundant facilities and/or overlapping functions among the Service component commands. DAFL. Combatant command (command authority); logistics.

Direct laying: Laying in which the sights of weapons are aligned directly on the target. Normally used in conjunction with mortars and sometimes artillery. Lay.

Direct liaison authorized: That authority granted by a commander (any level) to a subordinate to directly consult or coordinate an action with a command or agency within or outside of the granting command. Direct liaison authorized is more applicable to planning than operations and always carries with it the requirement of keeping the commander granting direct liaison authorized informed. Direct liaison authorized is a coordination relationship, not an authority through which command may be exercised. DIRLAUTH.

Direct support: A mission requiring a force to support another specific force and authorizing it to answer directly to the supported force's request for assistance. DS. Close support; general support; mission; mutual support; support.

Direct support artillery: Artillery whose primary task is to provide fire requested by the supported unit.

Direct supporting fire: Fire delivered in support of part of a force, as opposed to general supporting fire which is delivered in support of the force as a whole. Supporting fire.

Direct vendor delivery: A materiel acquisition and distribution method that requires vendor delivery directly to the customer. DVD. Distribution.

Disabling fire: The firing of ordnance by ships or aircraft at the steering or propulsion system of a vessel. The intent is to disable with minimum injury to personnel or damage to vessel.

Disaffected person: A person who is alienated or estranged from those in authority or lacks loyalty to the government; a state of mind.

Disarmament: The reduction of a military establishment to some level set by international agreement. Arms control agreement; arms control measure.

Disarmed mine: A mine for which the arming procedure has been reversed, rendering the mine inoperative. It is safe to handle and transport and can be rearmed by simple action.

Disaster assistance response team: United States Agency for International Development's (USAID) Office of United States Foreign Disaster Assistance provides this rapidly deployable team in response to international disasters. A disaster assistance response team provides specialists, trained in a variety of disaster relief skills, to assist US embassies and USAID missions with the management of US Government response to disasters. DART. Foreign disaster; foreign disaster relief.

Disaster control: Measures taken before, during, or after hostile action or natural or manmade disasters to reduce the probability of damage, minimize its effects, and initiate recovery. Area damage control; damage control.

Discriminating circuit: That part of the operating circuit of a sea mine which

distinguishes between the response of the detecting circuit to the passage of a ship and the response to other disturbances.

Disease and non battle injury: All illnesses and injuries not resulting from enemy or terrorist action or caused by conflict. Indigenous disease pathogens, biological warfare agents, heat and cold, hazardous noise, altitude, environmental, occupational, and industrial exposures, and other naturally occurring disease agents may cause disease and no battle injury. Disease and no battle injuries include injuries and illnesses resulting from training or from occupational, environmental, or recreational activities, and may result in short- or long-term, acute, or delayed illness, injury, disability, or death. DNBI.

Disease and no battle injury casualty: A person who is not a battle casualty but who is lost to the organization by reason of disease or injury, including persons dying of disease or injury, by reason of being missing where the absence does not appear to be voluntary, or due to enemy action or being interned. DNBI casualty.

Disengagement: In arms control, a general term for proposals that would result in the geographic separation of opposing nonindigenous forces without directly affecting indigenous military forces.

Dislocated civilian: A broad term primarily used by the Department of Defense that includes a displaced person, an evacuee, an expellee, an internally displaced person, a migrant, a refugee, or a stateless person. DC. Displaced person; evacuee; expellee; internally displaced person; migrant; refugee; stateless person.

Dispatch route: In road traffic, a roadway over which full control, both as to priorities of use and the regulation of movement of traffic in time and space, is exercised. Movement authorization is required for its use, even by a single vehicle. Route.

Dispenser: In air armament, a container or device which is used to carry and release sub munitions. Cluster bomb unit.

Dispersal: Relocation of forces for the purpose of increasing survivability. Dispersion.

Dispersal airfield: An airfield, military or civil, to which aircraft might move before H-hour on either a temporary duty or permanent change of station basis and be able to conduct operations. Airfield.

Dispersed movement pattern: A pattern for ship-to-shore movement which provides additional separation of landing craft both laterally and in depth. This pattern is used when nuclear weapon threat is a factor.

Dispersion: 1. A scattered pattern of hits around the mean point of impact of bombs and projectiles dropped or fired under identical conditions. 2. In antiaircraft gunnery, the scattering of shots in range and deflection about the mean point of explosion. 3. The spreading or separating of troops, materiel, establishments, or activities which are usually concentrated in limited areas to reduce vulnerability. 4. In chemical and biological operations, the dissemination of agents in liquid or aerosol form. 5. In airdrop operations, the scatter of personnel and/or cargo on the drop zone. 6. In naval control of shipping, the rebirthing of a ship in the periphery of the port area or in the vicinity of the port for its own protection in order to minimize the risk of damage from attack. See also circular error probable; convoy dispersal point; delivery error; deviation; dispersion error; horizontal error.

Dispersion error: The distance from the point of impact or burst of a round to the mean point of impact or burst.

Dispersion pattern: The distribution of a series of rounds fired from one weapon or a group of weapons under conditions as nearly identical as possible; the points of burst or impact being dispersed about a point called the mean point of impact.

Displaced person: A broad term used to refer to internally and externally displaced persons collectively. Evacuee; refugee.

Display: In military deception, a static portrayal of an activity, force, or equipment intended to deceive the adversary's visual observation.

Disposition: 1. Distribution of the elements of a command within an area; usually the exact location of each unit headquarters and the deployment of the forces subordinate to it. 2. A prescribed arrangement of the stations to be occupied by the several formations and single ships of a fleet, or major subdivisions of a fleet, for any purpose, such as cruising, approach, maintaining contact, or battle. 3. A prescribed arrangement of all the tactical units composing a flight or group of aircraft. See also deployment; dispersion. 4. (DOD only) The removal of a patient from a medical treatment facility by reason of return to duty, transfer to another treatment facility, death, or other termination of medical case.

Dissemination and integration: In intelligence usage, the delivery of intelligence to users in a suitable form and the application of the intelligence to appropriate missions, tasks, and functions. See also intelligence process.

Distance: 1. The space between adjacent individual ships or boats measured in any direction between foremasts. 2. The space between adjacent men, animals, vehicles, or units in a formation measured from front to rear. 3. The space between known reference points or a ground observer and a target, measured in meters (artillery), in yards (naval gunfire), or in units specified by the observer. Interval.

Distant retirement area: In amphibious operations, that sea area located to seaward of the landing area. This area is divided into a number of operating areas to which assault ships may retire and operate in the event of adverse weather or to prevent concentration of ships in the landing area. Amphibious operation; landing area; retirement.

Distant support area: In amphibious operations, the area located in the vicinity of the landing area but at considerable distance seaward of it. These areas are assigned to distant support forces, such as striking forces, surface action groups, surface action units, and their logistic groups. Amphibious operation; landing area.

Distressed person: An individual who requires search and rescue assistance to remove he or she from life-threatening or isolating circumstances in a permissive environment.

Distributed fire: Fire so dispersed as to engage most effectively an area target.

Distribution: 1. The arrangement of troops for any purpose, such as a battle, march, or maneuver. 2. A planned pattern of projectiles about a point. 3. A planned spread of fire to cover a desired frontage or depth. 4. An official delivery of anything, such as orders or supplies. 5. The operational process of synchronizing all elements of the logistic system to deliver the "right things" to the "right place" at the "right time" to support the geographic combatant commander. 6. The process of assigning military personnel to activities, units, or billets.

Distribution manager: The executive agent for managing distribution with the combatant commander's area of responsibility. Area of responsibility; distribution.

Distribution plan: A reporting system comprising reports, updates, and information systems feeds that articulate the requirements of the theater distribution system to the strategic and operational resources assigned responsibility for support to the theater. It portrays the interface of the physical, financial, information and communications networks for gaining visibility of the theater distribution system and communicates control activities necessary for optimizing capacity of the system. It depicts, and is continually updated to reflect changes in, infrastructure, support relationships, and customer locations to all elements of the distribution system. Distribution; distribution system; theater distribution; theater distribution system.

Distribution point: A point at which supplies and/or ammunition, obtained from supporting supply points by a division or other unit, are broken down for distribution to subordinate units. Distribution points usually carry no stocks; items drawn are issued completely as soon as possible.

Distribution system: That complex of facilities, installations, methods, and procedures designed to receive, store, maintain, distribute, and control the flow of military materiel between the point of receipt into the military system and the point of issue to using activities and units.

Ditching: Controlled landing of a distressed aircraft on water.

Diversion: 1. The act of drawing the attention and forces of an enemy from the point of the principal operation; an attack, alarm, or feint that diverts attention. 2. A change made in a prescribed route for operational or tactical reasons. A diversion order will not constitute a change of destination. 3. A rerouting of cargo or passengers to a new transshipment point or destination or on a different mode of transportation prior to arrival at ultimate destination. 4. In naval mine warfare, a route or channel bypassing a dangerous area. A diversion may connect one channel to another or it may branch from a channel and rejoin it on the other side of the danger. Demonstration.

Diversion airfield: An airfield with at least minimum essential facilities, which may be used as an emergency airfield or when the main or redeployment airfield is not usable or as required to facilitate tactical operations. Divert field. Airfield; departure airfield; main airfield; redeployment airfield.

Diversionary attack: An attack wherein a force attacks, or threatens to attack, a target other than the main target for the purpose of drawing enemy defenses away from the main effort. See also demonstration.

Diversionary landing: An operation in which troops are actually landed for the purpose of diverting enemy reaction away from the main landing.

Division: 1. A tactical unit/formation as follows: a. A major administrative and tactical unit/formation which combines in itself the necessary arms and services required for sustained combat, larger than a regiment/brigade and smaller than a corps. b. A number of naval vessels of similar type grouped together for operational and administrative command, or a tactical unit of a naval aircraft squadron, consisting of two or more sections. c. An air division is an air combat organization normally consisting of two or more wings with appropriate service units. The combat wings of an air division will normally contain similar type units. 2. An organizational part of a headquarters that handles military matters of a particular nature, such as personnel, intelligence, plans, and training, or supply and evacuation. 3. A number of personnel of a ship's complement grouped together for tactical and administrative control.

Division artillery: Artillery that is permanently an integral part of a division. For tactical purposes, all artillery placed under the command of a division commander is considered division artillery.

Doctrinal template: A model based on known or postulated adversary doctrine.

Doctrinal templates illustrate the disposition and activity of adversary forces and assets conducting a particular operation unconstrained by the effects of the battle space. They represent the application of adversary doctrine under ideal conditions. Ideally, doctrinal templates depict the threat's normal organization for combat, frontages, depths, boundaries and other control measures, assets available from other commands, objective depths, engagement areas, battle positions, and so forth. Doctrinal templates are usually scaled to allow ready use with geospatial products. Doctrine.

Doctrine: Fundamental principles by which the military forces or elements thereof guide their actions in support of national objectives. It is authoritative but requires judgment in application. Multinational doctrine; joint doctrine; multi-Service doctrine.

Dolly: Airborne data link equipment.

Domestic air traffic: Air traffic within the continental United States.

Domestic emergencies: Emergencies affecting the public welfare and occurring within the 50 states, District of Columbia, Commonwealth of Puerto Rico, US possessions and territories, or any political subdivision thereof, as a result of enemy attack, insurrection, civil disturbance, earthquake, fire, flood, or other public disasters or equivalent emergencies that endanger life and property or disrupt the usual process of government. Domestic emergencies include civil defense emergencies, civil disturbances, major disasters, and natural disasters. Civil defense emergency; civil disturbance; major disaster; natural disaster.

Domestic intelligence: Intelligence relating to activities or conditions within the United States that threaten internal security and that might require the employment of troops; and intelligence relating to activities of individuals or agencies potentially or actually dangerous to the security of the Department of Defense.

Dominant user: The Service or multinational partner who is the principal consumer of a particular common-user logistic supply or service within a joint or multinational operation. The dominant user will normally act as the lead Service to provide this particular common-user logistic supply or service to other Service components, multinational partners, other governmental agencies, or non governmental agencies as directed by the combatant commander. Common-user logistics; lead Service or agency for common-user logistics.

Dominant user concept: The concept that the Service that is the principal consumer will have the responsibility for performance of a support workload for all using Services.

Doppler effect: The phenomenon evidenced by the change in the observed frequency of a sound or radio wave caused by a time rate of change in the effective length of the path of travel between the source and the point of observation.

Doppler radar: A radar system that differentiates between fixed and moving targets by detecting the apparent change in frequency of the reflected wave due to motion of target or the observer.

Dormant: In mine warfare, the state of a mine during which a time delay feature in a mine prevents it from being actuated.

Dose rate contour line: A line on a map, diagram, or overlay joining all points at which the radiation dose rate at a given time is the same.

Dosimetry: The measurement of radiation doses. It applies to both the devices used (dosimeters) and to the techniques.

Double agent: Agent in contact with two opposing intelligence services, only one of which is aware of the double contact or quasi-intelligence services.

Double flow route: A route of at least two lanes allowing two columns of vehicles to proceed simultaneously, either in the same direction or in opposite directions. Single flow route.

Downgrade: To determine that classified information requires, in the interests of national security, a lower degree of protection against unauthorized disclosure than currently provided, coupled with a changing of the classification designation to reflect such a lower degree.

Downloading: An operation that removes airborne weapons or stores from an aircraft.

Draft: 1. The conscription of qualified citizens in military service. 2. The depth of water that a vessel requires to float freely; the depth of a vessel from the water line to the keel. Active duty; Military Service; watercraft.

Draft plan: A plan for which a draft plan has been coordinated and agreed with the other military headquarters and is ready for coordination with the nations involved, that is those nations who would be required to take national actions to support the plan. It may be used for future planning and exercises and may form the basis for an operation order to be implemented in time of emergency. Coordinated draft plan; final plan; initial draft plan; operation plan.

Drag: Force of aerodynamic resistance caused by the violent currents behind the shock front.

Drag loading: The force on an object or structure due to transient winds accompanying the passage of a blast wave. The drag pressure is the product of the dynamic pressure and the drag coefficient which is dependent upon the shape (or geometry) of the structure or object.

Drift: In ballistics, a shift in projectile direction due to gyroscopic action which results from gravitational and atmospherically induced torques on the spinning projectile.

Drill mine: An inert filled mine or mine-like body, used in loading, laying, or discharge practice and trials.

Drone: A land, sea, or air vehicle that is remotely or automatically controlled. Remotely piloted vehicle; unmanned aerial vehicle.

Drop altitude: The altitude above mean sea level at which airdrop is executed. Altitude; drop height.

Drop height: The vertical distance between the drop zone and the aircraft. Altitude; drop altitude.

Drop master: 1. An individual qualified to prepare, perform acceptance inspection, load, lash, and eject material for airdrop. 2. An aircrew member who, during parachute operations, will relay any required information between pilot and jumpmaster.

Drop message: A message dropped from an aircraft to a ground or surface unit.

Drop zone: A specific area upon which airborne troops, equipment, or supplies are airdropped. DZ.

Drug interdiction: A continuum of events focused on interrupting illegal drugs smuggled by air, sea, or land. Normally consists of several phases - cueing, detection, sorting, monitoring, interception, handover, disruption, endgame, and apprehension - some which may occur simultaneously. Counterdrug operations.

Dry deck shelter: A shelter module that attaches to the hull of a specially configured submarine to provide the submarine with the capability to launch and recover special operations personnel, vehicles, and equipment while submerged. The dry deck shelter provides a working environment at one atmosphere for the special operations element during transit and has structural integrity to the collapse depth of the host submarine. DDS.

D-to-P assets required on D-day: As applied to the D-to-P concept, this asset

requirement represents those stocks that must be physically available on D-day to meet initial allowance requirements, to fill the wartime pipeline between the producers and users, and to provide any required D to P consumption or production differential stockage. The D-to-P assets required on D day are also represented as the difference between the D-to-P materiel readiness gross requirements and the cumulative sum of all production deliveries during the D-to-P period. See also D-to-P concept.

D-to-P materiel readiness gross requirement: As applied to the D-to-P concept, the gross requirement for all supplies and materiel needed to meet all initial pipeline and anticipated expenditure requirements between D-day and P-day. Includes initial allowances, continental United States and overseas operating and safety levels, intransit levels of supply, and the cumulative sum of all items expended during the D-to-P period. D-to-P concept.

Dual agent: One who is simultaneously and independently employed by two or more intelligence agencies, covering targets for both.

Dual-capable aircraft: Allied and US fighter aircraft tasked and configured to perform either conventional or theater nuclear missions. DCA.

Dual-capable forces: Forces capable of employing dual-capable weapons.

Dual capable unit: A nuclear certified delivery unit capable of executing both conventional and nuclear missions.

Dual-firing circuit: An assembly comprising two independent firing systems, both electric or both non-electric, so that the firing of either system will detonate all charges.

Dual (multi)-capable weapons: 1. Weapons, weapon systems, or vehicles capable of selective equipage with different types or mixes of armament or firepower. 2.Sometimes restricted to weapons capable of handling either nuclear or non-nuclear munitions.

Dual (multi)-purpose weapons: Weapons which possess the capability for effective application in two or more basically different military functions and/or levels of conflict.

Dual-role tanker: Dual-role tankers carry support personnel, supplies, and equipment for the deploying force while escorting and/or refueling combat aircraft to the area of responsibility. Dual-role tankers can minimize the total lift requirement while providing critical cargo and personnel at the combat aircraft's time of arrival. Air refueling.

Dud: Explosive munitions which has not been armed as intended or which has failed to explode after being armed. Absolute dud; dwarf dud; flare dud; nuclear dud.

Dud probability: The expected percentage of failures in a given number of firings.

Due in: Quantities of materiel scheduled to be received from vendors, repair facilities, assembly operation, inter depot transfers, and other sources.

Dummy message: A message sent for some purpose other than its content, which may consist of dummy groups or may have a meaningless text.

Dummy minefield: In naval mine warfare, a minefield containing no live mines and presenting only a psychological threat.

Dummy run: Any simulated firing practice, particularly a dive bombing approach made without release of a bomb. Dry run.

Dump: A temporary storage area, usually in the open, for bombs, ammunition, equipment, or supplies.

Duplicate negative: A negative reproduced from a negative or diapositive.

Duty status: whereabouts unknown: A transitory casualty status, applicable only to military personnel, that is used when the responsible commander suspects the member may be a casualty whose absence is involuntary, but does not feel sufficient evidence currently exists to make a definite determination of missing or deceased. DUSTWUN. Casualty status.

Dwarf dud: A nuclear weapon that, when launched at or emplaced on a target, fails to provide a yield within a reasonable range of that which could be anticipated with normal operation of the weapon. This constitutes a dud only in a relative sense.

Dwell time: The time cargo remains in a terminal's in-transit storage area while awaiting shipment by clearance transportation. (2) The length of time a target is expected to remain in one location. Storage.

Dynamic targeting: Targeting that prosecutes targets identified too late, or not selected for action in time to be included in deliberate targeting.

Dynamic threat assessment: An intelligence assessment developed by the Defense Intelligence Agency that details the threat, capabilities, and intentions of adversaries in each of the priority plans in the Contingency Planning Guidance. DTA.

E

Earliest anticipated launch time: The earliest time expected for a special operations tactical element and its supporting platform to depart the staging or marshalling area together en route to the operations area. EALT.

Earliest arrival date: A day, relative to C-day, that is specified by a planner as the earliest date when a unit, a resupply shipment, or replacement personnel can be accepted at a port of debarkation during a deployment. Used with the latest arrival data, it defines a delivery window for transportation planning. EAD. Latest arrival date.

Early Spring: An anti reconnaissance satellite weapon system.

Early time: Span of detonation (atomic demolition munitions employment).

Early warning: Early notification of the launch or approach of unknown weapons or weapons carriers. EW. Attack assessment; tactical warning.

Earmarking of stocks: The arrangement whereby nations agree, normally in peacetime, to identify a proportion of selected items of their war reserve stocks to be called for by specified NATO commanders.

Earthling: The process of making a satisfactory electrical connection between the structure, including the metal skin, of an object or vehicle, and the mass of the Earth, to ensure a common potential with the Earth. Bonding.

Echelon: 1. A subdivision of a headquarters, i.e., forward echelon, rear echelon. 2.Separate level of command. As compared to a regiment, a division is a higher echelon, a battalion is a lower echelon. 3. A fraction of a command in the direction of depth to which a principal combat mission is assigned; i.e., attack echelon, support echelon, reserve echelon. 4. A formation in which its subdivisions are placed one behind another, with a lateral and even spacing to the same side.

Echeloned displacement: Movement of a unit from one position to another without discontinuing performance of its primary function. Normally, the unit divides into two functional elements; and, while the base continues to operate, the advance element displaces to a new site where, after it becomes operational, it is joined by the base element.

Economic action: The planned use of economic measures designed to influence the policies or actions of another state, e.g., to impair the war-making potential of a hostile power or to generate economic stability within a friendly power.

Economic order quantity: That quantity derived from a mathematical technique used to determine the optimum total variable costs required to order and hold inventory.

Economic potential: The total capacity of a nation to produce goods and services.

Economic potential for war: That share of the total economic capacity of a nation that can be used for the purposes of war.

Economic retention stock: That portion of the quantity of an item excess of the approved force retention level that has been determined will be more economical to retain for future peacetime issue in lieu of replacement of future issues by procurement. To warrant economic retention, items must have a reasonably predictable demand rate.

Economic warfare: Aggressive use of economic means to achieve national objectives.

Effect: 1. The physical or behavioral state of a system that results from an action, a set of actions, or another effect. 2. The result, outcome, or consequence of an action. 3. A change to a condition, behavior, or degree of freedom.

Effective damage: That damage necessary to render a target element inoperative, unserviceable, nonproductive, or uninhabitable.

Effective US controlled ships: US-owned foreign flagships that can be tasked by the Maritime Administration to support Department of Defense requirements when necessary. EUSCS.

Ejection: 1. Escape from an aircraft by means of an independently propelled seat or capsule. 2. In air armament, the process of forcefully separating an aircraft store from an aircraft to achieve satisfactory separation.

Ejection systems: a. command ejection system — A system in which the pilot of an aircraft or the occupant of the other ejection seat(s) initiates ejection resulting in the automatic ejection of all occupants. b. command select ejection system – A system permitting the optional transfer from one crew station to another of the control of a command ejection system for automatic ejection of all occupants. c. independent

Ejection system: An ejection system which operates independently of other ejection systems installed in one aircraft. d. sequenced ejection system – A system which ejects the aircraft crew in sequence to ensure a safe minimum total time of escape without collision.

Electrode sweep: In naval mine warfare, a magnetic cable sweep in which the water forms part of the electric circuit.

Electro-explosive device: An explosive or pyrotechnic component that initiates an explosive, burning, electrical, or mechanical train and is activated by the application of electrical energy. EED.

Electromagnetic compatibility: The ability of systems, equipment, and devices that utilize the electromagnetic spectrum to operate in their intended operational environments without suffering unacceptable degradation or causing unintentional degradation because of electromagnetic radiation or response. It involves the application of sound electromagnetic spectrum management; system, equipment, and device design configuration that ensures interference-free operation; and clear concepts and doctrines that maximize operational effectiveness. Also called EMC. See also electromagnetic spectrum; electromagnetic spectrum management; electronic warfare.

Electromagnetic deception: The deliberate radiation, re-radiation, alteration, suppression, absorption, denial, enhancement, or reflection of electromagnetic energy in a manner intended to convey misleading information to an enemy or to enemy electromagnetic dependent weapons, thereby degrading or neutralizing the enemy's combat capability. Electronic warfare.

Electromagnetic environment: The resulting product of the power and time distribution, in various frequency ranges, of the radiated or conducted electromagnetic emission levels that may be encountered by a military force, system, or platform when performing its assigned mission in its intended operational environment. It is the sum of electromagnetic interference;

electromagnetic pulse; hazards of electromagnetic radiation to personnel, ordnance, and volatile materials; and natural phenomena effects of lightning and precipitation static. EME.

Electromagnetic environmental effects: The impact of the electromagnetic environment upon the operational capability of military forces, equipment, systems, and platforms. It encompasses all electromagnetic disciplines, including electromagnetic compatibility and electromagnetic interference; electromagnetic vulnerability; electromagnetic pulse; electronic protection, hazards of electromagnetic radiation to personnel, ordnance, and volatile materials; and natural phenomena effects of lightning and precipitation static. E3.

Electromagnetic hardening: Action taken to protect personnel, facilities, and/or equipment by filtering, attenuating, grounding, bonding, and/or shielding against undesirable effects of electromagnetic energy. Electronic warfare.

Electromagnetic interference: Any electromagnetic disturbance that interrupts, obstructs, or otherwise degrades or limits the effective performance of electronics and electrical equipment. It can be induced intentionally, as in some forms of electronic warfare, or unintentionally, as a result of spurious emissions and responses, inter modulation products, and the like. EMI.

Electromagnetic intrusion: The intentional insertion of electromagnetic energy into transmission paths in any manner, with the objective of deceiving operators or of causing confusion. Electronic warfare.

Electromagnetic jamming: The deliberate radiation, re radiation, or reflection of electromagnetic energy for the purpose of preventing or reducing an enemy's effective use of the electromagnetic spectrum, and with the intent of degrading or neutralizing the enemy's combat capability. Electromagnetic spectrum; electromagnetic spectrum management; electronic warfare.

Electromagnetic pulse: The electromagnetic radiation from a strong electronic pulse, most commonly caused by a nuclear explosion that may couple with electrical or electronic systems to produce damaging current and voltage surges. Also called EMP. Electromagnetic radiation.

Electromagnetic radiation: Radiation made up of oscillating electric and magnetic fields and propagated with the speed of light. Includes gamma radiation, X-rays, ultraviolet, visible, and infrared radiation, and radar and radio waves.

Electromagnetic spectrum: The range of frequencies of electromagnetic radiation from zero to infinity. It is divided into 26 alphabetically designated bands. See also electronic warfare.

Electromagnetic spectrum management: Planning, coordinating, and managing joint use of the electromagnetic spectrum through operational, engineering, and administrative procedures. The objective of spectrum management is to enable electronic systems to perform their functions in the intended environment without causing or suffering unacceptable interference. Electromagnetic spectrum.

Electromagnetic vulnerability: The characteristics of a system that cause it to suffer a definite degradation (incapability to perform the designated mission) as a result of having been subjected to a certain level of electromagnetic environmental effects. EMV.

Electronic attack: Division of electronic warfare involving the use of electromagnetic energy, directed energy, or anti radiation weapons to attack personnel, facilities, or equipment with the intent of degrading, neutralizing, or destroying enemy combat capability and is considered a form of fires. Also called EA. See also electronic protection; electronic warfare; electronic warfare support.

Electronic imagery dissemination: The transmission of imagery or imagery products by any electronic means. This includes the following four categories. a. primary imagery dissemination system – The equipment and procedures used in the electronic transmission and receipt of un-exploited original or near-original quality Imagery in near real time. b. primary imagery dissemination: The electronic transmission and receipt of unexploited original or near-original quality imagery in near real time through a primary imagery dissemination system. c. secondary imagery

Electronic intelligence: Technical and geolocation intelligence derived from foreign non communications electromagnetic radiations emanating from other than nuclear detonations or radioactive sources. ELINT. Electronic warfare; foreign instrumentation signals intelligence; intelligence; signals intelligence.

Electronic line of sight: The path traversed by electromagnetic waves that is not subject to reflection or refraction by the atmosphere.

Electronic masking: The controlled radiation of electromagnetic energy on friendly frequencies in a manner to protect the emissions of friendly communications and electronic systems against enemy electronic warfare support measures/signals intelligence without significantly degrading the operation of friendly systems.

Electronic probing: Intentional radiation designed to be introduced into the devices or systems of potential enemies for the purpose of learning the functions and operational capabilities of the devices or systems.

Electronic protection: Division of electronic warfare involving actions taken to protect personnel, facilities, and equipment from any effects of friendly or enemy use of the electromagnetic spectrum that degrade, neutralize, or destroy friendly combat capability. EP. Electronic attack, electronic warfare; electronic warfare support.

Electronic reconnaissance: The detection, location, identification, and evaluation of foreign electromagnetic radiations. Electromagnetic radiation; reconnaissance.

Electronics security: The protection resulting from all measures designed to deny unauthorized persons information of value that might be derived from their interception and study of non communications electromagnetic radiations, e.g., radar.

Electronic warfare: Military action involving the use of electromagnetic and directed energy to control the electromagnetic spectrum or to attack the enemy. Electronic warfare consists of three divisions: electronic attack, electronic protection, and electronic warfare support. EW. Directed energy; electromagnetic spectrum; electronic attack; electronic protection; electronic warfare support.

Electronic warfare frequency deconfliction: Actions taken to integrate those frequencies used by electronic warfare systems into the overall frequency deconfliction process. Electronic warfare.

Electronic warfare reprogramming: The deliberate alteration or modification of electronic warfare or target sensing systems, or the tactics and procedures that employ them, in response to validated changes in equipment, tactics, or the electromagnetic environment. These changes may be the result of deliberate actions on the part of friendly, adversary or third parties; or may be brought about by electromagnetic interference or other inadvertent phenomena. The purpose of electronic warfare reprogramming is to maintain or enhance the effectiveness of electronic warfare and target sensing system equipment. Electronic warfare reprogramming includes changes to self defense systems, offensive weapons systems, and intelligence collection systems. Electronic warfare.

Electronic warfare support: Division of electronic warfare involving actions tasked by, or under direct control of, an operational commander to search for, intercept, identify, and locate or localize sources of intentional and unintentional radiated electromagnetic energy for the purpose of immediate threat recognition, targeting, planning and conduct of future operations. ES. Electronic attack; electronic protection; electronic warfare.

Electro-optical intelligence: Intelligence other than signals intelligence derived from the optical monitoring of the electromagnetic spectrum from ultraviolet (0.01 micrometers) through far infrared (1,000 micrometers).

ELECTRO-OPTINT: Intelligence; laser intelligence.

Electro-optics: The technology associated with those components, devices and systems which are designed to interact between the electromagnetic (optical) and the electric (electronic) state.

Element: An organization formed around a specific function within a designated directorate of a joint force commander's headquarters. The subordinate components of an element usually are functional cells.

Element set: Three lines of data which define the location of a satellite in space. ELSET.

Elevated causeway system: An elevated causeway pier that provides a means of delivering containers, certain vehicles, and bulk cargo ashore without the lighter age contending with the surf zone. Causeway.

Elevation: The vertical distance of a point or level on or affixed to the surface of the Earth measured from mean sea level. Altitude.

Elicitation (intelligence): Acquisition of information from a person or group in a manner that does not disclose the intent of the interview or conversation. A technique of human source intelligence collection, generally overt, unless the collector is other than he or she purports to be.

Eligible traffic: Traffic for which movement requirements are submitted and space is assigned or allocated. Such traffic must meet eligibility requirements specified in Joint Travel Regulations for the Uniformed Services and publications of the Department of Defense and Military Departments governing eligibility for land, sea, and air transportation, and be in accordance with the guidance of the Joint Chiefs of Staff.

Embarkation: The process of putting personnel and/or vehicles and their associated stores and equipment into ships and/or aircraft. Loading embarkation and tonnage table — A consolidated table showing personnel and cargo, by troop or naval units, loaded aboard a combat-loaded ship.

Embarkation area: An area ashore, including a group of embarkation points, in which final preparations for embarkation are completed and through which assigned personnel and loads for craft and ships are called forward to embark. Mounting area.

Embarkation element (unit) (group): A temporary administrative formation of personnel with supplies and equipment embarking or to be embarked (combat loaded) aboard the ships of one transport element (unit) (group). It is dissolved upon completion of the embarkation. An embarkation element normally consists of two or more embarkation teams: a unit, of two or more elements; and a group, of two or more units. Embarkation organization; embarkation team.

Embarkation officer: An officer on the staff of units of the landing force who advises the commander thereof on matters pertaining to embarkation planning and loading ships. Combat cargo officer.

Embarkation order: An order specifying dates, times, routes, loading diagrams, and methods of movement to shipside or aircraft for troops and their equipment. Movement table.

Embarkation organization: A temporary administrative formation of personnel with supplies and equipment embarking or to be embarked aboard amphibious shipping. Embarkation element; embarkation team.

Embarkation phase: In amphibious operations, the phase that encompasses the orderly assembly of personnel and materiel and their subsequent loading aboard ships and/or aircraft in a sequence designed to meet the requirements of the landing force concept of operations ashore.

Embarkation plans: The plans prepared by the landing force and appropriate subordinate commanders containing instructions and information concerning the organization for embarkation, assignment to shipping, supplies and equipment to be embarked, location and assignment of embarkation areas, control and communication arrangements, movement schedules and embarkation sequence, and additional pertinent instructions relating to the embarkation of the landing force.

Embarkation team: A temporary administrative formation of all personnel with supplies and equipment embarking or to be embarked aboard one ship. Embarkation element; embarkation organization.

Emergency action committee: An organization established at a foreign service post by the chief of mission or principal officer for the purpose of directing and coordinating the post's response to contingencies. It consists of consular representatives and members of other local US Government agencies in a foreign country who assist in the implementation of a Department of State emergency action plan. EAC.

Emergency anchorage: An anchorage, which may have a limited defense organization, for naval vessels, mobile support units, auxiliaries, or merchant ships. Assembly anchorage; holding anchorage; working anchorage.

Emergency-essential employee: A Department of Defense civilian employee whose assigned duties and responsibilities must be accomplished following the evacuation of non-essential personnel during a declared emergency or outbreak of war. The position occupied cannot be converted to a military billet because it requires uninterrupted performance so as to provide immediate and continuing support for combat operations and/or combat systems support functions. Evacuation.

Emergency interment: An interment, usually on the battlefield, when conditions do not permit either evacuation for interment in an interment site or interment according to national or international legal regulations. See also mortuary affairs; temporary interment; trench interment.

Emergency locator beacon: A generic term for all radio beacons used for emergency locating purposes. Crash locator beacon; personal locator beacon.

Emergency operations center: The physical location at which the coordination of information and resources to support domestic incident management activities normally takes place. An emergency operations center may be a temporary facility or may be located in a more central or permanently established facility, perhaps at a higher level of organization within a jurisdiction. Emergency operations centers may be organized by major functional disciplines, by jurisdiction, or by some combination thereof. EOC.

Emergency preparedness: Measures taken in advance of an emergency to reduce the loss of life and property and to protect a nation's institutions from all types of hazards through a comprehensive emergency management program of preparedness, mitigation, response, and recovery. EP.

Emergency preparedness liaison officer: A senior reserve officer who represents their Service at the appropriate joint field office conducting planning and coordination responsibilities in support of civil authorities. EPLO.

Emergency priority: A category of immediate mission request that takes precedence over all other priorities, e.g., an enemy breakthrough. Immediate mission request; priority of immediate mission requests.

Emergency relocation site: A site located where practicable outside a prime target area to which all or portions of a civilian or military headquarters may be moved. As a minimum, it is manned to provide for the maintenance of the facility, communications, and database. It should be capable of rapid activation, of supporting the initial requirements of the relocated headquarters for a predetermined period, and of expansion to meet wartime requirements of the relocated headquarters.

Emergency repair: The least amount of immediate repair to damaged facilities necessary for the facilities to support the mission. These repairs will be made using expedient materials and methods (such as AM-2 aluminum matting, cold-mix asphalt, plywood scabs, temporary utility lines, and emergency generators). Modular or kit-type facility substitutes would be appropriate if repairs cannot be made in time to meet mission requirements. Facility substitutes.

Emergency resupply: A resupply mission that occurs based on a predetermined set of circumstances and time interval should radio contact not be established or, once established, is lost between a special operations tactical element and its base. Automatic resupply; on-call resupply.

Emergency risk (nuclear): A degree of risk where anticipated effects may cause some temporary shock, casualties and may significantly reduce the unit's combat efficiency. Degree of risk; negligible risk (nuclear).

Emergency substitute: A product which may be used, in an emergency only, in place of another product, but only on the advice of technically qualified personnel of the nation using the product, who will specify the limitations.

Emergency support functions: A grouping of government and certain private-sector capabilities into an organizational structure to provide the support, resources, program implementation, and services that are most likely to be needed to save lives, protect property and the environment, restore essential services and critical infrastructure, and help victims and communities return to normal, when feasible, following domestic incidents. ESFs.

Emission control: The selective and controlled use of electromagnetic, acoustic, or other emitters to optimize command and control capabilities while minimizing, for operations security: a. detection by enemy sensors; b. mutual interference among friendly systems; and/or c. enemy interference with the ability to execute a military deception plan. EMCON. Electronic warfare.

Emission control orders: Orders used to authorize, control, or prohibit the use of electronic emission equipment. EMCON orders. Control of electromagnetic radiation.

Emission security: The component of communications security that results from all measures taken to deny unauthorized persons information of value that might be derived from intercept and analysis of compromising emanations from crypto equipment and telecommunications systems. Communications security.

Emplacement: 1. A prepared position for one or more weapons or pieces of equipment, for protection against hostile fire or bombardment, and from which they can execute their tasks. 2. The act of fixing a gun in a prepared position from which it may be fired.

Employment: The strategic, operational, or tactical use of forces.

Enabling force: Early deploying forces that establish critical capabilities to facilitate deployment and initial employment (including sustainment) of a force. Deployment; employment; force.

Enabling mine countermeasures: Countermeasures designed to counter mines once they have been laid. This includes both passive and active mine counter measures. Mine countermeasures.

Encipher: To convert plain text into unintelligible form by means of a cipher system.

End evening civil twilight: The time period when the sun has dropped 6 degrees beneath the western horizon; it is the instant at which there is no longer sufficient light to see objects with the unaided eye. Light intensification devices are recommended from this time until begin morning civil twilight. EECT.

End item — A final combination of end products, component parts, and/or materials that is ready for its intended use, e.g., ship, tank, mobile machine shop, or aircraft.

End of evening nautical twilight: Occurs when the sun has dropped 12 degrees below the western horizon, and is the instant of last available daylight for the visual control of limited ground operations. At end of evening nautical twilight there is no further sunlight available. Horizon.

End of mission: In artillery, mortar, and naval gunfire support, an order given to terminate firing on a specific target. Cease loading; call for fire; fire mission.

End state: The set of required conditions that defines achievement of the commander's objectives.

Endurance: The time an aircraft can continue flying, or a ground vehicle or ship can continue operating, under specified conditions, e.g., without refueling. Endurance distance.

Endurance distance: Total distance that a ground vehicle or ship can be self propelled at any specified endurance speed.

Endurance loading: The stocking aboard ship for a period of time, normally covering the number of months between overhauls, of items with all of the following characteristics: a. low price; b. low weight and cube; c. a predictable usage rate; and d. non deteriorative. Loading.

Enemy capabilities: Those courses of action of which the enemy is physically capable and that, if adopted, will affect accomplishment of the friendly mission. The term "capabilities" includes not only the general courses of action open to the enemy, such as attack, defense, reinforcement, or withdrawal, but also all the particular courses of action possible under each general course of action. "Enemy capabilities" are considered in the light of all known factors affecting military operations, including time, space, weather, terrain, and the strength and disposition of enemy forces. In strategic thinking, the capabilities of a nation represent the courses of action within the power of the nation for accomplishing its national objectives throughout the range of military operations. Capability; course of action; mission.

Enemy combatant: In general, a person engaged in hostilities against the United States or its coalition partners during an armed conflict. EC.

Engage: 1. In air defense, a fire control order used to direct or authorize units and/or weapon systems to fire on a designated target. Cease engagement; hold fire. 2. To bring the enemy under fire.

Engagement: 1. In air defense, an attack with guns or air-to-air missiles by an interceptor aircraft, or the launch of an air defense missile by air defense artillery and the missile's subsequent travel to intercept. 2. A tactical conflict, usually between opposing lower echelons maneuver forces. Battle; campaign.

Engineer support plan: An appendix to the logistics annex or separate annex of an operation plan that identifies the minimum essential engineering services and construction requirements required to support the commitment of military forces. ESP. Operation plan.

Enlisted terminal attack controller: Tactical air party member who assists in mission planning and provides final control of close air support aircraft in support of ground forces. ETAC. Close air support; mission; terminal.

En route care: Continuation of the provision of care during movement (evacuation) between the health service support capabilities in the continuum of care, without clinically compromising the patient's condition. Evacuation; patient.

Envelopment: An offensive maneuver in which the main attacking force passes around or over the enemy's principal defensive positions to secure objectives to the enemy's rear. Turning movement.

Environmental cleanup: The process of removing solid, liquid, and hazardous wastes, except for unexploded ordnance, resulting from the joint operation of US forces to a condition that approaches the one existing prior to operation as determined by the environmental baseline survey, if one was conducted. The extent of this process will depend upon the operational situation at the time that cleanup is accomplished.

Environmental considerations: The spectrum of environmental media, resources, or programs that may impact on, or are affected by, the planning and execution of military operations. Factors may include, but are not limited to, environmental compliance, pollution prevention, conservation, protection of historical and cultural sites, and protection of flora and fauna.

Environmental stewardship: The integration and application of environmental values into the military mission in order to sustain readiness, improve quality of life, strengthen civil relations, and preserve valuable natural resources.

Equipment: In logistics, all nonexpendable items needed to outfit or equip an individual or organization. Assembly; component; subassembly; supplies. equipment operationally ready – The status of an item of equipment in the possession of an operating unit that indicates it is capable of fulfilling its intended mission and in a system configuration that offers a high assurance of an effective, reliable, and safe performance.

Escalation: A deliberate or unpremeditated increase in scope or violence of a conflict.

Escapee: Any person who has been physically captured by the enemy and succeeds in getting free. Evasion and escape.

Escape line: A planned route to allow personnel engaged in clandestine activity to depart from a site or area when possibility of compromise or apprehension exists.

Escort: 1. A combatant unit(s) assigned to accompany and protect another force or convoy. 2. Aircraft assigned to protect other aircraft during a mission. 3. An armed guard that accompanies a convoy, a train, prisoners, etc. 4. An armed guard accompanying persons as a mark of honor. 5. To convoy. 6. A member of the Armed Forces assigned to accompany, assist, or guide an individual or group, e.g., an escort officer.

Escort forces: Combat forces of various types provided to protect other forces against enemy attack.

Espionage: The act of obtaining, delivering, transmitting, communicating, or receiving information about the national defense with an intent, or reason to believe, that the information may be used to the injury of the United States or to the advantage of any foreign nation. Espionage is a violation of 18 United States Code 792-798 and Article 106, Uniform Code of Military Justice. Counter intelligence.

Espionage against the United States: Overt, covert, or clandestine activity designed to obtain information relating to the national defense with intent or reason to believe that it will be used to the injury of the United States or to the advantage of a foreign nation. For espionage crimes see Chapter 37 of Title 18, United States Code.

Essential care: Medical treatment provided to manage the casualty throughout the range of care. This includes all care and treatment to either return the patient to duty (within the theater evacuation policy), or begin initial treatment required for optimization of outcome, and/or stabilization to ensure the patient can tolerate evacuation. En route care; first responders; forward resuscitative care; patient; theater.

Essential chemicals: In counterdrug operations, compounds that are required in the synthetic or extraction processes of drug production, but in most cases do not become part of the drug molecule. Essential chemicals are used in the production of cocaine or heroin.

Essential communications traffic: Transmissions (record or voice) of any precedence that must be sent electrically in order for the command or activity concerned to avoid a serious impact on mission accomplishment or safety or life.

Essential elements of friendly information: Key questions likely to be asked by adversary officials and intelligence systems about specific friendly intentions, capabilities, and activities, so they can obtain answers critical to their operational effectiveness. EEFI.

Essential elements of information: The most critical information requirements regarding the adversary and the environment needed by the commander by a particular time to relate with other available information and intelligence in order to assist in reaching a logical decision. EEIs.

Essential industry: Any industry necessary to the needs of a civilian or war economy. The term includes the basic industries as well as the necessary portions of those other industries that transform the crude basic raw materials into useful intermediate or end products, e.g., the iron and steel industry, the food industry, and the chemical industry.

Essential secrecy: The condition achieved from the denial of critical information to adversaries.

Essential task: In the context of joint operation planning, a specified or implied task that an organization must perform to accomplish the mission. An essential task is typically included in the mission statement. Implied task; specified task.

Establishment: An installation, together with its personnel and equipment, organized as an operating entity. Activity; base; equipment.

Estimate: 1. An analysis of a foreign situation, development, or trend that identifies its major elements, interprets the significance, and appraises the future possibilities and the prospective results of the various actions that might be taken. 2. An appraisal of the capabilities, vulnerabilities, and potential courses of action of a foreign nation or combination of nations in consequence of a specific national plan, policy, decision, or contemplated course of action. 3. An analysis of an actual or contemplated clandestine operation in relation to the situation in which it is or would be conducted in order to identify and appraise such factors as available as well as needed assets and potential obstacles, accomplishments, and consequences. Intelligence estimate.

Estimative intelligence: Intelligence that identifies, describes, and forecasts adversary capabilities and the implications for planning and executing military operations.

Evacuation control ship: In an amphibious operation, a ship designated as a control point for landing craft, amphibious vehicles, and helicopters evacuating casualties from the beaches. Medical personnel embarked in the evacuation control ship effect distribution of casualties throughout the attack force in accordance with ship's casualty capacities and specialized medical facilities available, and also perform emergency surgery.

Evacuation convoy: A convoy which is used for evacuation of dangerously exposed waters. Evacuation of dangerously exposed waters.

Evacuation of dangerously exposed waters: The movement of merchant ships under naval control from severely threatened coastlines and dangerously exposed waters to safer localities. Dangerously exposed waters.

Evacuation of port equipment: The transfer of mobile/movable equipment from a threatened port to another port or to a working anchorage.

Evacuee: A civilian removed from a place of residence by military direction for reasons of personal security or the requirements of the military situation. Displaced person; expellee; refugee.

Evader: Any person isolated in hostile or unfriendly territory who eludes capture.

Evaluation: In intelligence usage, appraisal of an item of information in terms of credibility, reliability, pertinence, and accuracy.

Evaluation and feedback: In intelligence usage, continuous assessment of intelligence operations throughout the intelligence process to ensure that the commander's intelligence requirements are being met. Intelligence process.

Evasion: The process whereby isolated personnel avoid capture with the goal of successfully returning to areas under friendly control.

Evasion aid: In personnel recovery, any piece of information or equipment designed to assist an individual in avoiding capture. Evasion aids include, but are not limited to, blood chits, pointee-talkees, evasion charts, barter items, and equipment designed to complement issued survival equipment. Blood chit; evasion; evasion chart; pointee-talkee; recovery; recovery operations.

Evasion and escape: The procedures and operations whereby military personnel and other selected individuals are enabled to emerge from an enemy-held or hostile area to areas under friendly control. E&E.

Evasion chart: A special map or chart designed as an evasion aid. EVC. Evasion; evasion aid. As Amended Through 17 March 2009

Evasion plan of action: A course of action, developed prior to executing a combat mission, that is intended to improve a potential isolated person's chances of successful evasion and recovery by providing the recovery forces with an additional source of information that can increase the predictability of the evader's action and movement. EPA. Course of action; evader; evasion; recovery force.

Event matrix: A description of the indicators and activity expected to occur in each named area of interest. It normally cross-references each named area of interest and indicator with the times they are expected to occur and the courses of action they will confirm or deny. There is no prescribed format. Activity; area of interest; indicator.

Event template: A guide for collection planning. The event template depicts the named areas of interest where activity, or its lack of activity, will indicate which course of action the adversary has adopted. Activity; area of interest; collection planning; course of action.

Exceptional transport: In railway terminology, transport of a load whose size,

weight, or preparation entails special difficulties vis-a-vis the facilities or equipment of even one of the railway systems to be used. Ordinary transport.

Excess property: The quantity of property in possession of any component of the Department of Defense that exceeds the quantity required or authorized for retention by that component.

Exclusion zone: A zone established by a sanctioning body to prohibit specific activities in a specific geographic area. The purpose may be to persuade nations or groups to modify their behavior to meet the desires of the sanctioning body or face continued imposition of sanctions, or use or threat of force.

Execute order: 1. An order issued by the Chairman of the Joint Chiefs of Staff, at the direction of the Secretary of Defense, to implement a decision by the President to initiate military operations. 2. An order to initiate military operations as directed. EXORD.

Executing commander (nuclear weapons): A commander to whom nuclear weapons are released for delivery against specific targets or in accordance with approved plans. Commander(s); releasing commander (nuclear weapons).

Execution planning: The Joint Operation Planning and Execution System translation of an approved course of action into an executable plan of action through the preparation of a complete operation plan or operation order. Execution planning is detailed planning for the commitment of specified forces and resources. During crisis action planning, an approved operation plan or other approved course of action is adjusted, refined, and translated into an operation order. Execution planning can proceed on the basis of prior contingency planning, or it can take place in the absence of prior planning. EP. Joint Operation Planning and Execution System.

Executive agent: A term used to indicate a delegation of authority by the Secretary of Defense to a subordinate to act on behalf of the Secretary of Defense. Designation as executive agent, in and of itself, confers no authority. The exact nature and scope of the authority delegated must be stated in the document designating the executive agent. An executive agent may be limited to providing only administration and support or coordinating common functions, or it may be delegated authority, direction, and control over specified resources for specified purposes. EA.

Exercise: A military maneuver or simulated wartime operation involving planning, preparation, and execution. It is carried out for the purpose of training and evaluation. It may be a multinational, joint, or single-Service exercise, depending on participating organizations. Command post exercise; field exercise; maneuver.

Exercise directing staff: A group of officers who by virtue of experience, qualifications, and a thorough knowledge of the exercise instructions, are selected to direct or control an exercise.

Exercise filled mine: In naval mine warfare, a mine containing an inert filling and an indicating device. Explosive filled mine; fitted mine; mine.

Exercise incident: An occurrence injected by directing staffs into the exercise which will have an effect on the forces being exercised, or their facilities, and which will require action by the appropriate commander and/or staff being exercised.

Exercise mine: In naval mine warfare, a mine suitable for use in mine warfare exercises, fitted with visible or audible indicating devices to show where and when it would normally fire. Drill mine; mine; practice mine.

Exercise specifications: The fundamental requirements for an exercise, providing in advance an outline of the concept, form, scope, setting, aim, objectives, force requirements, political implications, analysis arrangements, and costs.

Exercise sponsor: The commander who conceives a particular exercise and orders that it be planned and executed either by the commander's staff or by a subordinate headquarters.

Exercise study: An activity which may take the form of a map exercise, a war game, a series of lectures, a discussion group, or an operational analysis.

Exercise term: A combination of two words, normally unclassified, used exclusively to designate a test, drill, or exercise. An exercise term is employed to preclude the possibility of confusing exercise directives with actual operations directives.

Exfiltration: The removal of personnel or units from areas under enemy control by stealth, deception, surprise, or clandestine means. Special operations; unconventional warfare.

Existence load: Consists of items other than those in the fighting load that are required to sustain or protect the combat soldier. These items may be necessary for increased personal and environmental protection and are not normally carried by the individual. Fighting load.

Exoatmosphere: nuclear exoatmospheric burst.

Expedition: A military operation conducted by an armed force to accomplish a specific objective in a foreign country.

Expeditionary force: An armed force organized to accomplish a specific objective in a foreign country.

Expellee: A civilian outside the boundaries of the country of his or her nationality or ethnic origin who is being forcibly repatriated to that country or to a third country for political or other purposes. Displaced person; evacuee; refugee.

Expendable property: Property that may be consumed in use or loses its identity in use and may be dropped from stock record accounts when it is issued or used.

Expendable supplies and materiel: Supplies that are consumed in use, such as ammunition, paint, fuel, cleaning and preserving materials, surgical dressings, drugs, medicines, etc., or that lose their identity, such as spare parts, etc. Consumable supplies and materiel.

Exploder: A device designed to generate an electric current in a firing circuit after deliberate action by the user in order to initiate an explosive charge or charges.

Exploitation: 1. Taking full advantage of success in military operations, following up initial gains, and making permanent the temporary effects already achieved. 2. Taking full advantage of any information that has come to hand for tactical, operational, or strategic purposes. 3. An offensive operation that usually follows a successful attack and is designed to disorganize the enemy in depth. Attack; pursuit.

Exploratory hunting: In naval mine warfare, a parallel operation to search sweeping, in which a sample of the route or area is subjected to mine hunting procedures to determine the presence or absence of mines.

Explosive filled mine: In mine warfare, a mine containing an explosive charge but not necessarily the firing train needed to detonate it. Exercise filled mine; fitted mine.

Explosive hazard: Any hazard containing an explosive component. Explosive hazards include unexploded explosive ordnance (including land mines), booby traps, improvised explosive devices, captured enemy ammunition, and bulk explosives. EH.

Explosive ordnance: All munitions containing explosives, nuclear fission or fusion materials, and biological and chemical agents. This includes bombs and warheads; guided and ballistic missiles; artillery, mortar, rocket, and small arms ammunition; all mines, torpedoes, and depth charges; demolition charges; pyrotechnics; clusters and dispensers; cartridge and propellant actuated devices; electro-explosive devices; clandestine and improvised explosive devices; and all similar or related items or components explosive in nature.

Explosive ordnance disposal: The detection, identification, onsite evaluation, rendering safe, recovery, and final disposal of unexploded explosive ordnance. It may also include explosive ordnance which has become hazardous by damage or deterioration. EOD.

Explosive ordnance disposal incident: The suspected or detected presence of unexploded or damaged explosive ordnance which constitutes a hazard to operations, installations, personnel, or material. Not included in this definition are the accidental arming or other conditions that develop during the manufacture of high explosive material, technical service assembly operations or the laying of mines and demolition charges.

Explosive ordnance disposal unit: Personnel with special training and equipment who render explosive ordnance safe (such as bombs, mines, projectiles, and booby traps), make intelligence reports on such ordnance, and supervise the safe removal thereof.

Explosive train: A succession of initiating and igniting elements arranged to cause a charge to function.

Exposure dose: The exposure dose at a given point is a measurement of radiation in relation to its ability to produce ionization. The unit of measurement of the exposure dose is the roentgen.

Extended communications search: In search and rescue operations, consists of contacting all possible sources of information on the missing craft, including physically checking possible locations such as harbors, marinas, and airport ramps. An extended communications search is normally conducted after a preliminary communications search has yielded no results and when the mission is upgraded to the alert phase. EXCOM. Preliminary communications search; search and rescue incident classification, Subpart b.

Extent of a military exercise: The scope of an exercise in relation to the involvement of NATO and/or national commands. Intra-command exercise.

Extent of damage: The visible plan area of damage to a target element, usually expressed in units of 1,000 square feet, in detailed damage analysis and in approximate percentages in immediate-type damage assessment reports; e.g., 50 percent structural damage.

External audience: All people who are not part of the internal audience of US military members and civilian employees and their immediate families. Part of the concept of "publics." Includes many varied subsets that may be referred to as "audiences" or "publics." Internal audience; public.

External reinforcing force: A reinforcing force which is principally stationed in peacetime outside its intended Major NATO Command area of operations.

External support contract: Contract awarded by contracting organizations whose contracting authority does not derive directly from the theater support contracting head(s) of contracting activity or from systems support contracting authorities. Systems support contract; theater support contract.

Extraction parachute: An auxiliary parachute designed to release and extract and deploy cargo from aircraft in flight and deploy cargo parachutes. Gravity extraction.

Extraction zone: A specified drop zone used for the delivery of supplies and/or equipment by means of an extraction technique from an aircraft flying very close to the ground.

F

Fabricator: An individual or group who, usually without genuine resources, invents or inflates information for personal or political gain or political purposes.

Facility: A real property entity consisting of one or more of the following: a building, a structure, a utility system, pavement, and underlying land. Air facility.

Facility substitutes: Items such as tents and prepackaged structures requisitioned through the supply system that may be used to substitute for constructed facilities.

Fairway: A channel either from offshore, in a river, or in a harbor that has enough depth to accommodate the draft of large vessels. Draft; watercraft.

Fallout contours: Lines joining points which have the same radiation intensity that define a fallout pattern, represented in terms of roentgens per hour.

Fallout pattern: The distribution of fallout as portrayed by fallout contours.

Fallout prediction: An estimate, made before and immediately after a nuclear detonation, of the location and intensity of militarily significant quantities of radioactive fallout.

Fallout safe height of burst: The height of burst at or above which no militarily significant fallout will be reproduced as a result of a nuclear weapon detonation. Types of burst.

Fallout wind vector plot: A wind vector diagram based on the wind structure from the surface of the Earth to the highest altitude of interest.

False origin: A fixed point to the south and west of a grid zone from which grid distances are measured eastward and northward.

Fan camera photography: Photography taken simultaneously by an assembly of three or more cameras systematically installed at fixed angles relative to each other so as to provide wide lateral coverage with overlapping images. Tri-camera photography.

Fan cameras: An assembly of three or more cameras systematically disposed at fixed angles relative to each other so as to provide wide lateral coverage with overlapping images. Split cameras.

Fan marker beacon: A type of radio beacon, the emissions of which radiate in a vertical, fan-shaped pattern. The signal can be keyed for identification purposes. Radio beacon.

Farm gate type operations: Operational assistance and specialized tactical training provided to a friendly foreign air force by the Armed Forces of the United States to include, under certain specified conditions, the flying of operational missions in combat by combined United States and foreign aircrews as a part of the training being given when such missions are beyond the capability of the foreign air force.

Feasibility: The joint operation plan review criterion for assessing whether the assigned mission can be accomplished using available resources within the time contemplated by the plan. Acceptability; adequacy.

Feasibility assessment: A basic target analysis that provides an initial determination of the viability of a proposed target for special operations forces employment. FA.

Feasibility test: An operation plan review criteria to determine whether or not a plan is within the capacity of the resources that can be made available. Logistic implications test.

Federal coordinating officer: The federal officer who is appointed to manage Federal resource support activities related to Stafford Act disasters and emergencies. The federal coordinating officer is responsible for coordinating the timely delivery of federal disaster assistance resources and programs to the affected state and local governments, individual victims, and the private sector. FCO.

Federal service: A term applied to National Guard members and units when called to active duty to serve the Federal Government under Article I, Section 8 and Article II, Section 2 of the Constitution and the US Code, title 10 (Department of Defense), sections 12401 to 12408. Active duty; Reserve Components.

Federal supply class management: Those functions of materiel management that can best be accomplished by federal supply classification, such as cataloging, characteristic screening, standardization, interchangeability and substitution grouping, multi-item specification management, and engineering support of the foregoing.

Feint: In military deception, an offensive action involving contact with the adversary conducted for the purpose of deceiving the adversary as to the location and/or time of the actual main offensive action.

Fender: An object, usually made of rope or rubber, hung over the side of a vessel to protect the sides from damage caused by impact with wharves or other craft.

Ferret: An aircraft, ship, or vehicle especially equipped for the detection, location, recording, and analyzing of electromagnetic radiation.

Field army: Administrative and tactical organization composed of a headquarters, certain organic Army troops, service support troops, a variable number of corps, and a variable number of divisions. Army corps.

Field artillery: Equipment, supplies, ammunition, and personnel involved in the use of cannon, rocket, or surface-to-surface missile launchers. Field artillery cannons are classified according to caliber as follows.

Light – 120mm and less.
Medium – 121-160mm.
Heavy – 161-210mm.
Very heavy – greater than 210mm.
FA. Direct support artillery; general support artillery.

Field artillery observer: A person who watches the effects of artillery fire, adjusts the center of impact of that fire onto a target, and reports the results to the firing agency. Naval gunfire spotting team; spotter.

Field exercise: An exercise conducted in the field under simulated war conditions in which troops and armament of one side are actually present, while those of the other side may be imaginary or in outline. Command post exercise.

Field fortifications: An emplacement or shelter of a temporary nature which can be constructed with reasonable facility by units requiring no more than minor engineer supervisory and equipment participation.

Field of fire: The area which a weapon or a group of weapons may cover effectively with fire from a given position.

Field of view: 1. In photography, the angle between two rays passing through the perspective center (rear nodal point) of a camera lens to the two opposite sides of the format. Not to be confused with "angle of view." 2. The total solid angle available to the gunner when looking through the gun sight. FOV.

Field of vision: The total solid angle available to the gunner from his or her normal position. Field of view.

Field ordering officer: A Service member or Department of Defense civilian, who is appointed in writing and trained by a contracting officer and authorized to execute micro purchases in support of forces and/or designated civil-military operations. FOO.

Field press censorship: The security review of news material subject to the jurisdiction of the Armed Forces of the United States, including all information or material intended for dissemination to the public. FPC. Censorship.

Field training exercise: An exercise in which actual forces are used to train commanders, staffs, and individual units in basic, intermediate, and advanced-level warfare skills. FTX. Exercise; maneuver.

Fighter cover: The maintenance of a number of fighter aircraft over a specified area or force for the purpose of repelling hostile air activities. See also airborne alert; cover.

Fighter escort: An offensive counter air operation providing protection sorties by air-to-air capable fighters in support of other offensive air and air support missions over enemy territory, or in a defensive counter air role to protect high value airborne assets.

Fighter sweep: An offensive mission by fighter aircraft to seek out and destroy enemy aircraft or targets of opportunity in a designated area.

Fighting load: Consists of items of individual clothing, equipment, weapons, and ammunition that are carried by and are essential to the effectiveness of the combat soldier and the accomplishment of the immediate mission of the unit when the soldier is on foot. Existence load.

Filler: A substance carried in an ammunition container such as a projectile, mine, bomb, or grenade. A filler may be an explosive, chemical, or inert substance.

Filler personnel — Individuals of suitable grade and skill initially required to bring a unit or organization to its authorized strength.

Film badge: A photographic film packet to be carried by personnel, in the form of a badge, for measuring and permanently recording gamma-ray dosage.

Filter: In electronics, a device which transmits only part of the incident energy and may thereby change the spectral distribution of energy: a. High pass filters transmit energy above a certain frequency; b. Low pass filters transmit energy below a certain frequency; c. Band pass filters transmit energy of a certain bandwidth; d. Band stop filters transmit energy outside a specific frequency band.

Final approach: That part of an instrument approach procedure in which alignment and descent for landing are accomplished. a. In a non-precision approach it normally begins at the final approach fix or point and ends at the missed approach point or fix. b. In a precision approach the final approach commences at the glide path intercept point and ends at the decision height/ altitude.

Final destination: In naval control of shipping, the final destination of a convoy or of an individual ship irrespective of whether or not routing instructions have been issued.

Final governing standards: A comprehensive set of country-specific substantive environmental provisions, typically technical limitations on effluent, discharges, etc, or a specific management practice.

Final plan: A plan for which drafts have been coordinated and approved and which has been signed by or on behalf of a competent authority. Operation plan.

Final protective fire: An immediately available prearranged barrier of fire designed to impede enemy movement across defensive lines or areas.

Finance support: A financial management function to provide financial advice and recommendations, pay support, disbursing support, establishment of local depository accounts, essential accounting support, and support of the procurement process. Financial management.

Financial management: Financial management encompasses the two core functions of resource management and finance support. Also called FM. Finance support; resource management.

Fire: 1. The command given to discharge a weapon(s). 2. To detonate the main explosive charge by means of a firing system. Barrage fire; call fire; counter fire; counter preparation fire; covering fire; destruction fire; direct fire; direct supporting fire; distributed fire; grazing fire; harassing fire; indirect fire; neutralization fire; observed fire; preparation fire; radar fire; registration fire; scheduled fire; searching fire; supporting fire; suppressive fire.

Fireball: The luminous sphere of hot gases which forms a few millionths of a second after detonation of a nuclear weapon and immediately starts expanding and cooling.

Fire barrage (specify): An order to deliver a prearranged barrier of fire. Specification of the particular barrage may be by code name, numbering system, unit assignment, or other designated means.

Fire capabilities chart: A chart, usually in the form of an overlay, showing the areas which can be reached by the fire of the bulk of the weapons of a unit.

Fire control: The control of all operations in connection with the application of fire on a target.

Fire control radar: Radar used to provide target information inputs to a weapon fire control system.

Fire control system: A group of interrelated fire control equipments and/or instruments designed for use with a weapon or group of weapons.

Fire direction center: That element of a command post, consisting of gunnery and communications personnel and equipment, by means of which the commander exercises fire direction and/or fire control. The fire direction center receives target intelligence and requests for fire, and translates them into appropriate fire direction. The fire direction center provides timely and effective tactical and technical fire control in support of current operations. FDC.

Fire for effect: That volume of fires delivered on a target to achieve the desired effect. FFE. Final protective fire; fire mission; neutralize; suppression.

Fire mission: 1. Specific assignment given to a fire unit as part of a definite plan. 2. Order used to alert the weapon/battery area and indicate that the message following is a call for fire.

Fire plan: A tactical plan for using the weapons of a unit or formation so that their fire will be coordinated.

Firepower: 1. The amount of fire which may be delivered by a position, unit, or weapon system. 2. Ability to deliver fire.

Fires: The use of weapon systems to create a specific lethal or nonlethal effect on a target.

Fire storm: Stationary mass fire, generally in built-up urban areas, generating strong, inrushing winds from all sides; the winds keep the fires from spreading while adding fresh oxygen to increase their intensity.

Fire support: Fires that directly support land, maritime, amphibious, and special operations forces to engage enemy forces, combat formations, and facilities in pursuit of tactical and operational objectives. Fires.

Fire support area: An appropriate maneuver area assigned to fire support ships by the naval force commander from which they can deliver gunfire support to an amphibious operation.

FSA. amphibious operation; fire support; naval support area.

Fire support coordination: The planning and executing of fire so that targets are adequately covered by a suitable weapon or group of weapons.

Fire support coordination center: A single location in which are centralized communications facilities and personnel incident to the coordination of all forms of fire support. FSCC. Fire; fire support; fire support coordination; support; supporting arms coordination center.

Fire support coordination line: A fire support coordination measure that is established and adjusted by appropriate land or amphibious force commanders within their boundaries in consultation with superior, subordinate, supporting, and affected commanders. Fire support coordination lines facilitate the expeditious attack of surface targets of opportunity beyond the coordinating measure. A fire support coordination line does not divide an area of operations by defining a boundary between close and deep operations or a zone for close air support. The fire support coordination line applies to all fires of air, land, and sea-based weapon systems using any type of ammunition. Forces attacking targets beyond a fire support coordination line must inform all affected commanders in sufficient time to allow necessary reaction to avoid fratricide. Supporting elements attacking targets beyond the fire support coordination line must ensure that the attack will not produce adverse effects on, or to the rear of, the line. Short of a fire support coordination line, all air-to-ground and surface-to-surface attack operations are controlled by the appropriate land or amphibious force commander. The fire support coordination line should follow well-defined terrain features. Coordination of attacks beyond the fire support coordination line is especially critical to commanders of air, land, and special operations forces. In exceptional circumstances, the inability to conduct this coordination will not preclude the attack of targets beyond the fire support coordination line. However, failure to do so may increase the risk of fratricide and could waste limited resources. FSCL.

Fire support coordination measure: A measure employed by land or amphibious commanders to facilitate the rapid engagement of targets and simultaneously provide safeguards for friendly forces. FSCM. Fire support coordination.

Fire support element: That portion of the force tactical operations center at every echelon above company or troop (to corps) that is responsible for targeting coordination and for integrating fires delivered on surface targets by fire-support means under the control, or in support, of the force. Also called FSE. See also fire; fire support; force; support.

Fire support group: A temporary grouping of ships under a single commander charged with supporting troop operations ashore by naval gunfire. A fire support group may be further subdivided into fire support units and fire support elements.

Fire support officer: Senior field artillery officer assigned to Army maneuver battalions and brigades. Advises commander on fire-support matters. FSO. Field artillery; fire; fire support; support.

Fire support station: An exact location at sea within a fire support area from which a fire support ship delivers fire.

Fire support team: A team provided by the field artillery component to each maneuver company and troop to plan and coordinate all supporting fires available to the unit, including mortars, field artillery, naval surface fire support, and close air support integration. FIST. Close air support; field artillery; fire; fire support; support.

Firing area: In a sweeper-sweep combination it is the horizontal area at the depth of a particular mine in which the mine will detonate. The firing area has exactly the same dimensions as the interception area but will lie astern of it unless the mine detonates immediately when actuated.

Firing chart: Map, photo map, or grid sheet showing the relative horizontal and vertical positions of batteries, base points, base point lines, check points, targets, and other details needed in preparing firing data.

Firing circuit: 1. In land operations, an electrical circuit and/ or pyrotechnic loop designed to detonate connected charges from a firing point. 2. In naval mine warfare, that part of a mine circuit which either completes the detonator circuit or operates a ship counter.

Firing point: That point in the firing circuit where the device employed to initiate the detonation of the charges is located. FP.

Firing system: In demolition, a system composed of elements designed to fire the main charge or charges.

First light: The beginning of morning nautical twilight; i.e., when the center of the morning sun is 12 degrees below the horizon.

First responder care: The health care capability that provides immediate clinical care and stabilization to the patient in preparation for evacuation to the next health service support capability in the continuum of care.

First strike: The first offensive move of a war.

Fission products: A general term for the complex mixture of substances produced as a result of nuclear fission.

Fission to yield ratio: The ratio of the yield derived from nuclear fission to the total yield; it is frequently expressed in percent.

Fitted mine: In naval mine warfare, a mine containing an explosive charge, a primer, detonator, and firing system. Exercise filled mine; explosive filled mine.

Fix: A position determined from terrestrial, electronic, or astronomical data.

Fixed ammunition: Ammunition in which the cartridge case is permanently attached to the projectile. Munitions.

Fixed capital property: 1. Assets of a permanent character having continuing value. 2. As used in military establishments, includes real estate and equipment installed or in use, either in productive plants or in field operations. Synonymous with fixed assets.

Fixed medical treatment facility: A medical treatment facility which is designed to operate for an extended period of time at a specific site.

Fixed port: Water terminals with an improved network of cargo-handling facilities designed for the transfer of oceangoing freight. Water terminal.

Fixed price type contract: A type of contract that generally provides for a firm price or, under appropriate circumstances, may provide for an adjustable price for the supplies or services being procured. Fixed price contracts are of several types so designed as to facilitate proper pricing under varying circumstances.

Flag days (red or green): Red flag days are those during which movement requirements cannot be met; green flag days are those during which the requisite amount or a surplus of transportation capability exists.

Flag officer: A term applied to an officer holding the rank of general, lieutenant general, major general, or brigadier general in the US Army, Air Force or Marine Corps or admiral, vice admiral, or rear admiral in the US Navy or Coast Guard.

Flame field expedients: Simple, handmade devices used to produce flame or illumination. FFE.

Flame thrower: A weapon that projects incendiary fuel and has provision for ignition of this fuel.

Flank guard: A security element operating to the flank of a moving or stationary force to protect it from enemy ground observation, direct fire, and surprise attack.

Flanking attack: An offensive maneuver directed at the flank of an enemy. Frontal attack.

Flare: The change in the flight path of an aircraft so as to reduce the rate of descent for touchdown.

Flare dud: A nuclear weapon that, when launched at a target, detonates with anticipated yield but at an altitude appreciably greater than intended. This is not a dud insofar as yield is concerned, but it is a dud with respect to the effects on the target and the normal operation of the weapon.

Flash blindness: Impairment of vision resulting from an intense flash of light. It includes temporary or permanent loss of visual functions and may be associated with retinal burns. Dazzle.

Flash burn: A burn caused by excessive exposure (of bare skin) to thermal radiation.

Flash message: A category of precedence reserved for initial enemy contact messages or operational combat messages of extreme urgency. Brevity is mandatory. Precedence.

Flash ranging: Finding the position of the burst of a projectile or of an enemy gun by observing its flash.

Flash suppressor: Device attached to the muzzle of the weapon which reduces the amount of visible light or flash created by burning propellant gases.

Flash-to-bang time: The time from light being first observed until the sound of the nuclear detonation is heard.

Flatrack: Portable, open-topped, open-sided units that fit into existing below-deck container cell guides and provide a capability for container ships to carry oversized cargo and wheeled and tracked vehicles.

Flatted cargo: Cargo placed in the bottom of the holds, covered with planks and dunnage, and held for future use. Flatted cargo usually has room left above it for the loading of vehicles that may be moved without interfering with the flatted cargo. Frequently, flatted cargo serves in lieu of ballast. Sometimes called under stowed cargo.

Fleet: An organization of ships, aircraft, Marine forces, and shore-based fleet activities all under the command of a commander or commander in chief who may exercise operational as well as administrative control. major fleet; numbered fleet.

Fleet ballistic missile submarine: A nuclear-powered submarine designed to deliver ballistic missile attacks against assigned targets from either a submerged or surfaced condition. Designated as SSBN.

Fleet in being: A fleet (force) that avoids decisive action, but, because of its strength and location, causes or necessitates counter-concentrations and so reduces the number of opposing units available for operations elsewhere.

Fleet Marine Force: A balanced force of combined arms comprising land, air, and service elements of the US Marine Corps. A Fleet Marine Force is an integral part of a US fleet and has the status of a type command. FMF.

Flexible deterrent option: A planning construct intended to facilitate early decision making by developing a wide range of interrelated responses that begin with deterrent oriented actions carefully tailored to produce a desired effect. The flexible deterrent option is the means by which the various diplomatic, information, military, and economic deterrent measures available to the President are included in the joint operation planning process. FDO. Deterrent options.

Flexible response: The capability of military forces for effective reaction to any enemy threat or attack with actions appropriate and adaptable to the circumstances existing.

Flight: 1. In Navy and Marine Corps usage, a specified group of aircraft usually engaged in a common mission. 2. The basic tactical unit in the Air Force, consisting of four or more aircraft in two or more elements. 3. A single aircraft airborne on a nonoperational mission.

Flight advisory: A message dispatched to aircraft in flight or to interested stations to advise of any deviation or irregularity.

Flight deck: 1. In certain airplanes, an elevated compartment occupied by the crew for operating the airplane in flight. 2. The upper deck of an aircraft carrier that serves as a runway. The deck of an air-capable ship, amphibious aviation assault ship, or aviation ship used to launch and recover aircraft.

Flight deck officer: Officer responsible for the safe movement of aircraft on or about the flight deck of an aviation-capable ship. FDO.

Flight following: The task of maintaining contact with specified aircraft for the purpose of determining en route progress and/or flight termination.

Flight information center: A unit established to provide flight information service and alerting service.

Flight information region: An airspace of defined dimensions within which flight information service and alerting service are provided. FIR. Traffic control center; area control center.

Flight information service: A service provided for the purpose of giving advice and information useful for the safe and efficient conduct of flights. FIS.

Flight levels: Surfaces of constant atmospheric pressure which are related to a specific pressure datum, 1013.2 mb (29.92 in), and are separated by specific pressure intervals. (Flight levels are expressed in three digits that represent hundreds of feet; e.g., flight level 250 represents a barometric altimeter indication of 25,000 feet and flight level 255 is an indication of 25,500 feet.)

Flight path: The line connecting the successive positions occupied, or to be occupied, by an aircraft, missile, or space vehicle as it moves through air or space.

Flight plan: Specified information provided to air traffic services units relative to an intended flight or portion of a flight of an aircraft.

Flight plan correlation: A means of identifying aircraft by association with known flight plans.

Flight profile: Trajectory, or its graphic representation, followed by its altitude, speed, distance flown, and maneuver.

Flight quarters: A ship configuration that assigns and stations personnel at critical positions to conduct safe flight operations.

Flight readiness firing: A missile system test of short duration conducted with the propulsion system operating while the missile is secured to the launcher. Such a test is performed to determine the readiness of the missile system and launch facilities prior to flight test.

Flight surgeon: A physician specially trained in aviator medical practice whose primary duty is the medical examination and medical care of aircrew.

Flight test: Test of an aircraft, rocket, missile, or other vehicle by actual flight or launching. Flight tests are planned to achieve specific test objectives and gain operational information.

Flight visibility: The average forward horizontal distance from the cockpit of an aircraft in flight at which prominent unlighted objects may be seen and identified by day and prominent lighted objects may be seen and identified by night.

Floating base support: A form of logistic support in which supplies, repairs,

maintenance, and other services are provided in harbor or at an anchorage for operating forces from ships.

Floating craft company: A company-sized unit made up of various watercraft teams such as tugs, barges, and barge cranes. Watercraft.

Floating dump: Emergency supplies preloaded in landing craft, amphibious vehicles, or in landing ships. Floating dumps are located in the vicinity of the appropriate control officer, who directs their landing as requested by the troop commander concerned.

Floating mine: In naval mine warfare, a mine visible on the surface. Free mine; mine; watching mine.

Floating reserve: In an amphibious operation, reserve troops which remain embarked until needed. General reserve.

Flooder: In naval mine warfare, a device fitted to a buoyant mine which, on operation after a preset time, floods the mine case and causes it to sink to the bottom.

Flotation: The capability of a vehicle to float in water.

Fly-in echelon: Includes the balance of the initial assault force, not included in the assault echelon, and some aviation support equipment. FIE.

Foam path: A path of fire extinguisher foam laid on a runway to assist aircraft in an emergency landing.

Follow-up: In amphibious operations, the reinforcements and stores carried on transport ships and aircraft (not originally part of the amphibious force) that are offloaded after the assault and assault follow-on echelons have been landed. Amphibious operation; assault; assault follow-on echelon.

Follow-up echelon: In air transport operations, elements moved into the objective area after the assault echelon.

Follow-up shipping: Ships not originally a part of the amphibious task force but which deliver troops and supplies to the objective area after the assault phase has begun.

Follow-up supplies: Supplies delivered after the initial landings or airdrop to resupply units until routine supply procedures can be instituted. These supplies may be delivered either automatically or on an on-call basis and are prepared for delivery by supporting supply units. Resupply; routine supplies; supplies.

Footprint: 1. The area on the surface of the earth within a satellite's transmitter or sensor field of view. 2. The amount of personnel, spares, resources, and capabilities physically present and occupying space at a deployed location.

Force: 1. An aggregation of military personnel, weapon systems, equipment, and necessary support, or combination thereof. 2. A major subdivision of a fleet.

Force activity designators: Numbers used in conjunction with urgency of need designators to establish a matrix of priorities used for supply requisitions. Defines the relative importance of the unit to accomplish the objectives of the Department of Defense. FADs.

Force bed down: The provision of expedient facilities for troop support to provide a platform for the projection of force. These facilities may include modular or kit-type facility substitutes. Facility substitutes.

Force closure: The point in time when a supported joint force commander determines that sufficient personnel and equipment resources are in the assigned operational area to carry out assigned tasks. Closure; force.

Force enablement: Air refueling and other actions that increase an aircraft's range, payload, loiter time, and flexibility, to allow it to accomplish a wider range of missions. Air refueling.

Force extension: Tankers escorting fighters are force extended when they are refueled by other tankers en route to their destination. Force extension is normally required when tankers are acting in a dual-role capacity because their cargo will likely preclude carrying enough fuel for the tanker and receivers to reach the final destination. On global attack missions, force extension can also be used to extend the effective range, payload, and loiter time of combat aircraft due to the increased offload capacity of the force extended tanker. Air refueling; dual-role tanker.

Force health protection: Measures to promote, improve, or conserve the mental and physical well-being of Service members. These measures enable a healthy and fit force, prevent injury and illness, and protect the force from health hazards. FHP.

Force list: A total list of forces required by an operation plan, including assigned forces, augmentation forces, and other forces to be employed in support of the plan.

Force module: A grouping of combat, combat support, and combat service support forces, with their accompanying supplies and the required no unit resupply and personnel necessary to sustain forces for a minimum of 30 days. The elements of force modules are linked together or are uniquely identified so that they may be extracted from or adjusted as an entity in the Joint Operation Planning and Execution System databases to enhance flexibility and usefulness of the operation plan during a crisis. FM. Force module package.

Force module package: A force module with a specific functional orientation that include combat, associated combat support, and combat service support forces. Additionally, force module packages will contain sustainment in accordance with logistic policy contained in Joint Strategic Capabilities Plan Annex B. FMP. Force module.

Force multiplier: A capability that, when added to and employed by a combat force, significantly increases the combat potential of that force and thus enhances the probability of successful mission accomplishment.

Force planning: 1. Planning associated with the creation and maintenance of military capabilities. It is primarily the responsibility of the Military Departments, Services, and US Special Operations Command and is conducted under the administrative control that runs from the Secretary of Defense to the Military Departments and Services. 2. In the Joint Operation Planning and Execution System, the planning conducted by the supported combatant command and its components to determine required force capabilities to accomplish an assigned mission, as well as by the Military Departments, Services, and Service component commands of the combatant commands, to develop forces lists, source and tailor required force capabilities with actual units, identify and resolve shortfalls, and determine the routing and time-phasing of forces into the operational area.

Force projection: The ability to project the military instrument of national power from the United States or another theater, in response to requirements for military operations.

Force protection: Preventive measures taken to mitigate hostile actions against Department of Defense personnel resources, facilities, and critical information. Force protection does not include actions to defeat the enemy or protect against accidents, weather, or disease. FP. Force; force protection condition; protection.

Force protection working group: Cross-functional working group whose purpose is to conduct risk assessment and risk management and to recommend mitigating measures to the commander. FPWG.

Force rendezvous: A checkpoint at which formations of aircraft or ships join and become part of the main force. Group rendezvous.

Force requirement number: An alphanumeric code used to uniquely identify force entries in a given operation plan time-phased force and deployment data. FRN.

Force(s): Airborne force; armed forces; covering force; garrison force; multinational force; Navy cargo handling force; task force; underway replenishment force.

Force sequencing: The phased introduction of forces into and out of the operational area.

Force shortfall: A deficiency in the number or types of units available for planning within the time required for the performance of an assigned task.

Forces in being: Forces classified as being in state of readiness "A" or "B" as prescribed in the appropriate Military Committee document.

Force sourcing: The identification of the actual units, their origins, ports of embarkation, and movement characteristics to satisfy the time-phased force requirements of a supported commander.

Force tabs: With reference to war plans, the statement of time-phased deployments of major combat units by major commands and geographical areas.

Force tracking: The process of gathering and maintaining information on the location, status, and predicted movement of each element of a unit including the unit's command element, personnel, and unit-related supplies and equipment while in transit to the specified operational area.

Force visibility: The current and accurate status of forces; their current mission; future missions; location; mission priority; and readiness status. Force visibility provides information on the location, operational tempo, assets, and sustainment requirements of a force as part of an overall capability for a combatant commander.

Forcible entry: Seizing and holding of a military lodgment in the face of armed opposition. Lodgment.

Foreign assistance: Assistance to foreign nations ranging from the sale of military equipment to donations of food and medical supplies to aid survivors of natural and man-made disasters. US foreign assistance takes three forms: development assistance, humanitarian assistance, and security assistance. domestic emergencies; foreign disaster; foreign humanitarian assistance; security assistance.

Foreign consequence management: Assistance provided by the United States

Government to a host nation to mitigate the effects of a deliberate or inadvertent

chemical, biological, radiological, nuclear, or high-yield explosives attack or event and restore essential government services. FCM.

Foreign disaster: An act of nature (such as a flood, drought, fire, hurricane, earthquake, volcanic eruption, or epidemic), or an act of man (such as a riot, violence, civil strife, explosion, fire, or epidemic), which is or threatens to be of sufficient severity and magnitude to warrant United States foreign disaster relief to a foreign country, foreign persons, or to an intergovernmental organization. Foreign disaster relief.

Foreign disaster relief: Prompt aid that can be used to alleviate the suffering of foreign disaster victims. Normally it includes humanitarian services and transportation; the provision of food, clothing, medicine, beds, and bedding; temporary shelter and housing; the furnishing of medical materiel and medical and technical personnel; and making repairs to essential services. Foreign disaster.

Foreign humanitarian assistance: Department of Defense activities, normally in support of the United States Agency for International Development or Department of State, conducted outside the United States, its territories, and possessions to relieve or reduce human suffering, disease, hunger, or privation. FHA. Foreign assistance.

Foreign instrumentation signals intelligence: Technical information and intelligence derived from the intercept of foreign electromagnetic emissions associated with the testing and operational deployment of non-US aerospace, surface, and subsurface systems. Foreign instrumentation signals intelligence is a subcategory of signals intelligence. Foreign instrumentation signals include but are not limited to telemetry, beaconry, electronic interrogators, and video data links. FISINT. Signals intelligence.

Foreign intelligence: Information relating to capabilities, intentions, and activities of foreign powers, organizations, or persons, but not including counterintelligence, except for information on international terrorist activities. intelligence.

Foreign internal defense: Participation by civilian and military agencies of a government in any of the action programs taken by another government or other designated organization to free and protect its society from subversion, lawlessness, and insurgency. FID.

Foreign military sales: That portion of United States security assistance authorized by the Foreign Assistance Act of 1961, as amended, and the Arms Export Control Act of 1976, as amended. This assistance differs from the Military Assistance Program and the International Military Education and Training Program in that the recipient provides reimbursement for defense articles and services transferred. FMS.

Foreign military sales trainees: Foreign nationals receiving training conducted by the Department of Defense on a reimbursable basis, at the country's request.

Foreign national: Any person other than a US citizen, US permanent or temporary legal resident alien, or person in US custody.

Foreign nation support: Civil and/or military assistance rendered to a nation when operating outside its national boundaries during military operations based on agreements mutually concluded between nations or on behalf of intergovernmental organizations. Support may come from the nation in which forces are operating. Foreign nation support also may be from third party nations and include support or assistance, such as logistics, rendered outside the operational area. FNS. Host-nation support.

Foreign object damage: Rags, pieces of paper, line, articles of clothing, nuts, bolts, or tools that, when misplaced or caught by air currents normally found around aircraft operations (jet blast, rotor or prop wash, engine intake), cause damage to aircraft systems or weapons or injury to personnel. FOD.

Foreign service national: Foreign nationals who provide clerical, administrative, technical, fiscal, and other support at foreign service posts abroad and are not citizens of the United States. The term includes third country nationals who are individuals employed by a United States mission abroad and are neither a citizen of the US nor of the country to which assigned for duty. FSN.

Foreshore: That portion of a beach extending from the low water (datum) shoreline to the limit of normal high water wave wash.

Format: 1. In photography, the size and/or shape of a negative or of the print there from. 2. In cartography, the shape and size of a map or chart.

Formation: 1. An ordered arrangement of troops and/or vehicles for a specific purpose. 2. An ordered arrangement of two or more ships, units, or aircraft proceeding together under a commander.

Formatted message text: A message text composed of several sets ordered in a specified sequence, each set characterized by an identifier and containing information of a specified type, coded and arranged in an ordered sequence of character fields in accordance with the NATO message text formatting rules. It is designed to permit both manual and automated handling and processing. Free form message text; structured message text.

Formerly restricted data: Information removed from the restricted data category upon a joint determination by the Department of Energy and Department of Defense that such information relates primarily to the military utilization of atomic weapons and that such information can be adequately safeguarded as classified defense information. Restricted data.

Form lines: Lines resembling contours, but representing no actual elevations, which have been sketched from visual observation or from inadequate or unreliable map sources, to show collectively the configuration of the terrain.

Forward Aeromedical evacuation: That phase of evacuation which provides airlift for patients between points within the battlefield, from the battlefield to the initial point of treatment, and to subsequent points of treatment within the combat zone.

Forward air controller: An officer (aviator/pilot) member of the tactical air control party who, from a forward ground or airborne position, controls aircraft in close air support of ground troops. FAC. Close air support.

Forward air controller (airborne): A specifically trained and qualified aviation officer who exercises control from the air of aircraft engaged in close air support of ground troops. The forward air controller (airborne) is normally an airborne extension of the tactical air control party. FAC(A).

Forward area: An area in proximity to combat.

Forward arming and refueling point: A temporary facility – organized, equipped, and deployed by an aviation commander, and normally located in the main battle area closer to the area where operations are being conducted than the aviation unit's combat service area – to provide fuel and ammunition necessary for the employment of aviation maneuver units in combat. The forward arming and refueling point permits combat aircraft to rapidly refuel and rearm simultaneously. FARP.

Forward aviation combat engineering: A mobility operation in which engineers perform tasks in support of forward aviation ground facilities. Tasks include reconnaissance; construction of low altitude parachute extraction zones, landing strips, and airstrips; and providing berms, revetments, and trenches for forward arming and refueling points. FACE. Combat engineering; reconnaissance.

Forward edge of the battle area: The foremost limits of a series of areas in which ground combat units are deployed, excluding the areas in which the covering or screening forces are operating, designated to coordinate fire support, the positioning of forces, or the maneuver of units. FEBA.

Forward line of own troops: A line that indicates the most forward positions of friendly forces in any kind of military operation at a specific time. The forward line of own troops normally identifies the forward location of covering and screening forces. The forward line of own troops may be at, beyond, or short of the forward edge of the battle area. An enemy forward line of own troops indicates the forward-most position of hostile forces. FLOT.

Forward logistic site: Naval forward logistic site. FLS.

Forward-looking infrared: An airborne, electro-optical thermal imaging device that detects far-infrared energy, converts the energy into an electronic signal, and provides a visible image for day or night viewing. FLIR.

Forward oblique air photograph: Oblique photography of the terrain ahead of the aircraft.

Forward observer: An observer operating with front line troops and trained to adjust ground or naval gunfire and pass back battlefield information. In the absence of a forward air controller, the observer may control close air support strikes. FO. Forward air controller; spotter.

Forward operating base: An airfield used to support tactical operations without establishing full support facilities. The base may be used for an extended time period. Support by a main operating base will be required to provide backup support for a forward operating base. FOB.

Forward operating location: Primarily used for counterdrug operations. Similar to a forward operating base (FOB) but without the in-place infrastructure associated with a FOB. FOL.

Forward operating site: A scaleable location outside the United States and US territories intended for rotational use by operating forces. Such expandable "warm facilities" may be maintained with a limited US military support presence and possibly pre-positioned equipment. Forward operating sites support rotational rather than permanently stationed forces and are a focus for bilateral and regional training. FOS. Cooperative security location; main operating base.

Forward operations base: In special operations, a base usually located in friendly territory or afloat that is established to extend command and control or communications or to provide support for training and tactical operations. Facilities may be established for temporary or longer duration operations and may include an airfield or an unimproved airstrip, an anchorage, or a pier. A forward operations base may be the location of special operations component headquarters or a smaller unit that is controlled and/or supported by a main operations base. FOB. Advanced operations base; main operations base.

Forward recovery mission profile: A mission profile that involves the recovery of an aircraft at a neutral or friendly forward area airfield or landing site.

Forward resuscitative care: Care provided as close to the point of injury as possible based on current operational requirements to attain stabilization and achieve the most efficient use of life-and-limb saving medical treatment. Forward resuscitative care typically provides essential care for stabilization to ensure the patient can tolerate evacuation. FRC. Essential care; evacuation; medical treatment facility; patient.

Forward slope: Any slope which descends towards the enemy.

Forward tell: The transfer of information to a higher level of command. Track telling.

Foundation data: Specific information on essential features that change rarely or slowly, such as point positioning data, topographic features, elevation data, geodetic information, and safety of navigation data.

Four-round illumination diamond: A method of distributing the fire of illumination shells which, by a combination of lateral spread and range spread, provides illumination of a large area.

463L system: Aircraft pallets, nets, tie down, and coupling devices, facilities, handling equipment, procedures, and other components designed to interface with military and civilian aircraft cargo restraint systems. Though designed for airlift, system components may have to move intermodal via surface to support geographic combatant commander objectives.

Fragmentary order: An abbreviated form of an operation order issued as needed after an operation order to change or modify that order or to execute a branch or sequel to that order. FRAGORD.

Frame: In photography, any single exposure contained within a continuous sequence of photographs.

Free air anomaly: The difference between observed gravity and theoretical gravity that has been computed for latitude and corrected for elevation of the station above or below the geoids, by application of the normal rate of change of gravity for change of elevation, as in free air.

Free air overpressure: The unreflected pressure, in excess of the ambient atmospheric pressure, created in the air by the blast wave from an explosion. Overpressure.

Freedom of navigation operations: Operations conducted to demonstrate US or international rights to navigate air or sea routes.

Free drop: The dropping of equipment or supplies from an aircraft without the use of parachutes. Airdrop; air movement; free fall; high velocity drop; low velocity drop.

Free fall: A parachute maneuver in which the parachute is manually activated at the discretion of the jumper or automatically at a preset altitude. Airdrop; air movement; free drop; high velocity drop; low velocity drop.

Free-fire area: A specific area into which any weapon system may fire without additional coordination with the establishing headquarters. FFA.

Free form message text: A message text without prescribed format arrangements. It is intended for fast drafting as well as manual handling and processing. Also formatted message text; structured message text.

Free mail: Correspondence of a personal nature that weighs less than 11 ounces, to include audio and video recording tapes, from a member of the Armed Forces or designated civilian, mailed postage free from a Secretary of Defense approved free mail zone.

Free mine: In naval mine warfare, a moored mine whose mooring has parted or been cut.

Free rocket: A rocket not subject to guidance or control in flight.

Freight consolidating activity: A transportation activity that receives less than car- or truckload shipments of materiel for the purpose of assembling them into car- or truckload lots for onward movement to the ultimate consignee or to a freight distributing activity or other break bulk point. Freight distributing activity.

Frequency deconfliction: A systematic management procedure to coordinate the use of the electromagnetic spectrum for operations, communications, and intelligence functions. Frequency deconfliction is one element of electromagnetic spectrum management. Electromagnetic spectrum; electromagnetic spectrum management; electronic warfare.

Friendly: A contact positively identified as friendly. Hostile.

Friendly fire: In casualty reporting, a casualty circumstance applicable to persons killed in action or wounded in action mistakenly or accidentally by friendly forces actively engaged with the enemy, who are directing fire at a hostile force or what is thought to be a hostile force. Casualty.

Friendly force information requirement: Information the commander and staff need to understand the status of friendly force and supporting capabilities. FFIR.

Front: 1. The lateral space occupied by an element measured from the extremity of one flank to the extremity of the other flank. 2. The direction of the enemy. 3. The line of contact of two opposing forces. 4. When a combat situation does not exist or is not assumed, the direction toward which the command is faced.

Frontal attack: 1. An offensive maneuver in which the main action is directed against the front of the enemy forces. 2. In air intercept, an attack by an interceptor aircraft that terminates with a heading crossing angle greater than 135 degrees.

Frustrated cargo: Any shipment of supplies and/or equipment which, while en route to destination, is stopped prior to receipt and for which further disposition instructions must be obtained.

Full mission-capable: Material condition of any piece of military equipment, aircraft, or training device indicating that it can perform all of its missions. FMC. Deadline; mission-capable; partial mission-capable; partial mission-capable, maintenance; partial mission-capable, supply.

Functional component command: A command normally, but not necessarily, composed of forces of two or more Military Departments which may be established across the range of military operations to perform particular operational missions that may be of short duration or may extend over a period of time. Component; Service component command.

Functional damage assessment: The estimate of the effect of military force to degrade or destroy the functional or operational capability of the target to perform its intended mission and on the level of success in achieving operational objectives established against the target. This assessment is based upon all-source information, and includes an estimation of the time required for recuperation or replacement of the target function. Damage assessment; target.

Functional kill: To render a targeted installation, facility, or target system unable to fulfill its primary function.

Functions: The appropriate or assigned duties, responsibilities, missions, or tasks of an individual, office, or organization. As defined in the National Security Act of 1947, as amended, the term "function" includes functions, powers, and duties (5 United States Code 171n (a)).

Fusion: In intelligence usage, the process of examining all sources of intelligence and information to derive a complete assessment of activity.

Fuze cavity: A recess in a charge for receiving a fuze.

G

Gadget: Radar equipment (type of equipment may be indicated by a letter as listed in operation orders). May be followed by a color to indicate state of jamming. Colors will be used as follows: a. green — Clear of jamming. b. amber — Sector partially jammed. c. red — Sector completely jammed. d. blue — Completely jammed.

Gap: An area within a minefield or obstacle belt, free of live mines or obstacles, whose width and direction will allow a friendly force to pass through in tactical formation. Phoney minefield.

Gap filler radar: A radar used to supplement the coverage of the principal radar in areas where coverage is inadequate.

Gap (imagery): Any space where imagery fails to meet minimum coverage requirements. This might be a space not covered by imagery or a space where the minimum specified overlap was not obtained.

Gap marker: In landmine warfare, markers used to indicate a minefield gap. Gap markers at the entrance to, and exit from, the gap will be referenced to a landmark or intermediate marker. Marker.

Garble: An error in transmission, reception, encryption, or decryption that changes the text of a message or any portion thereof in such a manner that it is incorrect or undecryptable.

Garnishing: In surveillance, natural or artificial material applied to an object to achieve or assist camouflage.

Garrison force: All units assigned to a base or area for defense, development, operation, and maintenance of facilities. Force(s).

Gear: A general term for a collection of spars, ropes, blocks, and equipment used for lifting and stowing cargo and ships stores.

General agency agreement: A contract between the Maritime Administration and a steamship company which, as general agent, exercises administrative control over a government-owned ship for employment by the Military Sealift Command. GAA. Military Sealift Command.

General air cargo: Cargo without hazardous or dangerous properties and not requiring extra precautions for air transport.

General and complete disarmament: Reductions of armed forces and armaments by all states to levels required for internal security and for an international peace force. Connotation is "total disarmament" by all states.

General cargo: Cargo that is susceptible for loading in general, non specialized stowage areas or standard shipping containers; e.g., boxes, barrels, bales, crates, packages, bundles, and pallets.

General engineering: Those engineering capabilities and activities, other than combat engineering, that modify, maintain, or protect the physical environment. Examples include: the construction, repair, maintenance, and operation of infrastructure, facilities, lines of communication and bases; terrain modification and repair; and selected explosive hazard activities. GE.

General map: A map of small scale used for general planning purposes. Map.

General military intelligence: Intelligence concerning the (1) military capabilities of foreign countries or organizations or (2) topics affecting potential US or multinational military operations, relating to the following subjects: armed forces capabilities, including order of battle, organization, training, tactics, doctrine, strategy, and other factors bearing on military strength and effectiveness; area and terrain intelligence, including urban areas, coasts and landing beaches, and meteorological, oceanographic, and geological intelligence; transportation in all modes; military materiel production and support industries; military and civilian communications systems; military economics, including foreign military assistance; insurgency and terrorism; military political- sociological intelligence; location, identification, and description of military related installations; government control; escape and evasion; and threats and forecasts. GMI. Intelligence; military intelligence.

General orders: 1. Permanent instructions, issued in order form, that apply to all members of a command, as compared with special orders, which affect only individuals or small groups. General orders are usually concerned with matters of policy or administration. 2. A series of permanent guard orders that govern the duties of a sentry on post.

General purchasing agents: Agents who have been appointed in the principal overseas areas to supervise, control, coordinate, negotiate, and develop the local procurement of supplies, services, and facilities by Armed Forces of the United States, in order that the most effective utilization may be made of local resources and production.

General quarters: A condition of readiness when naval action is imminent. All battle stations are fully manned and alert; ammunition is ready for instant loading; guns and guided missile launchers.may be loaded.

General staff: A group of officers in the headquarters of Army or Marine divisions, Marine brigades, and aircraft wings, or similar or larger units that assist their commanders in planning, coordinating, and supervising operations. A general staff may consist of four or more principal functional sections: personnel (G-1), military intelligence (G-2), operations and training (G-3), logistics (G-4), and (in Army organizations) civil affairs and military government (G-5). (A particular section may be added or eliminated by the commander, dependent upon the need that has been demonstrated.) The comparable Air Force staff is found in the wing and larger units, with sections designated personnel, operations, etc. G-2 Air and G-3 Air are Army officers assigned to G-2 or G-3 at division, corps, and Army headquarters level who assist in planning and coordinating joint operations of ground and air units. Naval staffs ordinarily are not organized on these lines, but when they are, they are designated N-1, N-2, etc. Similarly, a joint staff may be designated J-1, J-2, etc. In Army brigades and smaller units and in Marine Corps units smaller than a brigade or aircraft wing, staff sections are designated S-1, S-2, etc., with corresponding duties; referred to as a unit staff in the Army and as an executive staff in the Marine Corps. Staff.

General stopping power: The percentage of a group of vehicles in battle formation likely to be stopped by mines when attempting to cross a minefield.

General support: 1. That support which is given to the supported force as a whole and not to any particular subdivision thereof. Close support; direct support; mutual support; support. 2. A tactical artillery mission. GS. Direct support; general support-reinforcing; reinforcing.

General support artillery: Artillery which executes the fire directed by the commander of the unit to which it organically belongs or is attached. It fires in support of the operation as a whole rather than in support of a specific subordinate unit. GSA. Direct support artillery; general support-reinforcing; reinforcing.

General support-reinforcing: General support-reinforcing artillery has the mission of supporting the force as a whole and of providing reinforcing fires for other artillery units. GSR. Direct support artillery; reinforcing.

General unloading period: In amphibious operations, that part of the ship-to-shore movement in which unloading is primarily logistic in character, and emphasizes speed and volume of unloading operations. It encompasses the unloading of units and cargo from the ships as rapidly as facilities on the beach permit. It proceeds without regard to class, type, or priority of cargo, as permitted by cargo handling facilities ashore. Initial unloading period.

General war: Armed conflict between major powers in which the total resources of the belligerents are employed, and the national survival of a major belligerent is in jeopardy.

Generation (photography): The preparation of successive positive and/or negative reproductions from an original negative and/or positive (first-generation). For example, the first positive produced from an original negative is a second-generation product; the negative made from this positive is a third-generation product; and the next positive or print from that negative is a fourth-generation product.

Geographic coordinates: The quantities of latitude and longitude which define the position of a point on the surface of the Earth with respect to the reference spheroid. Coordinates.

Geographic reference points: A means of indicating position, usually expressed either as double letters or as code words that are established in operation orders or by other means.

Georef: A worldwide position reference system that may be applied to any map or chart graduated in latitude and longitude regardless of projection. It is a method of expressing latitude and longitude in a form suitable for rapid reporting and plotting.

Geospatial engineering: Those engineering capabilities and activities that contribute to a clear understanding of the physical environment by providing geospatial information and services to commanders and staffs. Examples include: terrain analyses, terrain visualization, digitized terrain products, nonstandard tailored map products, precision survey, geospatial data management, baseline survey data, and force bed down analysis. Geospatial information and services.

Geospatial information: Information that identifies the geographic location and characteristics of natural or constructed features and boundaries on the Earth, including: statistical data and information derived from, among other things, remote sensing, mapping, and surveying technologies; and mapping, charting, geodetic data and related products.

Geospatial information and services: The collection, information extraction, storage, dissemination, and exploitation of geodetic, geomagnetic, imagery, gravimetric, aeronautical, topographic, hydrographic, littoral, cultural, and homonymic data accurately referenced to a precise location on the Earth's surface. Geospatial services include tools that enable users to access and manipulate data, and also include instruction, training, laboratory support, and guidance for the use of geospatial data. GI&S.

Geospatial intelligence: The exploitation and analysis of imagery and geospatial information to describe, assess, and visually depict physical features and geographically referenced activities on the Earth. Geospatial intelligence consists of imagery, imagery intelligence, and geospatial information. GEOINT.

Geospatial-intelligence contingency package: Preassembled package of selected maps, charts, and other geographic materials of various scales to support the planning and conduct of noncombatant evacuation operations in selected countries or areas. GCP. NOTE: Geospatial-intelligence contingency packages are replacing NEOPACKs when updated. Noncombatant evacuation operations; noncombatant evacuees.

Glide bomb: A bomb fitted with airfoils to provide lift and which is carried and released in the direction of a target by an airplane.

Glide mode: In a flight control system, a control mode in which an aircraft is automatically positioned to the center of the glide slope course.

Global Air Transportation Execution System: -The Air Mobility Command's aerial port operations and management information system designed to support automated cargo and passenger processing, the reporting of in-transit visibility data to the Global Transportation Network, and billing to Air Mobility Command's financial management directorate. GATES. Air Mobility Command; Global Transportation Network.

Global Combat Support System-Joint: The primary information technology application used to provide automation support to the joint logistician. GCSS-J.

Global Command and Control System: A deployable command and control system supporting forces for joint and multinational operations across the range of military operations with compatible, interoperable, and integrated communications systems. GCCS. Command and control; command and control system.

Global distribution: The process that synchronizes and integrates fulfillment of joint force requirements with employment of the joint force. It provides national resources (personnel and materiel) to support execution of joint operations. The ultimate objective of this process is the effective and efficient accomplishment of the joint force mission. distribution.

Global distribution of materiel: The process of providing materiel from the source of supply to its point of consumption or use on a worldwide basis. Global distribution.

Global Information Grid: The globally interconnected, end-to-end set of information capabilities, associated processes and personnel for collecting, processing, storing, disseminating, and managing information on demand to war fighters, policy makers, and support personnel. The Global Information Grid includes owned and leased communications and computing systems and services, software (including applications), data, security services, other associated services and National Security Systems. GIG. Grid; information.

Global Network Operations Center: United States Strategic Command operational element responsible for: providing global satellite communications system status; maintaining global situational awareness to include each combatant commander's planned and current operations as well as contingency plans; supporting radio frequency interference resolution management; supporting satellite anomaly resolution and management; facilitating satellite communications interface to the defense information infrastructure; and managing the regional satellite communications support centers. GNC.

Global Patient Movement Requirements Center: A joint activity reporting directly to the Commander, US Transportation Command, the Department of Defense single manager for the strategic and continental United States regulation and movement of uniformed services and other authorized patients. The Global Patient Movement Requirements Center provides medical regulating and Aeromedical evacuation scheduling for the continental United States and intratheater operations and provides support to the theater patient movement requirements centers. The Global Patient Movement Requirements Center coordinates with supporting resource providers to identify available assets and communicates transport to bed plans to the appropriate transportation agency for execution. GPMRC. medical treatment facility.

Global Positioning System: A satellite-based radio navigation system operated by the Department of Defense to provide all military, civil, and commercial users with precise positioning, navigation, and timing. GPS.

Global transportation management: The integrated process of satisfying transportation requirements using the Defense Transportation System to meet national security objectives. The process begins with planning, programming, and budgeting for transportation assets, services, and associated systems and continues through delivery of the users' transportation movement requirements. GTM. Defense Transportation System; Global Transportation Network.

Global Transportation Network: The automated support necessary to enable US Transportation Command and its components to provide global transportation management. The Global Transportation Network provides the integrated transportation data and systems necessary to accomplish global transportation planning, command and control, and in-transit visibility across the range of military operations. The designated Department of Defense in-transit visibility system provides customers with the ability to track the identity, status, and location of Department of Defense units and non-unit cargo, passengers, patients, forces, and military and commercial airlift, sealift, and surface assets from origin to destination across the range of military operations. The Global Transportation Network collects, integrates, and distributes transportation information to combatant commanders, Services, and other Department of Defense customers. Global Transportation Network provides US Transportation Command with the ability to perform command and control operations, planning and analysis, and business operations in tailoring customer requirements throughout the requirements process. GTN. See also global transportation management; in-transit visibility; United States Transportation Command.

Go no-go: The condition or state of operability of a component or system: "go," functioning properly; or "no-go," not functioning properly. Alternatively, a critical point at which a decision to proceed or not must be made.

Governing factors: In the context of joint operation planning, those aspects of the situation (or externally imposed factors) that the commander deems critical to the accomplishment of the mission.

Government-owned, contract-operated ships: Those ships to which the US Government holds title and which the Military Sealift Command operates under a contract (i.e., nongovernment-manned). These ships are designated United States Naval Ships and use the prefix "USNS" with the ship name and the letter "T" as a prefix to the ship classification. Military Sealift Command; United States Naval Ship.

Government-owned, Military Sealift Command-operated ships: Those ships to which the US Government holds title and which the Military Sealift Command operates with US Government employees. These ships are designated United States Naval Ships and use the prefix "USNS" with the ship name and the letter "T" as a prefix to the ship classification; United States Naval Ship.

Gradient: The rate of inclination to horizontal expressed as a ratio, such as 1:25, indicating a one unit rise to 25 units of horizontal distance.

Gradient circuit: In mine warfare, a circuit which is actuated when the rate of change, with time, of the magnitude of the influence is within predetermined limits.

Graphic: Any and all products of the cartographic and photogrammetric art. A graphic may be a map, chart, or mosaic or even a film strip that was produced using cartographic techniques.

Graphic scale: A graduated line by means of which distances on the map, chart, or photograph may be measured in terms of ground distance. Scale.

Grapnel: In naval mine warfare, a device fitted to a mine mooring designed to grapple the sweep wire when the mooring is cut.

Graticule: 1. In cartography, a network of lines representing the Earth's parallels of latitude and meridians of longitude. 2. In imagery interpretation, see reticle.

Graticule ticks: In cartography, short lines indicating where selected meridians and parallels intersect.

Graves registration program: A program that provides for search, recovery, tentative identification, and evacuation or temporary interment. Temporary interment is only authorized by the geographic combatant commander. Disposition of personal effects is included in this program. Personal effects.

Gravity extraction: The extraction of cargoes from the aircraft by influence of their own weight. Extraction parachute.

Grazing fire: Fire approximately parallel to the ground where the center of the cone of fire does not rise above one meter from the ground. Fire.

Grey propaganda: Propaganda that does not specifically identify any source. Propaganda.

Grid: 1. Two sets of parallel lines intersecting at right angles and forming squares; the grid is superimposed on maps, charts, and other similar representations of the Earth's surface in an accurate and consistent manner in order to permit identification of ground locations with respect to other locations and the computation of direction and distance to other points. 2. A term used in giving the location of a geographic point by grid coordinates. Military grid; military grid reference system.

Grid bearing: Bearing measured from grid north.

Grid convergence: The horizontal angle at a place between true north and grid north. It is proportional to the longitude difference between the place and the central meridian. Convergence.

Grid convergence factor: The ratio of the grid convergence angle to the longitude difference. In the Lambert Conical Orthomorphic projection, this ratio is constant for all charts based on the same two standard parallels. Convergence; grid convergence.

Grid coordinates: Coordinates of a grid coordinate system to which numbers and letters are assigned for use in designating a point on a gridded map, photograph, or chart. See also coordinates.

Grid coordinate system: A plane-rectangular coordinate system usually based on, and mathematically adjusted to, a map projection in order that geographic positions (latitudes and longitudes) may be readily transformed into plane coordinates and the computations relating to them may be made by the ordinary method of plane surveying. Coordinates.

Grid interval: The distance represented between the lines of a grid.

Grid magnetic angle: Angular difference in direction between grid north and magnetic north. It is measured east or west from grid north. Grid variation; grivation.

Grid navigation: A method of navigation using a grid overlay for direction reference. Navigational grid.

Grid north: The northerly or zero direction indicated by the grid datum of directional reference.

Grid ticks: Small marks on the neat line of a map or chart indicating additional grid reference systems included on that sheet. Grid ticks are sometimes shown on the interior grid lines of some maps for ease of referencing.

Grossly transportation feasible: A determination made by the supported commander that a draft operation plan can be supported with the apportioned transportation assets. This determination is made by using a transportation feasibility estimator to simulate movement of personnel and cargo from port of embarkation to port of debarkation within a specified time frame.

Gross weight: 1. Weight of a vehicle, fully equipped and serviced for operation, including the weight of the fuel, lubricants, coolant, vehicle tools and spares, crew, personal equipment, and load. 2. Weight of a container or pallet including freight and binding. WT. Net weight.

Ground alert: That status in which aircraft on the ground/ deck are fully serviced and armed, with combat crews in readiness to take off within a specified short period of time (usually 15 minutes) after receipt of a mission order. Airborne alert.

Ground combat element: The core element of a Marine air-ground task force (MAGTF) that is task-organized to conduct ground operations. It is usually constructed around an infantry organization but can vary in size from a small ground unit of any type, to one or more Marine divisions that can be independently maneuvered under the direction of the MAGTF commander. The ground combat element itself is not a formal command. GCE. Aviation combat element; combat service support element; command element; Marine air-ground task force; Marine expeditionary force; Marine expeditionary force; Marine expeditionary unit; special purpose Marine air-ground task force; task force.

Ground combat control: -A system of accurate measurements used to determine the distances and directions or differences in elevation between points on the Earth. Common control (artillery); control point; traverse.

Ground-controlled approach procedure: The technique for talking down, through the use of both surveillance and precision approach radar, an aircraft during its approach so as to place it in a position for landing. Automatic approach and landing.

Ground-controlled interception: A technique which permits control of friendly aircraft or guided missiles for the purpose of effecting interception. Air interception.

Ground fire: Small arms ground-to-air fire directed against aircraft.

Ground liaison officer: An officer trained in offensive air support activities. Ground liaison officers are normally organized into parties under the control of the appropriate Army commander to provide liaison to Air Force and naval units engaged in training and combat operations. GLO.

Ground observer center: A center to which ground observer teams report and which in turn will pass information to the appropriate control and/or reporting agency.

Ground return: The radar reflection from the terrain as displayed and/or recorded as an image.

Ground speed: The horizontal component of the speed of an aircraft relative to the Earth's surface. GS.

Ground visibility: Prevailing horizontal visibility near the Earth's surface as reported by an accredited observer.

Ground zero: The point on the surface of the Earth at, or vertically below or above, the center of a planned or actual nuclear detonation. Actual ground zero; desired ground zero.

Group: 1. A flexible administrative and tactical unit composed of either two or more battalions or two or more squadrons. The term also applies to combat support and combat service support units. 2. A number of ships and/or aircraft, normally a subdivision of a force, assigned for a specific purpose. 3. A long-standing functional organization that is formed to support a broad function within a joint force commander's headquarters. GP.

Group of targets: Two or more targets on which fire is desired simultaneously. A group of targets is designated by a letter/ number combination or a nickname.

Group rendezvous: A check point at which formations of the same type will join before proceeding. Force rendezvous.

Guard: 1. A form of security operation whose primary task is to protect the main force by fighting to gain time while also observing and reporting information, and to prevent enemy ground observation of and direct fire against the main body by reconnoitering, attacking, defending, and delaying. A guard force normally operates within the range of the main body's indirect fire weapons. 2. A radio frequency that is normally used for emergency transmissions and is continuously monitored. UHF band: 243.0 MHZ; VHF band: 121.5 MHZ. See also cover; flank guard; screen. 3. A military or civilian individual assigned to protect personnel, equipment, or installations, or to oversee a prisoner.

Guarded frequencies: Enemy frequencies that are currently being exploited for combat information and intelligence. A guarded frequency is time-oriented in that the guarded frequency list changes as the enemy assumes different combat postures. These frequencies may be jammed after the commander has weighed the potential operational gain against the loss of the technical information. Electronic warfare.

Guerrilla: A combat participant in guerrilla warfare. Unconventional warfare.

Guerrilla force: - A group of irregular, predominantly indigenous personnel organized along military lines to conduct military and paramilitary operations in enemy-held, hostile, or denied territory.

Guerrilla warfare: Military and paramilitary operations conducted in enemy-held or hostile territory by irregular, predominantly indigenous forces. GW. Unconventional warfare.

Guidance station equipment: The ground-based portion of a missile guidance system necessary to provide guidance during missile flight.

Guided missile: An unmanned vehicle moving above the surface of the Earth whose trajectory or flight path is capable of being altered by an external or internal mechanism. Aerodynamic missile; ballistic missile.

Guide specification: Minimum requirements to be used as a basis for the evaluation of a national specification covering a fuel, lubricant or associated product proposed for standardization action.

Guinea-pig: In naval mine warfare, a ship used to determine whether an area can be considered safe from influence mines under certain conditions or, specifically, to detonate pressure mines.

Gull: In electronic warfare, a floating radar reflector used to simulate a surface target at sea for deceptive purposes.

Gun: 1. A cannon with relatively long barrel, operating with relatively low angle of fire, and having a high muzzle velocity. 2. A cannon with tube length 30 calibers or more. Howitzer; mortar.

Gun carriage: A mobile or fixed support for a gun. It sometimes includes the elevating and traversing mechanisms. Carriage.

Gun-target line: An imaginary straight line from gun to target. GTL.

Gun-type weapon: A device in which two or more pieces of fissionable material, each less than a critical mass, are brought together very rapidly so as to form a supercritical mass that can explode as the result of a rapidly expanding fission chain.

Gyromagnetic compass: A directional gyroscope whose azimuth scale is maintained in alignment with the magnetic meridian by a magnetic detector unit.

H

Half-life: The time required for the activity of a given radioactive species to decrease to half of its initial value due to radioactive decay. The half-life is a characteristic property of each radioactive species and is independent of its amount or condition. The effective half-life of a given isotope is the time in which the quantity in the body will decrease to half as a result of both radioactive decay and biological elimination.

Half-residence time: As applied to delayed fallout, it is the time required for the amount of weapon debris deposited in a particular part of the atmosphere to decrease to half of its initial value.

Half thickness: Thickness of absorbing material necessary to reduce by one-half the intensity of radiation which passes through it.

Handling (ordnance): Applies to those individuals who engage in the breakout, lifting, or repositioning of ordnance or explosive devices in order to facilitate storage or stowage, assembly or disassembly, loading or down loading, or transporting. See also assembly; downloading; loading; ordnance.

Handover: The passing of control authority of an aircraft from one control agency to another control agency. Handover action may be accomplished between control agencies of separate Services when conducting joint operations or between control agencies within a single command and control system. Handover action is complete when the receiving controller acknowledges assumption of control authority. Hand-off.

Handover/crossover: In personnel recovery, the transfer of isolated personnel between two recovery forces. Evader; evasion; recovery; recovery operations.

Handover line: A control feature, preferably following easily defined terrain features, at which responsibility for the conduct of combat operations is passed from one force to another.

Hang fire: A malfunction that causes an undesired delay in the functioning of a firing system.

Harassing fire: Fire designed to disturb the rest of the enemy troops, to curtail movement, and, by threat of losses, to lower morale.

Harassment: An incident in which the primary objective is to disrupt the activities of a unit, installation, or ship, rather than to inflict serious casualties or damage.

Harbour: A restricted body of water, an anchorage, or other limited coastal water area and its mineable water approaches, from which shipping operations are projected or supported. Generally, a harbor is part of a base, in which case the harbor defense force forms a component element of the base defense force established for the local defense of the base and its included harbor.

Harbour defense: The defense of a harbor or anchorage and its water approaches against external threats such as: a. submarine, submarine-borne, or small surface craft attack; b. enemy mine laying operations; and c. sabotage. The defense of a harbor from guided missiles while such missiles are airborne is considered to be a part of air defense. Port security.

Hard beach: A portion of a beach especially prepared with a hard surface extending into the water, employed for the purpose of loading or unloading directly into or from landing ships or landing craft.

Hardened site: A site, normally constructed under rock or concrete cover, designed to provide protection against the effects of conventional weapons. It may also be equipped to provide protection against the side effects of a nuclear attack and against a chemical or a biological attack.

Hard missile base: A launching base that is protected against a nuclear explosion.

Hardstand: 1. A paved or stabilized area where vehicles are parked. 2. Open ground area having a prepared surface and used for the storage of materiel.

Hardware: 1. The generic term dealing with physical items as distinguished from its capability or function such as equipment, tools, implements, instruments, devices, sets, fittings, trimmings, assemblies, subassemblies, components, and parts. The term is often used in regard to the stage of development, as in the passage of a device or component from the design stage into the hardware stage as the finished object. 2. In data automation, the physical equipment or devices forming a computer and peripheral components. Software.

Harmonization: The process and/or results of adjusting differences or inconsistencies to bring significant features into agreement.

Hasty attack: In land operations, an attack in which preparation time is traded for speed in order to exploit an opportunity. Deliberate attack.

Hasty breaching: The rapid creation of a route through a minefield, barrier, or fortification by any expedient method.

Hasty breaching (land mine warfare): The creation of lanes through enemy minefields by expedient methods such as blasting with demolitions, pushing rollers or disabled vehicles through the minefields when the time factor does not permit detailed reconnaissance, deliberate breaching, or bypassing the obstacle.

Hasty crossing: The crossing of an inland water obstacle using the crossing means at hand or those readily available, and made without pausing for elaborate preparations. Deliberate crossing.

Hasty defense: A defense normally organized while in contact with the enemy or when contact is imminent and time available for the organization is limited. It is characterized by improvement of the natural defensive strength of the terrain by utilization of foxholes, emplacements, and obstacles. Deliberate defense.

Hatch: An opening in a ship's deck giving access to cargo holds.

Hatch list: A list showing, for each hold section of a cargo ship, a description of the items stowed, their volume and weight, the consignee of each, and the total volume and weight of materiel in the hold.

Hazard: A condition with the potential to cause injury, illness, or death of personnel; damage to or loss of equipment or property; or mission degradation. Injury; risk.

Hazards of electromagnetic radiation to fuels: The potential hazard that is created when volatile combustibles, such as fuel, are exposed to electromagnetic fields of sufficient energy to cause ignition. HERF.

Hazards of electromagnetic radiation to ordnance: The danger of accidental actuation of electro-explosive devices or otherwise electrically activating ordnance because of radio frequency electromagnetic fields. This unintended actuation could have safety (premature firing) or reliability consequences. HERO. Electromagnetic radiation; HERO SAFE ordnance; HERO UNSAFE ordnance; ordnance.

Hazards of electromagnetic radiation to personnel: The potential hazard that exists when personnel are exposed to an electromagnetic field of sufficient intensity to heat the human body. HERP.

Heading hold mode: In a flight control system, a control mode that automatically maintains an aircraft heading that exists at the instant of completion of a maneuver.

Heading indicator: An instrument which displays heading transmitted electrically from a remote compass system.

Heading select feature: A flight control system feature that permits selection or preselection of desired automatically controlled heading or headings of an aircraft.

Head of contracting activity: The official who has overall responsibility for managing the contracting activity. HCA.

Head-up display: A display of flight, navigation, attack, or other information superimposed upon the pilot's forward field of view. HUD. flight; horizontal situation display.

Health care provider: Any member of the Armed Forces, civilian employee of the Department of Defense, or personal services contract employee under Title 10 United States Code Section 1091 authorized by the Department of Defense to perform health care functions. The term does not include any contract provider who is not a personal services contract employee. DOD health care provider.

Health hazard assessment: An assessment that characterizes the possible health risks of occupational exposures of Service members during the course of their normal duties.

Health service logistic support: A functional area of logistic support that supports the joint force surgeon's health service support mission. It includes supplying Class VIII medical supplies (medical materiel to include medical peculiar repair parts used to sustain the health service support system), optical fabrication, medical equipment maintenance, blood storage and distribution, and medical gases. HSLS. Health service support; joint force surgeon.

Health service support: All services performed, provided, or arranged to promote, improve, conserve, or restore the mental or physical well-being of personnel. These services include, but are not limited to, the management of health services resources, such as manpower, monies, and facilities; preventive and curative health measures; evacuation of the wounded, injured, or sick; selection of the medically fit and disposition of the medically unfit; blood management; medical supply, equipment, and maintenance thereof; combat stress control; and medical, dental, veterinary, laboratory, optometric, nutrition therapy, and medical intelligence services. HSS.

Health surveillance: The regular or repeated collection, analysis, and interpretation of health-related data and the dissemination of information to monitor the health of a population and to identify potential health risks, thereby enabling timely interventions to prevent, treat, reduce, or control disease and injury. It includes occupational and environmental health surveillance and medical surveillance subcomponents.

Health threat: A composite of ongoing or potential enemy actions; adverse environmental, occupational, and geographic and meteorological conditions; endemic diseases; and employment of nuclear, biological, and chemical weapons (to include weapons of mass destruction) that have the potential to affect the short- or long-term health of personnel.

Heavy antitank weapon: A weapon capable of operating from ground or vehicle, used to defeat armor and other material targets.

Heavy drop: A system of delivery of heavy supplies and equipment by parachute.

Heavy-lift cargo: 1. Any single cargo lift, weighing over 5 long tons, and to be handled aboard ship. 2. In Marine Corps usage, individual units of cargo that exceed 800 pounds in weight or 100 cubic feet in volume.

Heavy-lift ship: A ship specially designed and capable of loading and unloading heavy and bulky items. It has booms of sufficient capacity to accommodate a single lift of 100 tons.

Height of burst: The vertical distance from the Earth's surface or target to the point of burst. HOB. Optimum height of burst; safe burst height; types of burst.

Helicopter direction center: In amphibious operations, the primary direct control agency for the helicopter group/unit commander operating under the overall control of the tactical air control center. HDC.

Helicopter landing zone: A specified ground area for landing assault helicopters to embark or disembark troops and/ or cargo. A landing zone may contain one or more landing sites. HLZ.

Helicopter support team: A task organization formed and equipped for employment in a landing zone to facilitate the landing and movement of helicopter-borne troops, equipment, and supplies, and to evacuate selected casualties and enemy prisoners of War. HST.

Helicopter transport area: Areas to the seaward and on the flanks of the outer transport and landing ship areas, but preferably inside the area screen, used for launching and/or recovering helicopters.

Helipad: A prepared area designated and used for takeoff and landing of helicopters.

Heliport: A facility designated for operating, basing, servicing, and maintaining helicopters.

Herbicide: A chemical compound that will kill or damage plants.

Hero Safe Ordnance: Any ordnance item that is percussion initiated, sufficiently shielded or otherwise so protected that all electro-explosive devices contained by the item are immune to adverse effects (safety or reliability) when the item is employed in its expected radio frequency environments, provided that the general hazards of electromagnetic radiation to ordnance requirements defined in the hazards from electromagnetic radiation manual are observed. Electromagnetic radiation; hazards of electromagnetic radiation to ordnance; HERO SUSCEPTIBLE ordnance; HERO UNSAFE ordnance; ordnance.

Hero Susceptible ordnance: Any ordnance item containing

electro-explosive devices proven by test or analysis to be adversely affected by radio frequency energy to the point that the safety and/or reliability of the system is in jeopardy when the system is employed in its expected radio frequency environment. See also electromagnetic radiation; hazards of electromagnetic radiation to ordnance; HERO SAFE ordnance; HERO UNSAFE ordnance; ordnance.

High airburst: The fallout safe height of burst for a nuclear weapon that increases damage to or casualties on soft targets, or reduces induced radiation contamination at actual ground zero. Types of burst.

High altitude bombing: Horizontal bombing with the height of release over 15,000 feet.

High altitude burst: The explosion of a nuclear weapon which takes place at a height in excess of 100,000 feet (30,000 meters). HAB. Types of burst.

High-altitude low-opening parachute technique: A method of delivering personnel, equipment, or supplies from airlift aircraft that must fly at altitudes above the threat umbrella. HALO.

High-altitude missile engagement zone: Weapon engagement zone.

High angle: In artillery and naval gunfire support, an order or request to obtain high angle fire.

High angle fire: Fire delivered at angles of elevation greater than the elevation that corresponds to the maximum range of the gun and ammunition concerned; fire, the range of which decreases as the angle of elevation is increased.

High-density airspace control zone: Airspace designated in an airspace control plan or airspace control order, in which there is a concentrated employment of numerous and varied weapons and airspace users. A high-density airspace control zone has defined dimensions which usually coincide with geographical features or navigational aids. Access to a high-density airspace control zone is normally controlled by the maneuver commander. The maneuver commander can also direct a more restrictive weapons status within the high-density airspace control zone. HIDACZ.

High explosive cargo: Cargo such as artillery ammunition, bombs, depth charges, demolition material, rockets, and missiles.

High-payoff target: A target whose loss to the enemy will significantly contribute to the success of the friendly course of action. High-payoff targets are those high-value targets that must be acquired and successfully attacked for the success of the friendly commander's mission. HPT. High-value target; target.

High-payoff target list: A prioritized list of high-payoff targets by phase of the joint operation. HPTL. High-payoff target; target.

High-risk personnel: Personnel who, by their grade, assignment, symbolic value, or relative isolation, are likely to be attractive or accessible terrorist targets. HRP. Antiterrorism.

High value asset control items: Items of supply identified for intensive management control under approved inventory management techniques designed to maintain an optimum inventory level of high investment items. Hi-value asset control items.

High-value target: A target the enemy commander requires for the successful completion of the mission. The loss of high-value targets would be expected to seriously degrade important enemy functions throughout the friendly commander's area of interest. HVT. High-payoff target; target.

High velocity drop: A drop procedure in which the drop velocity is greater than 30 feet per second (low velocity drop) and lower than free drop velocity. Airdrop.

High-water mark: Properly, a mark left on a beach by wave wash at the preceding high water. It does not necessarily correspond to the high-water line. Because it can be determined by simple observation, it is frequently used in place of the high-water line, which can be determined only by a survey. When so used, it is called the high-water line.

Hill shading: A method of representing relief on a map by depicting the shadows that would be cast by high ground if light were shining from a certain direction.

Hinterland, far: That region surrounding a beach or terminal operation to the extent that it has characteristics that affect the operation – normally within 100 miles.

Hinterland, near: The area of land within an operational area of a specific beach or terminal operation – usually within 5 miles.

Hoist: In helicopters, the mechanism by which external loads may be raised or lowered vertically.

Hold: 1. A cargo stowage compartment aboard ship. 2. To maintain or retain possession of by force, as a position or an area. 3. In an attack, to exert sufficient pressure to prevent movement or predisposition of enemy forces. 4. As applied to air traffic, to keep an aircraft within a specified space or location which is identified by visual or other means in accordance with Air Traffic Control instructions. Fix.

Holding attack: An attack designed to hold the enemy in position, to deceive the enemy as to where the main attack is being made, to prevent the enemy from reinforcing the elements opposing the main attack, and/ or to cause the enemy to commit the reserves prematurely at an indecisive location.

Holding point: A geographically or electronically defined location used in stationing aircraft in flight in a predetermined pattern in accordance with air traffic control clearance. Orbit point.

Holding position: A specified location on the airfield, close to the active runway and identified by visual means, at which the position of a taxiing aircraft is maintained in accordance with air traffic control instructions.

Homeland: The physical region that includes the continental United States, Alaska, Hawaii, United States possessions and territories, and surrounding territorial waters and airspace.

Homeland defense: The protection of United States sovereignty, territory, domestic population, and critical defense infrastructure against external threats and aggression or other threats as directed by the President. HD.

Homeland security: A concerted national effort to prevent terrorist attacks within the United States; reduce America's vulnerability to terrorism, major disasters, and other emergencies; and minimize the damage and recover from attacks, major disasters, and other emergencies that occur. HS.

Home recovery mission profile: A mission profile that involves the recovery of an aircraft at its permanent or temporarily assigned operating base.

Home station: The permanent location of active duty units and Reserve Component units (e.g., location of armory or reserve center). Active duty; Reserve Components.

Homing: The technique whereby a mobile station directs itself, or is directed, towards a source of primary or reflected energy, or to a specified point.

Homing guidance: A system by which a missile or torpedo steers itself towards a target by means of a self-contained mechanism which is activated by some distinguishing characteristics of the target. Active homing guidance; passive homing guidance; semi-active homing guidance.

Homing mine: In naval mine warfare, a mine fitted with propulsion equipment which homes on to a target.

Horizon: In general, the apparent or visible junction of the Earth and sky, as seen from any specific position. Also called the apparent, visible, or local horizon. A horizontal plane passing through a point of vision or perspective center. The apparent or visible horizon approximates the true horizon only when the point of vision is very close to sea level.

Horizontal action mine: In land mine warfare, a mine designed to produce a destructive effect in a plane approximately parallel to the ground.

Horizontal error: The error in range, deflection, or in radius, which a weapon may be expected to exceed as often as not. Horizontal error of weapons making a nearly vertical approach to the target is described in terms of circular error probable. Horizontal error of weapons producing elliptical dispersion pattern is expressed in terms of probable error. Circular error probable; delivery error; deviation; dispersion error.

Horizontal loading: Loading of items of like character in horizontal layers throughout the holds of a ship. Loading.

Horizontal situation display: An electronically generated display on which navigation information and stored mission and procedural data can be presented. Radar information and television picture can also be displayed either as a map overlay or as a separate image. Head-up display.

Horizontal situation indicator: An instrument which may display bearing and distance to a navigation aid, magnetic heading, track/course and track/course deviation.

Horizontal stowage: The lateral distribution of unit equipment or categories of supplies so that they can be unloaded simultaneously from two or more holds.

Horn: In naval mine warfare, a projection from the mine shell of some contact mines which, when broken or bent by contact, causes the mine to fire.

Hospital: A medical treatment facility capable of providing inpatient care. It is appropriately staffed and equipped to provide diagnostic and therapeutic services, as well as the necessary supporting services required to perform its assigned mission and functions. A hospital may, in addition, discharge the functions of a clinic.

Hostage: A person held as a pledge that certain terms or agreements will be kept.

Hostage rescue: A personnel recovery method used to recover isolated personnel who are specifically designated as hostages. Also called HR.

Host country: A nation which permits, either by written agreement or official invitation, government representatives and/or agencies of another nation to operate, under specified conditions, within its borders.

Hostile: In combat and combat support operations, an identity applied to a track declared to belong to any opposing nation, party, group, or entity, which by virtue of its behavior or information collected on it such as characteristics, origin, or nationality contributes to the threat to friendly forces. See also neutral; suspect; unknown.

Hostile act: An attack or other use of force against the US, US forces, or other designated persons or property. It also includes force used directly to preclude or impede the mission and/or duties of US forces, including the recovery of US personnel or vital US Government property.

Hostile casualty: A person who is the victim of a terrorist activity or who becomes a casualty "in action." "In action" characterizes the casualty as having been the direct result of hostile action, sustained in combat or relating thereto, or sustained going to or returning from a combat mission provided that the occurrence was directly related to hostile action. Included are persons killed or wounded mistakenly or accidentally by friendly fire directed at a hostile force or what is thought to be a hostile force. However, not to be considered as sustained in action and not to be interpreted as hostile casualties are injuries or death due to the elements, self-inflicted wounds, combat fatigue, and except in unusual cases, wounds or death inflicted by a friendly force while the individual is in an absent-without-leave, deserter, or dropped-from-rolls status or is voluntarily absent from a place of duty. Casualty; casualty type; non hostile casualty.

Hostile environment: Operational environment in which hostile forces have control as well as the intent and capability to effectively oppose or react to the operations a unit intends to conduct.

Hostile force: Any civilian, paramilitary, or military force or terrorist(s), with or without national designation, that have committed a hostile act, exhibited hostile intent, or have been declared hostile by appropriate US authority.

Hostile intent: The threat of imminent use of force by a foreign force, terrorist(s), or organization against the United States and US national interests, US forces and, in certain circumstances, US nationals, their property, US commercial assets, and other designated non-US forces, foreign nationals, and their property. When hostile intent is present, the right exists to use proportional force, including armed force, in self-defense by all necessary means available to deter or neutralize the potential attacker or, if necessary, to destroy the threat. A determination that hostile intent exists and requires the use of proportional force in self-defense must be based on evidence that an attack is imminent. Evidence necessary to determine hostile intent will vary depending on the state of international and regional political tension, military preparations, intelligence, and indications and warning information.

Host nation: A nation which receives the forces and/or supplies of allied nations and/or NATO organizations to be located on, to operate in, or to transit through its territory. HN.

Host-nation support: Civil and/or military assistance rendered by a nation to foreign forces within its territory during peacetime, crises or emergencies, or war based on agreements mutually concluded between nations. HNS. Host nation.

Host-nation support agreement: Basic agreement normally concluded at government-to-government or government- to-combatant commander level. These agreements may include general agreements, umbrella agreements, and memoranda of understanding. Host nation; host-nation support.

Hot spot: Region in a contaminated area in which the level of radioactive contamination is considerably greater than in neighboring regions in the area.

Hovering: A self-sustaining maneuver whereby a fixed, or nearly fixed, position is maintained relative to a spot on the surface of the Earth or underwater.

Hovering ceiling: The highest altitude at which the helicopter is capable of hovering in standard atmosphere. It is usually stated in two figures: hovering in ground effect and hovering out of ground effect.

Howitzer: 1. A cannon that combines certain characteristics of guns and mortars. The howitzer delivers projectiles with medium velocities, either by low or high trajectories. 2. Normally a cannon with a tube length of 20 to 30 calibers; however, the tube length can exceed 30 calibers and still be considered a howitzer when the high angle fire zoning solution permits range overlap between charges. gun; mortar.

Hub: An organization that sorts and distributes inbound cargo from wholesale supply sources (airlifted, sea lifted, and ground transportable) and/or from within the theater. Hub and spoke distribution; spoke.

Hub and spoke distribution: A physical distribution system developed and modeled on industry standards to provide cargo management for a theater. It is based on a "hub" moving cargo to and between several "spokes". It is designed to increase transportation efficiencies and in-transit visibility and reduce order ship time. Distribution; distribution system; hub; in-transit visibility; spoke.

Human factors: The psychological, cultural, behavioral, and other human attributes that influence decision-making, the flow of information, and the interpretation of information by individuals or groups.

Human intelligence: A category of intelligence derived from information collected and provided by human sources. HUMINT. human resources intelligence.

Humanitarian and civic assistance: -Assistance to the local populace provided by predominantly US forces in conjunction with military operations and exercises. This assistance is specifically authorized by Title 10, United States Code, section 401 and funded under separate authorities. HCA. Foreign humanitarian assistance.

Humanitarian assistance coordination center: A temporary center established by a geographic combatant commander to assist with interagency coordination and planning. A humanitarian assistance coordination center operates during the early planning and coordination stages of foreign humanitarian assistance operations by providing the link between the geographic combatant commander and other United States Government agencies, nongovernmental organizations, and international and regional organizations at the strategic level. HACC. Foreign humanitarian assistance; interagency coordination.

Humanitarian demining assistance: The activities related to the furnishing of education, training, and technical assistance with respect to the detection and clearance of land mines and other explosive remnants of war.

Humanitarian mine action: Activities that strive to reduce the social, economic, and environmental impact of land mines, unexploded ordnance and small arms ammunition - also characterized as explosive remnants of war.

Human resources intelligence: The intelligence derived from the intelligence collection discipline that uses human beings as both sources and collectors, and where the human being is the primary collection instrument. HUMINT.

Hung ordnance: Those weapons or stores on an aircraft that the pilot has attempted to drop or fire but could not because of a malfunction of the weapon, rack or launcher, or aircraft release and control system.

Hunter track: In naval mine warfare, the track to be followed by the hunter to ensure that the hunting gear passes over the lap track.

Hydrogen bomb: thermonuclear weapon.

Hydrographic chart: A nautical chart showing depths of water, nature of bottom, contours of bottom and coastline, and tides and currents in a given sea or sea and land area.

Hydrographic reconnaissance: Reconnaissance of an area of water to determine depths, beach gradients, the nature of the bottom, and the location of coral reefs, rocks, shoals, and manmade obstacles.

Hyperbaric chamber: A chamber used to induce an increase in ambient pressure as would occur in descending below sea level, in a water or air environment. It is the only type of chamber suitable for use in the treatment of decompression sickness in flying or diving. Compression chamber; diving chamber; recompression chamber.

Hyperbolic navigation system: A radio navigation system which enables the position of an aircraft equipped with a suitable receiver to be fixed by two or more intersecting hyperbolic position lines. The system employs either a time difference measurement of pulse transmissions or a phase difference measurement of phase-locked continuous wave transmissions. loran.

Hypergolic fuel: Fuel which will spontaneously ignite with an oxidizer, such as aniline with fuming nitric acid. It is used as the propulsion agent in certain missile systems.

Hypersonic: Of or pertaining to speeds equal to, or in excess of, five times the speed of sound. Speed of sound.

Hyperspectral imagery: Term used to describe the imagery derived from subdividing the electromagnetic spectrum into very narrow bandwidths. These narrow bandwidths may be combined with or subtracted from each other in various ways to form images useful in precise terrain or target analysis. HSI.

Hyperstereoscopy: Stereoscopic viewing in which the relief effect is noticeably

exaggerated, caused by the extension of the camera base. Exaggerated stereoscopy.

Hypobaric chamber: A chamber used to induce a decrease in ambient pressure as would occur in ascending to altitude. This type of chamber is primarily used for

training and experimental purposes. Altitude chamber; decompression chamber.

Hypsometric tinting: A method of showing relief on maps and charts bycoloring in different shades those parts which lie between selected levels. Altitude tint; elevation tint; layer tint.

I

Identification: 1. The process of determining the friendly or hostile character of an unknown detected contact. 2. In arms control, the process of determining which nation is responsible for the detected violations of any arms control measure. 3. In ground combat operations, discrimination between recognizable objects as being friendly or enemy, or the name that belongs to the object as a member of a class. ID.

Identification, friend or foe: A device that emits a signal positively identifying it as a friendly. IFF. Air defense.

Identification, friend or foe code: The discrete identification friend or foe code assigned to a particular aircraft, ship, or other vehicle for identification by electronic means.

Identification, friend or foe/selective identification feature procedures: The directives that govern the use of identification, friend or foe selective identification feature equipment. identification, friend or foe.

Identification maneuver: A maneuver performed for identification purposes.

Igloo space: Area in an earth-covered structure of concrete and/or steel designed for the storage of ammunition and explosives. Storage.

Image format: Actual size of negative, scope, or other medium on which image is produced.

Image motion compensation: Movement intentionally imparted to film at such a rate as to compensate for the forward motion of an air or space vehicle when photographing ground objects.

Imagery: A likeness or presentation of any natural or manmade feature or related object or activity, and the positional data acquired at the same time the likeness or representation was acquired, including: products produced by space-based national intelligence reconnaissance systems; and likeness and presentations produced by satellites, airborne platforms, unmanned aerial vehicles, or other similar means

Imagery collateral: The reference materials which support the imagery interpretation function.

Imagery correlation: The mutual relationship between the different signatures on imagery from different types of sensors in terms of position and the physical characteristics signified.

Imagery data recording: The transposing of information relating to the airborne vehicle and sensor, such as speed, height, tilt, position, and time, to the matrix block on the sensor record at the moment of image acquisition.

Imagery exploitation: The cycle of processing and printing imagery to the positive or negative state, assembly into imagery packs, identification, interpretation, mensuration, information extraction, the preparation of reports, and the dissemination of information.

Imagery intelligence: The technical, geographic, and intelligence information derived through the interpretation or analysis of imagery and collateral materials. IMINT. Intelligence; photographic intelligence.

Imagery interpretation: 1. The process of location, recognition, identification, and description of objects, activities, and terrain represented on imagery. 2. The extraction of information from photographs or other recorded images. photographic interpretation.

Imagery interpretation key: Any diagram, chart, table, list, or set of examples, etc., which is used to aid imagery interpreters in the rapid identification of objects visible on imagery.

Imagery pack: An assembly of the records from different imagery sensors covering a common target area.

Imitative communications deception: That division of deception involving the introduction of false or misleading but plausible communications into target systems that mimics or imitates the targeted communications. Deception; target system.

Imitative electromagnetic deception: electromagnetic deception. immediate airlift requests. Requests generated that, due to their time-critical nature, cannot be filled by a planned mission.

Immediate air support: Air support to meet specific requests which arise during the course of a battle and which by their nature cannot be planned in advance. Air support.

Immediate decontamination: Decontamination carried out by individuals immediately upon becoming contaminated to save lives, minimize casualties, and limit the spread of contamination. This may include decontamination of some personal clothing and/or equipment. Emergency decontamination. contamination; decontamination.

Immediate destination: The next destination of a ship or convoy, irrespective of whether or not onward routing instructions have been issued to it.

Immediate message: A category of precedence reserved for messages relating to situations that gravely affect the security of national and multinational forces or populace and that require immediate delivery to the addressee(s). Precedence.

Immediate mission request: A request for an air strike on a target that, by its nature, could not be identified sufficiently in advance to permit detailed mission coordination and planning. Preplanned mission request.

Immediate nuclear support: Nuclear support to meet specific requests that arise during the course of a battle, and that by their nature, cannot be planned in advance. Nuclear support; preplanned nuclear support.

Immediate operational readiness: Those operations directly related to the assumption of an alert or quick-reaction posture. Typical operations include strip alert, airborne alert and/or indoctrination, no-notice launch of an alert force, and the maintenance of missiles in an alert configuration. Nuclear weapon exercise; nuclear weapon maneuver.

Immediate response: Any form of immediate action taken to save lives, prevent human suffering, or mitigate great property damage under imminently serious conditions when time does not permit approval from a higher authority.

Impact action fuze: A fuze that is set in action by the striking of a projectile or bomb against an object, e.g., percussion fuze, contact fuze. Direct action fuze.

Impact area: An area having designated boundaries within the limits of which all ordnance will detonate or impact.

Impact pressure: The difference between pitot pressure and static pressure.

Implementation: Procedures governing the mobilization of the force and the deployment, employment, and sustainment of military operations in response to execution orders issued by the Secretary of Defense. IMP.

Implied task: In the context of joint operation planning, a task derived during mission analysis that an organization must perform or prepare to perform to accomplish a specified task or the mission, but which is not stated in the higher headquarters order. Essential task; specified task.

Implosion weapon: A weapon in which a quantity of fissionable material, less than a critical mass at ordinary pressure, has its volume suddenly reduced by compression so that it becomes supercritical, producing a nuclear explosion.

Imprest fund: A cash fund of a fixed amount established through an advance of funds, without appropriation change, to an authorized imprest fund cashier to effect immediate cash payments of relatively small amounts for authorized purchases of supplies and nonpersonal services.

Imprest funds: Funds issued by Army and Air Force Exchange Service (AAFES) to a military organization to purchase beginning inventory for the operation of an AAFES imprest fund activity. Army and Air Force Exchange Service imprest fund activity.

Imprint: Brief note in the margin of a map giving all or some of the following: date of publication, printing, name of publisher, printer, place of publication, number of copies printed, and related information.

Improved conventional munitions: Munitions characterized by the delivery of two or more antipersonnel or antimateriel and/or antiarmour sub munitions by a warhead or projectile.

Improvised early resupply: The onward movement of commodities which are available on land and which can be readily loaded into ships.

Improvised explosive device: A device placed or fabricated in an improvised manner incorporating destructive, lethal, noxious, pyrotechnic, or incendiary chemicals and designed to destroy, incapacitate, harass, or distract. It may incorporate military stores, but is normally devised from nonmilitary components. IED.

Improvised mine: A mine fabricated from available materials at or near its point of use.

Inactive aircraft inventory: Aircraft in storage or bailment and/ or government- furnished equipment on loan or lease outside of the Defense establishment or otherwise not available to the Military Services.

Inactive duty training: Authorized training performed by a member of a Reserve Component not on active duty or active duty for training and consisting of regularly scheduled unit training assemblies, additional training assemblies, periods of appropriate duty or equivalent training, and any special additional duties authorized for Reserve Component personnel by the Secretary concerned, and performed by them in connection with the prescribed activities of the organization in which they are assigned with or without pay. Does not include work or study associated with correspondence courses. IDT. Active duty for training.

Inactive National Guard: Army National Guard personnel in an inactive status not in the Selected Reserve who are attached to a specific National Guard unit but do not participate in training activities. Upon mobilization, they will mobilize with their units. In order for these personnel to remain members of the Inactive National Guard, they must muster once a year with their assigned unit. Like the Individual Ready Reserve, all members of the Inactive National Guard have legal, contractual obligations. Members of the Inactive National Guard may not train for retirement credit or pay and are not eligible for promotion. ING. Individual Ready Reserve; Selected Reserve.

Inactive status: Status of reserve members on an inactive status list of a Reserve Component or assigned to the Inactive Army National Guard. Those in an inactive status may not train for points or pay, and may not be considered for promotion.

Inbound traffic: Traffic originating in an area outside the continental United States destined for or moving in the general direction of the continental United States.

Incapacitating agent: A chemical agent, which produces temporary disabling conditions which (unlike those caused by riot control agents) can be physical or mental and persist for hours or days after exposure to the agent has ceased.

Incapacitating illness or injury: The casualty status of a person (a) whose illness or injury requires hospitalization but medical authority does not classify as very seriously ill or injured; or (b) seriously ill or injured and the illness or injury makes the person physically or mentally unable to communicate with the next of kin. III. Casualty status.

Incident: 1. In information operations, an assessed event of attempted entry, unauthorized entry, or an information attack on an automated information system. It includes unauthorized probing and browsing; disruption or denial of service; altered or destroyed input, processing, storage, or output of information; or changes to information system hardware, firmware, or software characteristics with or without the users' knowledge, instruction, or intent. 2. An occurrence, caused by either human action or natural phenomena, that requires action to prevent or minimize loss of life or damage to property and/or natural resources. Information operations.

Incident classification: Search and rescue incident classification.

Incident command post: The field location at which the primary tactical-level on-scene incident command functions are performed. It may be collocated with the incident base or other incident facilities and is normally identified by a green rotating or flashing light. ICP. Antiterrorism.

Incident command system: A standardized on-scene emergency management construct designed to aid in the management of resources during incidents. Consists of facilities, equipment, personnel, procedures, and communications established for this purpose. ICS.

Incident management: A national comprehensive approach to preventing, preparing for, responding to, and recovering from terrorist attacks, major disasters, and other emergencies. Incident management includes measures and activities performed at the local, state, and national levels and includes both crisis and consequence management activities.

Incident of national significance: An actual or potential high-impact event that requires a coordinated and effective response by and appropriate combination of Federal, state, local, tribal, nongovernmental, and/or private-sector entities in order to save lives and minimize damage, and provide the basis for long-term community recovery and mitigation activities.

Incidents: Brief clashes or other military disturbances generally of a transitory nature and not involving protracted hostilities.

In-company: Two or more units proceeding together under the command of a designated senior.

Incremental costs: Costs which are additional costs to the Service appropriations that would not have been incurred absent support of the contingency operation. Financial management.

Indefinite call sign: A call sign which does not represent a specific facility, command, authority, activity, or unit, but which may represent any one or any group of these. Call sign.

Independent: A merchant ship under naval control sailed singly and unescorted by a warship. Military independent.

Independent government estimate: The government's estimate of the resources and projected cost of the resources a contractor will incur in the performance of the contract. IGE.

Independent mine: A mine which is not controlled by the user after laying.

Independent review: In computer modeling and simulation, a review performed by competent, objective reviewers who are independent of the model developer. Independent review includes either (a) a detailed verification and/or validation of the model or simulation; or (b) an examination of the verification and/or validation performed by the model or simulation developer. Configuration management; validation; verification.

Indications: In intelligence usage, information in various degrees of evaluation, all of which bear on the intention of a potential enemy to adopt or reject a course of action.

Indications and warning: Those intelligence activities intended to detect and report time sensitive intelligence information on foreign developments that could involve a threat to the United States or allied and/or coalition military, political, or economic interests or to US citizens abroad. It includes forewarning of hostile actions or intentions against the United States, its activities, overseas forces, or allied and/or coalition nations. I&W. Information; intelligence.

Indicator: In intelligence usage, an item of information which reflects the intention or capability of an adversary to adopt or reject a course of action.

Indigenous populations and institutions: A generic term used to describe the civilian construct of an operational area to include its populations (legal citizens, legal and illegal immigrants, and all categories of dislocated civilians), governmental, tribal, commercial, and private organizations and entities. IPI.

Indirect fire: Fire delivered on a target that is not itself used as a point of aim for the weapons or the director.

Indirect laying: Aiming a gun either by sighting at a fixed object, called the aiming point, instead of the target or by using a means of pointing other than a sight, such as a gun director, when the target cannot be seen from the gun position.

Individual equipment: Referring to method of use: signifies personal clothing and equipment, for the personal use of the individual. Equipment.

Individual mobilization augmentee detachment: An administrative unit organized to train and manage individual mobilization augmentees.

Individual protective equipment: In chemical, biological, radiological, or nuclear

operations, the personal clothing and equipment required to protect an individual from chemical, biological, and radiological hazards and some nuclear hazards. IPE.

Individual Ready Reserve: A manpower pool consisting of individuals who have had some training or who have served previously in the Active Component or in the Selected Reserve, and may have some period of their military service obligation remaining. Members may voluntarily participate in training for retirement points and promotion with or without pay. IRR. Selected Reserve.

Individual reserves: The supplies carried on a soldier, animal, or vehicle for individual use in an emergency. See also reserve supplies.

Individual sponsored dependent: A dependent not entitled to travel to the overseas command at Government expense or who enters the command without endorsement of the appropriate overseas commander.

Induced environment: Any manmade or equipment-made environment that directly or indirectly affects the performance of man or materiel.

Induced radiation: Radiation produced as a result of exposure to radioactive

materials, particularly the capture of neutrons. Contamination; initial radiation; residual radiation; residual radioactivity.

Induction circuit: In naval mine warfare, a circuit actuated by the rate of change in a magnetic field due to the movement of the ship or the changing current in the sweep.

Industrial mobilization: The transformation of industry from its peacetime activity to the industrial program necessary to support the national military objectives. It includes the mobilization of materials, labor, capital, production facilities, and contributory items and services essential to the industrial program. Mobilization.

Industrial preparedness: The state of preparedness of industry to produce essential materiel to support the national military objectives.

Inert filling: A prepared non-explosive filling of the same weight as the explosive

filling.

Inertial guidance: A guidance system designed to project a missile over a predetermined path, wherein the path of the missile is adjusted after launching by devices wholly within the missile and independent of outside information. The system measures and converts accelerations experienced to distance traveled in a certain direction.

Inertial navigation system: A self-contained navigation system using inertial

detectors, which automatically provides vehicle position, heading, and velocity. INS.

Inert mine: A mine or replica of a mine incapable of producing an explosion. in extremis – A situation of such exceptional urgency that immediate action must be taken to minimize imminent loss of life or catastrophic degradation of the political or military situation.

Infiltration: 1. The movement through or into an area or territory occupied by either friendly or enemy troops or organizations. The movement is made, either by small groups or by individuals, at extended or irregular intervals. When used in connection with the enemy, it implies that contact is avoided. 2. In intelligence usage, placing an agent or other person in a target area in hostile territory. Usually involves crossing a frontier or other guarded line. Methods of infiltration are: black (clandestine); grey (through legal crossing point but under false documentation); and white (legal).

Inflammable cargo: Cargo such as drummed gasoline and oils.

In-flight phase: The flight of a missile or space vehicle from launch to detonation or impact.

In-flight report: The transmission from the airborne system of information obtained both at the target and en route.

Influence field: The distribution in space of the influence of a ship or minesweeping equipment.

Influence mine: A mine actuated by the effect of a target on some physical condition in the vicinity of the mine or on radiations emanating from the mine.

Influence release sinker: A sinker which holds a moored or rising mine at the sea-bed and releases it when actuated by a suitable ship influence.

Influence sweep: A sweep designed to produce an influence similar to that produced by a ship and thus actuate mines.

Information: 1. Facts, data, or instructions in any medium or form. 2. The meaning that a human assigns to data by means of the known conventions used in their representation.

Information assurance — Measures that protect and defend information and information systems by ensuring their availability, integrity, authentication, confidentiality, and nonrepudiation. This includes providing for restoration of information systems by incorporating protection, detection, and reaction capabilities. IA. Information; information operations; information system.

Information-based processes: Processes that collect, analyze, and disseminate

information using any medium or form. These processes may be stand-alone processes or subprocesses that, taken together, comprise a larger system or systems of processes. Information system.

Information box: A space on an annotated overlay, mosaic, map, etc., which is used for identification, reference, and scale information.

Information environment: The aggregate of individuals, organizations, and systems that collect, process, disseminate, or act on information. Information system.

Information management: The function of managing an organization's information resources by the handling of knowledge acquired by one or many different individuals and organizations in a way that optimizes access by all who have a share in that knowledge or a right to that knowledge.

Information operations: The integrated employment of the core capabilities of electronic warfare, computer network operations, psychological operations, military deception, and operations security, in concert with specified supporting and related capabilities, to influence, disrupt, corrupt or usurp adversarial human and automated decision making while protecting our own. IO. Computer network operations; electronic warfare; military deception; operations security; psychological operations.

Information report: Report used to forward raw information collected to fulfill intelligence requirements.

Information requirements: In intelligence usage, those items of information regarding the adversary and other relevant aspects of the operational environment that need to be collected and processed in order to meet the intelligence requirements of a commander. Priority intelligence requirement.

Information resources: Information and related resources, such as personnel, equipment, and information technology. Information.

Information security: The protection of information and information systems against unauthorized access or modification of information, whether in storage, processing, or transit, and against denial of service to authorized users. INFOSEC. Information system.

Information superiority: The operational advantage derived from the ability to collect, process, and disseminate an uninterrupted flow of information while exploiting or denying an adversary's ability to do the same. Information operations.

Information system: The entire infrastructure, organization, personnel, and components for the collection, processing, storage, transmission, display, dissemination, and disposition of information. Information; information operations.

Infrared imagery: That imagery produced as a result of sensing electromagnetic radiations emitted or reflected from a given target surface in the infrared position of the electromagnetic spectrum (approximately 0.72 to 1,000 microns).

Infrared line scan system: A passive airborne infrared recording system which scans across the ground beneath the flight path, adding successive lines to the record as the vehicle advances along the flight path. As Amended Through 17 March 2009

Infrared photography: Photography employing an optical system and direct image recording on film sensitive to near-infrared wavelength (infrared film). (Note: Not to be confused with "infrared imagery.")

Infrared pointer: A low power laser device operating in the near infrared light spectrum that is visible with light amplifying night vision devices. IR pointer.

Infrared radiation: Radiation emitted or reflected in the infrared portion of the electromagnetic spectrum.

Infrastructure: All building and permanent installations necessary for the support, redeployment, and military forces operations. Bilateral infrastructure; common infrastructure; national infrastructure.

Initial assessment: An assessment that provides a basic determination of the viability of the infiltration and Exfiltration portion of a proposed special operations forces mission. IA.

Initial draft plan: A plan which has been drafted and coordinated by the originating headquarters, and is ready for external coordination with other military headquarters. It cannot be directly implemented by the issuing commander, but it may form the basis for an operation order issued by the commander in the event of an emergency. Coordinated draft plan; draft plan; final plan; operation plan.

Initial early resupply: The onward movement of ships which are already loaded with cargoes which will serve the requirements after D-day. This includes such shipping deployed from major ports/major water terminals and subsequently dispersed to secondary ports/alternate water terminals and anchorages.

Initial entry into Military Service: Entry for the first time into military status induction, enlistment, or appointment in any Service of the Armed Forces of the United States. Appointment may be as a commissioned or warrant officer; as a cadet or midshipman at the Service academy of one of the armed forces; or as a midshipman, US Naval Reserve, for US Naval Reserve Officers' Training Corps training at a civilian institution.

Initial issues: The issue of materiel not previously furnished to an individual or organization, including new inductees and newly activated organizations, and the issue of newly authorized items of materiel.

Initial operational capability: The first attainment of the capability to employ effectively a weapon, item of equipment, or system of approved specific characteristics that is manned or operated by an adequately trained, equipped, and supported military unit or force. IOC.

Initial path sweeping: In naval mine warfare, initial sweeping to clear a path through a mined area dangerous to the following mine sweepers. Precursor sweeping.

Initial photo interpretation report: A first-phase interpretation report, subsequent to the Joint Tactical Air Reconnaissance/Surveillance Mission Report, presenting the results of the initial readout of new imagery to answer the specific requirements for which the mission was requested.

Initial point: 1. The first point at which a moving target is located on a plotting board. 2. A well-defined point, easily distinguishable visually and/or electronically, used as a starting point for the bomb run to the target. 3. airborne – A point close to the landing area where serials (troop carrier air formations) make final alterations in course to pass over individual drop or landing zones. 4. helicopter – An air control point in the vicinity of the landing zone from which individual flights of helicopters are directed to their prescribed landing sites. 5. Any designated place at which a column or element thereof is formed by the successive arrival of its various subdivisions, and comes under the control of the commander ordering the move. IP. Target approach point.

Initial programmed interpretation report: A standardized imagery interpretation report providing information on programmed mission objectives or other vital intelligence information which can be readily identified near these objectives, and which has not been reported elsewhere. IPIR.

Initial provisioning: The process of determining the range and quantity of items (i.e., spares and repair parts, special tools, test equipment, and support equipment) required to support and maintain an item for an initial period of service. Its phases include the identification of items of supply, the establishment of data for catalog, technical manual, and allowance list preparation, and the preparation of instructions to assure delivery of necessary support items with related end articles.

Initial radiation: The radiation, essentially neutrons and gamma rays, resulting from a nuclear burst and emitted from the fireball within one minute after burst. Induced radiation; residual radiation.

Initial reception point: In personnel recovery, a secure area or facility under friendly control where initial reception of recovered isolated personnel can safely take place. This point is ideally associated with a medical treatment facility, can safeguard recovered isolated personnel for up to 48 hours, and is where the reintegration process begins.

initial reserves: In amphibious operations, those supplies that normally are unloaded immediately following the assault waves; usually the supplies for the use of the beach organization, battalion landing teams, and other elements of regimental combat teams for the purpose of initiating and sustaining combat until higher supply installations are established. See also reserve supplies.

Initial response force: The first unit, usually military police, on the scene of a terrorist incident. Antiterrorism.

Initial unloading period: In amphibious operations, that part of the ship-to-shore movement in which unloading is primarily tactical in character and must be instantly responsive to landing force requirements. All elements intended to land during this period are serialized. See also general unloading period.

Initiating directive: An order to a subordinate commander to conduct military operations as directed. It is issued by the unified commander, sub unified commander, Service component commander, or joint force commander delegated overall responsibility for the operation.

Injury: A term comprising such conditions as fractures, wounds, sprains, strains, dislocations, concussions, and compressions. In addition, it includes conditions resulting from extremes of temperature or prolonged exposure. Acute poisonings (except those due to contaminated food) resulting from exposure to a toxic or poisonous substance are also classed as injuries. See also casualty; wounded.

Inland search and rescue region: The inland areas of the continental United States, except waters under the jurisdiction of the United States. Search and rescue region.

Inner transport area: In amphibious operations, an area as close to the landing beach as depth of water, navigational hazards, boat traffic, and enemy action permit, to which transports may move to expedite unloading. Outer transport area; transport area.

Innocent passage: The right of all ships to engage in continuous and expeditious surface passage through the territorial sea and archipelagic waters of foreign coastal states in a manner not prejudicial to its peace, good order, or security. Passage includes stopping and anchoring, but only if incidental to ordinary navigation or necessary by force majeure or distress, or for the purpose of rendering assistance to persons, ships, or aircraft in danger or distress.

Inshore patrol: A naval defense patrol operating generally within a naval defense coastal area and comprising all elements of harbor defenses, the coastal lookout system, patrol craft supporting bases, aircraft, and Coast Guard stations.

Inspection: In arms control, physical process of determining compliance with arms control measures.

Installation: A grouping of facilities, located in the same vicinity, which support particular functions. Installations may be elements of a base. Base; base complex.

Installation commander: The individual responsible for all operations performed by an installation. Antiterrorism; base commander; installation.

Installation complex: In the Air Force, a combination of land and facilities comprised of a main installation and its noncontiguous properties (auxiliary air fields, annexes, and missile fields) that provide direct support to or are supported by that installation. Installation complexes may comprise two or more properties, e.g., a major installation, a minor installation, or a support site, each with its associated annex(es) or support property(ies). Minor installation.

Instructional mine: An inert mine used for instruction and normally sectionalized for this purpose.

Instrument approach procedure: A series of predetermined maneuvers for the orderly transfer of an aircraft under instrument flight conditions from the beginning of the initial approach to a landing or to a point from which a landing may be made visually or the missed approach procedure is initiated.

Instrument meteorological conditions: Meteorological conditions expressed in terms of visibility, distance from cloud, and ceiling; less than minimums specified for visual meteorological conditions. IMC. Visual meteorological conditions.

Instruments of national power: All of the means available to the government in its pursuit of national objectives. They are expressed as diplomatic, economic, informational and military.

In support: An expression used to denote the task of providing artillery supporting fire to a formation or unit. Liaison and observation are not normally provided. At priority call; direct support.

In support of: Assisting or protecting another formation, unit, or organization while remaining under original control.

Insurgency: An organized movement aimed at the overthrow of a constituted government through use of subversion and armed conflict.

Insurgent: Member of a political party who rebels against established leadership. Antiterrorism; counterinsurgency; insurgency.

Integrated fire control system: A system that performs the functions of target acquisition, tracking, data computation, and engagement control, primarily using electronic means and assisted by electromechanical devices.

Integrated logistic support: A composite of all the support considerations necessary to assure the effective and economical support of a system for its life cycle. It is an integral part of all other aspects of system acquisition and operation. ILS.

Integrated materiel management: The exercise of total Department of Defense-level management responsibility for a federal supply group or class, commodity, or item for a single agency. It normally includes computation of requirements, funding, budgeting, storing, issuing, cataloging, standardizing, and procuring functions. IMM. Materiel; materiel management.

Integrated planning: In amphibious operations, the planning accomplished by commanders and staffs of corresponding echelons from parallel chains of command within the amphibious task force. Amphibious operation; amphibious task force.

Integrated priority list: A list of a combatant commander's highest priority requirements, prioritized across Service and functional lines, defining shortfalls in key programs that, in the judgment of the combatant commander, adversely affect the capability of the combatant commander's forces to accomplish their assigned mission. The integrated priority list provides the combatant commander's recommendations for programming funds in the planning, programming, and budgeting system process. IPL.

Integrated staff: A staff in which one officer only is appointed to each post on the establishment of the headquarters, irrespective of nationality and Service. Multinational staff; joint staff; parallel staff; staff.

Integrated warfare: The conduct of military operations in any combat environment wherein opposing forces employ non-conventional weapons in combination with conventional weapons.

Integration: 1. In force protection, the synchronized transfer of units into an operational commander's force prior to mission execution. 2. The arrangement of military forces and their actions to create a force that operates by engaging as a whole. 3. In photography, a process by which the average radar picture seen on several scans of the time base may be obtained on a print, or the process by which several photographic images are combined into a single image. Force protection.

Intelligence: The product resulting from the collection, processing, integration,

evaluation, analysis, and interpretation of available information concerning foreign nations, hostile or potentially hostile forces or elements, or areas of actual or potential operations. The term is also applied to the activity which results in the product and to the organizations engaged in such activity. Acoustic intelligence; all-source intelligence; basic intelligence; civil defense intelligence; combat intelligence; communications intelligence; critical intelligence; current intelligence; departmental intelligence; domestic intelligence; electronic intelligence; electro optical intelligence; foreign intelligence; foreign instrumentation signals intelligence; general military intelligence; human resources intelligence; imagery intelligence; joint intelligence; laser intelligence; measurement and signature intelligence; medical intelligence; merchant intelligence; military intelligence; national intelligence; nuclear intelligence; open-source intelligence; operational intelligence; photographic intelligence; political intelligence; radar intelligence; radiation intelligence; scientific and technical intelligence; security intelligence; strategic intelligence; tactical intelligence; target intelligence; technical intelligence; technical operational intelligence; terrain intelligence; unintentional radiation intelligence.

Intelligence annex: A supporting document of an operation plan or order that provides detailed information on the enemy situation, assignment of intelligence tasks, and intelligence administrative procedures.

Intelligence database: The sum of holdings of intelligence data and finished intelligence products at a given organization.

Intelligence data handling systems: Information systems that process and manipulate raw information and intelligence data as required. They are characterized by the application of general purpose computers, peripheral equipment, and automated storage and retrieval equipment for documents and photographs. While automation is a distinguishing characteristic of intelligence data handling systems, individual system components may be either automated or manually operated. IDHS.

Intelligence discipline:- A well defined area of intelligence planning, collection, processing, exploitation, analysis, and reporting using a specific category of technical or human resources. There are seven major disciplines: human intelligence, geospatial intelligence, measurement and signature intelligence, signals intelligence, open-source intelligence, technical intelligence, and counterintelligence. Counterintelligence; human intelligence; imagery intelligence; intelligence; measurement and signature intelligence; open-source intelligence; signals intelligence; technical intelligence.

Intelligence estimate: The appraisal, expressed in writing or orally, of available intelligence relating to a specific situation or condition with a view to determining the courses of action open to the enemy or adversary and the order of probability of their adoption.

Intelligence gathering: Collection of intelligence on other units or forces by own units or forces.

Intelligence information report: The primary vehicle used to provide human intelligence information to the consumer. It utilizes a message format structure that supports automated data entry into intelligence community databases. IIR.

Intelligence interrogation: -The systematic process of using approved interrogation approaches to question a captured or detained person to obtain reliable information to satisfy intelligence requirements, consistent with applicable law.

Intelligence journal: A chronological log of intelligence activities covering a stated period, usually 24 hours. It is an index of reports and messages that have been received and transmitted, important events that have occurred, and actions taken. The journal is a permanent and official record.

Intelligence operations: The variety of intelligence and counterintelligence tasks that are carried out by various intelligence organizations and activities within the intelligence process. Intelligence operations include planning and direction, collection, processing and exploitation, analysis and production, dissemination and integration, and evaluation and feedback. See also analysis and production; collection; dissemination and integration; evaluation and feedback; planning and direction; processing and exploitation.

Intelligence preparation of the battle space: An analytical methodology employed to reduce uncertainties concerning the enemy, environment, and terrain for all types of operations. Intelligence preparation of the battle space builds an extensive database for each potential area in which a unit may be required to operate. The database is then analyzed in detail to determine the impact of the enemy, environment, and terrain on operations and presents it in graphic form. Intelligence preparation of the battle space is a continuing process.

J

J-2X: The staff element of the intelligence directorate of a joint staff that combines and represents the principal authority for counterintelligence and human intelligence support. counterintelligence; human intelligence.

Jamming: Barrage jamming; electronic attack; electromagnetic jamming; selective jamming; spot jamming.

J-axis: A vertical axis in a system of rectangular coordinates; that line on which distances above or below (north or south) the reference line are marked, especially on a map, chart, or graph.

Jet advisory service: The service provided certain civil aircraft while operating within radar and non radar jet advisory areas. Within radar jet advisory areas, civil aircraft receiving this service are provided radar flight following, radar traffic information, and vectors around observed traffic. In nonradar jet advisory areas, civil aircraft receiving this service are afforded standard instrument flight rules separation from all other aircraft known to air traffic control to be operating within these areas.

Jet stream: A narrow band of high velocity wind in the upper troposphere or in the stratosphere.

Jettison: The selective release of stores from an aircraft other than normal attack.

Jettisoned mines:: Mines which are laid as quickly as possible in order to empty the minelayer of mines, without regard to their condition or relative positions.

Joiner: An independent merchant ship sailed to join a convoy. Joiner convoy; joiner section.

Joiner convoy:- A convoy sailed to join the main convoy. Also joiner; joiner section.

Joiner section: A joiner or joiner convoy, after rendezvous, and while maneuvering to integrate with the main convoy.

Joint: Connotes activities, operations, organizations, etc., in which elements of two or more Military Departments participate.

Joint acquisition review board: A joint task force or sub unified commander established board used to review and make recommendations for controlling critical common-user logistic supplies and services within the joint operational area and to recommend the proper sources of support for approved support requirements. JARB. Combatant commander logistic procurement support board; joint contracting support board.

Joint after action report: A report consisting of summary joint universal lessons learned. It describes a real world operation or training exercise and identifies significant lessons learned. JAAR.

Joint airborne advance party: An advance ground party that provides terminal guidance, air traffic control, ground control measures, intelligence gathering, and surface weather observation in the objective area of an airlift operation. It may consist of US Air Force combat control team members and a US Army long-range surveillance team or similar forces. JAAP.

Joint airborne training: Training operations or exercises involving airborne and

appropriate troop carrier units. This training includes: a. air delivery of personnel and equipment; b. assault operations by airborne troops and/or air transportable units; c. loading exercises and local orientation fights of short duration; and d. maneuvers and/or exercises as agreed upon by Services concerned and/or as authorized by the Joint Chiefs of Staff.

Joint air operations: Air operations performed with air capabilities/forces made available by components in support of the joint force commander's operation or campaign objectives, or in support of other components of the joint force.

Joint air operations center: A jointly staffed facility established for planning, directing, and executing joint air operations in support of the joint force commander's operation or campaign objectives. JAOC. Joint air operations.

Joint air operations plan: A plan for a connected series of joint air operations to achieve the joint force commander's objectives within a given time and joint operational area. JAOP. Joint air operations.

Joint amphibious operation: An amphibious operation conducted by significant elements of two or more Services.

Joint amphibious task force: A temporary grouping of units of two or more Services under a single commander, organized for the purpose of engaging in an amphibious landing for assault on hostile shores. JATF.

Joint base: For purposes of base defense operations, a joint base is a locality from which operations of two or more of the Military Departments are projected or supported and which is manned by significant elements of two or more Military Departments or in which significant elements of two or more Military Departments are located.

Joint captured materiel exploitation center: A physical location for deriving

intelligence information from captured enemy materiel. It is normally subordinate to the joint force. JCMEC.

Joint civil-military operations task force: A joint task force composed of civil-military operations units from more than one Service. It provides support to the joint force commander in humanitarian or nation assistance operations, theater campaigns, or civil-military operations concurrent with or subsequent to regional conflict. It can organize military interaction among many governmental and nongovernmental humanitarian agencies within the theater. JCMOTF. civil military operations; joint task force; task force.

Joint combined exchange training: A program conducted overseas to fulfill US forces training requirements and at the same time exchange the sharing of skills between US forces and host nation counterparts. Training activities are designed to improve US and host nation capabilities. JCET.

Joint communications network: The aggregation of all the joint communications systems in a theater. The joint communications network includes the joint multichannel trunking and switching system and the joint command and control communications system(s). JCN.

Joint deployable intelligence support system: A transportable workstation and communications suite that electronically extends a joint intelligence center to a joint task force or other tactical user. JDISS.

Joint Deployment and Distribution Enterprise: The complex of equipment,

procedures, doctrine, leaders, technical connectivity, information, shared knowledge, organizations, facilities, training, and materiel necessary to conduct joint distribution operations. JDDE.

Joint desired point of impact: A unique, alpha-numeric coded aim point identified by a three dimensional (latitude, longitude, elevation) mensurated point. It represents a weapon or capabilities desired point of impact or penetration and is used as the standard for identifying aim points. JDPI. Aim point; desired point of impact; desired mean point of impact.

Joint doctrine: Fundamental principles that guide the employment of US military forces in coordinated action toward a common objective. Joint doctrine contained in joint publications also includes terms, tactics, techniques, and procedures. It is authoritative but requires judgment in application. Chairman of the Joint Chiefs of Staff instruction; Chairman of the Joint Chiefs of Staff manual; doctrine; joint publication; joint test publication; multinational doctrine.

Joint Doctrine Planning Conference: A forum that meets semiannually to address and vote on project proposals; discuss key joint doctrinal and operational issues; discuss potential changes to the joint doctrine development process; keep up to date on the status of the joint publication projects and emerging publications; and keep abreast of other initiatives of interest to the members. The Joint Doctrine Planning Conference provides recommendations that are approved by the Joint Staff/ J-7, in the name of the Chairman of the Joint Chiefs of Staff. led JDPC.

Joint duty assignment: An assignment to a designated position in a multi-Service, jointor multinational command or activity that is involved in the integrated employment or support of the land, sea, and air forces of at least two of the three Military Departments. Such involvement includes, but is not limited to, matters relating to national military strategy, joint doctrine and policy, strategic planning, contingency planning, and command and control of combat operations under a unified or specified command. JDA.

Joint Duty Assignment List: Positions designated as joint duty assignments are reflected in a list approved by the Secretary of Defense and maintained by the Joint Staff. The Joint Duty Assignment List is reflected in the Joint Duty Assignment Management Information System. JDAL.

Joint Facilities Utilization Board: A joint board that evaluates and reconciles component requests for real estate, use of existing facilities, inter-Service support, and construction to ensure compliance with Joint Civil-Military Engineering Board priorities. JFUB.

Joint field office: A temporary multiagency coordination center established at the incident site to provide a central location for coordination of federal, state, local, tribal, nongovernmental, and private-sector organizations with primary responsibility for incident oversight, direction, and/or assistance to effectively coordinate protection, prevention, preparedness, response, and recovery actions. JFO.

Joint fires: Fires delivered during the employment of forces from two or more components in coordinated action to produce desired effects in support of a common objective. fires.

Joint fires element: An optional staff element that provides recommendations to the operations directorate to accomplish fires planning and synchronization. JFE. Fire support; joint fires.

Joint fire support: Joint fires that assist air, land, maritime, and special operations forces to move, maneuver, and control territory, populations, airspace, and key waters. Fire support; joint fires.

Joint flow and analysis system for transportation: System that determines the transportation feasibility of a course of action or operation plan; provides daily lift assets needed to move forces and resupply; advises logistic planners of channel and port inefficiencies; and interprets shortfalls from various flow possibilities. JFAST. Course of action; operation plan; system.

Joint force: A general term applied to a force composed of significant elements, assigned or attached, of two or more Military Departments operating under a single joint force commander. See also joint force commander.

Joint force commander: A general term applied to a combatant commander, sub unified commander, or joint task force commander authorized to exercise combatant command or operational control over a joint force. JFC. Joint force.

Joint force land component commander: The commander within a unified command, subordinate unified command, or joint task force responsible to the establishing commander for making recommendations on the proper employment of assigned, attached, and/or made available for tasking land forces; planning and coordinating land operations; or accomplishing such operational missions as may be assigned. The joint force land component commander is given the authority necessary to accomplish missions and tasks assigned by the establishing commander. JFLCC. Joint force commander.

Joint force maritime component commander: The commander within a unified command, subordinate unified command, or joint task force responsible to the establishing commander for making recommendations on the proper employment of assigned, attached, and/or made available for tasking maritime forces and assets; planning and coordinating maritime operations; or accomplishing such operational missions as may be assigned. The joint force maritime component commander is given the authority necessary to accomplish missions and tasks assigned by the establishing commander. JFMCC. Joint force commander.

Joint force surgeon: A general term applied to a Department of Defense medical department officer appointed by the joint force commander to serve as the joint force special staff officer responsible for establishing, monitoring, or evaluating joint force health service support. Also called JFS. Health service support; joint force.

Joint functions: Related capabilities and activities grouped together to help joint force commanders synchronize, integrate, and direct joint operations. Functions that are common to joint operations at all levels of war fall into six basic groups — command and control, intelligence, fires, movement and maneuver, protection, and sustainment.

Joint guidance, apportionment, and targeting team: A group that makes recommendations for air apportionment to engage targets, and provides other targeting support requiring component input at the joint force air component commander level. JGAT team. Air apportionment; apportionment; joint force air component commander; targeting.

Joint information bureau: Facility established by the joint force commander to serve as the focal point for the interface between the military and the media during the conduct of joint operations. When operated in support of multinational operations, a joint information bureau is called a "multinational information bureau." JIB. Public affairs.

Joint information system: Integrates incident information and public affairs into a cohesive organization designed to provide consistent, coordinated, timely information during a crisis or incident. JIS.

Joint integrated prioritized target list: A prioritized list of targets approved and maintained by the joint force commander. Targets and priorities are derived from the recommendations of components and other appropriate agencies, in conjunction with their proposed operations supporting the joint force commander's objectives and guidance. JIPTL. Target.

Joint intelligence: Intelligence produced by elements of more than one Service of the same nation.

Joint intelligence architecture: A dynamic, flexible structure that consists of the Defense Joint Intelligence Operations Center, combatant command joint intelligence operations centers, and subordinate joint task force intelligence operations centers or joint intelligence support elements. This architecture encompasses automated data processing equipment capabilities, communications and information requirements, and responsibilities to provide national, theater, and tactical commanders with the full range of intelligence required for planning and conducting operations. Architecture; intelligence.

Joint intelligence liaison element: A liaison element provided by the Central Intelligence Agency in support of a unified command or joint task force.

Joint intelligence operations center: An interdependent, operational intelligence organization at the Department of Defense, combatant command, or joint task force (if established) level, that is integrated with national intelligence centers, and capable of accessing all sources of intelligence impacting military operations planning, execution, and assessment. JIOC.

Joint intelligence support element: A subordinate joint force element whose focus is on intelligence support for joint operations, providing the joint force commander, joint staff, and components with the complete air, space, ground, and maritime adversary situation. JISE. Intelligence; joint force; joint operations.

Joint interagency coordination group: An interagency staff group that establishes regular, timely, and collaborative working relationships between civilian and military operational planners. Composed of US Government civilian and military experts accredited to the combatant commander and tailored to meet the requirements of a supported joint force commander, the joint interagency coordination group provides the joint force commander with the capability to coordinate with other US Government civilian agencies and departments. JIACG.

Joint interface control officer: The senior interface control officer for multi-tactical data link networks in the joint force. Responsible for development and validation of the architecture and the joint interoperability and management of the multi-tactical data link networks. Oversees operations of a joint interface control cell. JICO.

Joint interrogation and debriefing center: Physical location for the exploitation of intelligence information from detainees and other sources. JIDC. Information; intelligence.

Joint interrogation operations: 1. Activities conducted by a joint or interagency organization to extract information for intelligence purposes from enemy prisoners of war, dislocated civilians, enemy combatants, or other uncategorized detainees. 2. Activities conducted in support of law enforcement efforts to adjudicate enemy combatants who are believed to have committed crimes against US persons or property. JIO. Enemy combatant.

Joint line of communications security board: A board established to coordinate the security of all lines of communications (including that provided by allies or host nations) to support the concept of operations.. JLSB.

Joint logistics: The coordinated use, synchronization, and sharing of two or more Military Departments' logistic resources to support the joint force. Logistics.

Joint Logistics Operations Center: The Joint Logistics Operations Center is the current operations division within the Logistics Directorate of the Joint Staff. It monitors crisis, exercises, and interagency actions. It also works acquisition and cross-servicing agreements as well as international logistics. The Joint Logistics Operations Center reviews deployment orders produced by the Operations Directorate of the Joint Staff for logistic issues and ensures the correct airlift priority code is assigned. JLOC. Logistics.

Joint logistics over-the-shore commander: The joint logistics over-the-shore (JLOTS) commander is selected by the joint force commander (JFC) and is usually from either the Army or Navy components that are part of the JFC's task organization. This individual then builds a joint headquarters from personnel and equipment in theater to organize the efforts of all elements participating in accomplishing the JLOTS mission having either wet or dry cargo or both. JLOTS commanders will usually integrate members from each participating organization to balance the overall knowledge base in their headquarters. Joint logistics over-the-shore operations.

Joint logistics over-the-shore operations: Operations in which Navy and Army logistics over-the-shore forces conduct logistics over-the-shore operations together under a joint force commander. JLOTS operations. joint logistics; logistics over-the-shore operations.

Joint manpower program: The document that reflects an activity's mission, functions, organization, current and projected manpower needs and, when applicable, its required mobilization augmentation. A recommended joint manpower program also identifies and justifies any changes proposed by the commander or director of a joint activity for the next five fiscal years. JMP.

Joint Materiel Priorities and Allocation Board: The agency charged with performing duties for the Chairman of the Joint Chiefs of Staff in matters that establish materiel priorities or allocate resources. JMPAB. Materiel.

Joint meteorological and oceanographic coordination cell: A subset of a joint meteorological and oceanographic coordination organization which is delegated the responsibility of executing the coordination of meteorological and oceanographic support operations in the operational area. JMCC.

Joint meteorological and oceanographic coordination organization: A Service meteorological and oceanographic organization which is designated within the operations order as the lead organization responsible for coordinating meteorological and oceanographic operations support in the operational area. JMCO.

Joint meteorological and oceanographic officer: Officer designated to provide direct meteorological and oceanographic support to a joint force commander. JMO.

Joint mission-essential task: A mission task selected by a joint force commander deemed essential to mission accomplishment and defined using the common language of the universal joint task list in terms of task, condition, and standard. JMET. Condition, universal joint task list.

Joint Mobility Control Group: The Joint Mobility Control Group is the focal point for coordinating and optimizing transportation operations. This group is comprised of seven essential elements. The primary elements are US Transportation Command's Mobility Control Center, Joint Operational Support Airlift Center, Global Patient Movement Requirements Center, Tanker/Airlift Control Center, Military Sealift Command's Command Center, Military Traffic Management Command's Command Operations, and the Joint Intelligence Center-US Transportation Command. JMCG. Global Patient Movement Requirements Center; mobility; United States Transportation Command.

Joint mortuary affairs office: Plans and executes all mortuary affairs programs within a theater. Provides guidance to facilitate the conduct of all mortuary programs and to maintain data (as required) pertaining to recovery, identification, and disposition of all US dead and missing in the assigned theater. Serves as the central clearing point for all mortuary affairs and monitors the deceased and missing personal effects program. JMAO. Mortuary affairs; personal effects.

Joint movement center: The center established to coordinate the employment of all means of transportation (including that provided by allies or host nations) to support the concept of operations. This coordination is accomplished through establishment of transportation policies within the assigned operational area, consistent with relative urgency of need, port and terminal capabilities, transportation asset availability, and priorities set by a joint force commander. JMC. Concept of operations.

Joint Munitions Effectiveness Manual-Special Operations: A publication providing a single, comprehensive source of information covering weapon effectiveness, selection, and requirements for special operations munitions. In addition, the closely related fields of weapon characteristics and effects, target characteristics, and target vulnerability are treated in limited detail required by the mission planner. Although emphasis is placed on weapons that are currently in the inventory, information is also included for some weapons not immediately available but projected for the near future. JMEM-SO.

Joint network operations control center: An element of the J-6 established to support a joint force commander. The joint network operations control center serves as the single control agency for the management and direction of the joint force communications systems. The joint network operations control center may include plans and operations, administration, system control, and frequency management sections. JNCC.

Joint nuclear accident coordinating center: A combined Defense Special Weapons Agency and Department of Energy centralized agency for exchanging and maintaining information concerned with radiological assistance capabilities and coordinating that assistance in response to an accident or incident involving radioactive materials. JNACC.

Joint operation planning: Planning activities associated with joint military operations by combatant commanders and their subordinate joint force commanders in response to contingencies and crises. Joint operation planning includes planning for the mobilization, deployment, employment, sustainment, redeployment, and demobilization of joint forces. See also execution planning; Joint Operation Planning and Execution System; joint operation planning process.

Joint Operation Planning and Execution System: A system of joint policies,

procedures, and reporting structures, supported by communications and computer systems, that is used by the joint planning and execution community to monitor, plan, and execute mobilization, deployment, employment, sustainment, redeployment, and demobilization activities associated with joint operations. JOPES. Joint operation planning; joint operations; level of detail.

Joint operation planning process: An orderly, analytical process that consists of a logical set of steps to analyze a mission; develop, analyze, and compare alternative courses of action against criteria of success and each other; select the best course of action; and produce a joint operation plan or order. JOPP. Joint operation planning; Joint Operation Planning and Execution System.

Joint operations: A general term to describe military actions conducted by joint forces, or by Service forces in relationships (e.g., support, coordinating authority), which, of themselves, do not establish joint forces.

Joint operations area: An area of land, sea, and airspace, defined by a geographic combatant commander or subordinate unified commander, in which a joint force commander conducts military operations to accomplish a specific mission. JOA. Area of responsibility; joint special operations area.

Joint operations area forecast: -The official baseline meteorological and oceanographic forecast for operational planning and mission execution within the joint operations area. JOAF.

Joint operations center: A jointly manned facility of a joint force commander's headquarters established for planning, monitoring, and guiding the execution of the commander's decisions. JOC.

Joint patient movement requirements center: A joint activity established to coordinate the joint patient movement requirements function for a joint task force operating within a unified command area of responsibility. It coordinates with the theater patient movement requirements center for intratheater patient movement and the Global Patient Movement Requirements Center for inter theater patient movement. JPMRC. Health service support; joint force surgeon; joint operations area; medical treatment facility; patient.

Joint patient movement team: Teams comprised of personnel trained in medical regulating and movement procedures. These teams can supplement a global, theater, or joint patient movement requirements center staff. Joint patient movement teams are under the operational control of the Global Patient Movement Requirements Center until attached to a theater/joint patient movement requirements center or forward element supporting the respective joint operation or Federal Emergency Management Agency contingency. JPMT.

Joint personnel recovery center: The primary joint force organization responsible for planning and coordinating personnel recovery for military operations within the assigned operational area. JPRC. Combat search and rescue; search and rescue.

Joint personnel recovery support product: The basic reference document for personnel recovery-specific information on a particular country or region of interest. JPRSP.

Joint personnel training and tracking activity: The continental US center established (upon request of the supported combatant commander) to facilitate the reception, accountability, processing, training, and onward movement of both military and civilian individual augmentees preparing for overseas movement to support a joint military operation. JPTTA.

Joint planning and execution community: Those headquarters, commands, and agencies involved in the training, preparation, mobilization, deployment, employment, support, sustainment, redeployment, and demobilization of military forces assigned or committed to a joint operation. It consists of the Joint Staff, the Services and their major commands (including the Service wholesale logistics commands), the combatant commands (and their Service component commands), the subordinate unified commands and other subordinate joint forces of the combatant commands, and the combat support agencies. JPEC.

Joint planning group: A planning organization consisting of designated representatives of the joint force headquarters principal and special staff sections, joint force components (Service and/or functional), and other supporting organizations or agencies as deemed necessary by the joint force commander. JPG. Crisis action planning; joint operation planning.

Joint psychological operations task force: A joint special operations task force composed of headquarters and operational assets. It assists the joint force commander in developing strategic, operational, and tactical psychological operation plans for a theater campaign or other operations. Mission requirements will determine its composition and assigned or attached units to support the joint task force commander. JPOTF. Joint special operations task force; psychological operations; special operations.

Joint publication: A publication containing joint doctrine that is prepared under the direction and authority of the Chairman of the Joint Chiefs of Staff and applies to all Armed Forces of the United States. JP. Chairman of the Joint Chiefs of Staff instruction; Chairman of the Joint Chiefs of Staff manual; joint doctrine; joint test publication.

Joint reception complex: The group of nodes (air and/or sea) designated by the supported combatant command, in coordination with the host nation and United States Transportation Command, that receives, processes, services, supports, and facilitates onward movement of personnel, equipment, materiel, and units deploying into, out of, or within a theater line of communications. Group; node.

Joint reception coordination center: The organization, established by the Department of the Army as the designated Department of Defense executive agent for the repatriation of noncombatants, that ensures Department of Defense personnel and noncombatants receive adequate assistance and support for an orderly and expedient debarkation, movement to final destination in the US, and appropriate follow-on assistance at the final destination. JRCC.

Joint reception, staging, onward movement, and integration: A phase of joint force projection occurring in the operational area. This phase comprises the essential processes required to transition arriving personnel, equipment, and materiel into forces capable of meeting operational requirements. JRSOI. Integration; joint force; reception; staging.

Joint restricted frequency list: A time and geographically-oriented listing of TABOO, PROTECTED, and GUARDED functions, nets, and frequencies. It should be limited to the minimum number of frequencies necessary for friendly forces to accomplish objectives. JRFL. Electronic warfare; guarded frequencies; protected frequencies; TABOO frequencies.

Joint security area: A specific surface area, designated by the joint force commander to facilitate protection of joint bases that support joint operations. JSA.

Joint security coordination center: A joint operations center tailored to assist the joint security coordinator in meeting the security requirements in the joint operational area. JSCC.

Joint security coordinator: The officer with responsibility for coordinating the overall security of the operational area in accordance with joint force commander directives and priorities. JSC.

Joint servicing: That function performed by a jointly staffed and financed activity in support of two or more Military Services. Servicing.

Joint special operations air component commander: The commander within a joint force special operations command responsible for planning and executing joint special operations air activities. JSOACC.

Joint special operations area: An area of land, sea, and airspace assigned by a joint force commander to the commander of a joint special operations force to conduct special operations activities. It may be limited in size to accommodate a discrete direct action mission or may be extensive enough to allow a continuing broad range of unconventional warfare operations. JSOA.

Joint staff: 1. The staff of a commander of a unified or specified command, subordinate unified command, joint task force, or subordinate functional component, that includes members from the several Services comprising the force. These members should be assigned in such a manner as to ensure that the commander understands the tactics, techniques, capabilities, needs, and limitations of the component parts of the force. Positions on the staff should be divided so that Service representation and influence generally reflect the Service composition of the force. 2. The staff under the Chairman of the Joint Chiefs of Staff as provided for in Title 10, United States Code, Section 155. The Joint Staff assists the Chairman of the Joint Chiefs of Staff and, subject to the authority, direction, and control of the Chairman of the Joint Chiefs of Staff and the other members of the Joint Chiefs of Staff in carrying out their responsibilities. JS. staff.

Joint Staff doctrine sponsor: A Joint Staff directorate assigned to coordinate a specific joint doctrine project with the Joint Staff. Joint Staff doctrine sponsors assist the lead agent and primary review authority as requested and directed and process the final coordination for approval. JSDS. Joint doctrine.

Joint Strategic Capabilities Plan: The Joint Strategic Capabilities Plan provides

guidance to the combatant commanders and the Joint Chiefs of

Staff to accomplish tasks and missions based on current military capabilities. It apportions limited forces and resources to combatant commanders, based on military capabilities resulting from completed program and budget actions and intelligence assessments. The Joint Strategic Capabilities Plan provides a coherent framework for capabilities-based military advice provided to the President and Secretary of Defense. JSCP. Combatant commander; joint.

Joint strategic exploitation center: Theater-level physical location for an exploitation facility that functions under the direction of the joint force commander and is used to hold detainees with potential long-term strategic intelligence value, deemed to be of interest to counterintelligence or criminal investigators, or who may be a significant threat to the United States, its citizens or interests, or US allies. JSEC.

Joint Strategic Planning System: One of the primary means by which the Chairman of the Joint Chiefs of Staff, in consultation with the other members of the Joint Chiefs of Staff and the combatant commanders, carries out the statutory responsibilities to assist the President and Secretary of Defense in providing strategic direction to the Armed Forces; prepares strategic plans; prepares and reviews joint operation plans; advises the President and Secretary of Defense on requirements, programs, and budgets; and provides net assessment on the capabilities of the Armed Forces of the United States and its allies as compared with those of their potential adversaries. JSPS.

Joint suppression of enemy air defenses: A broad term that includes all suppression of enemy air defense activities provided by one component of the joint force in support of another. Also called J-SEAD. Suppression of enemy air defenses.

Joint table of allowances: A document that authorizes end-items of materiel for units operated jointly by two or more military assistance advisory groups and missions. JTA.

Joint table of distribution: A manpower document that identifies the positions and enumerates the spaces that have been approved for each organizational element of a joint activity for a specific fiscal year, and those spaces which have been accepted for planning and programming purposes for the four subsequent fiscal years. JTD. Joint manpower program.

Joint Tactical Air Reconnaissance/Surveillance Mission Report: A preliminary report of information from tactical reconnaissance aircrews rendered by designated debriefing personnel immediately after landing and dispatched prior to compilation of the initial photo interpretation report. It provides a summary of the route conditions, observations, and aircrew actions and identifies sensor products. MISREP.

Joint targeting coordination board: A group formed by the joint force commander to accomplish broad targeting oversight functions that may include but are not limited to coordinating targeting information, providing targeting guidance and priorities, and refining the joint integrated prioritized target list. The board is normally comprised of representatives from the joint force staff, all components, and if required, component subordinate units. JTCB. joint integrated prioritized target list; targeting.

Joint targeting steering group: A group formed by a combatant commander to assist in developing targeting guidance and reconciling competing requests for assets from multiple joint task forces. JTSG. Group; joint; targeting.

Joint target list: A consolidated list of selected targets, upon which there are no restrictions placed, considered to have military significance in the joint force commander's operational area. JTL. joint; target.

Joint task force: A joint force that is constituted and so designated by the Secretary of Defense, a combatant commander, a sub unified commander, or an existing joint task force commander. JTF.

Joint Task Force-Civil Support: A standing joint task force established to plan and integrate Department of Defense support to the designated lead federal agency for domestic chemical, biological, radiological, nuclear, and high-yield explosives consequence management operations. JTF-CS.

Joint task force counterintelligence coordinating authority: An authority that affects the overall coordination of counterintelligence (CI) activities (in a joint force intelligence directorate counterintelligence and human intelligence staff element, joint task force configuration), with subordinate command CI elements, other supporting CI organizations, and supporting agencies to ensure full CI coverage of the task force operational area. TFCICA. Counter intelligence; counterintelligence activities; joint task force.

joint technical augmentation cell: A tailored team that, when directed, deploys to a supported combatant commander's area of responsibility to provide chemical, biological, radiological, and nuclear technical advice and planning assistance for executing foreign consequence management. JTAC.

Joint Technical Coordinating Group for Munitions Effectiveness: A Joint Staff-level organization tasked to produce generic target vulnerability and weaponeering studies. The special operations working group is a subordinate organization specializing in studies for special operations. JTCG-ME.

Joint test publication: A proposed publication produced for the purpose of field-testing an emergent concept that has been validated through the Joint Experimentation Program or a similar joint process. JTP. Chairman of the Joint Chiefs of Staff instruction; joint doctrine; joint publication.

Joint total asset visibility: The capability designed to consolidate source data from a variety of joint and Service automated information systems to provide joint force commanders with visibility over assets in-storage, in-process, and in-transit. JTAV.

Joint Transportation Board: Responsible to the Chairman of the Joint Chiefs of Staff, the Joint Transportation Board assures that common-user transportation resources assigned or available to the Department of Defense are allocated as to achieve maximum benefit in meeting Department of Defense objectives. JTB. Common-user transportation.

Joint urban operations: All joint operations planned and conducted across the range of military operations on or against objectives on a topographical complex and its adjacent natural terrain where manmade construction or the density of noncombatants are the dominant features. JUOs. Joint operations.

Joint war fighting capabilities assessment: A team of war fighting and functional area experts from the Joint Staff, unified commands, Services, Office of the Secretary of Defense, and Defense agencies tasked by the Joint Requirements Oversight Council with completing assessments and providing military recommendations to improve joint war fighting capabilities. JWCA.

Joint Worldwide Intelligence Communications System: The sensitive, compartmented information portion of the Defense Information Systems Network. It incorporates advanced networking technologies that permit point-to-point or multipoint information exchange involving voice, text, graphics, data, and video teleconferencing. JWICS.

Joint zone (air, land, or sea): An area established for the purpose of permitting friendly surface, air, and subsurface forces to operate simultaneously.

Join up: To form separate aircraft or groups of aircraft into a specific formation.

judge advocate: An officer of the Judge Advocate General's Corps of the Army, Air Force, Marine Corps, and the United States Coast Guard who is designated as a judge advocate. JA.

Jumpmaster: The assigned airborne qualified individual who controls paratroops from the time they enter the aircraft until they exit. Stick commander (air transport).

Jump speed: The airspeed at which paratroops can jump with comparative safety from an aircraft.

K

K-day: The basic date for the introduction of a convoy system on any particular convoy lane. D-day; M-day.

Key employee: Any Reservist identified by his or her employer, private or public, as filling a key position.

Key facilities list: A register of selected command installations and industrial facilities of primary importance to the support of military operations or military production programs. It is prepared under the policy direction of the Joint Chiefs of Staff.

Key point: A concentrated site or installation, the destruction or capture of which would seriously affect the war effort or the success of operations.

Key position: A civilian position, public or private (designated by the employer and approved by the Secretary concerned), that cannot be vacated during war or national emergency.

Keystone publications: Joint doctrine publications that establish the doctrinal foundation for a series of joint publications in the hierarchy of joint publications. These publications are signed by the Chairman of the Joint Chiefs of Staff. Keystone publications are provided for joint personnel support, intelligence support, operations, logistic support, plans, and communications systems support. Capstone publications; joint publication.

Key terrain: Any locality, or area, the seizure or retention of which affords a marked advantage to either combatant. Vital ground.

Kill box: A three-dimensional area used to facilitate the integration of joint fires.

Killed in action: A casualty category applicable to a hostile casualty, other than the victim of a terrorist activity, who is killed outright or who dies as a result of wounds or other injuries before reaching a medical treatment facility.KIA. Casualty category.

Killing zone: An area in which a commander plans to force the enemy to concentrate so as to be destroyed with conventional weapons or the tactical employment of nuclear weapons.

Kill probability: A measure of the probability of destroying a target.

Kiloton weapon: A nuclear weapon, the yield of which is measured in terms of

thousands of tons of trinitrotoluene explosive equivalents, producing yields from 1 to 999 kilotons. Megaton weapon; nominal weapon; subkiloton weapon.

Kite: In naval mine warfare, a device which when towed, submerges and planes at a predetermined level without sideways displacement.

L

Land control operations: The employment of ground forces, supported by naval and air forces (as appropriate) to achieve military objectives in vital land areas. Such operations include destruction of opposing ground forces, securing key terrain, protection of vital land lines of communications, and establishment of local military superiority in areas of land operations. Sea control operations.

Land forces: Personnel, weapon systems, vehicles, and support elements operating on land to accomplish assigned missions and tasks.

Landing aid: Any illuminating light, radio beacon, radar device, communicating device, or any system of such devices for aiding aircraft in an approach and landing.

Landing area — 1. That part of the operational area within which are conducted the landing operations of an amphibious force. It includes the beach, the approaches to the beach, the transport areas, the fire support areas, the airspace occupied by close supporting aircraft, and the land included in the advance inland to the initial objective. 2. (Airborne) The general area used for landing troops and materiel either by airdrop or air landing. This area includes one or more drop zones or landing strips. 3. Any specially prepared or selected surface of land, water, or deck designated or used for takeoff and landing of aircraft. Airfield; amphibious force; landing beach; landing force.

Landing attack: An attack against enemy defenses by troops landed from ships, aircraft, boats, or amphibious vehicles. Assault.

Landing beach: That portion of a shoreline usually required for the landing of a battalion landing team. However, it may also be that portion of a shoreline constituting a tactical locality (such as the shore of a bay) over which a force larger or smaller than a battalion landing team may be landed.

Landing craft: A craft employed in amphibious operations, specifically designed for carrying troops and their equipment and for beaching, unloading, and retracting. It is also used for resupply operations.

landing craft and amphibious vehicle assignment table: A table showing the

assignment of personnel and materiel to each landing craft and amphibious vehicle and the assignment of the landing craft and amphibious vehicles to waves for the ship-to-shore movement. landing craft availability table – A tabulation of the type and number of landing craft that will be available from each ship of the transport group. The table is the basis for the assignment of landing craft to the boat groups for the ship-to-shore movement.

landing diagram: A graphic means of illustrating the plan for the ship-to-shore movement.

landing force support party: A temporary landing force organization composed of Navy and landing force elements, that facilitates the ship-to-shore movement and provides initial combat support and combat service support to the landing force. The landing force support party is brought into existence by a formal activation order issued by the commander, landing force. LFSP. Combat service support; combat support; landing force; ship-to-shore movement.

Landing group: In amphibious operations, a subordinate task organization of the landing force capable of conducting landing operations, under a single tactical command, against a position or group of positions.

Landing group commander: In amphibious operations, the officer designated by the commander, landing force as the single tactical commander of a subordinate task organization capable of conducting landing operations against a position or group of positions. See also amphibious operation; commander, landing force.

Landing mat: A prefabricated, portable mat so designed that any number of planks (sections) may be rapidly fastened together to form surfacing for emergency runways, landing beaches, etc.

Landing plan: 1. In amphibious operations, a collective term referring to all individually prepared naval and landing force documents that, taken together, present in detail all instructions for execution of the ship-to-shore movement. 2. In airlift operations, the sequence, method of delivery, and place of arrival of troops and materiel.

Landing point: A point within a landing site where one helicopter or vertical takeoff and landing aircraft can land. Airfield.

Landing roll: The movement of an aircraft from touchdown through deceleration to taxi speed or full stop.

Landing schedule: In an amphibious operation, a schedule that shows the beach, hour, and priorities of landing of assault units, and which coordinates the movements of landing craft from the transports to the beach in order to execute the scheme of maneuver ashore.

Landing sequence table: A document that incorporates the detailed plans for ship-to-shore movement of nonscheduled units.

Landing ship: An assault ship which is designed for long sea voyages and for rapid unloading over and on to a beach.

Landing ship dock: A ship designed to transport and launch loaded amphibious craft and/or amphibian vehicles with their crews and embarked personnel and/or equipment and to render limited docking and repair services to small ships and craft. LSD.

Landing signalman enlisted: Enlisted man responsible for ensuring that helicopters, on signal, are safely started, engaged, launched, recovered, and shut down. LSE.

Landing signals officer: Officer responsible for the visual control of aircraft in the terminal phase of the approach immediately prior to landing. LSO. Terminal phase.

Landing site: 1. A site within a landing zone containing one or more landing points. Airfield. 2. In amphibious operations, a continuous segment of coastline over which troops, equipment and supplies can be landed by surface means.

Landing threshold: The beginning of that portion of a runway usable for landing.

Landing zone: Any specified zone used for the landing of aircraft. LZ. Airfield.

Landing zone control: Pathfinder drop zone control.

Landing zone control party: Personnel specially trained and equipped to establish and operate communications devices from the ground for traffic control of aircraft/helicopters for a specific landing zone.

Landmark: A feature, either natural or artificial, that can be accurately determined on the ground from a grid reference.

Land search: The search of terrain by Earth-bound personnel.

Lane marker: In land mine warfare, sign used to mark a minefield lane. Lane markers, at the entrance to and exit from the lane, may be referenced to a landmark or intermediate marker. Marker; minefield lane.

Lap: In naval mine warfare, that section or strip of an area assigned to a single sweeper or formation of sweepers for a run through the area.

Lap course: In naval mine warfare, the true course desired to be made good during a run along a lap.

Lap track: In naval mine warfare, the center line of a lap; ideally, the track to be

followed by the sweep or detecting gear.

Lap turn: In naval mine warfare, the maneuver a minesweeper carries out during the period between the completion of one run and the commencement of the run immediately following.

Lap width: In naval mine warfare, the swept path of the ship or formation divided by the percentage coverage being swept to.

Large-lot storage: A quantity of material that will require four or more pallet columns stored to maximum height. Usually accepted as stock stored in carload or greater quantities. Storage.

Large-scale map: A map having a scale of 1:75,000 or larger. Map.

Large spread: A report by an observer or a spotter to the ship to indicate that the distance between the bursts of a salvo is excessive.

Laser: Any device that can produce or amplify optical radiation primarily by the process of controlled stimulated emission. A laser may emit electromagnetic radiation from the ultraviolet portion of the spectrum through the infrared portion. Also, an acronym for "light amplification by stimulated emission of radiation."

Laser footprint: The projection of the laser beam and buffer zone on the ground or target area. The laser footprint may be part of the laser surface danger zone if that footprint lies within the nominal visual hazard distance of the laser. Buffer zone; laser.

Laser guidance unit: A device which incorporates a laser seeker to provide guidance commands to the control system of a missile, projectile or bomb.

Laser illuminator: A device for enhancing the illumination in a zone of action by irradiating with a laser beam.

Laser intelligence: Technical and geo-location intelligence derived from laser systems; a subcategory of electro-optical intelligence. LASINT. electro-optical intelligence; intelligence.

Laser linescan system: An active airborne imagery recording system which uses a laser as the primary source of illumination to scan the ground beneath the flight path, adding successive across-track lines to the record as the vehicle advances. Infrared linescan system.

Laser pulse duration: The time during which the laser output pulse power remains continuously above half its maximum value.

Laser rangefinder: A device which uses laser energy for determining the distance from the device to a place or object.

Laser seeker: A device based on a direction sensitive receiver which detects the energy reflected from a laser designated target and defines the direction of the target relative to the receiver. Laser guided weapon.

Laser spot: The area on a surface illuminated by a laser. Laser; spot.

Laser spot tracker: A device that locks on to the reflected energy from a laser-marked or designated target and defines the direction of the target relative to itself. LST.

Laser target designating system: A system which is used to direct (aim or point) laser energy at a target. The system consists of the laser designator or laser target marker with its display and control components necessary to acquire the target and direct the beam of laser energy thereon.

Laser target designator: A device that emits a beam of laser energy which is used to mark a specific place or object. LTD. Laser; target.

Laser-target/gun-target angle: The angle between the laser-to-target line and the laser guided weapon/gun-target line at the point where they cross the target. Laser; laser guided weapon; target.

Laser-target line: An imaginary straight line from the laser designator to the target with respect to magnetic north. Laser; laser target designator; target.

Lashing: tie down. restraint of loads.

Lashing point: tie down point.

Late: In artillery and naval gunfire support, a report made to the observer or spotter, whenever there is a delay in reporting "shot" by coupling a time in seconds with the report.

Lateral gain: The amount of new ground covered laterally by successive photographic runs over an area.

Lateral route: A route generally parallel to the forward edge of the battle area, which crosses, or feeds into, axial routes. Route.

Lateral spread: A technique used to place the mean point of impact of two or more units 100 meters apart on a line perpendicular to the gun-target line.

Latest arrival date: A day, relative to C-Day, that is specified by the supported combatant commander as the latest date when a unit, a resupply shipment, or replacement personnel can arrive at the port of debarkation and support the concept of operations. Used with the earliest arrival date, it defines a delivery window for transportation planning. LAD.

Late time: span of detonation (atomic demolition munitions employment), Part 3.

Lattice: A network of intersecting positional lines printed on a map or chart from which a fix may be obtained.

Launch pad: A concrete or other hard surface area on which a missile launcher is positioned.

Launch time: The time at which an aircraft or missile is scheduled to be airborne. Airborne order.

Launch under attack: Execution by the President of Single Integrated Operational Plan forces subsequent to tactical warning of strategic nuclear attack against the United States and prior to first impact. LUA.

Launch window: The earliest and latest time a rocket may launch.

Laundering: In counterdrug operations, the process of transforming drug money into a more manageable form while concealing its illicit origin. Foreign bank accounts and dummy corporations are used as shelters. Counterdrug operations.

Law enforcement agency: Any of a number of agencies (outside the Department of Defense) chartered and empowered to enforce US laws in the following jurisdictions: The United States, a state (or political subdivision) of the United States, a territory (or political subdivision) of the United States, a federally recognized Native American tribe or Alaskan Native Village, or within the borders of a host nation. LEA.

Law of war: That part of international law that regulates the conduct of armed hostilities. the law of armed conflict. rules of engagement.

Lay: 1. Direct or adjust the aim of a weapon. 2. Setting of a weapon for a given range, a given direction, or both. 3. To drop one or more aerial bombs or aerial mines onto the surface from an aircraft. 4. To spread a smoke screen on the ground from an aircraft. 5. To calculate or project a course. 6. To lay on: a. to execute a bomber strike; b. to set up a mission.

Lay down bombing: A very low level bombing technique wherein delay fuzes and/or devices are used to allow the attacker to escape the effects of the bomb.

Layer depth: The depth from the surface of the sea to the point above the first major negative thermo cline at which sound velocity is maximum.

Lay reference number: In naval mine warfare, a number allocated to an individual mine by the minefield planning authority to provide a simple means of referring to it.

Lead agency: Designated among US Government agencies to coordinate the interagency oversight of the day-to-day conduct of an ongoing operation. The lead agency is to chair the interagency working group established to coordinate policy related to a particular operation. The lead agency determines the agenda, ensures cohesion among the agencies, and is responsible for implementing decisions.

Lead agent: 1. An individual Service, combatant command, or Joint Staff directorate assigned to develop and maintain a joint publication. 2. In medical materiel management, the designated unit or organization to coordinate or execute day-to-day conduct of an ongoing operation or function. LA.

Lead aircraft: 1. The airborne aircraft designated to exercise command of other aircraft within the flight. 2. An aircraft in the van of two or more aircraft.

Lead federal agency: The federal agency that leads and coordinates the overall federal response to an emergency. Designation and responsibilities of a lead federal agency vary according to the type of emergency and the agency's statutory authority. LFA.

Lead nation: One nation assumes the responsibility for procuring and providing a broad spectrum of logistic support for all or a part of the multinational force and/or headquarters. Compensation and/or reimbursement will then be subject to agreements between the parties involved. The lead nation may also assume the responsibility to coordinate logistics of the other nations within its functional and regional area of responsibility. See also logistic support; multinational force.

Leapfrog: Form of movement in which like supporting elements are moved

successively through or by one another along the axis of movement of supported

forces.

Leaver: A merchant ship which breaks off from a convoy to proceed to a different destination and becomes independent. Also called convoy leaver. See also leaver convoy; leaver section.

Leaver convoy: A convoy which has broken off from the main convoy and is

proceeding to a different destination. Leaver; leaver section.

Leaver section: A group of ships forming part of the main convoy which will

subsequently break off to become leavers or a leaver convoy. See also leaver; leaver convoy.

Left (or right): 1. Terms used to establish the relative position of a body of troops. The person using the terms "left" or "right" is assumed to be facing in the direction of the enemy regardless of whether the troops are advancing towards or withdrawing from the enemy. 2. Correction used in adjusting fire to indicate that a lateral shift of the mean point of impact perpendicular to the reference line or spotting line is desired.

Left (right) bank: That bank of a stream or river on the left (right) of the observer when facing in the direction of flow or downstream.

Letter of assist: A contractual document issued by the United Nations to a government authorizing it to provide goods or services to a peacekeeping operation; the United Nations agrees either to purchase the goods or services or authorizes the government to supply them subject to reimbursement by the United Nations. A letter of assist typically details specifically what is to be provided by the contributing government and establishes a funding limit that cannot be exceeded. Also called LOA. Peacekeeping.

Letter of authorization: A document issued by the procuring contracting officer or designee that authorizes contractor personnel authorized to accompany the force to travel to, from, and within the operational area; and, outlines government furnished support authorizations within the operational area. LOA.

Letter of offer and acceptance: Standard Department of Defense form on which the US Government documents its offer to transfer to a foreign government or international organization US defense articles and services via foreign military sales pursuant to the Arms Export Control Act. LOA. Foreign military sales.

Level-of-effort munitions: In stockpile planning, munitions stocked on the basis of expected daily expenditure rate, the number of combat days, and the attrition rate assumed, to counter targets the number of which is unknown. Threat-oriented munitions.

Level of effort-oriented items: Items for which requirements computations are based on such factors as equipment and personnel density and time and rate of use. See also combination mission/level of effort-oriented items; mission-oriented items.

Leverage — In the context of joint operation planning, a relative advantage in combat power and/or other circumstances against the adversary across one or more domains (air, land, sea, and space) and/or the information environment sufficient to exploit that advantage. Leverage is an element of operational design. Operational art; operational design.

Liaison: That contact or intercommunication maintained between elements of military forces or other agencies to ensure mutual understanding and unity of purpose and action.

Liberated territory: Any area, domestic, neutral, or friendly, which, having been occupied by an enemy, is retaken by friendly forces.

Licensed production: A direct commercial arrangement between a US company and a foreign government, international organization, or foreign company, providing for the transfer of production information which enables the foreign government, international organization, or commercial producer to manufacture, in whole or in part, an item of US defense equipment. A typical license production arrangement would include the functions of production engineering, controlling, quality assurance and determining of resource requirements. It may or may not include design engineering information and critical materials production and design information. A licensed production arrangement is accomplished under the provisions of a manufacturing license agreement per the US International Traffic in Arms Regulation.

Life cycle: The total phases through which an item passes from the time it is initially developed until the time it is either consumed in use or disposed of as being excess to all known materiel requirements.

Lifeguard submarine: A submarine employed for rescue in an area which cannot be adequately covered by air or surface rescue facilities because of enemy opposition, distance from friendly bases, or other reasons. It is stationed near the objective and sometimes along the route to be flown by the strike aircraft.

Life support equipment: Equipment designed to sustain aircrew members and passengers throughout the flight environment, optimizing their mission effectiveness and affording a means of safe and reliable escape, descent, survival, and recovery in emergency situations.

Lightening: The operation (normally carried out at anchor) of transferring crude oil cargo from a large tanker to a smaller tanker, so reducing the draft of the larger tanker to enable it to enter port.

Lighterage: The process in which small craft are used to transport cargo or personnel from ship to shore. Lighterage may be performed using amphibians, landing craft, discharge lighters, causeways, and barges.

Light filter:- An optical element such as a sheet of glass, gelatine, or plastic dyed in a specific manner to absorb selectively light of certain colors.

light line: A designated line forward of which vehicles are required to use black-out lights at night.

Lightweight amphibious container handler: A United States Marine Corps piece of equipment usually maneuvered by a bulldozer and used to retrieve 20-foot equivalent containers from landing craft in the surf and place them on flatbed truck trailers. Container.

Limited production-type item: An item under development, commercially available or available from other Government agencies, for which an urgent operational requirement exists and for which no other existing item is suitable. Such an item appears to fulfill an approved materiel requirement or other Military Department approved requirements and to be promising enough operationally to warrant initiating procurement and/or production for service issue prior to completion of development and/or test or adoption as a standard item.

Limited standard item: An item of supply determined by standardization action as authorized for procurement only to support in-service military materiel requirements.

Limited war: Armed conflict short of general war, exclusive of incidents, involving the overt engagement of the military forces of two or more nations.

Limiting factor: A factor or condition that, either temporarily or permanently, impedes mission accomplishment. Illustrative examples are transportation network deficiencies, lack of in-place facilities, malpositioned forces or materiel, extreme climatic conditions, distance, transit or over flight rights, political conditions, etc.

Limit of fire: 1. The boundary marking off the area on which gunfire can be delivered. 2. Safe angular limits for firing at aerial targets.

Line of communications: A route, either land, water, and/or air, that connects an operating military force with a base of operations and along which supplies and military forces move. LOC. Base of operations; route.

Line of demarcation: A line defining the boundary of a buffer zone or area of limitation. A line of demarcation may also be used to define the forward limits of disputing or belligerent forces after each phase of disengagement or withdrawal has been completed. Area of limitation; buffer zone; disengagement; peace operations.

Line of departure: 1. In land warfare, a line designated to coordinate the departure of attack elements. 2. In amphibious warfare, a suitably marked offshore coordinating line to assist assault craft to land on designated beaches at scheduled times. LD.

Line of operations: 1. A logical line that connects actions on nodes and/or decisive points related in time and purpose with an objective(s). 2. A physical line that defines the interior or exterior orientation of the force in relation to the enemy or that connects actions on nodes and/ or decisive points related in time and space to an objective(s). LOO.

Line-route map: A map or overlay for signal communications operations that shows the actual routes and types of construction of wire circuits in the field. It also gives the locations of switchboards and telegraph stations.

Line search: Reconnaissance along a specific line of communications, such as a road, railway or waterway, to detect fleeting targets and activities in general.

Link encryption: The application of online crypto-operation to a link of a communications system so that all information passing over the link is encrypted in its entirety.

Link-lift vehicle: The conveyance, together with its operating personnel, used to satisfy a movement requirement between nodes.

Link-route segments: Route segments that connect nodes wherein link-lift vehicles perform the movement function.

Liquid explosive: Explosive which is fluid at normal temperatures.

Liquid propellant: Any liquid combustible fed to the combustion chamber of a rocket engine.

listening watch: A continuous receiver watch established for the reception of traffic addressed to, or of interest to, the unit maintaining the watch, with complete log optional.

Litter: A basket or frame utilized for the transport of injured persons. litter patient — A patient requiring litter accommodations while in transit.

Littoral: The littoral comprises two segments of battle space: 1. Seaward: the area from the open ocean to the shore, which must be controlled to support operations ashore. 2. Landward: the area inland from the shore that can be supported and defended directly from the sea.

Load: The total weight of passengers and/or freight carried on board a ship, aircraft, train, road vehicle, or other means of conveyance. Airlift capability; airlift requirement; allowable load.

Load control group: Personnel who are concerned with organization and control of loading within the pick-up zone.

Loading: The process of putting personnel, materiel, supplies and other freight on board ships, aircraft, trains, road vehicles, or other means of conveyance. Embarkation.

Loading chart (aircraft): Any one of a series of charts carried in an aircraft that shows the proper location for loads to be transported and that pertains to check-lists, balance records, and clearances for weight and balance.

Loading plan: All of the individually prepared documents which, taken together,

present in detail all instructions for the arrangement of personnel, and the loading of equipment for one or more units or other special grouping of personnel or material moving by highway, water, rail, or air transportation. Ocean manifest.

Loading point: A point where one aircraft can be loaded or unloaded.

Loading site: An area containing a number of loading points.

Loading time: In airlift operations, a specified time, established jointly by the airlift and airborne commanders concerned, when aircraft and loads are available and loading is to begin.

Loadmaster: An Air Force technician qualified to plan loads, to operate auxiliary materials handling equipment, and to supervise loading and unloading of aircraft.

Load signal: In personnel recovery, a visual signal displayed in a covert manner to indicate the presence of an individual or object at a given location. Evasion; recovery operations; signal.

Load spreader: Material used to distribute the weight of a load over a given area to avoid exceeding designed stress.

Localizer: A directional radio beacon which provides to an aircraft an indication of its lateral position relative to a predetermined final approach course. See also instrument landing system.

Local mean time: The time interval elapsed since the mean sun's transit of the observer's anti-meridian.

Local procurement: The process of obtaining personnel, services, supplies, and

equipment from local or indigenous sources.

Local purchase: The function of acquiring a decentralized item of supply from sources outside the Department of Defense.

Lock on: Signifies that a tracking or target-seeking system is continuously and automatically tracking a target in one or more coordinates (e.g., range, bearing, elevation).

Lodgment: A designated area in a hostile or potentially hostile operational area that, when seized and held, makes the continuous landing of troops and materiel possible and provides maneuver space for subsequent operations. Hostile.

Loft bombing: A method of bombing in which the delivery plane approaches the target at a very low altitude, makes a definite pull-up at a given point, releases the bomb at a predetermined point during the pull-up, and tosses the bomb onto the target. Toss bombing.

Logistic assessment: An evaluation of: a. the logistic support required to support particular military operations in a theater, country, or area; and b. the actual and/or potential logistic support available for the conduct of military operations either within the theater, country, or area, or located elsewhere.

Logistic estimate of the situation: An appraisal resulting from an orderly examination of the logistic factors influencing contemplated courses of action in order to provide conclusions concerning the degree and manner of that influence.

Logistics: Planning and executing the movement and support of forces. It includes those aspects of military operations that deal with: a. design and development, acquisition, storage, movement, distribution, maintenance, evacuation, and disposition of materiel; b. movement, evacuation, and hospitalization of personnel; c. acquisition or construction, maintenance, operation, and disposition of facilities; and d. acquisition or furnishing of services.

Logistics over-the-shore operation area: That geographic area required to conduct a logistics over-the-shore operation. LOA. Logistics over-the shore operations.

Logistics over-the-shore operations: The loading and unloading of ships without the benefit of deep draft-capable, fixed port facilities; or as a means of moving forces closer to tactical assembly areas dependent on threat force capabilities. LOTS operations. Joint logistics over-the-shore operations.

Logistic sourcing: The identification of the origin and determination of the availability of the time-phased force and deployment data non unit logistic requirements.

Logistic support: Support that encompasses the logistic services, materiel, and transportation required to support the continental United States-based and worldwide deployed forces.

Logistic support (medical): Medical care, treatment, hospitalization, and evacuation as well as the furnishing of medical services, supplies, materiel, and adjuncts thereto.

Long-range bomber aircraft: A bomber designed for a tactical operating radius over 2,500 nautical miles at design gross weight and design bomb load.

Look: In mine warfare, a period during which a mine circuit is receptive of an influence.

Loran: A long-range radio navigation position fixing system using the time difference of reception of pulse type transmissions from two or more fixed stations. This term is derived from the words long-range electronic navigation.

Lot Number: Specifically, a quantity of material all of which was manufactured under identical conditions and assigned an identifying lot number.

Low airburst: The fallout safe height of burst for a nuclear weapon which maximizes damage to or casualties on surface targets. Types of burst.

Low-altitude missile engagement zone: Weapon engagement zone.

Low-altitude parachute extraction system: A low-level, self-contained system capable of delivering heavy loads into an area where air landing is not feasible from an optimum aircraft wheel altitude of 5 to 10 feet above ground level. One or more platforms may be dropped. LAPES.

Low angle: In artillery and naval gunfire support, an order or request to obtain low angle fire.

Low angle fire: Fire delivered at angles of elevation below the elevation that corresponds to the maximum range of the gun and ammunition concerned.

Low angle loft bombing: Type of loft bombing of free fall bombs wherein weapon release occurs at an angle less than 35 degrees above the horizontal. Loft bombing.

Low dollar value item: An item that normally requires considerably less management effort than those in the other management intensity groupings.

Low level transit route: A temporary corridor of defined dimensions established in the forward area to minimize the risk to friendly aircraft from friendly air defenses or surface forces. LLTR.

Low velocity drop: A drop procedure in which the drop velocity does not exceed 30 feet per second.

Low visibility operations: Sensitive operations wherein the political-military restrictions inherent in covert and clandestine operations are either not necessary or not feasible; actions are taken as required to limit exposure of those involved and/or their activities. Execution of these operations is undertaken with the knowledge that the action and/or sponsorship of the operation may preclude plausible denial by the initiating power.

M

Mach number: The ratio of the velocity of a body to that of sound in the surrounding medium.

Magnetic compass: An instrument containing a freely suspended magnetic element which displays the direction of the horizontal component of the Earth's magnetic field at the point of observation.

Magnetic declination: The angle between the magnetic and geographical meridians at any place, expressed in degrees east or west to indicate the direction of magnetic north from true north. In nautical and aeronautical navigation, the term magnetic variation is used instead of magnetic declination and the angle is termed variation of the compass or magnetic variation. Magnetic declination is not otherwise synonymous with magnetic variation which refers to regular or irregular change with time of the magnetic declination, dip, or intensity. Magnetic variation.

Magnetic equator: A line drawn on a map or chart connecting all points at which the magnetic inclination (dip) is zero for a specified epoch. A clinic line.

Magnetic mine: A mine which responds to the magnetic field of a target.

Magnetic mine hunting: The process of using magnetic detectors to determine the presence of mines or mine like objects.

Magnetic north: The direction indicated by the north seeking pole of a freely

suspended magnetic needle, influenced only by the Earth's magnetic field.

Magnetic tape: A tape or ribbon of any material impregnated or coated with magnetic or other material on which information may be placed in the form of magnetically polarized spots.

Magnetic variation: 1. In navigation, at a given place and time, the horizontal angle between the true north and magnetic north measured east or west according to whether magnetic north lies east or west of true north. See also magnetic declination. 2. In cartography, the annual change in direction of the horizontal component of the Earth's magnetic field.

Mail embargo: A temporary shutdown or redirection of mail flow to or from a specific location.

Main airfield: An airfield planned for permanent occupation in peacetime, also suitable for use in wartime and having sufficient operational facilities for full use of its combat potential. See also airfield; departure airfield; diversion airfield; redeployment airfield.

Main armament: The request of the observer or spotter to obtain fire from the largest guns installed on the fire support ship.

Main attack: The principal attack or effort into which the commander throws the full weight of the offensive power at his disposal. An attack directed against the chief objective of the campaign, major operation, or battle.

Main convoy: The convoy as a whole which sails from the convoy assembly port/anchorage to its destination. It may be supplemented by joiners or joiner convoys, and leavers or leaver convoys may break off.

Main deck: The highest deck running the full length of a vessel (except for an aircraft carrier's hanger deck). Watercraft.

Main detonating line: In demolition, a line of detonating cord used to transmit the detonation wave to two or more branches.

Main line of resistance: A line at the forward edge of the battle position, designated for the purpose of coordinating the fire of all units and supporting weapons, including air and naval gunfire. It defines the forward limits of a series of mutually supporting defensive areas, but it does not include the areas occupied or used by covering or screening forces.

Main operations base: In special operations, a base established by a joint force special operations component commander or a subordinate special operations component commander in friendly territory to provide sustained command and control, administration, and logistic support to special operations activities in designated areas. MOB. Advanced operations base; forward operations base.

Main supply route: The route or routes designated within an operational area upon which the bulk of traffic flows in support of military operations. MSR.

Maintenance area: A general locality in which are grouped a number of maintenance activities for the purpose of retaining or restoring materiel to a serviceable condition.

Maintenance engineering: The application of techniques, engineering skills, and effort, organized to ensure that the design and development of weapon systems and equipment provide adequately for their effective and economical maintenance.

Maintenance (materiel): 1. All action taken to retain materiel in a serviceable condition or to restore it to serviceability. It includes inspection, testing, servicing, classification as to serviceability, repair, rebuilding, and reclamation. 2. All supply and repair action taken to keep a force in condition to carry out its mission. 3. The routine recurring work required to keep a facility (plant, building, structure, ground facility, utility system, or other real property) in such condition that it may be continuously used at its original or designed capacity and efficiency for its intended purpose.

Maintenance status: 1. A non operating condition, deliberately imposed, with adequate personnel to maintain and preserve installations, materiel, and facilities in such a condition that they may be readily restored to operable condition in a minimum time by the assignment of additional personnel and without extensive repair or overhaul. 2. That condition of materiel that is in fact, or is administratively classified as, unserviceable, pending completion of required servicing or repairs. 3. A condition of materiel readiness that reports the level of operational readiness for a piece of equipment.

Major combat element: Those organizations and units described in the Joint Strategic Capabilities Plan that directly produce combat capability. The size of the element varies by Service, force capability, and the total number of such elements available. Examples are Army divisions and separate brigades, Air Force squadrons, Navy task forces, and Marine expeditionary forces. Major force.

Major fleet: A principal, permanent subdivision of the operating forces of the Navy with certain supporting shore activities. Presently there are two such fleets: the Pacific Fleet and the Atlantic Fleet. Fleet.

Major force: A military organization comprised of major combat elements and associated combat support, combat service support, and sustainment increments. The major force is capable of sustained military operations in response to plan employment requirements. Major combat element.

Major nuclear power: Any nation that possesses a nuclear striking force capable of posing a serious threat to every other nation.

Major operation: A series of tactical actions conducted by combat forces of a single or several Services, coordinated in time and place, to achieve strategic or operational objectives in an operational area. These actions are conducted simultaneously or sequentially in accordance with a common plan and are controlled by a single commander. For noncombat operations, a reference to the relative size and scope of a military operation. Operation.

Major weapon system: One of a limited number of systems or subsystems that for reasons of military urgency, criticality, or resource requirements, is determined by the Department of Defense as being vital to the national interest.

Make safe: One or more actions necessary to prevent or interrupt complete function of the system. Among the necessary actions are: (1) install (safety devices such as pins or locks); (2) disconnect; (3) bleed (accumulators, reservoirs); (4) remove (explosive devices such as initiators, fuzes, detonators); and (5) intervene.

Management and control system (mobility): Those elements of organizations and/or activities that are part of, or are closely related to, the mobility system, and which authorize requirements to be moved, to obtain and allocate lift resources, or to direct the operation of link lift vehicles.

Maneuverable reentry vehicle: A reentry vehicle capable of performing preplanned flight maneuvers during the reentry phase. Multiple independently targetable reentry vehicle; multiple reentry vehicle; reentry vehicle.

Manifest: A document specifying in detail the passengers or items carried for a specific destination.

Manipulative electromagnetic deception: Electromagnetic deception.

Manpower management: The means of manpower control to ensure the most efficient and economical use of available manpower.

Manpower management survey: Systematic evaluation of a functional area utilizing expert knowledge, manpower scaling guides, experience, and other practical considerations in determining the validity and managerial efficiency of the function's present or proposed manpower establishment.

Manpower requirements: Human resources needed to accomplish specified work loads of organizations.

Manpower resources: Human resources available to the Services that can be applied against manpower requirements.

Man space: The space and weight factor used to determine the combat capacity of vehicles, craft, and transport aircraft, based on the requirements of one person with individual equipment. The person is assumed to weigh between 222-250 pounds and to occupy 13.5 cubic feet of space. Boat space.

Man transportable: Items that are usually transported on wheeled, tracked, or air vehicles, but have integral provisions to allow periodic handling by one or more individuals for limited distances (100-500 meters). Upper weight limit: approximately 65 pounds per individual.

Map: A graphic representation, usually on a plane surface and at an established scale, of natural or artificial features on the surface of a part or the whole of the Earth or other planetary body. The features are positioned relative to a coordinate reference system. Administrative map; chart index; chart series; chart sheet; controlled map; general map; large-scale map; line-route map; map chart; map index; map series; map sheet; medium-scale map; operation map; planimetric map; situation map; small-scale map; strategic map; tactical map; topographic map; traffic circulation map.

Map chart: A representation of a land-sea area, using the characteristics of a map to represent the land area and the characteristics of a chart to represent the sea area, with such special characteristics as to make the map-chart most useful in military operations, particularly amphibious operations.

Map convergence: The angle at which one meridian is inclined to another on a map or chart. Convergence.

Map exercise: An exercise in which a series of military situations is stated and solved on a map.

Map index: Graphic key primarily designed to give the relationship between sheets of a series, their coverage, availability, and further information on the series.

Map reference: A means of identifying a point on the surface of the Earth by relating it to information appearing on a map, generally the graticule or grid.

Map reference code: A code used primarily for encoding grid coordinates and other information pertaining to maps. This code may be used for other purposes where the encryption of numerals is required.

Map series: A group of maps or charts usually having the same scale and cartographic specifications, and with each sheet appropriately identified by producing agency as belonging to the same series.

Map sheet: An individual map or chart either complete in itself or part of a series.

Margin: In cartography, the area of a map or chart lying outside the border

Marginal data: All explanatory information given in the margin of a map or chart

which clarifies, defines, illustrates, and/or supplements the graphic portion of the sheet.

Marine base: A base for support of Marine ground forces, consisting of activities or facilities for which the Marine Corps has operating responsibilities, together with interior lines of communications and the minimum surrounding area necessary for local security. (Normally, not greater than an area of 20 square miles.) Base complex.

Marine Corps special operations forces – Those Active Component Marine Corps

forces designated by the Secretary of Defense that are specifically organized, trained, and equipped to conduct and support special operations. MARSOF.

Marine division and wing team: A Marine Corps air-ground team consisting of one division and one aircraft wing, together with their normal reinforcements.

Marine environment: The oceans, seas, bays, estuaries, and other major water bodies, including their surface interface and interaction, with the atmosphere and with the land seaward of the mean high water mark.

Marine expeditionary brigade: A Marine air-ground task force that is constructed around a reinforced infantry regiment, a composite Marine aircraft group, and a combat logistics regiment. The Marine expeditionary brigade, commanded by a general officer, is task-organized to meet the requirements of a specific situation. It can function as part of a joint task force, as the lead echelon of the Marine expeditionary force, or alone. It varies in size and composition, and is larger than a Marine expeditionary unit but smaller than a Marine expeditionary force. The Marine expeditionary brigade is capable of conducting missions across the full range of military operations. MEB. Brigade; Marine air-ground task force; Marine expeditionary force.

Marine expeditionary force (forward): A designated lead echelon of a Marine expeditionary force (MEF), task-organized to meet the requirements of a specific situation. A Marine expeditionary force (forward) varies in size and composition, and may be commanded by the MEF commander personally or by another designated commander. It may be tasked with preparing for the subsequent arrival of the rest of the MEF/joint/multinational forces, and/or the conduct of other specified tasks, at the discretion of the MEF commander. A Marine expeditionary force (forward) may also be a stand-alone Marine air-ground task force (MAGTF), task-organized for a mission in which an MEF is not required. MEF (FWD). Aviation combat element; combat service support element; command element; ground combat element; Marine air-ground task force; Marine expeditionary force; Marine expeditionary unit; Marine expeditionary unit; special purpose Marine air-ground task force; task force.

Marine expeditionary unit: A Marine air-ground task force (MAGTF) that is constructed around an infantry battalion reinforced, a helicopter squadron reinforced, and a task-organized combat service support element. It normally fulfills Marine Corps forward sea-based deployment requirements. The Marine expeditionary unit provides an immediate reaction capability for crisis response and is capable of limited combat operations. Also called MEU. See also aviation combat element; combat service support element; command element; ground combat element; Marine air-ground task force; Marine expeditionary force; Marine expeditionary force (forward); Marine expeditionary unit (special operations capable); special purpose Marine air-ground task force; task force.

Marine Logistics Command: The US Marines may employ the concept of the Marine Logistics Command (MLC) in major regional contingencies to provide operational logistic support, which will include arrival and assembly operations. The combat service support operations center will be the MLC's primary combat service support coordination center for units undergoing arrival and assembly. MLC. Combat service support operations center.

Maritime Administration Ready Reserve Force: The Maritime Administration (MARAD) Ready Reserve Force is composed of 68 surge sealift assets owned and operated by the US Department of Transportation/ MARAD and crewed by civilian mariners. In time of contingency or exercises, the ships are placed under the operational command of the Military Sealift Command. National Defense Reserve Fleet.

Maritime control area: An area generally similar to a defensive sea area in purpose except that it may be established any place on the high seas. Maritime control areas are normally established only in time of war. Defensive sea area.

Maritime defense sector: One of the subdivisions of a coastal area.

Maritime domain: The oceans, seas, bays, estuaries, islands, coastal areas, and the airspace above these, including the littorals.

Maritime domain awareness: The effective understanding of anything associated with the maritime domain that could impact the security, safety, economy, or environment of a nation.

Maritime environment: The complex union and interaction between oceans, seas, bays, estuaries, and other major water bodies, with the atmosphere and land seaward of the mean high water mark.

Maritime forces: Forces that operate on, under, or above the sea to gain or exploit command of the sea, sea control, or sea denial and/or to project power from the sea.

Maritime interception operations: Efforts to monitor, query, and board merchant vessels in international waters to enforce sanctions against other nations such as those in support of United Nations Security Council Resolutions and/or prevent the transport of restricted goods. MIO.

Maritime power projection: Power projection in and from the maritime environment, including a broad spectrum of offensive military operations to destroy enemy forces or logistic support or to prevent enemy forces from approaching within enemy weapons' range of friendly forces. Maritime power projection may be accomplished by amphibious assault operations, attack of targets ashore, or support of sea control operations.

Maritime pre-positioning force operation: A rapid deployment and assembly of a Marine expeditionary force in a secure area using a combination of inter theater airlift and forward-deployed maritime pre-positioning ships. Marine expeditionary force; maritime pre-positioning ships.

Maritime pre-positioning ships: Civilian-crewed, Military Sealift Command-chartered ships that are organized into three squadrons and are usually forward-deployed. These ships are loaded with pre-positioned equipment and 30 days of supplies to support three Marine expeditionary brigades. MPS. Navy cargo handling battalion.

Maritime search and rescue region: The waters subject to the jurisdiction of the United States; the territories and possessions of the United States (except Canal Zone and the inland area of Alaska), and designated areas of the high seas. Search and rescue region.

Maritime special purpose force: A task-organized force formed from elements of a Marine expeditionary unit (special operations capable) and naval special warfare forces that can be quickly tailored to a specific mission. The maritime special purpose force can execute on short notice a wide variety of missions in a supporting, supported, or unilateral role. It focuses on operations in a maritime environment and is capable of operations in conjunction with or in support of special operations forces. The maritime special purpose force is integral to and directly relies upon the Marine expeditionary unit for all combat and combat service support. MSPF.

Maritime superiority: That degree of dominance of one force over another that permits the conduct of maritime operations by the former and its related land, maritime, and air forces at a given time and place without prohibitive interference by the opposing force.

Maritime supremacy: That degree of maritime superiority wherein the opposing force is incapable of effective interference.

Marker: 1. A visual or electronic aid used to mark a designated point. 2. In land mine warfare: See gap marker; intermediate marker; lane marker; row marker; strip marker. 3. In naval operations, a maritime unit which maintains an immediate offensive or obstructive capability against a specified target.

Marker ship: In an amphibious operation, a ship which takes accurate station on a designated control point. It may fly identifying flags by day and show lights to seaward by night.

Marking: To maintain contact on a target from such a position that the marking unit has an immediate offensive capability.

Marking error: In naval mine warfare, the distance and bearing of a marker from a target.

Marking fire: Fire placed on a target for the purpose of identification.

Marking panel: A sheet of material displayed for visual communication, usually between friendly units. Panel code.

Married failure: In naval mine warfare, a moored mine lying on the seabed connected to its sinker from which it has failed to release owing to defective mechanism.

Marshalling: 1. The process by which units participating in an amphibious or airborne operation group together or assemble when feasible or move to temporary camps in the vicinity of embarkation points, complete preparations for combat, or prepare for loading. 2. The process of assembling, holding, and organizing supplies and/or equipment, especially vehicles of transportation, for onward movement. Stage; staging area.

Marshalling area: A location in the vicinity of a reception terminal or pre-positioned equipment storage site where arriving unit personnel, equipment, materiel, and accompanying supplies are reassembled, returned to the control of the unit commander, and prepared for onward movement. The joint complex commander designating the location will coordinate the use of the facilities with other allied commands and the host nation, and will provide life support to the units while in the marshalling area.

Mass: 1. The concentration of combat power. 2. The military formation in which units are spaced at less than the normal distances and intervals.

Mass casualty: Any large number of casualties produced in a relatively short period of time, usually as the result of a single incident such as a military aircraft accident, hurricane, flood, earthquake, or armed attack that exceeds local logistic support capabilities. Casualty.

Massed fire: -1. The fire of the batteries of two or more ships directed against a single target. 2. Fire from a number of weapons directed at a single point or small area.

Master: The commanding officer of a United States Naval Ship, a commercial ship, or a government-owned general agency agreement ship operated for the Military Sealift Command by a civilian company to transport Department of Defense cargo. MA.

Master air attack plan: A plan that contains key information that forms the foundation of the joint air tasking order. Sometimes referred to as the air employment plan or joint air tasking order shell. Information that may be found in the plan includes joint force commander guidance, joint force air component commander guidance, support plans, component requests, target update requests, availability of capabilities and forces, target information from target lists, aircraft allocation, etc. MAAP. air attack; target.

Master film: The earliest generation of imagery (negative or positive) from which subsequent copies are produced.

Master plot: A portion of a map or overlay on which are drawn the outlines of the areas covered by an air photographic sortie. Latitude and longitude, map, and sortie information are shown. Sortie plot.

Materials handling: The movement of materials to, through, and from productive processes; in warehouses and storage; and in receiving and shipping areas.

Materials handling equipment: Mechanical devices for handling of supplies with greater ease and economy. MHE. Materials handling.

Materiel: All items (including ships, tanks, self-propelled weapons, aircraft, etc., and related spares, repair parts, and support equipment, but excluding real property, installations, and utilities) necessary to equip, operate, maintain, and support military activities without distinction as to its application for administrative or combat purposes. Equipment; personal property.

Materiel cognizance: Denotes responsibility for exercising supply management over items or categories of materiel.

Materiel inventory objective: The quantity of an item required to be on hand and on order on M-day in order to equip, provide a materiel pipeline, and sustain the approved US force structure and those Allied forces designated for US materiel support, through the period prescribed for war materiel planning purposes. It is the quantity by which the war materiel requirement exceeds the war materiel procurement capability and the war materiel requirement adjustment. It includes the M-day force materiel requirement and the war reserve materiel requirement

Materiel pipeline: The quantity of an item required in the worldwide supply system to maintain an uninterrupted replacement flow.

Materiel readiness: The availability of materiel required by a military organization to support its wartime activities or contingencies, disaster relief, or other emergencies.

Materiel release confirmation: A notification from a shipping or storage activity advising the originator of a materiel release order of the positive action taken on the order. It will also be used with appropriate shipment status document identifier codes as a reply to a follow up initiated by the inventory control point.

Materiel release order: An order issued by an accountable supply system manager directing a non-accountable activity within the same supply distribution complex to release and ship materiel.

Materiel requirements: Those quantities of items of equipment and supplies necessary to equip, provide a materiel pipeline, and sustain a Service, formation, organization, or unit in the fulfillment of its purposes or tasks during a specified period.

Maximum effective range: The maximum distance at which a weapon may be expected to be accurate and achieve the desired effect.

Maximum elevation figure: A figure, shown in each quadrangle bounded by ticked graticule lines on aeronautical charts, which represents the height in thousands and hundreds of feet, above mean sea level, of the highest known natural or manmade feature in that quadrangle, plus suitable factors to allow for inaccuracy and incompleteness of the topographical heighting information.

Maximum enlisted amount: For any month, the sum of: a. the highest rate of basic pay payable for such month to any enlisted member of the Armed Forces of the United States at the highest pay grade applicable to enlisted members; and b. in the case of officers entitled to special pay under Title 37, United States Code, for such month, the amount of such special pay payable to such officers for such month.

Maximum landing weight: The maximum gross weight due to design or operational limitations at which an aircraft is permitted to land.

Maximum operating depth: The keel depth that a submarine is not to exceed during operations. This depth is determined by the submarine's national naval authority. Test depth.

Maximum ordinate: In artillery and naval gunfire support, the height of the highest point in the trajectory of a projectile above the horizontal plane passing through its origin. vertex height.

Maximum permissible concentration: Radioactivity concentration guide.

Maximum permissible dose: That radiation dose which a military commander or

other appropriate authority may prescribe as the limiting cumulative radiation dose to be received over a specific period of time by members of the command, consistent with current operational military considerations.

Maximum range: The greatest distance a weapon can fire without consideration of dispersion.

Maximum sustained speed: In road transport, the highest speed at which a vehicle, with its rated payload, can be driven for an extended period on a level first-class highway without sustaining damage.

Maximum take-off weight: The maximum gross weight due to design or operational limitations at which an aircraft is permitted to take off.

M-day force materiel requirement: The quantity of an item required to be on hand and on order (on M-day minus one day) to equip and provide a materiel pipeline for the approved peacetime US force structure, both active and reserve.

Meaconing: A system of receiving radio beacon signals and rebroadcasting them on the same frequency to confuse navigation. The meaconing stations cause inaccurate bearings to be obtained by aircraft or ground stations.

Mean lethal dose: 1. The amount of nuclear irradiation of the whole body which would be fatal to 50 percent of the exposed personnel in a given period of time. 2. The dose of chemical agent that would kill 50 percent of exposed, unprotected, and untreated personnel.

Mean line of advance: In naval usage, the direction expected to be made good over a sustained period.

Mean point of impact: The point whose coordinates are the arithmetic means of the coordinates of the separate points of impact/burst of a finite number of projectiles fired or released at the same aiming point under a given set of conditions.

Mean sea level: The average height of the surface of the sea for all stages of the tide; used as a reference for elevations. MSL.

Measured mile: In maritime navigation, distance precisely measured and marked, used by a vessel to calibrate its log.

Measurement and signature intelligence: Intelligence obtained by quantitative and qualitative analysis of data derived from specific technical sensors for the purpose of identifying any distinctive features associated with the emitter or sender, and to facilitate subsequent identification and/or measurement of the same. The detected feature may be either reflected or emitted. MASINT. Intelligence; scientific and technical intelligence.

Measurement and Signature Intelligence Requirements System: A system for the management of theater and national measurement and signature intelligence (MASINT) collection requirements. It provides automated tools for users in support of submission, review, and validation of MASINT nominations of requirements to be tasked for national and Department of Defense MASINT collection, production, and exploitation resources. Called MRS. Measurement and signature intelligence.

Measurement ton: The unit of volumetric measurement of equipment associated with surface-delivered cargo. Measurement tons equal total cubic feet divided by 40 (1MTON = 40 cubic feet). M/T, MT, MTON.

Measure of effectiveness: A criterion used to assess changes in system behavior, capability, or operational environment that is tied to measuring the attainment of an end state, achievement of an objective, or creation of an effect. MOE. Combat assessment; mission.

Measure of performance: A criterion used to assess friendly actions that is tied to measuring task accomplishment. MOP.

Mechanical sweep: In naval mine warfare, any sweep used with the object of

physically contacting the mine or its appendages.

Median incapacitating dose: The amount or quantity of chemical agent which when introduced into the body will incapacitate 50 percent of exposed, unprotected personnel.

Media pool: A limited number of news media who represent a larger number of news media organizations for purposes of news gathering and sharing of material during a specified activity. Pooling is typically used when news media support resources cannot accommodate a large number of journalists. News media representative; public affairs.

Medical civil-military operations: All military health-related activities in support of a joint force commander that establish, enhance, maintain or influence relations between the joint or multinational force and host nation, multinational governmental and nongovernmental civilian organizations and authorities, and the civilian populace in order to facilitate military operations, achieve US operational objectives, and positively impact the health sector. MCMO.

Medical evacuees: Personnel who are wounded, injured, or ill and must be moved to or between medical facilities.

Medical intelligence: That category of intelligence resulting from collection, evaluation, analysis, and interpretation of foreign medical, bio-scientific, and environmental information that is of interest to strategic planning and to military medical planning and operations for the conservation of the fighting strength of friendly forces and the formation of assessments of foreign medical capabilities in both military and civilian sectors. MEDINT. Intelligence.

Medical intelligence preparation of the operational environment: A systematic continuing process that analyzes information on medical and disease threats, enemy capabilities, terrain, weather, local medical infrastructure, potential humanitarian and refugee situations, transportation issues, and political, religious and social issues for all types of operations. Medical intelligence preparation of the operational environment is a component of the health service support mission analysis process, and the resulting statistics serves as a basis for developing health service support estimates and plans. It includes: defining the operational environment, describing the operational environment effects on health service support operations, evaluating the operational environmental threats, and determining courses of action to meet actual and potential threats. MIPOE.

Medical officer: Physician with officer rank. MO.

Medical protocols: Directives issued by competent military authority that delineate the circumstances and limitations under which United States medical forces will initiate medical care and support to those individuals that are not Department of Defense health care beneficiaries or designated eligible for care in a military medical treatment facility by the Secretary of Defense.

Medical regulating: The actions and coordination necessary to arrange for the movement of patients through the levels of care. This process matches patients with a medical treatment facility that has the necessary health service support capabilities and available bed space. Health service support; medical treatment facility.

Medical surveillance: The ongoing, systematic collection, analysis, and interpretation of data derived from instances of medical care or medical evaluation, and the reporting of population-based information for characterizing and countering threats to a population's health, well-being and performance. Surveillance.

Medical treatment facility: A facility established for the purpose of furnishing medical and/ or dental care to eligible individuals. MTF.

Medium-angle loft bombing: Type of loft bombing wherein weapon release occurs at an angle between 35 and 75 degrees above the horizontal.

Medium-lot storage: Generally defined as a quantity of material that will require one to three pallet stacks, stored to maximum height. Thus, the term refers to relatively small lots as distinguished from definitely large or small lots. Storage. medium-range ballistic missile — A ballistic missile with a range capability from about 600 to 1,500 nautical miles.

Medium-range bomber aircraft: A bomber designed for a tactical operating radius of under 1,000 nautical miles at design gross weight and design bomb load.

Medium-range transport aircraft: Transport aircraft.

Medium-scale map: A map having a scale larger than 1:600,000 and smaller than 1:75,000. Map.

Meeting engagement: A combat action that occurs when a moving force, incompletely deployed for battle, engages an enemy at an unexpected time and place.

Megaton weapon: A nuclear weapon, the yield of which is measured in terms of millions of tons of trinitrotoluene explosive equivalents. Kiloton weapon; nominal weapon; sub kiloton weapon.

Mensuration:- The process of measurement of a feature or location on the earth to determine an absolute latitude, longitude, and elevation. For targeting applications, the errors inherent in both the source for measurement as well as the measurement processes must be understood and reported.

Merchant convoy: A convoy consisting primarily of merchant ships controlled by the naval control of shipping organization.

Merchant intelligence: In intelligence handling, communication instructions for reporting by merchant vessels of vital intelligence sightings. MERINT.

Merchant ship: A vessel engaged in mercantile trade except river craft, estuarial

craft, or craft which operate solely within harbor limits.

Merchant ship casualty report: A report by message, or other means, of a casualty to a merchant ship at sea or in port. Merchant ship casualty reports are sent by the escort force commander or other appropriate authority to the operational control authority in whose area the casualty occurred.

Merchant ship communications system: A worldwide system of communications to and from merchant ships using the peacetime commercial organization as a basis but under operational control authority, with the ability to employ the broadcast mode to ships when the situation makes radio silence necessary. Also called mercomms system.

Merchant ship control zone: A defined area of sea or ocean inside which it may be necessary to offer guidance, control, and protection to Allied shipping.

Merchant ship reporting and control message system: A worldwide message system for reporting the movements of and information relating to the control of merchant ships.

Mercomms system: Merchant ship communications system.

Message: Any thought or idea expressed briefly in a plain or secret language and prepared in a form suitable for transmission by any means of communication.

Message (telecommunications): Record information expressed in plain or encrypted language and prepared in a format specified for intended transmission by a telecommunications system.

Meteorological and oceanographic: A term used to convey all meteorological, oceanographic, and space environmental factors as provided by Services, support agencies, and other sources. These factors include the whole range of atmospheric (weather) and oceanographic phenomena, from the sub-bottom of the earth's oceans up to the space environment (space weather). METOC.

Meteorological and oceanographic data: Measurements or observations of meteorological and oceanographic variables.

Meteorological and oceanographic environment: The surroundings, which include conditions, resources, and natural phenomena, in and through which the joint force operates. The complete environment extends from the sub-bottom of the Earth's oceans, through maritime, land areas, airspace, ionosphere, and outward into space.

Meteorology: The study dealing with the phenomena of the atmosphere including the physics, chemistry, and dynamics extending to the effects of the atmosphere on the Earth's surface and the oceans.

Microform: A generic term for any form, whether film, video tape, paper, or other medium, containing miniaturized or otherwise compressed images which cannot be read without special display devices.

Midcourse guidance: The guidance applied to a missile between termination of the boost phase and the start of the terminal phase of flight.

Midcourse phase: That portion of the flight of a ballistic missile between the boost phase and the terminal phase. Ballistic trajectory; boost phase; terminal phase.

Migrant: A person who (1) belongs to a normally migratory culture who may cross national boundaries, or (2) has fled his or her native country for economic reasons rather than fear of political or ethnic persecution.

Militarily significant fallout: Radioactive contamination capable of inflicting radiation doses on personnel which may result in a reduction of their combat effectiveness.

Military Affiliate Radio System: A program conducted by the Departments of the Army, Navy, and Air Force in which amateur radio stations and operators participate in and contribute to the mission of providing auxiliary and emergency communications on a local, national, or international basis as an adjunct to normal military communications. MARS.

Military assistance advisory group: A joint Service group, normally under the military command of a commander of a unified command and representing the Secretary of Defense, which primarily administers the US military assistance planning and programming in the host country. MAAG.

Military Assistance Articles and Services List: A Department of Defense publication listing source, availability, and price of items and services for use by the unified commands and Military Departments in preparing military assistance plans and programs.

Military assistance for civil disturbances: A mission of civil support involving Department of Defense support, normally based on the direction of the President, to suppress insurrections, rebellions, and domestic violence, and provide federal supplemental assistance to the states to maintain law and order. MACDIS.

Military Assistance Program: That portion of the US security assistance authorized by the Foreign Assistance Act of 1961, as amended, which provides defense articles and services to recipients on a non reimbursable (grant) basis. MAP.

Military Assistance Program training: International military education and training.

Military assistance to civil authorities: The broad mission of civil support consisting of the three mission subsets of military support to civil authorities, military support to civilian law enforcement agencies, and military assistance for civil disturbances. MACA.

Military capability: The ability to achieve a specified wartime objective (win a war or battle, destroy a target set). It includes four major components: force structure, modernization, readiness, and sustainability. a. **force structure** – Numbers, size, and composition of the units that comprise US defense forces; e.g., divisions, ships, air wings. b. **modernization** – Technical sophistication of forces, units, weapon systems, and equipments. c. **unit readiness** – The ability to provide capabilities required by the combatant commanders to execute their assigned missions. This is derived from the ability of each unit to deliver the outputs for which it was designed. d. **sustainability** – The ability to maintain the necessary level and duration of operational activity to achieve military objectives. Sustainabilit is a function of providing for and maintaining those levels of ready forces, materiel, and consumables necessary to support military effort. readiness.

Military characteristics: -Those characteristics of equipment upon which depends its ability to perform desired military functions. Military characteristics include physical and operational characteristics but not technical characteristics.

Military civic action: The use of preponderantly indigenous military forces on projects useful to the local population at all levels in such fields as education, training, public works, agriculture, transportation, communications, health, sanitation, and others contributing to economic and social development, which would also serve to improve the standing of the military forces with the population. (US forces may at times advise or engage in military civic actions in overseas areas.)

Military construction: Any construction, alteration, development, conversion, or extension of any kind carried out with respect to a military installation. MILCON.

Military container moved via ocean: Commercial or Government owned (or leased) shipping containers that are moved via ocean transportation without bogey wheels attached, i.e., lifted on and off the ship. SEAVAN.

Military damage assessment: An appraisal of the effects of an attack on a nation's military forces to determine residual military capability and to support planning for recovery and reconstitution. See also damage assessment.

Military deception: Actions executed to deliberately mislead adversary military decision makers as to friendly military capabilities, intentions, and operations, thereby causing the adversary to take specific actions (or inactions) that will contribute to the accomplishment of the friendly mission. MILDEC. Deception.

Military Department: One of the departments within the Department of Defense created by the National Security Act of 1947, as amended. MILDEP. Department of the Air Force; Department of the Army; Department of the Navy.

Military designed vehicle: A vehicle having military characteristics resulting from military research and development processes, designed primarily for use by forces in the field in direct connection with, or support of, combat or tactical operations.

Military education: The systematic instruction of individuals in subjects that will

enhance their knowledge of the science and art of war. Military training.

Military engagement: Routine contact and interaction between individuals or elements of the Armed Forces of the United States and those of another nation's armed forces, or foreign and domestic civilian authorities or agencies to build trust and confidence, share information, coordinate mutual activities, and maintain influence.

Military geographic documentation: Military geographic information that has been evaluated, processed, summarized, and published.

Military geographic information: Information concerning physical aspects, resources, and artificial features of the terrain that is necessary for planning and operations.

Military geography: The specialized field of geography dealing with natural and manmade physical features that may affect the planning and conduct of military operations.

Military government ordinance: An enactment on the authority of a military governor promulgating laws or rules regulating the occupied territory under such control.

Military governor: The military commander or other designated person who, in an occupied territory, exercises supreme authority over the civil population subject to the laws and usages of war and to any directive received from the commander's government or superior.

Military grid: Two sets of parallel lines intersecting at right angles and forming

squares; the grid is superimposed on maps, charts, and other similar representations of the surface of the Earth in an accurate and consistent manner to permit identification of ground locations with respect to other locations and the computation of direction and distance to other points. Also military grid reference system.

Military grid reference system: A system which uses a standard-scaled grid square, based on a point of origin on a map projection of the surface of the Earth in an accurate and consistent manner to permit either position referencing or the computation of direction and distance between grid positions. MGRS. Military grid.

Military health system: A health system that supports the military mission by fostering, protecting, sustaining, and restoring health. It also provides the direction, resources, health care providers, and other means necessary for promoting the health of the beneficiary population. These include developing and promoting health awareness issues to educate customers, discovering and resolving environmentally based health threats, providing health services, including preventive care and problem intervention, and improving the means and methods for maintaining the health of the beneficiary population, by constantly evaluating the performance of the health care services system.

Military independent: A merchant ship or auxiliary sailed singly but controlled and reported as a military unit. See also independent.

Military intelligence: Intelligence on any foreign military or military-related situation or activity which is significant to military policymaking or the planning and conduct of military operations and activities. MI.

Military Intelligence Board: A decision-making forum which formulates Department of Defense intelligence policy and programming priorities. MIB. Intelligence; military intelligence.

Military intervention: The deliberate act of a nation or a group of nations to introduce its military forces into the course of an existing controversy.

Military journalist: A US Service member or Department of Defense civilian employee providing photographic, print, radio, or television command information for military internal audiences. See also command information.

Military land transportation resources: All military-owned transportation resources, designated for common-user, over the ground, point-to-point use.

Military load classification: A standard system in which a route, bridge, or raft is assigned class number(s) representing the load it can carry. Vehicles are also assigned number(s) indicating the minimum class of route, bridge, or raft they are authorized to use. Route classification.

Military necessity: The principle whereby a belligerent has the right to apply any

measures which are required to bring about the successful conclusion of a military operation and which are not forbidden by the laws of war.

Military nuclear power: A nation which has nuclear weapons and the capability for their employment.

Military occupation: A condition in which territory is under the effective control of a foreign armed force. Occupied territory; phases of military government.

Military options: A range of military force responses that can be projected to accomplish assigned tasks. Options include one or a combination of the following: civic action, humanitarian assistance, civil affairs, and other military activities to develop positive relationships with other countries; confidence building and other measures to reduce military tensions; military presence; activities to convey threats to adversaries as well as truth projections; military deceptions and psychological operations; quarantines, blockades, and harassment operations; raids; intervention operations; armed conflict involving air, land, maritime, and strategic warfare operations; support for law enforcement authorities to counter international criminal activities (terrorism, narcotics trafficking, slavery, and piracy); support for law enforcement authorities to suppress domestic rebellion; and support for insurgency, counterinsurgency, and civil war in foreign countries. Civil affairs; foreign humanitarian assistance; military civic action.

Military ordinary mail: A special military airlift service for ordinary official mail being sent to, from, or between overseas areas. MOM.

Military performance specification container: A container that meets specific written standards. Aviation and Troop Command, US Army, procures military performance specification containers for the Army and will perform like services for othér Department of Defense components on request. MILSPEC container.

Military post office: A branch of a designated US-based post office such as New York, San Francisco, Miami, or Seattle established by US Postal Service authority and operated by one of the Military Services. The term includes Army, Air Force, Navy, Marine Corps, and established Coast Guard post offices MPO.

Military postal clerk: A person of the US Armed Forces officially designated to perform postal duties.

Military Postal Service: The command, organization, personnel, and facilities established to provide, through military post offices, a means for the transmission of mail to and from the Department of Defense, members of the US Armed Forces, and other authorized agencies and individuals. MPS.

Military Postal Service Agency: -The single manager operating agency established to manage the Military Postal Service. MPSA.

Military posture: The military disposition, strength, and condition of readiness as it affects capabilities.

Military requirement: An established need justifying the timely allocation of resources to achieve a capability to accomplish approved military objectives, missions, or tasks. Also called operational requirement. Objective force level.

Military resources: Military and civilian personnel, facilities, equipment, and supplies under the control of a Department of Defense component.

Military Sealift Command: A major command of the US Navy reporting to Commander Fleet Forces Command, and the US Transportation Command's component command responsible for designated common-user sealift transportation services to deploy, employ, sustain, and redeploy US forces on a global basis. MSC. Transportation component command.

Military Sealift Command-controlled ships: Those ships assigned by the Military

Sealift Command (MSC) for a specific operation. They may be MSC nucleus fleet ships, contract-operated MSC ships, MSC-controlled time or voyage-chartered commercial ships, or MSC-controlled ships allocated by the Maritime Administration to MSC to carry out Department of Defense objectives.

Military Sealift Command force: The Military Sealift Command force common-user sealift consists of three subsets: the Naval Fleet Auxiliary Force, common-user ocean transportation, and the special mission support force. These ship classes include government-owned ships (normally civilian-manned) and ships acquired by Military Sealift Command charter or allocated from other government agencies. Common-user sealift; Military Sealift Command.

Military Service: A branch of the Armed Forces of the United States, established by act of Congress, in which persons are appointed, enlisted, or inducted for military service, and which operates and is administered within a military or executive department. The Military Services are: the United States Army, the United States Navy, the United States Air Force, the United States Marine Corps, and the United States Coast Guard.

Military source operations: Refers to the collection, from, by and/or via humans, of foreign and military and military-related intelligence.

Military standard requisitioning and issue procedure: A uniform procedure

established by the Department of Defense for use within the Department of Defense to govern requisition and issue of materiel within standardized priorities. MILSTRIP.

Military standard transportation and movement procedures: Uniform and standard transportation data, documentation, and control procedures applicable to all cargo movements in the Department of Defense transportation system. MILSTAMP.

Military support to civil authorities: A mission of civil support consisting of support for natural or man-made disasters, chemical, biological, radiological, nuclear, or high-yield explosive consequence management, and other support as required. MSCA.

Military support to civilian law enforcement agencies: A mission of civil support that includes support to civilian law enforcement agencies. This includes but is not limited to: combating terrorism, counterdrug operations, national security special events, and national critical infrastructure and key asset protection. MSCLEA.

Military symbol: A graphic sign used, usually on map, display or diagram, to represent a particular military unit, installation, activity, or other item of military interest.

Military technician: A Federal civilian employee providing full-time support to a National Guard, Reserve, or Active Component organization for administration, training, and maintenance of the Selected Reserve. MILTECH.

Military traffic: Department of Defense personnel, mail, and cargo to be, or being, transported.

Military training: 1. The instruction of personnel to enhance their capacity to perform specific military functions and tasks. 2. The exercise of one or more military units conducted to enhance their combat readiness. Military education.

Military van (container): Military-owned, demountable container, conforming to US and international standards, operated in a centrally controlled fleet for movement of military cargo. MILVAN.

MILSPEC container: Military performance specification containers.

MILVAN chassis: The compatible chassis to which the military van (container) is

attached by coupling the lower four standard corner fittings of the container to compatible mounting blocks in the chassis to permit road movement.

Mine: 1. In land mine warfare, an explosive or other material, normally encased, designed to destroy or damage ground vehicles, boats, or aircraft, or designed to wound, kill, or otherwise incapacitate personnel. It is designed to be detonated by the action of its victim, by the passage of time, or by controlled means. 2. In naval mine warfare, an explosive device laid in the water with the intention of damaging or sinking ships or of deterring shipping from entering an area. Land mine warfare; mine warfare.

Mineable waters: Waters where naval mines of any given type may be effective against any given target.

Mine clearance: The process of removing all mines from a route or area.

Mine-cluster: A number of mines (not to exceed five) laid within a two-meter semicircle of the central mine.

Mine countermeasures; - All methods for preventing or reducing damage or danger from mines. MCM.

Mined area: An area declared dangerous due to the presence or suspected presence of mines.

Mine disposal: The operation by suitably qualified personnel designed to render safe, neutralize, recover, remove, or destroy mines.

Minefield: 1. In land warfare, an area of ground containing mines emplaced with or without a pattern. 2. In naval warfare, an area of water containing mines laid with or without a pattern. Land mine warfare; mine; mine warfare.

Minefield breaching: In land mine warfare, the process of clearing a lane through a minefield under tactical conditions. Minefield lane.

Minefield density: In land mine warfare, the average number of mines per meter of minefield front, or the average number of mines per square meter of minefield. In naval warfare, the average number of mines per nautical mile.

Minefield lane: A marked lane, unmined, or cleared of mines, leading through a minefield.

Minefield marking: Visible marking of all points required in laying a minefield and indicating the extent of such minefields.

Minefield record: A complete written record of all pertinent information concerning a minefield, submitted on a standard form by the officer in charge of the laying operations.

Minefield report: An oral, electronic, or written communication concerning mining activities (friendly or enemy) submitted in a standard format by the fastest secure means available.

Mine hunting: Employment of sensor and neutralization systems, whether air, surface, or subsurface, to locate and dispose of individual mines. Mine hunting is conducted to eliminate mines in a known field when sweeping is not feasible or desirable, or to verify the presence or absence of mines in a given area. Minesweeping.

Mine row: A single row of mines or clusters of mines. Mine strip.

Mine spotting : In naval mine warfare, the process of visually observing a mine or minefield.

Mine strip: In land mine warfare, two parallel mine rows laid simultaneously six meters or six paces apart.

Minesweeping: The technique of clearing mines using either mechanical, explosive, or influence sweep equipment. Mechanical sweeping removes, disturbs, or otherwise neutralizes the mine; explosive sweeping causes sympathetic detonations in, damages, or displaces the mine; and influence sweeping produces either the acoustic and/or magnetic influence required to detonate the mine. Mine hunting.

Mine warfare: The strategic, operational, and tactical use of mines and mine countermeasures. Mine warfare is divided into two basic subdivisions: the laying of mines to degrade the enemy's capabilities to wage land, air, and maritime warfare; and the countering of enemy-land mines to permit friendly maneuver or use of selected land or sea areas. MIW.

Mine warfare chart: A special naval chart, at a scale of 1:50,000 or larger (preferably 1:25,000 or larger) designed for planning and executing mine warfare operations, either based on an existing standard nautical chart, or produced to special specifications.

Mine warfare forces (naval): Navy forces charged with the strategic, operational, and tactical use of naval mines and their countermeasures. Such forces are capable of offensive and defensive measures in connection with laying and clearing mines.

Mine warfare group: A task organization of mine warfare units for the conduct of mine laying and/or mine countermeasures in maritime operations.

Mine watching: In naval mine warfare, the mine countermeasures procedure to detect, record and, if possible, track potential minelayers and to detect, find the position of, and/or identify mines during the actual mine laying.

Mine weapons: The collective term for all weapons which may be used in mine warfare.

Minimize: A condition wherein normal message and telephone traffic is drastically reduced in order that messages connected with an actual or simulated emergency shall not be delayed.

Minimum aircraft operating surface: The minimum surface on an airfield which is essential for the movement of aircraft. It includes the aircraft dispersal areas, the minimum operating strip, and the taxiways between them. Minimum operating strip.

Minimum attack altitude: The lowest altitude determined by the tactical use of weapons, terrain consideration, and weapons effects that permits the safe conduct of an air attack and/or minimizes effective enemy counteraction.

Minimum crossing altitude: The lowest altitude at certain radio fixes at which an aircraft must cross when proceeding in the direction of a higher minimum en route instrument flight rules altitude.

Minimum essential equipment: That part of authorized allowances of Army equipment, clothing, and supplies needed to preserve the integrity of a unit during movement without regard to the performance of its combat or service mission. Items common within this category will normally be carried by or accompany troops to the port and will be placed aboard the same ships with the troops. As used in movement directives, minimum essential equipment refers to specific items of both organizational and individual clothing and equipment.

Minimum force: Those minimum actions, including the use of armed force, sufficient to bring a situation under control or to defend against hostile act or hostile intent. All actions must cease as soon as the target complies with instructions or ceases hostile action. The firing of weapons is to be considered as a means of last resort.

Minimum nuclear safe distance: The sum of the radius of safety and the buffer distance.

Minimum nuclear warning time: The sum of system reaction time and personnel reaction time.

Minimum obstruction clearance altitude: The specified altitude in effect between radio fixes on very high frequency omnirange airways, off-airway routes, or route segments, which meets obstruction-clearance requirements for the entire route segment, and that assures acceptable navigational signal coverage only within 22 miles of a very high frequency omnirange.

Minimum operating strip: A runway which meets the minimum requirements for operating assigned and/or allocated aircraft types on a particular airfield at maximum or combat gross weight. Minimum aircraft operating surface.

Minimum range: 1. Least range setting of a gun at which the projectile will clear an obstacle or friendly troops between the gun and the target. 2. Shortest distance to which a gun can fire from a given position. 3. The range at which a projectile or fuse will be armed.

Minimum reception altitude: The lowest altitude required to receive adequate signals to determine specific very high frequency omnirange and tactical air navigation fixes.

Minimum residual radioactivity weapon : A nuclear weapon designed to have

optimum reduction of unwanted effects from fallout, rainout, and burst site

radioactivity. Salted weapon.

Minimum-risk route: A temporary corridor of defined dimensions recommended for use by high-speed, fixed-wing aircraft that presents the minimum known hazards to low-flying aircraft transiting the combat zone. MRR.

Minimum safe altitude: The altitude below which it is hazardous to fly owing to presence of high ground or other obstacles.

Minor control: Photogrammetric control.

Minor installation: In the Air Force, a facility operated by an Active, Reserve, or Guard unit of at least squadron size that does not otherwise satisfy all the criteria for a major installation. This category includes Air Force stations; air stations; Air Reserve stations; and Air Guard stations. Examples of minor installations are Active, Reserve, or Guard flying operations that are located at civilian-owned airports. Installation complex.

Minor port: A port having facilities for the discharge of cargo from coasters or lighters only.

Misfire: 1. Failure to fire or explode properly. 2. Failure of a primer or the propelling charge of a round or projectile to function wholly or in part.

Missed approach: An approach which is not completed by landing.

Missile assembly checkout facility: A building, van, or other type structure located near the operational missile launching location and designed for the final assembly and checkout of the missile system.

Missile control system: A system that serves to maintain attitude stability and to correct deflections. See also missile guidance system.

Missile defense: Defensive measures designed to destroy attacking enemy missiles, or to nullify or reduce the effectiveness of such attack.

Missile destruct: Intentional destruction of a missile or similar vehicle for safety or other reasons.

Missile destruct system: A system which, when operated by external command or preset internal means, destroys the missile or similar vehicle.

Missile guidance system: A system which evaluates flight information, correlates it with target data, determines the desired flight path of a missile, and communicates the necessary commands to the missile flight control system. Missile control system.

Missile release line: The line at which an attacking aircraft could launch an air-to-surface missile against a specific target.

Mission: 1. The task, together with the purpose, that clearly indicates the action to be taken and the reason therefore. 2. In common usage, especially when applied to lower military units, a duty assigned to an individual or unit; a task. 3. The dispatching of one or more aircraft to accomplish one particular task.

Mission assignment: The vehicle used by the Department of Homeland Security/Emergency Preparedness and Response/ Federal Emergency Management Agency to support federal operations in a Stafford Act major disaster or emergency declaration that orders immediate, short-term emergency response assistance when an applicable state or local government is overwhelmed by the event and lacks the capability to perform, or contract for, the necessary work.

Mission-capable;- Material condition of an aircraft indicating it can perform at least one and potentially all of its designated missions. Mission-capable is further defined as the sum of full mission-capable and partial mission-capable. Also called MC. Full mission-capable; partial mission-capable; partial mission-capable, maintenance; partial mission-capable, supply.

Mission-essential material: 1. That materiel authorized and available to combat, combat support, combat service support, and combat readiness training forces in order to accomplish their assigned missions. 2. For the purpose of sizing organic industrial facilities, that Service-designated materiel authorized to combat, combat support, combat service support, and combat readiness training forces and activities, including Reserve and National Guard activities, that is required to support approved emergency and/or war plans, and where the materiel is used to: a. destroy the enemy or the enemy's capacity to continue war; b. provide battlefield protection of personnel; c. communicate under war conditions; d. detect, locate, or maintain surveillance over the enemy; e. provide combat transportation and support of men and materiel; and f. support training functions. Mission-essential materiel should also be suitable for employment under emergency plans to meet the purposes enumerated above.

Mission needs statement: A formatted non-system-specific statement containing operational capability needs and written in broad operational terms. It describes required operational capabilities and constraints to be studied during the Concept Exploration and Definition Phase of the Requirements Generation Process. MNS.

Mission-oriented items: Items for which requirements computations are based upon the assessment of enemy capabilities expressed as a known or estimated quantity of total targets to be destroyed. See also combination mission/level of effort-oriented items; level of effort-oriented items.

Mission-oriented protective posture: A flexible system of protection against chemical, biological, radiological, and nuclear contamination. This posture requires personnel to wear only that protective clothing and equipment (mission-oriented protective posture gear) appropriate to the threat level, work rate imposed by the mission, temperature, and humidity. MOPP. Mission-oriented protective posture gear.

Mission-oriented protective posture gear: Military term for individual protective equipment including suit, boots, gloves, mask with hood, first aid treatments, and decontamination kits issued to military members. MOPP gear. Decontamination; mission-oriented protective posture.

Mission review report (photographic interpretation): An intelligence report containing information on all targets covered by one photographic sortie.

Mission specific data sets: Further densification of global geospatial foundation data. Information created to support specific operations, operation plans, training, or system development. Information conforms to established Department of Defense data specifications. MSDS. Geospatial information and services.

Mission statement: A short sentence or paragraph that describes the organization's essential task (or tasks) and purpose – a clear statement of the action to be taken and the reason for doing so. The mission statement contains the elements of who, what, when, where, and why, but seldom specifies how.

Mission type order: 1. An order issued to a lower unit that includes the accomplishment of the total mission assigned to the higher headquarters. 2. An order to a unit to perform a mission without specifying how it is to be accomplished.

Mixed: In artillery and naval gunfire support, a spotting, or an observation, by a

spotter or an observer to indicate that the rounds fired resulted in an equal number of air and impact bursts.

Mixed bag: In naval mine warfare, a collection of mines of various types, firing

systems, sensitivities, arming delays and ship counter settings.

Mixed minefield: A minefield containing both antitank and antipersonnel mines. Minefield.

Mobile defense: Defense of an area or position in which maneuver is used with organization of fire and utilization of terrain to seize the initiative from the enemy.

Mobile inshore undersea warfare unit: A Navy surveillance unit that provides seaward security to joint logistics over-the-shore operations from either a port or harbor complex or unimproved beach sites. The mobile inshore undersea warfare unit is equipped with mobile radar, sonar, and communications equipment located within a mobile van. MIUWU. joint logistics over-the-shore operations.

Mobile mine: In naval mine warfare, a mine designed to be propelled to its proposed laying position by propulsion equipment like a torpedo. It sinks at the end of its run and then operates like a mine.

Mobile security force: A dedicated security force designed to defeat Level I and II threats on a base and/or base cluster. MSF.

Mobile support group (naval): Provides logistic support to ships at an anchorage; in effect a naval base afloat, although certain of its supporting elements may be located ashore.

Mobile training team: A team consisting of one or more US military or civilian personnel sent on temporary duty, often to a foreign nation, to give instruction. The mission of the team is to train indigenous personnel to operate, maintain, and employ weapons and support systems, or to develop a self-training capability in a particular skill. The Secretary of Defense may direct a team to train either military or civilian indigenous personnel, depending upon host-nation requests. MTT.

Mobility: A quality or capability of military forces which permits them to move from place to place while retaining the ability to fulfill their primary mission.

Mobility Air Forces: The Mobility Air Forces are comprised of those air components and Service components that are assigned air mobility forces and/or that routinely exercise command authority over their operations. MAF.

Mobility analysis: An in-depth examination of all aspects of transportation planning in support of operation plan and operation order development.

Mobility corridor: Areas where a force will be canalized due to terrain restrictions. They allow military forces to capitalize on the principles of mass and speed and are therefore relatively free of obstacles.

Mobility echelon: A subordinate element of a unit that is scheduled for deployment separately from the parent unit.

Mobility system support resources: Those resources that are required to: a. complement the airlift and sealift forces; and/or b. perform those work functions directly related to the origination, processing, or termination of a movement requirement.

Mobilization base: The total of all resources available, or that can be made available, to meet foreseeable wartime needs. Such resources include the manpower and materiel resources and services required for the support of essential military, civilian, and survival activities, as well as the elements affecting their state of readiness, such as (but not limited to) the following: manning levels, state of training, modernization of equipment, mobilization materiel reserves and facilities, continuity of government, civil defense plans and preparedness measures, psychological preparedness of the people, international agreements, planning with industry, dispersion, and standby legislation and controls.

Mobilization exercise: An exercise involving, either completely or in part, the implementation of mobilization plans.

Mobilization site: The designated location where a Reserve Component unit or individual mobilizes or moves after mobilization for further processing, training, and employment. This differs from a mobilization station in that it is not necessarily a military installation. Mobilization; mobilization station; Reserve Components.

Mobilization staff officer: The action officer assigned the principle responsibility or additional duties related to Reserve Component mobilization actions. mobilization; Reserve Components.

Mobilization station: The designated military installation to which a Reserve Component unit or individual is moved for further processing, organizing, equipping, training, and employment and from which the unit or individual may move to an aerial port of embarkation or seaport of embarkation. Mobilization; mobilization site; Reserve Components.

Mock-up: A model, built to scale, of a machine, apparatus, or weapon, used in studying the construction of, and in testing a new development, or in teaching personnel how to operate the actual machine, apparatus, or weapon.

Mode (identification, friend or foe): The number or letter referring to the specific pulse spacing of the signals transmitted by an interrogator o transponder.

Mode of transport: The various modes used for a movement. For each mode, there are several means of transport. They are: a. inland surface transportation (rail, road, and inland waterway); b. sea transport (coastal and ocean); c. air transportation; and d. pipelines.

Modernized Integrated Database: The national level repository for the general military intelligence available to the entire Department of Defense Intelligence Information System community and, through Global Command and Control System integrated imagery and intelligence, to tactical units. This data is maintained and updated by the Defense Intelligence Agency. Commands and Services are delegated responsibility to maintain their portion of the database. MIDB. Database.

Rank Abbreviations	Meaning
MOD	Modified
MOD	Modify
MOD	Ministry Of Defense
MOD	Ministry Of Defence (British)
MOD	Modernization
MOD	Massachusetts Office on Disability
MOD	Mission Operations Directorate
MOD	Maximum Operating Depth
MOD	Maps on Demand
MOD	Military of Defence
MOD	Memorandum of Decision
MOD	Money-Of the-Day
MOD	Mayor's Office on Disability
MOD	Ministry of Overseas Development
MOD	Miscellaneous Obligation Document
MOD	Maritime Operations Division
MOD	Marine Operations Division
MOD	Manufacturers Operations Division
MOD	Management Operations Directorate
MOD	MARS Operating Directive
MOD	Management and Organization Division
MOD	Maintenance Overhaul Designator
MOD	Memorandum Obligation Document
MOD	Management and Operations Division

Modified combined obstacle overlay: A joint intelligence preparation of the battle space product used to portray the effects of each battle space dimension on military operations. It normally depicts militarily significant aspects of the battle space environment, such as obstacles restricting military movement, key geography, and military objectives. MCOO. joint intelligence preparation of a battle space.

Moment: In air transport, the weight of a load multiplied by its distance from a

reference point in the aircraft.

Monitoring: 1. The act of listening, carrying out surveillance on, and/or recording the emissions of one's own or allied forces for the purposes of maintaining and improving procedural standards and security, or for reference, as applicable. 2. The act of listening, carrying out surveillance on, and/or recording of enemy emissions for intelligence purposes. 3. The act of detecting the presence of radiation and the measurement thereof with radiation measuring instruments. Also called radiological monitoring.

Monitoring service: The general surveillance of known air traffic movements by reference to a radar scope presentation or other means, for the purpose of passing advisory information concerning conflicting traffic or providing navigational assistance. Direct supervision or control is not exercised, nor is positive separation provided.

Moored: Lying with both anchors down or tied to a pier, anchor buoy, or mooring buoy.

Moored mine: A contact or influence-operated mine of positive buoyancy held below the surface by a mooring attached to a sinker or anchor on the bottom. See also mine.

Mopping up: The liquidation of remnants of enemy resistance in an area that has been surrounded or isolated, or through which other units have passed without eliminating all active resistance.

Mortar: A muzzle-loading, indirect fire weapon with either a rifled or smooth bore. It usually has a shorter range than a howitzer, employs a higher angle of fire, and has a tube with a length of 10 to 20 calibers. Gun; howitzer.

Mortuary affairs: Covers the search for, recovery, identification, preparation, and disposition of remains of persons for whom the Services are responsible by status and Executive Order. Joint mortuary affairs office.

Mosaic: An assembly of overlapping photographs that have been matched to form a continuous photographic representation of a portion of the surface of the Earth. Controlled mosaic; semi-controlled mosaic.

Most capable Service or agency: The organization that is best suited to provide common supply commodity or logistic service support within a specific joint operation. In this context, "best suited" could mean the Service or agency that has required or readily available resources and/or expertise. The most capable Service may or may not be the dominant user in any particular operation. Agency.

Motorized unit: A unit equipped with complete motor transportation that enables all of its personnel, weapons, and equipment to be moved at the same time without assistance from other sources.

Mounting: 1. All preparations made in areas designated for the purpose, in anticipation of an operation. It includes the assembly in the mounting area, preparation and maintenance within the mounting area, movement to loading points, and subsequent embarkation into ships, craft, or aircraft if applicable. 2. A carriage or stand upon which a weapon is placed.

Mounting area: A general locality where assigned forces of an amphibious or airborne operation, with their equipment, are assembled, prepared, and loaded in shipping and/or aircraft preparatory to an assault. Embarkation area.

Movement control: 1. The planning, routing, scheduling, and control of personnel and cargo movements over lines of communications. 2. An organization responsible for the planning, routing, scheduling, and control of personnel and cargo movements over lines of communications. Called movement control center or MCC. Consumer logistics; line of communications; movement control center; movement control teams; non-unit-related cargo; non-unit-related personnel.

Movement control post: The post through which the control of movement is exercised by the commander, depending on operational requirements.

Movement credit: The allocation granted to one or more vehicles in order to move over a controlled route in a fixed time according to movement instructions.

Movement directive: The basic document published by the Department of the Army or the Department of the Air Force (or jointly) that authorizes a command to take action to move a designated unit from one location to another.

Movement group: Those ships and embarked units that load out and proceed to

rendezvous in the objective area.

Movement order: An order issued by a commander covering the details for a move of the command.

Movement phase: In amphibious operations, the period during which various elements of the amphibious force move from points of embarkation to the operational area. This move may be via rehearsal, staging, or rendezvous areas. The movement phase is completed when the various elements of the amphibious force arrive at their assigned positions in the operational area. Amphibious force; amphibious operation.

Movement plan: In amphibious operations, the naval plan providing for the movement of the amphibious task force to the objective area. It includes information and instructions concerning departure of ships from embarkation points, the passage at sea, and the approach to and arrival in assigned positions in the objective area. Amphibious operation; amphibious task force.

Movement report control center: The controlling agency for the entire movement report system. It has available all information relative to the movements of naval ships and other ships under naval control.

Movement report system: A system established to collect and make available to certain commands vital information on the status, location, and movement of flag commands, commissioned fleet units, and ships under operational control of the Navy.

Movement requirement: A stated movement mode and time-phased need for the transport of units, personnel, and/or materiel from a specified origin to a specified destination.

Movement restriction: A restriction temporarily placed on traffic into and/or out of areas to permit clearance of or prevention of congestion.

Movement table: A table giving detailed instructions or data for a move. When necessary it will be qualified by the words road, rail, sea, air, etc., to signify the type of movement. Normally issued as an annex to a movement order or instruction.

Movement to contact: A form of the offense designed to develop the situation and to establish or regain contact. Meeting engagement; reconnaissance in force.

Moving havens: Restricted areas established to provide a measure of security to submarines and surface ships in transit through areas in which the existing attack restrictions would be inadequate to prevent attack by friendly forces. Moving submarine haven; moving surface ship haven.

Moving map display: A display in which a symbol, representing the vehicle, remains stationary while the map or chart image moves beneath the symbol so that the display simulates the horizontal movement of the vehicle in which it is installed. Occasionally the design of the display is such that the map or chart image remains stationary while the symbol moves across a screen. Projected map display.

Moving submarine haven: An area established by a submarine operating authority to prevent mutual interference among friendly submarines, or between friendly submarines and ships operating with towed bodies or arrays.

Moving surface ship haven: Established by surface ship notices, a moving surface ship haven will normally be a circle with a specified radius centered on the estimated position of the ship or the guide of a group of ships. Moving havens.

Moving target indicator: A radar presentation which shows only targets which are in motion. Signals from stationary targets are subtracted out of the return signal by the output of a suitable memory circuit.

Multichannel: Pertaining to communications, usually full duplex, on more than one channel simultaneously. Multichannel transmission may be accomplished by either time-, frequency-, code-, and phase-division multiplexing or space diversity.

Multi-modal: In transport operations, a term applied to the movement of passengers and cargo by more than one method of transport.

Multinational: Between two or more forces or agencies of two or more nations or coalition partners. Alliance; coalition.

Multinational doctrine: Fundamental principles that guide the employment of forces of two or more nations in coordinated action toward a common objective. It is ratified by participating nations. See also doctrine; joint doctrine; multi-Service doctrine.

Multinational exercise: An exercise containing one or more non-US participating force(s). See also exercise.

Multinational force: A force composed of military elements of nations who have formed an alliance or coalition for some specific purpose. MNF. Multinational force commander; multinational operations.

Multinational force commander: A general term applied to a commander who exercises command authority over a military force composed of elements from two or more nations. The extent of the multinational force commander's command authority is determined by the participating nations. MNFC. Multinational force.

Multinational integrated logistic support: Two or more nations agree to provide logistic assets to a multinational force under operational control of a multinational force commander for the logistic support of a multinational force. Logistic support; multinational integrated logistic support unit; multinational logistics; multinational logistic support arrangement.

Multinational integrated logistic support unit: An organization resulting when two or more nations agree to provide logistics assets to a multinational logistic force under the operational control of a multinational commander for the logistic support of a multinational force. MILU. Logistic support; multinational; multinational integrated logistic support.

Multinational logistics: Any coordinated logistic activity involving two or more nations supporting a multinational force conducting military operations under the auspices of an alliance or coalition, including those conducted under United Nations mandate. Multinational logistics includes activities involving both logistic units provided by participating nations designated for use by the multinational force commander as well as a variety of multinational logistic support arrangements that may be developed and used by participating forces. Logistics; multinational; multinational logistic support arrangement.

Multinational logistic support arrangement: Any arrangement involving two or more nations that facilitates the logistic support of a force (either the forces of the countries participating in the arrangement or other countries). Logistic support; multinational; multinational logistics.

Multinational operations: A collective term to describe military actions conducted by forces of two or more nations, usually undertaken within the structure of a coalition or alliance. Alliance; coalition; coalition action.

Multinational staff: A staff composed of personnel of two or more nations within the structure of a coalition or alliance. See also integrated staff; joint staff; parallel staff.

Multinational warfare: Warfare conducted by forces of two or more nations, usually undertaken within the structure of a coalition or alliance.

Multiple drill: Multiple unit training assemblies.

Multiple inactive duty training periods: Two scheduled inactive duty training periods performed in one calendar day, each at least four hours in duration. No more than two inactive duty training periods may be performed in one day.

Multiple independently targetable reentry vehicle: A reentry vehicle carried by a delivery system that can place one or more reentry vehicles over each of several separate targets. See also maneuverable reentry vehicle; multiple reentry vehicle; reentry vehicle.

Multiple reentry vehicle: The reentry vehicle of a delivery system that places more than one reentry vehicle over an individual target. See also maneuverable reentry vehicle; multiple independently targetable reentry vehicle; reentry vehicle.

Multiple unit training assemblies: Two or more unit training assemblies executed during one or more consecutive days. No more than two unit training assemblies may be performed in one calendar day.

Multiple warning phenomenology: Deriving warning information from two or more systems observing separate physical phenomena associated with the same events to attain high credibility while being less susceptible to false reports or spoofing.

Multiplexer: A device that combines (multiplexes) multiple input signals (information channels) into an aggregate signal (common channel) for transmission.

Multi-point refueling system: A limited number of KC-135 aircraft can be equipped with external wing-mounted pods to conduct drogue air refueling, while still maintaining boom air refueling capability on the same mission. This dual refueling capability makes KC-135s with multi-point refueling systems ideal for use as ground alert aircraft. MPRS. Air refueling.

Multispectral imagery: The image of an object obtained simultaneously in a number of discrete spectral bands. MSI.

Multi-spot ship: Those ships certified to have two or more adjacent landing areas. Spot.

Mutual support: That support which units render each other against an enemy,

because of their assigned tasks, their position relative to each other and to the enemy, and their inherent capabilities. Close support; direct support; support.

Muzzle brake: A device attached to the muzzle of a weapon that utilizes escaping gas to reduce recoil.

Muzzle compensator: A device attached to the muzzle of a weapon that utilizes escaping gas to control muzzle movement.

Muzzle velocity: The velocity of a projectile with respect to the muzzle at the instant the projectile leaves the weapon.

Named area of interest: The geographical area where information that will satisfy a specific information requirement can be collected. Named areas of interest are usually selected to capture indications of adversary courses of action, but also may be related to conditions of the battle space. NAI. Area of interest.

N

Napalm — 1. Powdered aluminum soap or similar compound used to gelatinize oil or gasoline for use in napalm bombs or flame throwers. 2. The resultant gelatinized substance.

Narcoterrorism: Terrorism that is linked to illicit drug trafficking.

National Air Mobility System: A broad and comprehensive system of civilian and military capabilities and organizations that provides the President and Secretary of Defense and combatant commanders with rapid global mobility. This system effectively integrates the management of airlift, air refueling, and air mobility support assets, processes, and procedures into an integrated whole. NAMS. Airlift; air mobility; air refueling.

National capital region: A geographic area encompassing the District of Columbia and eleven local jurisdictions in the State of Maryland and the Commonwealth of Virginia. NCR.

National censorship: The examination and control under civil authority of communications entering, leaving, or transiting the borders of the United States, its territories, or its possessions. Censorship.

National Communications System: The telecommunications system that results from the technical and operational integration of the separate telecommunications systems of the several executive branch departments and agencies having a significant telecommunications capability. NCS.

National critical infrastructure and key assets: The infrastructure and assets vital to a nation's security, governance, public health and safety, economy, and public confidence. They include telecommunications, electrical power systems, gas and oil distribution and storage, water supply systems, banking and finance, transportation, emergency services, industrial assets, information systems, and continuity of government operations. NCI&KA.

National defense area: An area established on non-Federal lands located within the United States or its possessions or territories for the purpose of safeguarding classified defense information or protecting Department of Defense (DOD) equipment and/or materiel. Establishment of a national defense area temporarily places such non-Federal lands under the effective control of the Department of Defense and results only from an emergency event. The senior DOD representative at the scene will define the boundary, mark it with a physical barrier, and post warning signs. The landowner's consent and cooperation will be obtained whenever possible; however, military necessity will dictate the final decision regarding location, shape, and size of the national defense area. NDA.

National defense strategy: A document approved by the Secretary of Defense for applying the Armed Forces of the United States in coordination with Department of Defense agencies and other instruments of national power to achieve national security strategy objectives. NDS.

National detainee reporting center: National-level center that obtains and stores information concerning enemy prisoners of war, civilian internees, and retained personnel and their confiscated personal property. May be established upon the outbreak of an armed conflict or when persons are captured or detained by U.S. military forces in the course of the full range of military operations. Accounts for all persons who pass through the care, custody, and control of the U.S. Department of Defense. NDRC.

National Disaster Medical System: A coordinated partnership between Departments of Homeland Security, Health and Human Services, Defense, and Veterans Affairs established for the purpose of responding to the needs of victims of a public health emergency. NDMS.

National emergency: A condition declared by the President or the Congress by virtue of powers previously vested in them that authorize certain emergency actions to be undertaken in the national interest. Action to be taken may include partial, full, or total mobilization of national resources. Mobilization.

National Incident Management System: A national crisis response system that provides a consistent, nationwide approach for Federal, state, local, and tribal governments; the private sector; and nongovernmental organizations to work effectively and efficiently together to prepare for, respond to, and recover from domestic incidents, regardless of cause, size, or complexity. NIMS.

National information infrastructure: The nationwide interconnection of communications networks, computers, databases, and consumer electronics that make vast amounts of information available to users. The national information infrastructure encompasses a wide range of equipment, including cameras, scanners, keyboards, facsimile machines, computers, switches, compact disks, video and audio tape, cable, wire, satellites, fiber-optic transmission lines, networks of all types, televisions, monitors, printers, and much more. The friendly and adversary personnel who make decisions and handle the transmitted information constitute a critical component of the national information infrastructure. NII. Defense information infrastructure; global information infrastructure; information.

National infrastructure: Infrastructure provided and financed by a NATO member in its own territory solely for its own forces (including those forces assigned to or designated for NATO). Infrastructure.

National intelligence: The terms "national intelligence" and "intelligence related to the national security" each refers to all intelligence, regardless of the source from which derived and including information gathered within or outside of the United States, which pertains, as determined consistent with any guidelines issued by the President, to the interests of more than one department or agency of the Government; and that involves (a) threats to the United States, its people, property, or interests; (b) the development, proliferation, or use of weapons of mass destruction; or (c) any other matter bearing on United States national or homeland security.

National intelligence estimate: A strategic estimate of the capabilities, vulnerabilities, and probable courses of action of foreign nations produced at the national level as a composite of the views of the intelligence community. NIE.

National intelligence support team: A nationally sourced team composed of intelligence and communications experts from Defense Intelligence Agency, Central Intelligence Agency, National Geospatial-Intelligence Agency, National Security Agency, or other intelligence community agencies as required. NIST. Intelligence; national intelligence.

National intelligence surveys: Basic intelligence studies produced on a coordinated interdepartmental basis and concerned with characteristics, basic resources, and relatively unchanging natural features of a foreign country or other area.

National interagency fire center: A facility located in Boise, Idaho, that is jointly operated by several federal agencies and is dedicated to coordination, logistic support, and improved weather services in support of fire management operations throughout the United States. NIFC.

National Military Command System: The priority component of the Global Command and Control System designed to support the President, Secretary of Defense and Joint Chiefs of Staff in the exercise of their responsibilities. NMCS.

National Military Strategy: A document approved by the Chairman of the Joint Chiefs of Staff for distributing and applying military power to attain national security strategy and national defense strategy objectives. Also called NMS. National Security Strategy; strategy; theater strategy.

National operations center: The primary national hub for domestic incident management operational coordination and situational awareness. A standing 24 hours a day, 7 days a week interagency organization fusing law enforcement, national intelligence, emergency response, and private-sector reporting. NOC.

National policy: A broad course of action or statements of guidance adopted by the government at the national level in pursuit of national objectives.

National Reconnaissance Office: A Department of Defense agency tasked to ensure that the United States has the technology and space borne and airborne assets needed to acquire intelligence worldwide, including support to such functions as monitoring of arms control agreements, indications and warning, and the planning and conducting of military operations. This mission is accomplished through research and development, acquisition, and operation of space borne and airborne intelligence data collection systems. NRO.

National response coordination center: A multiagency center that provides overall federal response and recovery coordination for incidents of national significance and emergency management program implementation. This center is a functional component of the national operations center. NRCC.

National security: A collective

term encompassing both national defense and foreign relations of the United States. Specifically, the condition provided by: a. a military or defense advantage over any foreign nation or group of nations; b. a favorable foreign relations position; or c. a defense posture capable of successfully resisting hostile or destructive action from within or without, overt or covert. Security.

National Security Council: A governmental body specifically designed to assist the President in integrating all spheres of national security policy. The President, Vice President, Secretary of State, and Secretary of Defense are statutory members. The Chairman of the Joint Chiefs of Staff; Director, Central Intelligence Agency; and the Assistant to the President for National Security Affairs serve as advisers. NSC.

National security interests: The foundation for the development of valid national objectives that define US goals or purposes. National security interests include preserving US political identity, framework, and institutions; fostering economic well-being; and bolstering international order supporting the vital interests of the United States and its allies.

National Security Strategy: A document approved by the President of the United States for developing, applying, and coordinating the instruments of national power to achieve objectives that contribute to national security. NSS. National Military Strategy; strategy; theater strategy.

National shipping authority: The organization within each Allied government responsible in time of war for the direction of its own merchant shipping. NSA.

National special security event: A designated event that, by virtue of its political, economic, social, or religious significance, may be the target of terrorism or other criminal activity. NSSE.

National support element: Any national organization or activity that supports national forces that are a part of a multinational force. Their mission is nation-specific support to units and common support that is retained by the nation. NSE. Multinational force; support.

National System for Geospatial Intelligence: The combination of technology, policies, capabilities, doctrine, activities, people, data, and communities necessary to produce geospatial intelligence in an integrated, multi-intelligence environment. NSG.

Nation assistance: Civil and/or military assistance rendered to a nation by foreign forces within that nation's territory during peacetime, crises or emergencies, or war based on agreements mutually concluded between nations. Nation assistance programs include, but are not limited to, security assistance, foreign internal defense, other Title 10, US Code programs, and activities performed on a reimbursable basis by Federal agencies or intergovernmental organizations.

Natural Disaster: An emergency situation posing significant danger to life and property that results from a natural cause. Domestic emergencies.

Nautical mile: A measure of distance equal to one minute of arc on the Earth's surface. The United States has adopted the international nautical mile equal to 1,852 meters or 6,076.11549 feet. nm.

Nautical plotting chart: An outline chart, devoid of hydrographic information, of a specific scale and projection, usually portraying a graticule and compass rose, designed to be ancillary to standard nautical charts, and produced either as an individual chart or a part of a coordinated series.

Naval Air Training and Operating Procedures Standardization manual: Series of general and specific aircraft procedural manuals that govern the operations of naval aircraft. NATOPS manual.

Naval base: A naval base primarily for support of the forces afloat, contiguous to a port or anchorage, consisting of activities or facilities for which the Navy has operating responsibilities, together with interior lines of communications and the minimum surrounding area necessary for local security. Base complex.

Naval beach group: A permanently organized naval command within an amphibious force comprised of a commander and staff, a beach master unit, an amphibious construction battalion, and assault craft units, designed to provide an administrative group from which required naval tactical components may be made available to the attack force commander and to the amphibious landing force commander. NBG. Shore party.

Naval coastal warfare: Coastal sea control, harbor defense, and port security, executed both in coastal areas outside the United States in support of national policy and in the United States as part of this Nation's defense. NCW.

Naval coastal warfare commander: An officer designated to conduct naval coastal warfare missions within a designated operational area. NCWC.

Naval construction force: The combined construction units of the Navy, including primarily the mobile construction battalions and the amphibious construction battalions. These units are part of the operating forces and represent the Navy's capability for advanced base construction. NCF.

Naval coordination and protection of shipping: Control exercised by naval authorities of movement, routing, reporting, convoy organization, and tactical diversion of allied merchant shipping. It does not include the employment or active protection of such shipping. NCAPS.

Naval coordination and protection of shipping officer: A naval officer appointed to form merchant convoys and control and coordinate the routing and movements of such convoys, independently sailed merchant ships, and hospital ships in and out of a port or base.

Naval coordination and protection of shipping organization: The organization within the Navy which carries out the specific responsibilities of the Chief of Naval Operations to provide for the control and protection of movements of merchant ships in time of war. NCAPS organization.

Naval gunfire operations center: The agency established in a ship to control the execution of plans for the employment of naval gunfire, process requests for naval gunfire support, and to allot ships to forward observers. Ideally located in the same ship as the supporting arms coordination center.

Naval gunfire spotting team: The unit of a shore fire control party that designates targets; controls commencement, cessation, rate, and types of fire; and spots fire on the target. Field artillery observer; spotter.

Naval gunfire support: Fire provided by Navy surface gun systems in support of a unit or units tasked with achieving the commander's objectives. A subset of naval surface fire support. NGFS. Naval surface fire support.

Naval mobile environmental team: A team of naval personnel organized, trained, and equipped to support maritime special operations by providing weather, oceanography, mapping, charting, and geodesy support. NMET.

Naval operation: 1. A naval action (or the performance of a naval mission) that may be strategic, operational, tactical, logistic, or training. 2. The process of carrying on or training for naval combat in order to gain the objectives of any battle or campaign.

Naval port control office: The authority established at a port or port complex to coordinate arrangements for logistic support and harbor services to ships under naval control and to otherwise support the naval control of shipping organization.

Naval special warfare: A designated naval warfare specialty that conducts operations in the coastal, riverine, and maritime environments. Naval special warfare emphasizes small, flexible, mobile units operating under, on, and from the sea. These operations are characterized by stealth, speed, and precise, violent application of force. NSW.

Naval special warfare forces: Those Active and Reserve Component Navy forces designated by the Secretary of Defense that are specifically organized, trained, and equipped to conduct and support special operations. NSW forces or NAVSOF.

Naval special warfare special operations component: The Navy special operations component of a unified or subordinate unified command or joint special operations task force. NAVSOC.

Naval special warfare task element: A provisional subordinate element of a naval special warfare task unit, employed to extend the command and control and support capabilities of its parent task unit. NSWTE. Naval special warfare task unit.

Naval special warfare task group: A provisional naval special warfare organization that plans, conducts, and supports special operations in support of fleet commanders and joint force special operations component commanders. NSWTG.

Naval special warfare task unit: A provisional subordinate unit of a naval special warfare task group. NSWTU. Naval special warfare task group.

Naval special warfare unit: A permanent Navy organization forward based to control and support attached naval special warfare forces. NSWU.

Naval stores: Any articles or commodities used by a naval ship or station, such as equipment; consumable supplies; clothing; petroleum, oils, and lubricants; medical supplies; and ammunition.

Naval support area: A sea area assigned to naval ships detailed to support an amphibious operation. Fire support area.

Naval surface fire support: Fire provided by Navy surface gun and missile systems in support of a unit or units. NSFS. Fire support.

Naval tactical data system: A complex of data inputs, user consoles, converters, adapters, and radio terminals interconnected with high-speed, general-purpose computers and its stored programs. Combat data is collected, processed, and composed into a picture of the overall tactical situation that enables the force commander to make rapid, accurate evaluations and decisions.

Navigational grid: A series of straight lines, superimposed over a conformal projection and indicating grid north, used as an aid to navigation. The interval of the grid lines is generally a multiple of 60 or 100 nautical miles. Military grid.

Navigation head: A transshipment point on a waterway where loads are transferred between water carriers and land carriers. A navigation head is similar in function to a railhead or truck head.

Navigation mode: In a flight control system, a control mode in which the flight path of an aircraft is automatically maintained by signals from navigation equipment.

Navy cargo handling force: The combined cargo handling units of the Navy, including primarily the Navy cargo handling and port group, the Naval Reserve cargo handling training battalion, and the Naval Reserve cargo handling battalion. These units are part of the operating forces and represent the Navy's capability for open ocean cargo handling. NCHF. Navy cargo handling battalion.

Navy special operations component: The Navy component of a joint force special operations component. NAVSOC. Air Force special operations component; Army special operations component.

Navy support element: The maritime pre-positioning force element that is composed of naval beach group staff and subordinate unit personnel, a detachment of Navy cargo handling force personnel, and other Navy components, as required. It is tasked with conducting the off-load and ship-to-shore movement of maritime pre-positioned equipment and/or supplies. NSE.

Navy tactical air control center: Tactical air control center.

Navy-unique fleet essential aircraft: Combatant commander-controlled airlift assets deemed essential for providing air transportation in support of naval operations' transportation requirements. This capability is intended to provide a balance and supplement to other airlift assets to ensure the Navy's ability to respond to emergency and wartime requirements. NUFEA.

Near miss (aircraft) : Any circumstance in flight where the degree of separation between two aircraft is considered by either pilot to have constituted a hazardous situation involving potential risk of collision.

Near real time: Pertaining to the timeliness of data or information which has been delayed by the time required for electronic communication and automatic data processing. This implies that there are no significant delays. NRT. Real time.

Neat lines: The lines that bound the body of a map, usually parallels and meridians. Graticule.

Need to know: A criterion used in security procedures that requires the custodians of classified information to establish, prior to disclosure, that the intended recipient must have access to the information to perform his or her official duties.

Negation: Measures to deceive, disrupt, deny, degrade, or destroy an adversary's space systems and services or any other space system or service used by an adversary that hostile to US national interests. Space control.

Negative phase of the shock wave: The period during which the pressure falls below ambient and then returns to the ambient value. Positive phase of the shock wave.

Negative photo plane: The plane in which a film or plate lies at the moment of

exposure.

Negligible risk (nuclear): A degree of risk where personnel are reasonably safe, with the exceptions of dazzle or temporary loss of night vision. Emergency risk (nuclear).

Nerve agent: A potentially lethal chemical agent which interferes with the transmission of nerve impulses.

Net call sign: A call sign which represents all stations within a net. Call sign.

Net (communications): An organization of stations capable of direct communications on a common channel or frequency.

Net control station: A communications station designated to control traffic and enforce circuit discipline within a given net. NCS.

Net explosive weight: The actual weight in pounds of explosive mixtures or compounds, including the trinitrotoluene equivalent of energetic material, that is used in determination of explosive limits and explosive quantity data arcs. NEW.

Net inventory assets: That portion of the total materiel assets that is designated to meet the materiel inventory objective. It consists of the total materiel assets less the peacetime materiel consumption and losses through normal appropriation and procurement lead time periods.

Net sweep: In naval mine warfare, a two-ship sweep, using a netlike device, designed to collect drifting mines or scoop them up from the sea bottom.

Net weight: -Weight of a ground vehicle without fuel, engine oil, coolant, on-vehicle materiel, cargo, or operating personnel.

Network operations: Activities conducted to operate and defend the Global Information Grid. NETOPS.

Neutral: In combat and combat support operations, an identity applied to a track whose characteristics, behavior, origin, or nationality indicate that it is neither supporting nor opposing friendly forces. Hostile; suspect; unknown.

Neutrality: In international law, the attitude of impartiality during periods of war adopted by third states toward a belligerent and subsequently recognized by the belligerent, which creates rights and duties between the impartial states and the belligerent. In a United Nations enforcement action, the rules of neutrality apply to impartial members of the United Nations except so far as they are excluded by the obligation of such members under the United Nations Charter.

Neutralization: In mine warfare, a mine is said to be neutralized when it has been rendered, by external means, incapable of firing on passage of a target, although it may remain dangerous to handle.

Neutralization fire: Fire which is delivered to render the target ineffective or unusable.

Neutralize: 1. As pertains to military operations, to render ineffective or unusable. 2. To render enemy personnel or material incapable of interfering with a particular operation. 3. To render safe mines, bombs, missiles, and booby traps. 4. To make harmless anything contaminated with a chemical agent.

Neutral state: In international law, a state that pursues a policy of neutrality during war. Neutrality.

Neutron induced activity: Radioactivity induced in the ground or an object as a result of direct irradiation by neutrons.

News media representative: An individual employed by a civilian radio or television station, newspaper, newsmagazine, periodical, or news agency to gather and report on a newsworthy event. NMR. Public affairs.

Nickname: A combination of two separate unclassified words that is assigned an unclassified meaning and is employed only for unclassified administrative, morale, or public information purposes.

Night effect: An effect mainly caused by variations in the state of polarization of reflected waves, which sometimes result in errors in direction finding bearings. The effect is most frequent at nightfall.

Night vision device: Any electro-optical device that is used to detect visible and infrared energy and provide a visible image. Night vision goggles, forward-looking infrared, thermal sights, and low-light level television are night vision devices. NVD. Forward-looking infrared; night vision goggles(s).

Night vision goggle(s): An electro-optical image intensifying device that detects visible and near-infrared energy, intensifies the energy, and provides a visible image for night viewing. Night vision goggles can be either hand-held or helmet-mounted. NVG. Night vision device.

Node: 1. A location in a mobility system where a movement requirement is originated, processed for onward movement, or terminated. 2. In communications and computer systems, the physical location that provides terminating, switching, and gateway access services to support information exchange. 3. An element of a system that represents a person, place, or physical thing.

Nominal filter: A filter capable of cutting off a nominated minimum percentage by weight of solid particles greater than a stated micron size.

Nominal focal length: An approximate value of the focal length, rounded off to some standard figure, used for the classification of lenses, mirrors, or cameras.

Nominal weapon: A nuclear weapon producing a yield of approximately 20 kilotons. Kiloton weapon; megaton weapon; subkiloton weapon.

Nonair transportable: That which is not transportable by air by virtue of dimension, weight, or special characteristics or restrictions.

Nonaligned state: A state that pursues a policy of nonalignment.

Nonalignment: The political attitude of a state that does not associate or identify itself with the political ideology or objective espoused by other states, groups of states, or international causes, or with the foreign policies stemming there from. It does not preclude involvement, but expresses the attitude of no precommitment to a particular state (or block) or policy before a situation arises.

Non appropriated funds: Funds generated by DOD military and civilian personnel and their dependents and used to augment funds appropriated by the Congress to provide a comprehensive, morale-building welfare, religious, educational, and recreational program, designed to improve the well-being of military and civilian personnel and their dependents.

Non battle injury: A person who becomes a casualty due to circumstances not directly attributable to hostile action or terrorist activity. NBI.

Noncombatant evacuation operations: Operations directed by the Department of State or other appropriate authority, in conjunction with the Department of Defense, whereby noncombatants are evacuated from foreign countries when their lives are endangered by war, civil unrest, or natural disaster to safe havens or to the United States. NEOs. Evacuation; geospatial-intelligence contingency package; noncombatant evacuees; operation; safe haven.

Nonconventional assisted recovery: Personnel recovery conducted by indigenous/surrogate personnel that are trained, supported, and led by special operations forces, unconventional warfare ground and maritime forces, or other government agencies' personnel that have been specifically trained and directed to establish and operate indigenous or surrogate infrastructures. NAR.

Nondeferrable issue demand: Issue demand related to specific periods of time that will not exist after the close of those periods, even though not satisfied during the period.

Nonexpendable supplies and materiel: Supplies not consumed in use that retain their original identity during the period of use, such as weapons, machines, tools, and equipment.

Nonfixed medical treatment facility: A medical treatment facility designed to be moved from place to place, including medical treatment facilities afloat.

Nongovernmental organization: A private, self-governing, not-for-profit organization dedicated to alleviating human suffering; and/or promoting education, health care, economic development, environmental protection, human rights, and conflict resolution; and/or encouraging the establishment of democratic institutions and civil society. NGO.

Nonhostile casualty: A person who becomes a casualty due to circumstances not directly attributable to hostile action or terrorist activity. Casualties due to the elements, self-inflicted wounds, and combat fatigue are non hostile casualties. NHCS.

Nonlethal weapon: A weapon that is explicitly designed and primarily employed so as to incapacitate personnel or materiel, while minimizing fatalities, permanent injury to personnel, and undesired damage to property and the environment. NLW.

Non-linear approach: In approach and landing systems, a final approach in which the nominal flight path is not a straight line.

Nonorganic transportation requirement: Unit personnel and cargo for which the transportation source must be an outside agency, normally a component of US Transportation Command.

Nonprior service personnel: Individuals without any prior military service, who have not completed basic inactive duty training, and who receive a commission in or enlist directly into an Armed Force of the United States.

Nonproliferation: Those actions (e.g., diplomacy, arms control, multilateral agreements, threat reduction assistance, and export controls) taken to prevent the proliferation of weapons of mass destruction by dissuading or impeding access to, or distribution of, sensitive technologies, material, and expertise. NP.

Nonrecurring demand: A request by an authorized requisitioner to satisfy a materiel requirement known to be a one-time occurrence. This material is required to provide initial stockage allowances, to meet planned program requirements, or to satisfy a one-time project or maintenance requirement. Nonrecurring demands normally will not be considered by the supporting supply system in the development of demand-based elements of the requirements computation.

Non-registered publication: A publication which bears no register number and for which periodic accounting is not required.

Nonscheduled units: Units of the landing force held in readiness for landing during the initial unloading period, but not included in either scheduled or on-call waves. This category usually includes certain of the combat support units and most of the combat service support units with higher echelon (division and above) reserve units of the landing force. Their landing is directed when the need ashore can be predicted with a reasonable degree of accuracy.

Nonstandard item: An item of supply determined by standardization action as not authorized for procurement.

Nonstandard unit: A force requirement identified in a time-phased force and deployment data for which movement characteristics have not been described in the type unit characteristics file. The planner is required to submit detailed movement characteristics for these units.

Nonstocked item: An item that does not meet the stockage criteria for a given activity, and therefore is not stocked at the particular activity.

Nonstrategic nuclear forces: Those nuclear-capable forces located in an operational area with a capability to employ nuclear weapons by land, sea, or air forces against opposing forces, supporting installations, or facilities. Such forces may be employed, when authorized by competent authority, to support operations that contribute to the accomplishment of the commander's mission within the theater of operations.

Non-unit record: A time-phased force and deployment data file entry for non-unit-related cargo and personnel. Characteristics include using and providing organization, type of movement, routing data, cargo category, weight, volume, area required, and number of personnel requiring transportation.

Non-unit-related cargo: All equipment and supplies requiring transportation to an operational area, other than those identified as the equipment or accompanying supplies of a specific unit (e.g., resupply, military support for allies, and support for nonmilitary programs, such as civil relief). NURC.

Non-unit-related personnel: All personnel requiring transportation to or from an operational area, other than those assigned to a specific unit (e.g., filler personnel; replacements; temporary duty/temporary additional duty personnel; civilians; medical evacuees; and retrograde personnel). NRP or NUP.

Non-US forces: Includes all armed forces of states other than US forces. US forces may act in defense of non-US forces when so designated by the President or Secretary of Defense.

Normal charge: Charge employing a standard amount of propellant to fire a gun under ordinary conditions, as compared with a reduced charge. Reduced charge. normal impact effect — Cardinal point effect.

North American Aerospace Defense Command: A bi-national command of the US and Canada that provides aerospace surveillance, warning and assessment of aerospace attack, and maintains the sovereignty of US and Canadian airspace. NORAD.

No-strike list: A list of objects or entities characterized as protected from the effects of military operations under international law and/or rules of engagement. Attacking these may violate the law of armed conflict or interfere with friendly relations with indigenous personnel or governments. NSL. Law of armed conflict.

Notice to airmen: A notice containing information concerning the establishment, condition, or change in any aeronautical facility, service, procedures, or hazard, the timely knowledge of which is essential to personnel concerned with flight operations. NOTAM.

Notional ship: -A theoretical or average ship of any one category used in transportation planning (e.g., a Liberty ship for dry cargo; a T-2 tanker for bulk petroleum, oils, and lubricants; a personnel transport of 2,400 troop spaces).

Not mission capable, maintenance: Material condition indicating that systems and equipment are not capable of performing any of their assigned missions because of maintenance requirements. NMCM. Not mission capable, supply.

Not mission capable, supply: Material condition indicating that systems and equipment are not capable of performing any of their assigned missions because of maintenance work stoppage due to a supply shortage. NMCS. Not mission capable, maintenance.

Not seriously injured: The casualty status of a person whose injury may or may not require hospitalization; medical authority does not classify as very seriously injured, seriously injured, or incapacitating illness or injury; and the person can communicate with the next of kin. NSI. Casualty status.

Nuclear airburst: The explosion of a nuclear weapon in the air, at a height greater than the maximum radius of the fireball. See also types of burst.

Nuclear bonus effects: Desirable damage or casualties produced by the effects from friendly nuclear weapons that cannot be accurately calculated in targeting as the uncertainties involved preclude depending on them for a militarily significant result.

Nuclear certifiable: Indicates a unit or vehicle possessing the potential of passing functional tests and inspections of all normal and emergency systems affecting the nuclear weapons.

Nuclear certified: Nuclear certified delivery unit; nuclear certified delivery vehicle.

Nuclear certified delivery vehicle: A delivery vehicle whose compatibility with anuclear weapon has been certified by the applicable nuclear power through formal procedures. See also nuclear delivery vehicle.

Nuclear cloud: An all-inclusive term for the volume of hot gases, smoke, dust, and other particulate matter from the nuclear bomb itself and from its environment, which is carried aloft in conjunction with the rise of the fireball produced by the detonation of the nuclear weapon.

Nuclear collateral damage: Undesired damage or casualties produced by the effects from friendly nuclear weapons.

Nuclear column: A hollow cylinder of water and spray thrown up from an underwater burst of a nuclear weapon, through which the hot, high-pressure gases formed in the explosion are vented to the atmosphere. A somewhat similar column of dirt is formed in an underground explosion.

Nuclear commitment: A statement by a NATO member that specific forces have

been committed or will be committed to NATO in a nuclear only or dual capable role.

Nuclear contact surface burst: An explosion of a nuclear weapon whose center of energy is at the surface of land or water.

Nuclear coordination: A broad term encompassing all the actions involved with planning nuclear strikes, including liaison between commanders, for the purpose of satisfying support requirements or because of the extension of weapons effects into the territory of another.

Nuclear damage: 1. **Light Damage** — Damage which does not prevent the immediate use of equipment or installations for which it was intended. Some repair by the user may be required to make full use of the equipment or installations. 2. **Moderate Damage** — Damage which prevents the use of equipment or installations until extensive repairs are made. 3. **Severe Damage** — Damage which prevents use of equipment or installations permanently.

Nuclear damage assessment: The determination of the damage effect to the population, forces, and resources resulting from actual nuclear attack. It is performed during and after an attack. The operational significance of the damage is not evaluated in this assessment.

Nuclear delivery unit: Any level of organization capable of employing a nuclear weapon system or systems when the weapon or weapons have been released by proper authority.

Nuclear delivery vehicle: That portion of the weapon system which provides the means of delivery of a nuclear weapon to the target.

Nuclear detonation detection and reporting system: A system deployed to provide surveillance coverage of critical friendly target areas, and indicate place, height of burst, yield, and ground zero of nuclear detonations. NUDETS.

Nuclear dud: A nuclear weapon that, when launched at or emplaced on a target, fails to provide any explosion of that part of the weapon designed to produce the nuclear yield.

Nuclear energy: All forms of energy released in the course of a nuclear fission or nuclear transformation.

Nuclear exoatmospheric burst: The explosion of a nuclear weapon above the sensible atmosphere (above 120 kilometers) where atmospheric interaction is minimal.

Nuclear incident: An unexpected event involving a nuclear weapon, facility, or component, resulting in any of the following, but not constituting a nuclear weapon(s) accident: a. an increase in the possibility of explosion or radioactive contamination; b. errors committed in the assembly, testing, loading, or transportation of equipment, and/or the malfunctioning of equipment and materiel which could lead to an unintentional operation of all or part of the weapon arming and/or firing sequence, or which could lead to a substantial change in yield, or increased dud probability;

and c. any act of God, unfavorable environment, or condition resulting in damage to the weapon, facility, or component.

Nuclear intelligence: Intelligence derived from the collection and analysis of radiation and other effects resulting from radioactive sources. NUCINT.

Nuclear logistic movement: The transport of nuclear weapons in connection with supply or maintenance operations. Under certain specified conditions, combat aircraft may be used for such movements.

Nuclear nation: Military nuclear powers and civil nuclear powers.

Nuclear parity: A condition at a given point in time when opposing forces possess nuclear offensive and defensive systems approximately equal in overall combat effectiveness.

Nuclear planning system: A system composed of personnel, directives, and electronic data processing systems to directly support geographic nuclear combatant commanders in developing, maintaining, and disseminating nuclear operation plans.

Nuclear proximity-surface burst: An explosion of a nuclear weapon at a height less than the maximum radius of its fireball, but low enough to facilitate cratering and/or the propagation of a shock wave into the ground.

Nuclear radiation: Particulate and electromagnetic radiation emitted from atomic nuclei in various nuclear processes. The important nuclear radiations, from the weapon standpoint, are alpha and beta particles, gamma rays, and neutrons.

Nuclear reactor: A facility in which fissile material is used in a self-supporting chain reaction to produce heat and/or radiation for both practical application and research and development.

Nuclear safety line: A line selected, if possible, to follow well-defined topographical features and used to delineate levels of protective measures, degrees of damage or risk to friendly troops, and/or to prescribe limits to which the effects of friendly weapons may be permitted to extend.

Nuclear stalemate: A concept that postulates a situation wherein the relative strength of opposing nuclear forces results in mutual deterrence against employment of nuclear forces.

Nuclear strike warning: A warning of impending friendly or suspected enemy nuclear attack.

Nuclear support: The use of nuclear weapons against hostile forces in support of friendly air, land, and naval operations. Immediate nuclear support; preplanned nuclear support.

Nuclear transmutation: Artificially induced modification of the constituents of certain nuclei, thus giving rise to different nuclides.

Nuclear underground burst: The explosion of a nuclear weapon in which the center of the detonation lies at a point beneath the surface of the ground.

Nuclear underwater burst: The explosion of a nuclear weapon in which the center of the detonation lies at a point beneath the surface of the water.

Nuclear vulnerability assessment: The estimation of the probable effect on population, forces, and resources from a hypothetical nuclear attack. It is performed predominantly in the preattack period; however, it may be extended to the transattack or postattack periods.

Nuclear warfare: Warfare involving the employment of nuclear weapons. Postattack period; transattack period.

Nuclear warning message: A warning message that must be disseminated to all affected friendly forces any time a nuclear weapon is to be detonated if effects of the weapon will have impact upon those forces.

Nuclear weapon: A complete assembly, in its intended ultimate configuration which, upon completion of the prescribed arming, fusing, and firing sequence, is capable of producing the intended nuclear reaction and release of energy.

Nuclear weapon degradation: The degeneration of a nuclear warhead to such an extent that the anticipated nuclear yield is lessened.

Nuclear weapon employment time: The time required for delivery of a nuclear weapon after the decision to fire has been made.

Nuclear weapon exercise: An operation not directly related to immediate operational readiness. It includes removal of a weapon from its normal storage location, preparing for use, delivery to an employment unit, and the movement in a ground training exercise, to include loading aboard an aircraft or missile and return to storage. It may include any or all of the operations listed above, but does not include launching or flying operations. Typical exercises include aircraft generation exercises, ground readiness exercises, ground tactical exercises, and various categories of inspections designed to evaluate the capability of the unit to perform its prescribed mission. Immediate operational readiness; nuclear weapon maneuver.

Nuclear weapons surety: Material, personnel, and procedures that contribute to the security, safety, and reliability of nuclear weapons and to the assurance that there will be no nuclear weapon accidents, incidents, unauthorized weapon detonations, or degradation in performance at the target.

Nuclear yields: The energy released in the detonation of a nuclear weapon, measured in terms of the kilotons or megatons of trinitrotoluene required to produce the same energy release. Yields are categorized as follows:

very low – less than 1 kiloton;

low – 1 kiloton to 10 kilotons;

medium – over 10 kilotons to 50 kilotons;

high – over 50 kilotons to 500 kilotons;

very high – over 500 kilotons.

Nominal weapon; subkiloton weapon.

Nuisance minefield: A minefield laid to delay and disorganize the enemy and to hinder the use of an area or route. Minefield.

Numbered beach: In amphibious operations, a subdivision of a colored beach, designated for the assault landing of a battalion landing team or similarly sized unit, when landed as part of a larger force.

Numbered fleet: A major tactical unit of the Navy immediately subordinate to a major fleet command and comprising various task forces, elements, groups, and units for the purpose of prosecuting specific naval operations.

O

Objective: 1. The clearly defined, decisive, and attainable goal toward which every operation is directed. 2. The specific target of the action taken (for example, a definite terrain feature, the seizure or holding of which is essential to the commander's plan, or, an enemy force or capability without regard to terrain features).

Objective area: A defined geographical area within which is located an objective to be captured or reached by the military forces. This area is defined by competent authority for purposes of command and control. OA.

Objective force level: The level of military forces that needs to be attained within a finite time frame and resource level to accomplish approved military objectives, missions, or tasks. Military requirement.

Obligated reservist: An individual who has a statutory requirement imposed by the Military Selective Service Act of 1967 or Section 651, Title 10, United States Code, to serve on active duty in the armed forces or to serve while not on active duty in a Reserve Component for a period not to exceed that prescribed by the applicable statute.

Oblique air photograph: An air photograph taken with the camera axis directed between the horizontal and vertical planes. Commonly referred to as an "oblique." a. High Oblique. One in which the apparent horizon appears. b. Low Oblique. One in which the apparent horizon does not appear.

Oblique air photograph strip: Photographic strip composed of oblique air photographs.

Obliquity: The characteristic in wide-angle or oblique photography that portrays the terrain and objects at such an angle and range that details necessary for interpretation are seriously masked or are at a very small scale, rendering interpretation difficult or impossible.

Observation helicopter: Helicopter used primarily for observation and reconnaissance, but which may be used for other roles.

Observation post: A position from which military observations are made, or fire directed and adjusted, and which possesses appropriate communications; may be airborne. OP.

Observed fire: Fire for which the point of impact or burst can be seen by an observer. The fire can be controlled and adjusted on the basis of observation.

Observed fire procedure: A standardized procedure for use in adjusting indirect fire on a target.

Observer-target line: An imaginary straight line from the observer/spotter to the target. See also spotting line.

Observer-target range: The distance along an imaginary straight line from the observer or spotter to the target.

Obstacle: Any obstruction designed or employed to disrupt, fix, turn, or block the movement of an opposing force, and to impose additional losses in personnel, time, and equipment on the opposing force. Obstacles can exist naturally or can be man-made, or can be a combination of both.

Obstacle belt: A brigade-level command and control measure, normally given graphically, to show where within an obstacle zone the ground tactical commander plans to limit friendly obstacle employment and focus the defense. It assigns an intent to the obstacle plan and provides the necessary guidance on the overall effect of obstacles within a belt. See also obstacle.

Obstacle clearing: The total elimination or neutralization of obstacles.

Obstacle intelligence: Those collection efforts to detect the presence of enemy (and natural) obstacles, determine their types and dimensions, and provide the necessary information to plan appropriate combined arms breaching, clearance, or bypass operations to negate the impact on the friendly scheme of maneuver. It is typically related to the tactical level of intelligence. OBSTINTEL.

Obstacle restricted areas: A command and control measure used to limit the type or number of obstacles within an area. Obstacle.

Obstacle zone: A division-level command and control measure, normally done graphically, to designate specific land areas where lower echelons are allowed to employ tactical obstacles.

Obstructor: In naval mine warfare, a device laid with the sole object of obstructing or damaging mechanical minesweeping equipment.

Occupational and environmental health surveillance: The regular or repeated collection, analysis, archiving, interpretation, and dissemination of occupational and environmental health-related data for monitoring the health of, or potential health hazard impact on, a population and individual personnel, and for intervening in a timely manner to prevent, treat, or control the occurrence of disease or injury when determined necessary.

Occupational and environmental health threats: Threats to the health of military personnel and to military readiness created by exposure to hazardous agents, environmental contamination, or toxic industrial materials. Health threat. Occupied territory: Territory under the authority and effective control of a belligerent armed force. The term is not applicable to territory being administered pursuant to peace terms, treaty, or other agreement, express or implied, with the civil authority of the territory.

Ocean Cargo Clearance Authority: The Surface Deployment and Distribution Command activity that books Department of Defense sponsored cargo and passengers for surface movement, performs related contract administration, and accomplishes export and import surface traffic management functions for Department of Defense cargo moving within the Defense Transportation System. OCCA.

Ocean convoy: A convoy whose voyage lies, in general, outside the continental shelf. Convoy.

Ocean manifest: A detailed listing of the entire cargo loaded into any one ship showing all pertinent data which will readily identify such cargo and where and how the cargo is stowed.

Ocean station ship: A ship assigned to operate within a specified area to provide several services, including search and rescue, meteorological information, navigational aid, and communications facilities.

Offensive counter air: Offensive operations to destroy, disrupt, or neutralize enemy aircraft, missiles, launch platforms, and their supporting structures and systems both before and after launch, but as close to their source as possible. Offensive counter air operations range throughout enemy territory and are generally conducted at the initiative of friendly forces. These operations include attack operations, suppression of enemy air defenses, fighter escort, and fighter sweep. OCA. Counter air; defensive counter air; operation.

Offensive counter air attack operations: Offensive action in support of the offensive counter air mission against surface targets which contribute to the enemy's air power capabilities. Any part of the joint force may be tasked to conduct or support offensive counter air attack operations. OCA attack ops. Counter air; offensive counter air.

Offensive minefield: In naval mine warfare, a minefield laid in enemy territorial water or waters under enemy control.

Offensive space control: Those operations to prevent an adversary's hostile use of US/third party space capabilities and services or negate (disrupt, deny, degrade, deceive, or destroy) an adversary's space capabilities.

Office: An enduring organization that is formed around a specific function within a joint force commander's headquarters to coordinate and manage support requirements.

Officer in tactical command: In maritime usage, the senior officer present eligible to assume command, or the officer to whom the senior officer has delegated tactical command. OTC.

Official information: Information that is owned by, produced for or by, or is subject to the control of the United States Government.

Off-load preparation party: A temporary task organization of Navy and Marine maintenance, embarkation, equipment operators, and cargo-handling personnel deployed to the maritime pre-positioning ship before or during its transit to the objective area to prepare the ship's off-load systems and embarked equipment for offload. OPP.

Offset bombing: Any bombing procedure which employs a reference or aiming point other than the actual target.

Offset costs: Costs for which funds have been appropriated that may not be incurred as a result of a contingency operation. Those funds may then be applied to the cost of the operation. Contingency operation.

Offset distance (nuclear: The distance the desired ground zero or actual ground zero is offset from the center of an area target or from a point target.

Offset lasing: The technique of aiming a laser designator at a point other than the target and, after laser acquisition, moving the laser to designate the target for terminal attack guidance. Laser target designator.

Offshore assets: Oil and gas facilities, mining and industrial installations, ocean thermal energy conversion facilities, deep water ports, aids to navigation, and nuclear power plants located or in operation seaward of the coastline.

Offshore bulk fuel system: The system used for transferring fuel from points offshore to reception facilities on the beach. It consists of two subsystems: amphibious bulk liquid transfer system and the offshore petroleum discharge system. Amphibious bulk liquid transfer system; offshore petroleum discharge system.

Offshore patrol: A naval defense patrol operating in the outer areas of navigable coastal waters. It is a part of the naval local defense forces consisting of naval ships and aircraft and operates outside those areas assigned to the inshore patrol.

Oiler: A naval or merchant tanker specially equipped and rigged for replenishing other ships at sea.

On berth: Said of a ship when it is properly moored to a quay, wharf, jetty, pier, or buoy or when it is at anchor and available for loading or discharging passengers and cargo.

On-call: 1. A term used to signify that a prearranged concentration, air strike, or final protective fire may be called for. 2. Preplanned, identified force or materiel requirements without designated time-phase and destination information. Such requirements will be called forward upon order of competent authority.

On-call resupply: A resupply mission planned before insertion of a special operations team into the operations area but not executed until requested by the operating team.

On-call target: Planned target upon which fires or other actions are determined using deliberate targeting and triggered, when detected or located, using dynamic targeting.

On-call target (nuclear): A planned nuclear target other than a scheduled nuclear target for which a need can be anticipated but which will be delivered upon request rather than at a specific time. Coordination and warning of friendly troops and aircraft are mandatory.

One day's supply: A unit or quantity of supplies adopted as a standard of measurement, used in estimating the average daily expenditure under stated conditions. It may also be expressed in terms of a factor, e.g., rounds of ammunition per weapon per day.

One-look circuit: A mine circuit which requires actuation by a given influence once only.

On hand: The quantity of an item that is physically available in a storage location and contained in the accountable property book records of an issuing activity.

On-scene commander: 1. An individual in the immediate vicinity of an isolating event who temporarily assumes command of the incident. 2. The federal officer designated to direct federal crisis and consequence management efforts at the scene of a terrorist or weapons of mass destruction incident. OSC.

On-station time: The time an aircraft can remain on station. May be determined by endurance or orders.

Open improved storage space: Open area that has been graded and hard surfaced or prepared with topping of some suitable material so as to permit effective materials handling operations. Storage.

Open ocean: Ocean limit defined as greater than 12 nautical miles (nm) from shore, as compared with high seas that are over 200 nm from shore.

Open route: A route not subject to traffic or movement control restrictions.

Open-source intelligence: Information of potential intelligence value that is available to the general public. OSINT.

Open unimproved wet space: That water area specifically allotted to and usable for storage of floating equipment. Storage.

Operating forces: Those forces whose primary missions are to participate in combat and the integral supporting elements thereof. Combat forces; combat service support element; combat support elements.

Operating level of supply: The quantities of materiel required to sustain operations in the interval between requisitions or the arrival of successive shipments. These quantities should be based on the established replenishment period.

Operation: 1. A military action or the carrying out of a strategic, operational, tactical, service, training, or administrative military mission. 2. The process of carrying on combat, including movement, supply, attack, defense, and maneuvers needed to gain the objectives of any battle or campaign.

Operational architecture: - Descriptions of the tasks, operational elements, and information flows required to accomplish or support a war fighting function.

Operational art: The application of creative imagination by commanders and staffs — supported by their skill, knowledge, and experience — to design strategies, campaigns, and major operations and organize and employ military forces. Operational art integrates ends, ways, and means across the levels of war.

Operational authority: That authority exercised by a commander in the chain of command, defined further as combatant command, operational control, tactical control, or a support relationship. Combatant command; in support of; operational control; support; tactical control.

Operational characteristics: Those military characteristics that pertain primarily to the functions to be performed by equipment, either alone or in conjunction with other equipment; e.g., for electronic equipment, operational characteristics include such items as frequency coverage, channeling, type of modulation, and character of emission.

Operational contract support: The process of planning for and obtaining supplies, services, and construction from commercial sources in support of joint operations along with the associated contractor management functions.

Operational control authority: The naval commander responsible within a specified geographical area for the naval control of all merchant shipping under Allied naval control. OCA.

Operational decontamination: Decontamination carried out by an individual and/or a unit, restricted to specific parts of operationally essential equipment, materiel and/or working areas, in order to minimize contact and transfer hazards and to sustain operations. This may include decontamination of the individual beyond the scope of immediate decontamination, as well as decontamination of mission-essential spares and limited terrain decontamination.

Operational design: The conception and construction of the framework that underpins a campaign or major operation plan and its subsequent execution. Campaign; major operation.

Operational design element: A key consideration used in operational design.

Operational documentation: Visual information documentation of activities to convey information about people, places, and things. It is general purpose documentation normally accomplished in peacetime. OPDOC.

Operational environment: A composite of the conditions, circumstances, and influences that affect the employment of capabilities and bear on the decisions of the commander.

Operational evaluation: The test and analysis of a specific end item or system, insofar as practicable under Service operating conditions, in order to determine if quantity production is warranted considering: a. the increase in military effectiveness to be gained; and b. its effectiveness as compared with currently available items or systems, consideration being given to: (1) personnel capabilities to maintain and operate the equipment; (2) size, weight, and location considerations; and (3) enemy capabilities in the field. See also technical evaluation.

Operational intelligence: Intelligence that is required for planning and conducting campaigns and major operations to accomplish strategic objectives within theaters or operational areas. Intelligence; strategic intelligence; tactical intelligence.

Operationally ready: 1. A unit, ship, or weapon system capable of performing the missions or functions for which organized or designed. Incorporates both equipment readiness and personnel readiness. 2. Personnel available and qualified to perform assigned missions or functions.

Operational necessity: A mission associated with war or peacetime operations in which the consequences of an action justify the risk of loss of aircraft and crew. mission.

Operational pause: A temporary halt in operations.

Operational procedures: The detailed methods by which headquarters and units carry out their operational tasks.

Operational reach: The distance and duration across which a unit can successfully employ military capabilities.

Operational readiness: The capability of a unit/formation, ship, weapon system, or equipment to perform the missions or functions for which it is organized or designed. May be used in a general sense or to express a level or degree of readiness. OR. Combat readiness.

Operational readiness evaluation: An evaluation of the operational capability and effectiveness of a unit or any portion thereof.

Operational Requirements Document: A formatted statement containing performance and related operational parameters for the proposed concept or system. Prepared by the user or user's representative at each milestone beginning with Milestone I, Concept Demonstration Approval of the Requirements Generation Process. ORD.

Operational reserve: An emergency reserve of men and/or materiel established for the support of a specific operation. Reserve supplies.

Operational route: Land route allocated to a command for the conduct of a specific operation; derived from the corresponding basic military route network.

Operational support airlift: Operational support airlift (OSA) missions are movements of high-priority passengers and cargo with time, place, or mission-sensitive requirements. OSA aircraft are those fixed-wing aircraft acquired and/or retained exclusively for OSA missions, as well as any other Department of Defense-owned or controlled aircraft, fixed- or rotary-wing, used for OSA purposes. OSA.

Operational testing; - A continuing process of evaluation that may be applied to either operational personnel or situations to determine their validity or reliability.

Operational training: -Training that develops, maintains, or improves the operational readiness of individuals or units.

Operation and maintenance: Maintenance and repair of real property, operation of utilities, and provision of other services such as refuse collection and disposal, entomology, snow removal, and ice alleviation. O&M.

Operation annexes; - Those amplifying instructions that are of such a nature, or are so voluminous or technical, as to make their inclusion in the body of the plan or order undesirable.

Operation map: A map showing the location and strength of friendly forces involved in an operation. It may indicate predicted movement and location of enemy forces.

Operation order: A directive issued by a commander to subordinate commanders for the purpose of effecting the coordinated execution of an operation. OPORD.

Operations center: The facility or location on an installation, base, or facility used by the commander to command, control, and coordinate all operational activities. OC.

Operations research: The analytical study of military problems undertaken to provide responsible commanders and staff agencies with a scientific basis for decision on action to improve military operations. operational research; operations analysis.

Operations security: A process of identifying critical information and subsequently analyzing friendly actions attendant to military operations and other activities to: a. identify those actions that can be observed by adversary intelligence systems; b. determine indicators that adversary intelligence systems might obtain that could be interpreted or pieced together to derive critical information in time to be useful to adversaries; and c. select and execute measures that eliminate or reduce to an acceptable level the vulnerabilities of friendly actions to adversary exploitation. OPSEC.

Operations security indicators: Friendly detectable actions and open-source information that can be interpreted or pieced together by an adversary to derive critical information. operations security measures — Methods and means to gain and maintain essential secrecy about critical information.

Operations security vulnerability: A condition in which friendly actions provide

operations security indicators that may be obtained and accurately evaluated by an adversary in time to provide a basis for effective adversary decision making.

Operations support element: An element that is responsible for all administrative, operations support and services support functions within the counterintelligence and human intelligence staff element of a joint force intelligence directorate. OSE.

Operations to restore order: Operations intended to halt violence and support, reinstate, or establish civil authorities. They are designed to return an unstable and lawless environment to the point where indigenous police forces can effectively enforce the law and restore civil authority.

Opportune lift: That portion of lift capability available for use after planned requirements have been met.

Opposite numbers: Officers (including foreign) having corresponding duty assignments within their respective Military Services or establishments.

Optical axis: In a lens element, the straight line which passes through the centers of curvature of the lens surfaces. In an optical system, the line formed by the coinciding principal axes of the series of optical elements.

Optical mine hunting: The use of an optical system (e.g., television or towed diver) to detect and classify mines or mine like objects on or protruding from the seabed.

Optimum height: The height of an explosion which will produce the maximum effect against a given target.

Optimum height of burst: For nuclear weapons and for a particular target (or area), the height at which it is estimated a weapon of a specified energy yield will produce a certain desired effect over the maximum possible area.

Orbital injection: The process of providing a space vehicle with sufficient velocity to establish an orbit.

Orbit determination: The process of describing the past, present, or predicted position of a satellite in terms of orbital parameters.

Order: A communication, written, oral, or by signal, which conveys instructions from a superior to a subordinate. In a broad sense, the terms "order" and "command" are synonymous. However, an order implies discretion as to the details of execution whereas a command does not.

Order of battle: The identification, strength, command structure, and disposition of the personnel, units, and equipment of any military force. OB; OOB.

Order time: 1. The time elapsing between the initiation of stock replenishment action and submittal of requisition or order. 2. The time elapsing between the submittal of requisition or order and shipment of materiel by the supplying activity.

Ordinary transport: In railway terminology, transport of a load whose size, weight, or preparation does not entail special difficulties vis-à-vis the facilities or equipment of the railway systems to be used.

Ordnance: Explosives, chemicals, pyrotechnics, and similar stores, e.g., bombs, guns and ammunition, flares, smoke, or napalm.

Organic: Assigned to and forming an essential part of a military organization. Organic parts of a unit are those listed in its table of organization for the Army, Air Force, and Marine Corps, and are assigned to the administrative organizations of the operating forces for the Navy.

Organizational equipment: Referring to method of use: signifies that equipment (other than individual equipment) used in furtherance of the common mission of an organization or unit. Equipment.

Organizational maintenance: That maintenance that is the responsibility of and performed by a using organization on its assigned equipment. Its phases normally consist of inspecting, servicing, lubricating, and adjusting, as well as the replacing of parts, minor assemblies, and subassemblies.

Organization for combat: In amphibious operations, task organization of landing force units for combat, involving combinations of command, ground and aviation combat, combat support, and combat service support units for accomplishment of missions ashore. Amphibious operation; task organization.

Organization for landing; - In amphibious operations, the specific tactical grouping of the landing force for the assault.

Organization of the ground: The development of a defensive position by strengthening the natural defenses of the terrain and by assignment of the occupying troops to specific localities.

Originating medical facility: A medical facility that initially transfers a patient to another medical facility.

Oropesa sweep: In naval mine warfare, a form of sweep in which a length of sweep wire is towed by a single ship, lateral displacement being caused by an otter and depth being controlled at the ship end by a kite and at the other end by a float and float wire.

Orthomorphic projection: A projection in which the scale, although varying throughout the map, is the same in all directions at any point, so that very small areas are represented by correct shape and bearings are correct.

Oscillating mine: A mine, hydrostatically controlled, which maintains a pre-set depth below the surface of the water independently of the rise and fall of the tide.

Other detainee: Person in the custody of the US Armed Forces who has not been classified as an enemy prisoner of war (article 4, Geneva Convention of 1949 Relative to the Treatment of Prisoners of War (GPW)), retained personnel, or civilian internee. OD.

Other war reserve materiel requirement, protectable: The portion of the other war reserve materiel requirement that is protected for purposes of procurement, funding, and inventory management.

Otter: In naval mine warfare, a device which, when towed, displaces itself sideways to a predetermined distance.

Outer transport area: In amphibious operations, an area inside the antisubmarine screen to which assault transports proceed initially after arrival in the objective area. inner transport area; transport area.

Outline map: A map which represents just sufficient geographic information to permit the correlation of additional data placed upon it.

Outline plan: A preliminary plan which outlines the salient features or principles of a course of action prior to the initiation of detailed planning.

Overhaul: The restoration of an item to a completely serviceable condition as prescribed by maintenance serviceability standards.

overhead clearance: The vertical distance between the route surface and any obstruction above it.

Overlay: A printing or drawing on a transparent or semi-transparent medium at the same scale as a map, chart, etc., to show details not appearing or requiring special emphasis

on the original.

Overpressure: The pressure resulting from the blast wave of an explosion. It is referred to as "positive" when it exceeds atmospheric pressure and "negative" during the passage of the wave when resulting pressures are less than atmospheric pressure.

Overprint: Information printed or stamped upon a map or chart, in addition to that originally printed, to show data of importance or special use.

Overseas: All locations, including Alaska and Hawaii, outside the continental United States.

Overseas search and rescue region: Overseas unified command areas (or portions thereof not included within the inland region or the maritime region).

Over the beach operations: logistics over-the-shore operations. over-the-horizon amphibious operations — An operational initiative launched from beyond visual and radar range of the shoreline.

Over-the-horizon radar: A radar system that makes use of the atmospheric reflection and refraction phenomena to extend its range of detection beyond line of sight. Over-the-horizon radars may be either forward scatter or back scatter systems.

Overt operation: An operation conducted openly, without concealment. clandestine operation; covert operation.

Overt peacetime psychological operations programs: Those programs developed by combatant commands, in coordination with the chiefs of US diplomatic missions, that plan, support, and provide for the conduct of psychological operations, during military operations other than war, in support of US regional objectives, policies, interests, and theater military missions. OP3. psychological operations.

P

Pace: For ground forces, the speed of a column or element regulated to maintain a prescribed average speed.

Pace setter: An individual, selected by the column commander, who travels in the lead vehicle or element to regulate the column speed and establish the pace necessary to meet the required movement order.

Packaged petroleum product: A petroleum product normally packaged by a manufacturer and procured, stored, transported, and issued in containers having a fill capacity of 55 United States gallons (or 45 Imperial gallons, or 205 liters) or less.

Pack up kit: Service-provided maintenance gear including spare parts and consumables most commonly needed by the deployed helicopter detachment. Supplies are sufficient for a short-term deployment but do not include all material needed for every maintenance task. PUK.

Padding: Extraneous text added to a message for the purpose of concealing its beginning, ending, or length.

Palletized load system: A truck with hydraulic load handling mechanism, trailer, and flat rack system capable of self-loading and -unloading. Truck and companion trailer each have a 16.5 ton payload capacity. PLS.

Palletized load system flat rack: Topless, side less container component of palletized load system, some of which conform to International Organization for Standardization specifications. Palletized load system.

Palletized unit load: Quantity of any item, packaged or unpackaged, which is arranged on a pallet in a specified manner and securely strapped or fastened thereto so that the whole is handled as a unit.

Panel code: A prearranged code designed for visual communications, usually between friendly units, by making use of marking panels. See also marking panel.

Panoramic camera: 1. In aerial photography, a camera which, through a system of moving optics or mirrors, scans a wide area of the terrain, usually from horizon to horizon. The camera may be mounted vertically or obliquely within the aircraft, to scan across or along the line of flight. 2. In ground photography, a camera which photographs a wide expanse of terrain by rotating horizontally about the vertical axis through the center of the camera lens.

Parachute deployment height: The height above the intended impact point at which the parachute or parachutes are fully deployed.

Para drop: Delivery by parachute of personnel or cargo from an aircraft in flight.

Parallel sheaf: In artillery and naval gunfire support, a sheaf in which the planes (lines) of fire of all pieces are parallel.

Parallel staff: A staff in which one officer from each nation, or Service, working in parallel is appointed to each post.

Parrot: Identification friend or foe transponder equipment.

Partial mission-capable: Material condition of an aircraft or training device indicating that it can perform at least one but not all of its missions. PMC.

Partial mission-capable, maintenance: Material condition of an aircraft or training device indicating that it can perform at least one but not all of its missions because of maintenance requirements existing on the inoperable subsystem(s). PMCM.

Partial mission-capable, supply: Material condition of an aircraft or training device indicating it can perform at least one but not all of its missions because maintenance required to clear the discrepancy cannot continue due to a supply shortage. PMCS.

Partial storage monitoring: A periodic inspection of major assemblies or components for nuclear weapons, consisting mainly of external observation of humidity, temperatures, and visual damage or deterioration during storage. This type of inspection is also conducted prior to and upon completion of a movement.

Partisan warfare: Not to be used. See guerrilla warfare. partner nation. Those nations that the United States works with to disrupt the production, transportation, distribution, and sale of illicit drugs, as well as the money involved with this illicit activity. PN.

Part number: A combination of numbers, letters, and symbols assigned by a designer, a manufacturer, or vendor to identify a specific part or item of materiel.

Pass: 1. A short tactical run or dive by an aircraft at a target. 2. A single sweep through or within firing range of an enemy air formation.

Passage of lines: An operation in which a force moves forward or rearward through another force's combat positions with the intention of moving into or out of contact with the enemy. A passage may be designated as a forward or rearward passage of lines.

Passenger mile: One passenger transported one mile. For air and ocean transport, use

nautical miles; for rail, highway, and inland waterway transport in the continental United States, use statute miles.

Passive: In surveillance, an adjective applied to actions or equipments which emit no energy capable of being detected.

Passive defence: Measures taken to reduce the probability of and to minimize the effects of damage caused by hostile action without the intention of taking the initiative. Active defense.

Passive homing guidance: A system of homing guidance wherein the receiver in the missile utilizes radiation from the target.

Passive mine: 1. A mine whose anti counter mining device has been operated preventing the firing mechanism from being actuated. The mine will usually remain passive for a comparatively short time. 2. A mine which does not emit a signal to detect the presence of a target. Active mine.

Pass time: In road transport, the time that elapses between the moment when the leading vehicle of a column passes a given point and the moment when the last vehicle passes the same point.

Password: A secret word or distinctive sound used to reply to a challenge. Challenge; countersign.

Pathfinder drop zone control: The communication and operation center from which pathfinders exercise aircraft guidance. pathfinder landing zone control – See pathfinder drop zone control.

Patient movement: The act or process of moving a sick, injured, wounded, or other person to obtain medical and/r dental care or treatment. Functions include medical regulating, patient evacuation, and en route medical care.

Patient movement items: The medical equipment and supplies required to support patients during aero medical evacuation. PMIs.

Patient movement requirements center: Term used to represent any theater, joint or the Global Patient Movement Requirements Center function. A joint activity that coordinates patient movement. It is the functional merging of joint medical regulating processes, Services' medical regulating processes, and patient movement evacuation requirements planning (transport to bed plan). PMRC.

Patrol: A detachment of ground, sea, or air forces sent out for the purpose of gathering information or carrying out a destructive, harassing, mopping-up, or security mission.

Pattern bombing: The systematic covering of a target area with bombs uniformly distributed according to a plan.

Pattern laying : In land mine warfare, the laying of mines in a fixed relationship to each other.

Payload: 1. The sum of the weight of passengers and cargo that an aircraft can carry. Load. 2. The warhead, its container, and activating devices in a military missile. 3. The satellite or research vehicle of a space probe or research missile. 4. The load which the vehicle is designed to transport under specified conditions of operation, in addition to its unladen weight.

Payload build-up (missile and space): The process by which the scientific instrumentation and necessary mechanical and electronic subassemblies are assembled into a complete operational package capable of achieving the scientific objectives of the mission.

Payload integration (missile and space): The compatible installation of a complete payload package into the spacecraft and space vehicle..

P-day: That point in time at which the rate of production of an item available for military consumption equals the rate at which the item is required by the Armed Forces.

Peacemaking: The process of diplomacy, mediation, negotiation, or other forms of peaceful settlements that arranges an end to a dispute and resolves issues that led to it.

Peacetime force materiel assets: That portion of total materiel assets that is designated to meet the peacetime force materiel requirement. War reserves.

Peacetime force materiel requirement: The quantity of an item required to equip, provide a materiel pipeline, and sustain the United States force structure and those allied forces designated for United States peacetime support in current Secretary of Defense guidance and to support the scheduled establishment through normal appropriation and procurement lead time periods.

Peacetime materiel consumption and losses: The quantity of an item consumed, lost, or worn out beyond economical repair through normal appropriation and procurement lead time periods.

Peacetime operating stocks: Logistic resources on hand or on order necessary to support day-to-day operational requirements, and which, in part, can also be used to offset sustaining requirements. POS.

Peak overpressure: The maximum value of overpressure at a given location which is generally experienced at the instant the shock (or blast) wave reaches that location.

Pencil beam: A searchlight beam reduced to, or set at, its minimum width.

Penetration: In land operations, a form of offensive which seeks to break through the enemy's defense and disrupt the defensive system.

Penetration aids: Techniques and/or devices employed by offensive aerospace weapon systems to increase the probability of penetration of enemy defenses.

Penetration (intelligence): The recruitment of agents within or the infiltration of agents or technical monitoring devices in an organization or group for the purpose of acquiring information or of influencing its activities.

Percentage clearance: In mine warfare, the estimated percentage of mines of specified characteristics which have been cleared from an area or channel.

Performance work statement: A statement of work for performance based acquisitions that describe the results in clear, specific, and objective terms with measurable outcomes. PWS.

Perils of the sea: Accidents and dangers peculiar to maritime activities, such as storms, waves, and wind; collision; grounding; fire, smoke and noxious fumes; flooding, sinking and capsizing; loss of propulsion or steering; and any other hazards resulting from the unique environment of the sea.

Perimeter defense: A defense without an exposed flank, consisting of forces deployed along the perimeter of the defended area.

Periodic intelligence summary: A report of the intelligence situation in a tactical operation usually at intervals of 24 hours, or as directed by the commander. PERINTSUM.

Period: The time it takes for a satellite to complete one orbit around the earth.

Period of interest: A period of time in which a launch of a missile is expected. POI.

Perishable cargo: Cargo requiring refrigeration, such as meat, fruit, fresh vegetables, and medical department biological.

Permafrost: Permanently frozen subsoil.

Permissive environment: Operational environment in which host country military and law enforcement agencies have control as well as the intent and capability to assist operations that a unit intends to conduct.

Persistency: In biological or chemical warfare, the characteristic of an agent which pertains to the duration of its effectiveness under determined conditions after its dispersal.

Persistent agent: A chemical agent that, when released, remains able to cause casualties for more than 24 hours to several days or weeks.

Personal effects: All privately owned moveable, personal property of an individual. PE. Mortuary affairs; personal property.

Personal locator beacon: An emergency radio locator beacon with a two-way speech

facility carried by crew members, either on their person or in their survival equipment,

and capable of providing homing signals to assist search and rescue operations. PLB.

Personal property: Property of any kind or any interest therein, except real property,

records of the Federal Government, and naval vessels of the following categories:

surface combatants, support ships, and submarines.

Person authorized to direct disposition of human remains: A person, usually primary next of kin, who is authorized to direct disposition of human remains.

PADD. Mortuary affairs.

Person eligible to receive effects: The person authorized by law to receive the personal effects of a deceased military member. Receipt of personal effects does not constitute ownership. Also called PERE.

Person in custody: Any person under the direct control and protection of US forces.

Personnel: Those individuals required in either a military or civilian capacity to accomplish the assigned mission.

Personnel increment number: A seven-character, alphanumeric field that uniquely describes a non-unit-related personnel entry (line) in a Joint Operation Planning and Execution System time-phased force and deployment data. PIN.

Personnel locator system: A system that provides rough range and bearing to isolated personnel by integrating the survival radio with an airborne locating system, based on an encrypted communications homing system. PLS.

Personnel locator system code: A six digit number programmed into survival radios and used by recovery forces to covertly locate isolated personnel. PLS Code.

Personnel reaction time (nuclear): The time required by personnel to take prescribed protective measures after receipt of a nuclear strike warning.

Personnel recovery: The sum of military, diplomatic, and civil efforts to prepare for and execute the recovery and reintegration of isolated personnel. PR.

Personnel recovery coordination cell: The primary joint force component organization responsible for coordinating and controlling component personnel recovery missions.

PRCC.

Personnel recovery task force: A force comprised of US or multinational military forces and/or other US agencies formed to execute a specific personnel recovery mission to locate, support, and recover isolated personnel. PRTF.

Perspective grid: A network of lines, drawn or superimposed on a photograph, to represent the perspective of a systematic network of lines on the ground or datum plane.

Petroleum intersectional service: An intersectional or inter zonal service in a theater of operations that operates pipelines and related facilities for the supply of bulk petroleum products to theater Army elements and other forces as directed.

Petroleum, oils and lubricants: A broad term that includes all petroleum and associated products used by the Armed Forces. POL.

Phase: In joint operation planning, a definitive stage of an operation or campaign during which a large portion of the forces and capabilities are involved in similar or mutually supporting activities for a common purpose.

Phase line: A line utilized for control and coordination of military operations, usually an easily identified feature in the operational area. PL.

Phonetic alphabet: A list of standard words used to identify letters in a message transmitted by radio or telephone. The following are the authorized words, listed in order, for each letter in the alphabet: ALFA, BRAVO, CHARLIE, DELTA, ECHO, FOXTROT, GOLF, HOTEL, INDIA, JULIETT, KILO, LIMA, MIKE, NOVEMBER, OSCAR, PAPA, QUEBEC, ROMEO, SIERRA, TANGO, UNIFORM, VICTOR, WHISKEY, X-RAY, YANKEE, and ZULU.

Phony minefield: An area free of live mines used to simulate a minefield, or section of a minefield, with the object of deceiving the enemy.

Photoflash bomb: A bomb designed to produce a brief and intense illumination for medium altitude night photography.

Photoflash cartridge: A pyrotechnic cartridge designed to produce a brief and intense illumination for low altitude night photography.

Photogrammetric control: Control established by photogrammetric methods as distinguished from control established by ground methods.

Photogrammetry: The science or art of obtaining reliable measurements from photographic images.

Photographic intelligence: The collected products of photographic interpretation, classified and evaluated for intelligence use. PHOTINT.

Photographic interpretation: Imagery interpretation.

Photographic panorama: A continuous photograph or an assemblage of overlapping oblique or ground photographs that have been matched and joined together to form a continuous photographic representation of the area.

Photographic reading: The simple recognition of natural or manmade features from photographs not involving imagery interpretation techniques.

Photographic strip: Series of successive overlapping photographs taken along a selected course or direction.

Photo interpretation key: Imagery interpretation key.

Photomap: A reproduction of a photograph or photo mosaic upon which the grid lines, marginal data, contours, place names, boundaries, and other data may be added.

Photo nadir: The point at which a vertical line through the perspective center of the camera lens intersects the photo plane.

Physical characteristics: Those military characteristics of equipment that are primarily physical in nature, such as weight, shape, volume, water-proofing, and sturdiness.

Physical damage assessment: The estimate of the quantitative extent of physical damage to a target resulting from the application of military force. This assessment is based upon observed or interpreted damage.

Pictomap: A topographic map in which the photographic imagery of a standard mosaic has been converted into interpretable colors and symbols by means of a Pictomap process.

Pictorial symbolization: The use of symbols which convey the visual character of the features they represent.

Pierson-Moskowitz scale: A scale that categorizes the force of progressively higher wind speeds.

Pillbox: A small, low fortification that houses machine guns, antitank weapons, etc. A pillbox is usually made of concrete, steel, or filled sandbags.

Pilot's trace: A rough overlay to a map made by the pilot of a photographic reconnaissance aircraft during or immediately after a sortie. It shows the location, direction, number, and order of photographic runs made, together with the camera(s) used on each run.

Pinpoint photograph: A single photograph or a stereo pair of a specific object or target.

Pinpoint target: In artillery and naval gunfire support, a target less than 50 meters in diameter.

Pipeline: In logistics, the channel of support or a specific portion thereof by means of which materiel or personnel flow from sources of procurement to their point of use.

Piracy: An illegal act of violence, depredation, or detention in or over international waters committed for private ends by the crew or passengers of a private ship or aircraft against another ship or aircraft or against persons or property on board such ship or aircraft.

Pitch: 1. The movement of an aircraft or ship about its transverse axis. 2. In air photography, the camera rotation about the transverse axis of the aircraft.

Pitch angle: The angle between the aircraft's longitudinal axis and the horizontal plane. Also called inclination angle.

Plan for landing: In amphibious operations, a collective term referring to all individually prepared naval and landing force documents which, taken together, present in detail all instructions for execution of the ship-to-shore movement.

Planimetric map: A map representing only the horizontal position of features. Sometimes called a line map.

Plan information capability: The capability that allows a supported command to enter and update key elements of information in an operation plan stored in the Joint Operation Planning and Execution System.

Planned airlift requests: Requests generated to meet airlift requirements that can be forecast or where requirements can be anticipated and published in the air tasking order.

Planning and direction: In intelligence usage, the determination of intelligence requirements, development of appropriate intelligence architecture, preparation of a collection plan, and issuance of orders and requests to information collection agencies. See also intelligence process.

Planning factor: A multiplier used in planning to estimate the amount and type of effort involved in a contemplated operation. Planning factors are often expressed as rates, ratios, or lengths of time.

Planning order: A planning directive that provides essential planning guidance and directs the initiation of execution planning before the directing authority approves a military course of action. PLANORD.

Planning phase: In amphibious operations, the phase normally denoted by the period extending from the issuance of the order initiating the amphibious operation up to the embarkation phase. The planning phase may occur during movement or at any other time upon receipt of a new mission or change in the operational situation.

Planning team: A functional element within a joint force commander's headquarters established to solve problems related to a specific task or requirement. The planning team is not enduring and dissolves upon completion of the assigned task.

Plan position indicator: A cathode ray tube on which radar returns are so displayed as to bear the same relationship to the transmitter as the objects giving rise to them.

Plant equipment: Personal property of a capital nature, consisting of equipment, furniture, vehicles, machine tools, test equipment, and accessory and auxiliary items, but excluding special tooling and special test equipment, used or capable of use in the manufacture of supplies or for any administrative or general plant purpose.

Plastic zone: The region beyond the rupture zone associated with crater formation resulting from an explosion in which there is no visible rupture, but in which the soil is permanently deformed and compressed to a high density.

Plate: 1. In cartography: a. a printing plate of zinc, aluminum, or engraved copper; b. collective term for all "states" of an engraved map reproduced from the same engraved printing plate; c. all detail to appear on a map or chart which will be reproduced from a single printing plate. 2. In photography, a transparent medium, usually glass, coated with a photographic emulsion.

Platform drop: The airdrop of loaded platforms from rear loading aircraft with roller conveyors. See also airdrop; airdrop platform.

Plot: 1. Map, chart, or graph representing data of any sort. 2. Representation on a diagram or chart of the position or course of a target in terms of angles and distances from positions; location of a position on a map or a chart. 3. The visual display of a single location of an airborne object at a particular instant of time. 4. A portion of a map or overlay on which are drawn the outlines of the areas covered by one or more photographs.

Point defense: The defense or protection of special vital elements and installations.

Point designation grid: A system of lines, having no relation to the actual scale, or orientation, drawn on a map, chart, or air photograph dividing it into squares so that points can be more readily located.

Pointee-talkee: A language aid containing selected phrases in English opposite a translation in a foreign language. It is used by pointing to appropriate phrases.

Point of no return: A point along an aircraft track beyond which its endurance will not permit return to its own or some other associated base on its own fuel supply.

Point-to-point sealift: The movement of troops and/or cargo in Military Sealift Command nucleus or commercial shipping between established ports, in administrative landings, or during logistics over-the-shore operations.

Poised mine: A mine in which the ship counter setting has been run down to "one" and which is ready to detonate at the next actuation.

Polar coordinates: 1. Coordinates derived from the distance and angular measurements from a fixed point. 2. In artillery and naval gunfire support, the direction, distance, and vertical correction from the observer/spotter position to the target.

Polar orbit: A satellite orbit in which the satellite passes over the North and South Poles on each orbit, and eventually passes over all points on the earth. The angle of inclination between the equator and a polar orbit is 90 degrees.

Polar plot: The method of locating a target or point on the map by means of polar coordinates.

Political intelligence: Intelligence concerning foreign and domestic policies of governments and the activities of political movements.

Political warfare: Aggressive use of political means to achieve national objectives.

Politico-military gaming: Simulation of situations involving the interaction of political, military, sociological, psychological, economic, scientific, and other appropriate factors.

Pool: 1. Maintenance and control of a supply of resources or personnel upon which other activities may draw. The primary purpose of a pool is to promote maximum efficiency of use of the pooled resources or personnel, e.g., a petroleum pool or a labor and equipment pool. 2. Any combination of resources which serves a common purpose.

Population at risk: The strength in personnel of a given force structure in terms of which casualty rates are stated. PAR.

Port capacity: The estimated capacity of a port or an anchorage to clear cargo in 24 hours usually expressed in tons. Beach capacity; clearance capacity.

Port designator: A group of letters identifying ports in convoy titles or messages.

Port evacuation of cargoes: The removal of cargoes from a threatened port to alternative storage sites.

Port evacuation of shipping : The movement of merchant ships from a threatened port for their own protection.

Port security: The safeguarding of vessels, harbors, ports, waterfront facilities, and cargo from internal threats such as destruction, loss, or injury from sabotage or other subversive acts; accidents; thefts; or other causes of similar nature. Harbor defense; physical security; security.

Positive control: A method of airspace control that relies on positive identification, tracking, and direction of aircraft within an airspace, conducted with electronic means by an agency having the authority and responsibility therein.

Positive identification and radar advisory zone: A specified area established for identification and flight following of aircraft in the vicinity of a fleet-defended area. PIRAZ.

Positive phase of the shock wave: The period during which the pressure rises very sharply to a value that is higher than ambient and then decreases rapidly to the ambient pressure. See also negative phase of the shock wave.

Posse Comitatus Act: Prohibits search, seizure, or arrest powers to US military personnel. Amended in 1981 under Public Law 97-86 to permit increased Department of Defense support of drug interdiction and other law enforcement activities.

Postattack period: In nuclear warfare, that period which extends from the termination of the final attack until political authorities agree to terminate hostilities.

Post hostilities period: That period subsequent to the date of ratification by political authorities of agreements to terminate hostilities.

Post strike reconnaissance: Missions undertaken for the purpose of gathering information used to measure results of a strike.

Practice mine: 1. In land mine warfare, an inert mine to which is fitted a fuze and a device to indicate, in a non-lethal fashion, that the fuze has been activated.

2. In naval mine warfare, an inert-filled mine but complete with assembly, suitable for instruction and for practice in preparation.

Pre assault operation: Operations conducted by the amphibious force upon its arrival in the operational area and prior to H-hour and/or L-hour. Amphibious force; times.

Precautionary launch: The launching of nuclear loaded aircraft under imminent nuclear attack so as to preclude friendly aircraft destruction and loss of weapons on the ground and/or carrier.

Precautionary personnel recovery: The planning and pre-positioning of aircraft, ships, or ground forces and facilities before an operation to provide personnel recovery assistance if needed. Precautionary postures include: duck butt; lifeguard; airborne alert; and quick response posture. Precautionary PR.

Precipitation static: Charged precipitation particles that strike antennas and gradually charge the antenna, which ultimately discharges across the insulator, causing a burst of static. P-STATIC.

Precise frequency: A frequency requirement accurate to within one part in 1,000,000,000.

Precise time and time interval: A reference value of time and time interval (frequency). Standards are maintained through traceable measurements referenced to a primary timing or frequency standard. The Department of Defense standard for precise time and time interval is Universal Coordinated Time as maintained by the United States Naval Observatory.

Precision bombing : Bombing directed at a specific point target.

Precision-guided munitions: A weapon that uses a seeker to detect electromagnetic energy reflected from a target or reference point and, through processing, provides guidance commands to a control system that guides the weapon to the target. PGM.

Precursor: Any chemical reactant which takes place at any stage in the production by whatever method of a toxic chemical. This includes any key component of a binary or multicomponent chemical system.

Precursor chemical: Compounds that are required in the synthetic or extraction processes of drug production, and become incorporated into the drug molecule. Not used in the production of cocaine or heroin.

Precursor front: An air pressure wave which moves ahead of the main blast wave for some distance as a result of a nuclear explosion of appropriate yield and low burst height over a heat-absorbing surface. The pressure at the precursor front increases more gradually than in a true shock wave, so that the behavior in the precursor region is said to be non-ideal.

Precursor sweeping. The sweeping of an area by relatively safe means in order to reduce the risk to mine countermeasures vessels in subsequent operations.

Predicted fire: Fire that is delivered without adjustment.

Predominant height: In air reconnaissance, the height of 51 percent or more of the structures within an area of similar surface material.

Preemptive attack: An attack initiated on the basis of incontrovertible evidence that an enemy attack is imminent.

Pre initiation: The initiation of the fission chain reaction in the active material of a nuclear weapon at any time earlier than that at which either the designed or the maximum compression or degree of assembly is attained.

Pre-launch survivability: The probability that a delivery and/ or launch vehicle will survive an enemy attack under an established condition of warning.

Preliminary communications search: In search and rescue operations, consists of contacting and checking major facilities within the areas where the craft might be or might have been seen. A preliminary communications search is normally conducted during the uncertainty phase. PRECOM.

Preliminary demolition target: A target, other than a reserved demolition target, which is earmarked for demolition and which can be executed immediately after preparation, provided that prior authority has been granted. Demolition target; reserved demolition target.

Preload loading: The loading of selected items aboard ship at one port prior to the main loading of the ship at another.

Preparation fire: Fire delivered on a target preparatory to an assault.

Prepare to deploy order: An order issued by competent authority to move forces or

prepare forces for movement. PTDO.

Preplanned air support: Air support in accordance with a program, planned in advance of operations.

Preplanned mission request: A request for an air strike on a target that can be anticipated sufficiently in advance to permit detailed mission coordination and planning.

Preplanned nuclear support: Nuclear support planned in advance of operations. Immediate nuclear support; nuclear support.

Pre-position: To place military units, equipment, or supplies at or near the point of planned use or at a designated location to reduce reaction time, and to ensure timely support of a specific force during initial phases of an operation.

Pre-positioned war reserve materiel requirement, balance: That portion of the pre-positioned war reserve materiel requirement that has not been acquired or funded. This level consists of the pre-positioned war reserve materiel requirement, less the prepositioned war reserve requirement, protectable.

Pressure breathing: The technique of breathing which is required when oxygen is supplied direct to an individual at a pressure higher than the ambient barometric pressure.

Pressure mine: 1. In land mine warfare, a mine whose fuse responds to the direct pressure of a target. 2. In naval mine warfare, a mine whose circuit responds to the hydrodynamic pressure field of a target.

Pressurized cabin: The occupied space of an aircraft in which the air pressure has been increased above that of the ambient atmosphere by compression of the ambient atmosphere into the space.

Prestrike reconnaissance: Missions undertaken for the purpose of obtaining complete information about known targets for use by the strike force.

Prevention: 1. The security procedures undertaken by the public and private sectors in order to discourage terrorist acts. 2. In space usage, measures to preclude an adversary's hostile use of United States or third-party space systems and services. Prevention can include diplomatic, economic, and political measures.

Prevention of stripping equipment: Anti recovery device.

Preventive deployment: The deployment of military forces to deter violence at the interface or zone of potential conflict where tension is rising among parties. Forces may be employed in such a way that they are indistinguishable from a peace operations force in terms of equipment, force posture, and activities.

Preventive diplomacy: Diplomatic actions taken in advance of a predictable crisis to prevent or limit violence.

Preventive maintenance: The care and servicing by personnel for the purpose of maintaining equipment and facilities in satisfactory operating condition by providing for systematic inspection, detection, and correction of incipient failures either before they occur or before they develop into major defects.

Preventive war: A war initiated in the belief that military conflict, while not imminent, is inevitable, and that to delay would involve greater risk.

Prewithdrawal demolition target: A target prepared for demolition preliminary to a withdrawal, the demolition of which can be executed as soon after preparation as convenient on the orders of the officer to whom the responsibility for such demolitions has been delegated.

Primary agency: The federal department or agency assigned primary responsibility for managing and coordinating a specific emergency support function in the National Response Plan.

Primary aircraft authorization: The number of aircraft authorized to a unit for performance of its operational mission. The primary authorization forms the basis for the allocation of operating resources to include manpower, support equipment, and flying-hour funds. PAA.

Primary aircraft inventory: The aircraft assigned to meet the primary aircraft authorization. PAI.

Primary censorship: Armed forces censorship performed by personnel of a company, battery, squadron, ship, station, base, or similar unit on the personal communications of persons assigned, attached, or otherwise under the jurisdiction of a unit.

Primary control officer: In amphibious operations, the officer embarked in a primary control ship assigned to control the movement of landing craft, amphibious vehicles, and landing ships to and from a colored beach. PCO.

Primary control ship: In amphibious operations, a ship of the task force designated to provide support for the primary control officer and a combat information center control team for a colored beach. PCS.

Primary flight control: The controlling agency on aviation ships and amphibious aviation assault ships that is responsible for air traffic control of aircraft within 5 nautical miles of the ship. On most Coast Guard cutters, primary flight control duties are performed by a combat information center, and the term "PRIFLY" is not used. PRIFLY. Amphibious aviation assault ship; aviation ship.

Primary imagery dissemination: See electronic imagery dissemination. primary imagery dissemination system — See electronic imagery dissemination.

Primary interest: Principal, although not exclusive, interest and responsibility for accomplishment of a given mission, including responsibility for reconciling the activities of other agencies that possess collateral interest in the program.

Primary review authority: The organization, within the lead agent's chain of command, that is assigned by the lead agent to perform the actions and coordination necessary to develop and maintain the assigned joint publication under the cognizance of the lead agent. PRA. Joint publication; lead agent.

Prime contract: A contract or contractual action entered into by the United States Government for the purpose of obtaining supplies, materials, equipment, or services of any kind.

Primed charge: A charge ready in all aspects for ignition.

Prime mover: A vehicle, including heavy construction equipment, possessing military characteristics, designed primarily for towing heavy, wheeled weapons and frequently providing facilities for the transportation of the crew of, and ammunition for, the weapon.

Prime vendor: A contracting process that provides commercial products to regionally grouped military and federal customers from commercial distributors using electronic commerce. Customers typically receive materiel delivery through the vendor's commercial distribution system. PV.

Principal building: A building aboard a diplomatic or consular compound where classified information may be handled, stored, discussed, or processed, but that does not house the offices of the chief of mission or principal officer.

Principal federal official: The federal official designated by the Secretary of Homeland Security to act as his/her representative locally to oversee, coordinate, and execute the Secretary's incident management responsibilities under Homeland Security Presidential Directive 5 for incidents of national significance. PFO.

Principal officer: The officer in charge of a diplomatic mission, consular office, or other Foreign Service post, such as a United States Liaison Office.

Principal parallel: On an oblique photograph, a line parallel to the true horizon and passing through the principal point.

Principal plane: A vertical plane which contains the principal point of an oblique photograph, the perspective center of the lens, and the ground nadir.

Principal scale: In cartography, the scale of a reduced or generating globe representing the sphere or spheroid, defined by the fractional relation of their respective radii. Also called nominal scale.

Principal vertical: On an oblique photograph, a line perpendicular to the true horizon and passing through the principal point.

Printing size of a map or chart: The dimensions of the smallest rectangle which will contain a map or chart, including all the printed material in its margin.

Print reference: A reference to an individual print in an air photographic sortie.

Priority intelligence requirement: An intelligence requirement, stated as a priority for intelligence support, that the commander and staff need to understand the adversary or the operational environment. PIR. Information requirements; intelligence; intelligence process; intelligence requirement.

Priority message: A category of precedence reserved for messages that require expeditious action by the addressee(s) and/or furnish essential information for the conduct of operations in progress when routine precedence will not suffice.

Priority of immediate mission requests: Emergency priority; urgent priority.

Prior permission: Permission granted by the appropriate authority prior to the commencement of a flight or a series of flights landing in or flying over the territory of the nation concerned.

Prisoner of war branch camp: A subsidiary camp under the supervision and administration of a prisoner of war camp.

Prisoner of war camp: An installation established for the internment and administration of prisoners of war.

Prisoner of war censorship: The censorship of the communications to and from enemy prisoners of war and civilian internees held by the United States Armed Forces. Censorship.

Prisoner of war compound: A subdivision of a prisoner of war enclosure.

Prisoner of war enclosure: A subdivision of a prisoner of war camp.

Prisoner of war personnel record: A form for recording the photograph, fingerprints, and other pertinent personal data concerning the prisoner of war, including that required by the Geneva Convention.

Private sector: An umbrella term that may be applied in the United States and in foreign countries to any or all of the nonpublic or commercial individuals and businesses, specified nonprofit organizations, most of academia and other scholastic institutions, and selected nongovernmental organizations.

Privity of contract: The legal relationship that exists between two contracting parties, for example, between the government and the prime contractor.

Proactive measures: In antiterrorism, measures taken in the preventive stage of antiterrorism designed to harden targets and detect actions before they occur.

Proactive mine countermeasures: Measures intended to prevent the enemy from successfully laying mines.

Probability of damage: The probability that damage will occur to a target expressed as a percentage or as a decimal. PD.

Probable error: Horizontal error.

Probable error deflection: Error in deflection that is exceeded as often as not.

Probable error height of burst: Error in height of burst that projectile and/or missile fuzes may be expected to exceed as often as not.

Probable error range: Error in range that is exceeded as often as not.

Probably destroyed: In air operations, a damage assessment on an enemy aircraft seen to break off combat in circumstances which lead to the conclusion that it must be a loss although it is not actually seen to crash.

Probe: In information operations, any attempt to gather information about an automated information system or its on-line users. Information; information operations; information system.

Procedural control: A method of airspace control which relies on a combination of previously agreed and promulgated orders and procedures.

Procedures: Standard, detailed steps that prescribe how to perform specific tasks. tactics; techniques.

Procedure turn: An aircraft maneuver in which a turn is made away from a designated track followed by a turn in the opposite direction, both turns being executed at a constant rate so as to permit the aircraft to intercept and proceed along the reciprocal of the designated track.

Procedure word: A word or phrase limited to radio telephone procedure used to facilitate communication by conveying information in a condensed standard form.

Processing: 1. In photography, the operations necessary to produce negatives, diapositives, or prints from exposed films, plates, or paper. 2. A system of operations designed to convert raw data into useful information.

Processing and exploitation: In intelligence usage, the conversion of collected information into forms suitable to the production of intelligence. Intelligence process.

Process owner: The head of a Department of Defense component assigned a responsibility by the Secretary of Defense when process improvement involves more than one Military Service or Department of Defense component.

Proclamation: A document published to the inhabitants of an area that sets forth the basis of authority and scope of activities of a commander in a given area and which defines the obligations, liabilities, duties, and rights of the population affected.

Procurement lead time: The interval in time between the initiation of procurement action and receipt into the supply system of the production model (excludes prototypes) purchased as the result of such actions. It is composed of two elements, production lead time and administrative lead time. Production lead time; receipt into the supply system.

Procuring contracting officer: A contracting officer who initiates and signs the contract. PCO.

Administrative contracting officer; contracting officer.

Producer countries: In counterdrug operations, countries where naturally occurring plants such as coca, cannabis, or poppies are cultivated for later refinement into illicit drugs. See also counterdrug operations.

Production base: The total national industrial production capacity available for the manufacture of items to meet materiel requirements.

Production lead time: The time interval between the placement of a contract and receipt into the supply system of materiel purchased. Two entries are provided: a. initial —The time interval if the item is not under production as of the date of contract

Placement; and b. reorder: The time interval if the item is under production as of the date of contract placement. See also procurement lead time.

Production loss appraisal: An estimate of damage inflicted on an industry in terms of quantities of finished products denied the enemy from the moment of attack through the period of reconstruction to the point when full production is resumed.

Proficiency training aircraft: Aircraft required to maintain the proficiency of pilots and other aircrew members who are assigned to nonflying duties.

Program aircraft: The total of the active and reserve aircraft. Aircraft.

Programmed Forces: The forces that exist for each year of the Future Years Defense Program. They contain the major combat and tactical support forces that are expected to execute the national strategy within manpower, fiscal, and other constraints. See also current force; force; Intermediate Force Planning Level.

Prohibited area: A specified area within the land areas of a state or its internal waters, archipelagic waters, or territorial sea adjacent thereto over which the flight of aircraft is prohibited. May also refer to land or sea areas to which access is prohibited. Closed area; danger area; restricted area.

Projected map display: The displayed image of a map or chart projected through an optical or electro-optical system onto a viewing surface.

Projection print: An enlarged or reduced photographic print made by projection of the image of a negative or a transparency onto a sensitized surface.

Proliferation (nuclear weapons): The process by which one nation after another comes into possession of, or into the right to determine the use of, nuclear weapons; each nation becomes potentially able to launch a nuclear attack upon another nation.

Proofing: The verification that a breached lane is free of live mines by passing a mine roller or other mine-resistant vehicle through as the lead vehicle.

Propaganda: Any form of communication in support of national objectives designed to influence the opinions, emotions, attitudes, or behavior of any group in order to benefit the sponsor, either directly or indirectly. Black propaganda; grey propaganda; white propaganda.

Proper authority: An authority authorized to call an opposing force hostile; may be either the President, the Secretary of Defense, the affected combatant commander, and/or any commander so delegated by either the President, Secretary of Defense or the combatant commander.

Proper clearance: A clearance for entry of units into specified defense areas by civil or military authorities having responsibility for granting such clearance.

Property: 1. Anything that may be owned. 2. As used in the military establishment, this term is usually confined to tangible property, including real estate and materiel. For special purposes and as used in certain statutes, this term may exclude such items as the public domain, certain lands, certain categories of naval vessels, and records of the Federal Government.

Property account: A formal record of property and property transactions in terms of quantity and/or cost, generally by item. An official record of Government property required to be maintained.

Proportional navigation: A method of homing navigation in which the missile turn rate is directly proportional to the turn rate in space of the line of sight.

Protected emblems: The red cross, red crescent, and other symbols that designate that persons, places, or equipment so marked have a protected status under the law of war.

Protected site: A facility which is protected by the use of camouflage or concealment, selective siting, construction of facilities decision.

Q

Q-message: A classified message relating to navigational dangers, navigational aids, mined areas, and searched or swept channels.

Q-route: A system of preplanned shipping lanes in mined or potentially mined waters used to minimize the area the mine countermeasures commander has to keep clear of mines in order to provide safe passage for friendly shipping.

Quadrant elevation: The angle between the horizontal plane and the axis of the bore when the weapon is laid. It is the algebraic sum of the elevation, angle of site, and complementary angle of site.

Quadruple container: A quadruple container box 57.5" x 96" x 96" with a metal frame, pallet base, and International Organization for Standardization (ISO) corner fittings. Four of these boxes can be lashed together to form a 20- foot American National Standards Institute and/ or ISO intermodal container. QUADCON.

Quay: A structure of solid construction along a shore or bank that provides berthing and generally provides cargo-handling facilities. A similar facility of open construction is called a wharf.

Quick response force: A company-sized force providing responsive, mission-tailored, lightly armed ground units that can deploy on short notice, with minimal lift assets, and capable of providing immediate or emergency response. QRF

R

Radar: A radio detection device that provides information on range, azimuth, and/or elevation of objects.

Radar advisory: The term used to indicate that the provision of advice and information is based on radar observation.

Radar altimetry area: A large and comparatively level terrain area with a defined elevation which can be used in determining the altitude of airborne equipment by the use of radar.

Radar beacon: A receiver-transmitter combination that sends out a coded signal when triggered by the proper type of pulse, enabling determination of range and bearing information by the interrogating station or aircraft. RB.

Radar camouflage: The use of radar absorbent or reflecting materials to change the radar echoing properties of a surface of an object.

Radar clutter: Unwanted signals, echoes, or images on the face of the display tube which interfere with observation of desired signals.

Radar countermeasures: Electronic warfare; chaff.

Radar coverage: The limits within which objects can be detected by one or more radar stations.

Radar danning: In naval mine warfare, a method of navigating by using radar to keep the required distance from a line of dan buoys.

Radar deception: Electromagnetic deception.

Radar fire: Gunfire aimed at a target which is tracked by radar.

Radar guardship: Any ship which has been assigned the task by the officer in tactical command of maintaining the radar watch.

Radar horizon: The locus of points at which the rays from a radar antenna become tangential to the Earth's surface. On the open sea this locus is horizontal, but on land it varies according to the topographical features of the terrain.

Radar imagery: Imagery produced by recording radar waves reflected from a given target surface.

Radar intelligence: Intelligence derived from data collected by radar. RADINT. Intelligence.

Radar netting: The linking of several radars to a single center to provide integrated target information.

Radar netting station: A center which can receive data from radar tracking stations and exchange this data among other radar tracking stations, thus forming a radar netting system. Radar netting unit; radar tracking station.

Radar netting unit: Optional electronic equipment that converts the operations central of certain air defense fire distribution systems to a radar netting station. Radar netting station.

Radar picket: Any ship, aircraft, or vehicle, stationed at a distance from the force protected, and integrated into a common operational picture for the purpose of increasing the radar detection range.

Radar reconnaissance: Reconnaissance by means of radar to obtain information on enemy activity and to determine the nature of terrain.

Radarscope overlay: A transparent overlay for placing on the radarscope for comparison and identification of radar returns.

Radarscope photography: A film record of the returns shown by a radar screen.

Radar silence: An imposed discipline prohibiting the transmission by radar of electromagnetic signals on some or all frequencies.

Radar spoking: Periodic flashes of the rotating time base on a radial display. Sometimes caused by mutual interference.

Radar tracking station: A radar facility that has the capability of tracking moving targets.

Radial: A magnetic bearing extending from a very high frequency omni-range and/or tactical air navigation station.

Radial displacement: On vertical photographs, the apparent "leaning out," or the apparent displacement of the top of any object having height in relation to its base. The direction of displacement is radial from the principal point on a true vertical, or from the isocenter on a vertical photograph distorted by tip or tilt.

Radiation dose: The total amount of ionizing radiation absorbed by material or tissues. Exposure dose.

Radiation dose rate: Measurement of radiation dose per unit of time.

Radiation exposure state: The condition of a unit, or exceptionally an individual, deduced from the cumulative whole body radiation dose(s) received. It is expressed as a symbol which indicates the potential for future operations and the degree of risk if exposed to additional nuclear radiation.

Radiation exposure status: Criteria to assist the commander in measuring unit exposure to radiation based on total past cumulative dose, normally expressed in centigray. RES.

Radiation intelligence: Intelligence derived from the collection and analysis of non-information-bearing elements extracted from the electromagnetic energy unintentionally emanated by foreign devices, equipments, and systems, excluding those generated by the detonation of atomic or nuclear weapons.

Radioactive decay: The decrease in the radiation intensity of any radioactive material with respect to time.

Radioactive decay curve: A graph line representing the decrease of radioactivity with the passage of time.

Radioactive decay rate: The time rate of the disintegration of radioactive material generally accompanied by the emission of particles and/or gamma radiation.

Radioactivity: The spontaneous emission of radiation, generally alpha or beta particles, often accompanied by gamma rays, from the nuclei of an unstable isotope.

Radioactivity concentration guide: The amount of any specified radioisotope that is acceptable in air and water for continuous consumption. radio and wire integration – The combining of wire circuits with radio facilities. RWI.

Radio approach aids: Equipment making use of radio to determine the position of an aircraft with considerable accuracy from the time it is in the vicinity of an airfield or carrier until it reaches a position from which landing can be carried out.

Radio beacon: A radio transmitter which emits a distinctive or characteristic signal used for the determination of bearings, courses, or location. radio countermeasures.

Radio deception: The employment of radio to deceive the enemy. Radio deception includes sending false dispatches, using deceptive headings, employing enemy call signs, etc. Electronic warfare.

Radio detection: The detection of the presence of an object by radio-location without precise determination of its position.

Radio direction finding: Radiolocation in which only the direction of a station is determined by means of its emissions.

Radio direction finding database: The aggregate of information, acquired by both airborne and surface means, necessary to provide support to radio direction-finding operations to produce fixes on target transmitters and/or emitters. The resultant bearings and fixes serve as a basis for tactical decisions concerning military operations, including exercises, planned or underway.

Radio fix: The location of a ship or aircraft by determining the direction of radio signals coming to the ship or aircraft from two or more sending stations, the locations of which are known.

Radio frequency countermeasures: Any device or technique employing radio frequency materials or technology that is intended to impair the effectiveness of enemy activity, particularly with respect to precision guided weapons and sensor systems. RF CM.

Radio guard: A ship, aircraft, or radio station designated to listen for and record transmissions and to handle traffic on a designated frequency for a certain unit or units.

Radiological accident: A loss of control over radiation or radioactive material that presents a hazard to life, health, or property or that may result in any member of the general population exceeding exposure limits for ionizing radiation.

Radiological defense: Defensive measures taken against the radiation hazards resulting from the employment of nuclear and radiological weapons.

Radiological dispersal device: An improvised assembly or process, other than a nuclear explosive device, designed to disseminate radioactive material in order to cause destruction, damage, or injury. RDD.

Radiological environment: Conditions found in an area resulting from the presence of a radiological hazard.

Radiological exposure device: A radioactive source placed to cause injury or death. RED.

Radiological operation: The employment of radioactive materials or radiation producing devices to cause casualties or restrict the use of terrain. It includes the intentional employment of fallout from nuclear weapons.

Radiological survey: The directed effort to determine the distribution and dose rates of radiation in an area.

Radiological survey flight altitude: The altitude at which an aircraft is flown during an aerial radiological survey.

Radio magnetic indicator: An instrument which displays aircraft heading and bearing to selected radio navigation aids.

Radio navigation: Radio-location intended for the determination of position or direction or for obstruction warning in navigation.

Radio range finding: Radio-location in which the distance of an object is determined by means of its radio emissions, whether independent, reflected, or retransmitted on the same or other wavelength.

Radio range station: A radio navigation land station in the aeronautical radio navigation service providing radio equi-signal zones.

Radio silence: A condition in which all or certain radio equipment capable of radiation is kept inoperative.

Radio telegraphy: The transmission of telegraphic codes by means of radio.

Radio telephony: The transmission of speech by means of modulated radio waves.

Radius of action: The maximum distance a ship, aircraft, or vehicle can travel away from its base along a given course with normal combat load and return without refueling, allowing for all safety and operating factors.

Radius of damage: The distance from ground zero at which there is a 0.50 probability of achieving the desired damage.

Radius of integration: The distance from ground zero that indicates the area within which the effects of both the nuclear detonation and conventional weapons are to be integrated.

Radius of safety: The horizontal distance from ground zero beyond which the weapon effects on friendly troops are acceptable.

Raid: An operation to temporarily seize an area in order to secure information, confuse an adversary, capture personnel or equipment, or to destroy a capability. It ends with a planned withdrawal upon completion of the assigned mission.

Railhead: A point on a railway where loads are transferred between trains and other means of transport. Navigation head.

Railway line capacity: The maximum number of trains which can be moved in each direction over a specified section of track in a 24 hour period.

Railway loading ramp: A sloping platform situated at the end or beside a track and rising to the level of the floor of the rail cars or wagons.

Rainfall (nuclear): The water that is precipitated from the base surge clouds after an underwater burst of a nuclear weapon. This rain is radioactive and presents an important secondary effect of such a burst.

Rainout: Radioactive material in the atmosphere brought down by precipitation.

Ramjet: A jet-propulsion engine containing neither compressor nor turbine which depends for its operation on the air compression accomplished by the forward motion of the engine. Pulsejet.

Random mine laying: In land mine warfare, the laying of mines without regard to pattern.

Range marker: A single calibration blip fed onto the time base of a radial display. The rotation of the time base shows the single blips as a circle on the plan position indicator scope. It may be used to measure range.

Range markers: Two upright markers that may be lighted at night and placed so that, when aligned, the direction indicated assists in piloting. They may be used in amphibious operations to aid in beaching landing ships or craft.

Rangers: Rapidly deployable airborne light infantry organized and trained to conduct highly complex joint direct action operations in coordination with or in support of other special operations units of all Services. Rangers also can execute direct action operations in support of conventional nonspecial operations missions conducted by a combatant commander and can operate as conventional light infantry when properly augmented with other elements of combined arms.

Range spread: The technique used to place the mean point of impact of two or more units 100 meters apart on the gun-target line.

Ranging: The process of establishing target distance. Types of ranging include echo, intermittent, manual, navigational, explosive echo, optical, radar, etc. See also spot.

Rapid and precise response: Rapid and precise response is the ability of the defense supply chain to meet the constantly changing needs of the joint force.

Rapid global mobility: The timely movement, positioning, and sustainment of military forces and capabilities across the range of military operations. Mobility.

Rapid response force: A battalion minus-sized force providing responsive, mission tailored, lightly armed ground units that can deploy on short notice, with minimal lift assets, and capable of providing immediate or emergency response. RRF.

Rated load: The designed safe operating load for the equipment under prescribed conditions.

Rate of fire: The number of rounds fired per weapon per minute.

Rate of march: The average number of miles or kilometers to be traveled in a given period of time, including all ordered halts. It is expressed in miles or kilometers in the hour. Pace.

Ratio print: A print the scale of which has been changed from that of the negative by photographic enlargement or reduction.

Ratline: An organized effort for moving personnel and/or material by clandestine means across a denied area or border.

Ready position: In helicopter operations, a designated place where a helicopter load of troops and/or equipment waits for pick-up.

Ready Reserve: The Selected Reserve, Individual Ready Reserve, and Inactive National Guard liable for active duty as prescribed by law (title 10, US Code, sections 10142, 12301, and 12302). Active duty; Inactive National Guard; Individual Ready Reserve; Selected Reserve.

Ready-to-load date: The date when a unit will be ready to move from the origin, i.e., mobilization station. RLD.

Reallocation authority: The authority given to NATO commanders and normally negotiated in peacetime, to reallocate in an "emergency in war" national logistic resources controlled by the combat forces under their command, and made available by nations, in order to influence the battle logistically.

Real property: Lands, buildings, structures, utilities systems, improvements, and appurtenances thereto. Includes equipment attached to and made part of buildings and structures but not movable equipment.

Real time: Pertaining to the timeliness of data or information which has been delayed only by the time required for electronic communication. This implies that there are no noticeable delays. Near real time.

Rear area: For any particular command, the area extending forward from its rear boundary to the rear of the area assigned to the next lower level of command. This area is provided primarily for the performance of support functions. Army service area.

Rear area operations center/ rear tactical operations center: A command and control facility that serves as an area and/or subarea commander's planning, coordinating, monitoring, advising, and directing agency for area security operations.

Rear echelon: Elements of a force which are not required in the objective area.

Rearming: 1. An operation that replenishes the prescribed stores of ammunition, bombs, and other armament items for an aircraft, naval ship, tank, or armored vehicle in order to make it ready for combat service. 2. Resetting the fuze on a bomb or on an artillery, mortar, or rocket projectile so that it will detonate at the desired time.

Rebuild: The restoration of an item to a standard as nearly as possible to its original condition in appearance, performance, and life expectancy.

Receipt: A transmission made by a receiving station to indicate that a message has been satisfactorily received.

Receipt into the supply system: That point in time when the first item or first quantity of the item of the contract has been received at or is en route to point of first delivery after inspection and acceptance.

Receiving ship: The ship in a replenishment unit that receives the rig(s).

Reclama: A request to duly constituted authority to reconsider its decision or its proposed action.

Recognition signal: Any prearranged signal by which individuals or units may identify each other.

Reconnaissance: A mission undertaken to obtain, by visual observation or other detection methods, information about the activities and resources of an enemy or adversary, or to secure data concerning the meteorological, hydrographic, or geographic characteristics of a particular area. RECON.

Reconnaissance by fire: A method of reconnaissance in which fire is placed on a suspected enemy position to cause the enemy to disclose a presence by movement or return of fire.

Reconnaissance exploitation report: A standard message format used to report the results of a tactical air reconnaissance mission. Whenever possible the report should include the interpretation of sensor imagery. RECCEXREP.

Reconnaissance in force: An offensive operation designed to discover and/or test the enemy's strength or to obtain other information.

Reconnaissance photography: Photography taken to obtain information on the results of bombing, or on enemy movements, concentrations, activities, and forces. The primary purposes do not include making maps, charts, or mosaics.

Record information: All forms (e.g., narrative, graphic, data, computer memory) of information registered in either temporary or permanent form so that it can be retrieved, reproduced, or preserved.

Recoverable item: An item that normally is not consumed in use and is subject to return for repair or disposal. Reparable item.

Recovery: 1. In air (aviation) operations, that phase of a mission which involves the return of an aircraft to a land base or platform afloat. 2. The retrieval of a mine from the location where emplaced. 3. In personnel recovery, actions taken to physically gain custody of isolated personnel and return them to the initial reception point. 4. Actions taken to extricate damaged or disabled equipment for return to friendly control or repair at another location.

Recovery airfield: Any airfield, military or civil, at which aircraft might land post-H-hour. It is not expected that combat missions would be conducted from a recovery airfield.

Recovery force: In personnel recovery, an organization consisting of personnel and equipment with a mission of locating, supporting, and recovering isolated personnel, and returning them to friendly control.

Recovery mechanism: Designated indigenous or surrogate infrastructure that is specifically developed, trained, and directed by US forces to contact, authenticate, support, move, and exfiltrate designated isolated personnel from uncertain or hostile areas back to friendly control. Recovery mechanisms may operate with other US or multinational personnel recovery capabilities. RM.

Recovery operations: Operations conducted to search for, locate, identify, recover, and return isolated personnel, human remains, sensitive equipment, or items critical to national security.

Recovery procedures: Explosive ordnance disposal procedures.

Recovery site: In personnel recovery, an area from which isolated personnel can be recovered. See also escapee; evader; evasion; evasion and escape.

Recovery team: In personnel recovery, designated US or US-directed forces, who are specifically trained to operate in conjunction with indigenous or surrogate forces, and are tasked to contact, authenticate, support, move, and exfiltrate isolated personnel. RT.

Recovery vehicle: In personnel recovery, the vehicle on which isolated personnel are boarded and transported from the recovery site.

Recovery zone: A designated geographic area from which special operations forces can be extracted by air, boat, or other means. RZ.

Rectification: In photogrammetry, the process of projecting a tilted or oblique photograph on to a horizontal reference plane.

Redeployment airfield: An airfield not occupied in its entirety in peacetime, but available immediately upon outbreak of war for use and occupation by units redeployed from their peacetime locations. It must have substantially the same standard of operational facilities as the main airfield.

Red Horse: Air Force units wartime-structured to provide a heavy engineer capability. They have a responsibility across the operational area, are not tied to a specific base, and are not responsible for base operation and maintenance. These units are mobile, rapidly deployable, and largely self-sufficient for limited periods of time.

Redistribution: The utilization of logistic resources after Transfer of Authority necessary for the fulfillment of the commander's combat missions. The logistic resources are designated in peacetime and will become assigned to the NATO commander in crisis and conflict.

Red team: An organizational element comprised of trained and educated members that provide an independent capability to fully explore alternatives in plans and operations in the context of the operational environment and from the perspective of adversaries and others.

Reduction: The creation of lanes through a minefield or obstacle to allow passage of the attacking ground force.

Reduction (photographic): The production of a negative, diapositive, or print at a scale smaller than the original.

Reefer: 1. A refrigerator. 2. A motor vehicle, railroad freight car, ship, aircraft, or other conveyance, so constructed and insulated as to protect commodities from either heat or cold.

Reentry vehicle: That part of a space vehicle designed to re-enter the Earth's atmosphere in the terminal portion of its trajectory. RV. Maneuverable reentry vehicle; multiple reentry vehicle.

Reference diversion point: One of a number of positions selected by the routing authority on both sides of the route of a convoy or independent to facilitate diversion at sea.

Reference point: A prominent, easily located point in the terrain.

Reflex sight: An optical or computing sight that reflects a reticle image (or images) onto a combining glass for superimposition on the target.

Refraction: The process by which the direction of a wave is changed when moving into shallow water at an angle to the bathymetric contours. The crest of the wave advancing in shallower water moves more slowly than the crest still advancing in deeper water, causing the wave crest to bend toward alignment with the underwater contours.

Refuge area: A coastal area considered safe from enemy attack to which merchant ships may be ordered to proceed when the shipping movement policy is implemented. Safe anchorage.

Refugee: A person who owning to a well-founded fear of being persecuted for reasons of race, religion, nationality, membership of a particular social group or political opinion, is outside the country of his or her nationality and is unable or, owing to such fear, is unwilling to avail himself or herself of the protection of that country. Dislocated civilian; displaced person; evacuee; expellee; stateless person.

Regimental landing team: A task organization for landing comprised of an infantry regiment reinforced by those elements that are required for initiation of its combat function ashore.

Regional response coordination center: A standing facility that is activated to coordinate regional response efforts, until a joint field office is established and/or the principal federal official, federal or coordinating officer can assume their National Response Plan coordination responsibilities. RRCC.

Regional security officer: A security officer responsible to the chief of mission (ambassador), for security functions of all US embassies and consulates in a given country or group of adjacent countries. RSO.

Register: In cartography, the correct position of one component of a composite map image in relation to the other components, at each stage of production.

Registration: The adjustment of fire to determine firing data corrections.

Registration fire: Fire delivered to obtain accurate data for subsequent effective engagement of targets.

Registration point: Terrain feature or other designated point on which fire is adjusted for the purpose of obtaining corrections to firing data.

Regrade: To determine that certain classified information requires, in the interests of national defense, a higher or a lower degree of protection against unauthorized disclosure than currently provided, coupled with a changing of the classification designation to reflect such higher or lower degree.

Regulated item: Any item whose issue to a user is subject to control by an appropriate authority for reasons that may include cost, scarcity, technical or hazardous nature, or operational significance.

Regulating point: An anchorage, port, or ocean area to which assault and assault follow on echelons and follow-up shipping proceed on a schedule, and at which they are normally controlled by the commander, amphibious task force, until needed in the transport area for unloading.

Regulating station: A command agency established to control all movements of personnel and supplies into or out of a given area.

Reinforcing: A support mission in which the supporting unit assists the supported unit to accomplish the supported unit's mission. Only like units can be given a reinforcing/reinforced mission.

Reinforcing obstacles: Those obstacles specifically constructed, emplaced, or detonated through military effort and designed to strengthen existing terrain to disrupt, fix, turn, or block enemy movement.

Reintegrate: In personnel recovery, the task of conducting appropriate debriefings and reintegrating recovered isolated personnel back to duty and their family.

Relateral tell: The relay of information between facilities through the use of a third facility. This type of telling is appropriate between automated facilities in a degraded communications environment.

Relative biological effectiveness: The ratio of the number of rads of gamma (or X) radiation of a certain energy that will produce a specified biological effect to the number of rads of another radiation required to produce the same effect measures the "relative biological effectiveness" of the latter radiation.

Release: In air armament, the intentional separation of a free-fall aircraft store, from its suspension equipment, for purposes of employment of the store.

Release altitude: Altitude of an aircraft above the ground at the time of release of bombs, rockets, missiles, tow targets, etc.

Release point (road): A well-defined point on a route at which the elements composing a column return under the authority of their respective commanders, each one of these elements continuing its movement towards its own appropriate destination.

Releasing commander (nuclear weapons): A commander who has been delegated authority to approve the use of nuclear weapons within prescribed limits.

Releasing officer: A properly designated individual who may authorize the sending of a message for and in the name of the originator.

Reliability diagram: In cartography, a diagram showing the dates and quality of the source material from which a map or chart has been compiled.

Relief: Inequalities of evaluation and the configuration of land features on the surface of the Earth which may be represented on maps or charts by contours, hypsometric tints, shading, or spot elevations.

Relief in place: An operation in which, by direction of higher authority, all or part of a unit is replaced in an area by the incoming unit. The responsibilities of the replaced elements for the mission and the assigned zone of operations are transferred to the incoming unit. The incoming unit continues the operation as ordered.

Religious support: The entire spectrum of professional duties that a chaplain provides and performs in the dual role of religious leader and staff officer assisted by enlisted support personnel. Combatant command chaplain; command chaplain; lay leader; religious support plan; religious support team.

Religious support plan: A plan that describes how religious support will be provided to all members of a joint force. When approved by the commander, it may be included as an annex to an operation plan. RSP.

Remain-behind equipment: Unit equipment left by deploying forces at their bases when they deploy.

Remaining forces: The total surviving United States forces at any given stage of combat operations.

Remote delivery: In mine warfare, the delivery of mines to a target area by any means other than direct emplacement. The exact position of mines so laid may not be known.

Remotely piloted vehicle: An unmanned vehicle capable of being controlled from a distant location through a communication link. It is normally designed to be recoverable. Drone.

Render safe procedures: Explosive ordnance disposal procedures.

Rendezvous area: In an amphibious operation, the area in which the landing craft and amphibious vehicles rendezvous to form waves after being loaded, and prior to movement to the line of departure.

Reorder cycle: The interval between successive reorder (procurement) actions.

Reorder point: 1. That point at which time a stock replenishment requisition would be submitted to maintain the predetermined or calculated stockage objective. 2. The sum of the safety level of supply plus the level for order and shipping time equals the reorder point.

Repair: The restoration of an item to serviceable condition through correction of a specific failure or unserviceable condition. Overhaul; rebuild.

Repair cycle: The stages through which a reparable item passes from the time of its removal or replacement until it is reinstalled or placed in stock in a serviceable condition.

Repair cycle aircraft: Aircraft in the active inventory that are in or awaiting depot maintenance, including those in transit to or from depot maintenance.

Reparable item: An item that can be reconditioned or economically repaired for reuse when it becomes unserviceable.

Repatriate: A person who returns to his or her country or citizenship, having left said native country either against his or her will, or as one of a group who left for reason of politics, religion, or other pertinent reasons.

Replacement demand: A demand representing replacement of items consumed or worn out.

Replacement factor: The estimated percentage of equipment or repair parts in use that will require replacement during a given period due to wearing out beyond repair, enemy action, abandonment, pilferage, and other causes except catastrophes.

Replacements: Personnel required to take the place of others who depart a unit.

Replenishment at sea: Those operations required to make a transfer of personne land/or supplies when at sea.

Reportable incident: Any suspected or alleged violation of Department of Defense policy or of other related orders, policies, procedures or applicable law, for which there is credible information.

Reported unit: A unit designation that has been mentioned in an agent report, captured document, or interrogation report, but for which available information is insufficient to include the unit in accepted order of battle holdings.

Reporting post: An element of the control and reporting system used to extend the radar coverage of the control and reporting center. It does not undertake the control of aircraft.

Reporting time interval: 1. In surveillance, the time interval between the detection of an event and the receipt of a report by the user. 2. In communications, the time for transmission of data or a report from the originating terminal to the end receiver. Near real time.

Representative downwind direction: During the forecast period, the mean surface downwind direction in the hazard area towards which the cloud travels.

Representative downwind speed: The mean surface downwind speed in the hazard area during the forecast period.

Representative fraction: The scale of a map, chart, or photograph expressed as a fraction or ratio.

Request for assistance: A request based on mission requirements and expressed in terms of desired outcome, formally asking the Department of Defense to provide assistance to a local, state, tribal, or other federal agency. RFA.

Request modify: In artillery and naval gunfire support, a request by any person, other than the person authorized to make modifications to a fire plan, for a modification.

Required delivery date: The date that a force must arrive at the destination and complete unloading. RDD.

Requirements capability: This capability provides a Joint Operation Planning and Execution System user with the ability to identify, update, review, and delete data on forces and sustainment required to support an operation plan or course of action.

Requirements management system: A system for the management of theater and national imagery collection requirements that provides automated tools for users in support of submission, review, and validation of imagery nominations as requirements to be tasked on national or Department of Defense imagery collection, production, and exploitation resources. RMS.

Requiring activity: A military or other designated supported organization that identifies and receives contracted support during military operations. Supported unit.

Requisition: 1. An authoritative demand or request especially for personnel, supplies, or services authorized but not made available without specific request. 2. To demand or require services from an invaded or onquered nation.

Requisitioning objective: The maximum quantities of materiel to be maintained on hand and on order to sustain current operations. It will consist of the sum of stocks represented by the operating level, safety level, and the order and shipping time or procurement lead time, as appropriate.

Rescue combat air patrol: An aircraft patrol provided over that portion of an objective area in which recovery operations are being conducted for the purpose of intercepting and destroying hostile aircraft. RESCAP.

Rescue ship: In shipping control, a ship of a convoy stationed at the rear of a convoy column to rescue survivors.

Research: All effort directed toward increased knowledge of natural phenomena and environment and toward the solution of problems in all fields of science. This includes basic and applied research.

Reseau: A grid system of a standard size in the image plane of a photographic system used for mensuration purposes.

Reservation: The stated qualification by a nation that describes the part of a standardization agreement that it will not implement or will implement only with limitations. Implementation; ratification; subscription.

Reserve: 1. Portion of a body of troops that is kept to the rear, or withheld from action at the beginning of an engagement, in order to be available for a decisive movement. 2. Members of the Military Services who are not in active service but who are subject to call to active duty. 3. Portion of an appropriation or contract authorization held or set aside for future operations or contingencies and, in respect to which, administrative authorization to incur commitments or obligations has been withheld. Aero rational reserve; reserve supplies.

Reserve aircraft: Those aircraft that have been accumulated in excess of immediate needs for active aircraft and are retained in the inventory against possible future needs. Aircraft.

Reserve component category: The category that identifies an individual's status in a reserve component. The three reserve component categories are Ready Reserve, Standby Reserve, and Retired Reserve. Each reservist is identified by a specific reserve component category designation.

Reserve Components: Reserve Components of the Armed Forces of the United States are: a. the Army National Guard of the United States; b. the Army Reserve; c. the Naval Reserve; d. the Marine Corps Reserve; e. the Air National Guard of the United States; f. the Air Force Reserve; and g. the Coast Guard Reserve. RCs.

Reserved demolition target: A target for demolition, the destruction of which must be controlled at a specific level of command because it plays a vital part in the tactical, operational, or strategic plan, or because of the importance of the structure itself, or because the demolition may be executed in the face of the enemy.

Reserved obstacles: Those demolition obstacles that are deemed critical to the plan for which the authority to detonate is reserved by the designating commander.

Reserved route: In road traffic, a specific route allocated exclusively to an authority or formation.

Reserve supplies: Supplies accumulated in excess of immediate needs for the purpose of ensuring continuity of an adequate supply. Reserves. Battle reserves; beach reserves; contingency retention stock; economic retention stock; individual reserves; initial reserves; unit reserves.

Resettled person: A refugee or an internally displaced person wishing to return somewhere other than his or her previous home or land within the country or area of original displacement.

Residual capabilities assessment: Provides an automated or manual crisis action capability to assess the effects of weapons of mass destruction events for operations planning. Residual capabilities assessment tasks include, but are not limited to, assessment of infrastructure and facility damage, fallout prediction, weapons effect analysis, population impact assessment, and tracking strategic assets.

Residual contamination: Contamination which remains after steps have been taken to remove it. These steps may consist of nothing more than allowing the contamination to decay normally.

Residual forces: Unexpended portions of the remaining United States forces that have an immediate combat potential for continued military operations, and that have been deliberately withheld from utilization.

Residual radiation: Nuclear radiation caused by fallout, artificial dispersion of radioactive material, or irradiation which results from a nuclear explosion and persists longer than one minute after burst. Contamination; induced radiation; initial radiation.

Resistance movement: An organized effort by some portion of the civil population of a country to resist the legally established government or an occupying power and to disrupt civil order and stability.

Resolution: 1. A measurement of the smallest detail that can be distinguished by a sensor system under specific conditions. 2. A formal expression of an official body such as Congress, the United Nations Security Council, or North Atlantic Treaty Organization North Atlantic Committee that may provide the basis for or set limits on a military operation.

Resources: The forces, materiel, and other assets or capabilities apportioned or allocated to the commander of a unified or specified command.

Response force: A mobile force with appropriate fire support designated, usually by the area commander, to deal with Level II threats in the rear area. RF.

Responsibility: 1. The obligation to carry forward an assigned task to a successful conclusion. With responsibility goes authority to direct and take the necessary action to ensure success. 2. The obligation for the proper custody, care, and safekeeping of property or funds entrusted to the possession or supervision of an individual. See also accountability.

Responsor: An electronic device used to receive an electronic challenge and display a reply thereto.

Rest and recuperation: The withdrawal of individuals from combat or duty in a combat area for short periods of rest and recuperation. R&R.

Restitution: The process of determining the true planimetric position of objects whose images appear on photographs.

Restraint: In the context of joint operation planning, a requirement placed on the command by a higher command that prohibits an action, thus restricting freedom of action. See also constraint; operational limitation.

Restraint of loads: The process of binding, lashing, and wedging items into one unit or into its transporter in a manner that will ensure immobility during transit.

Restricted area: 1. An area in which there are special restrictive measures employed to prevent or minimize interference between friendly forces. 2. An area under military jurisdiction in which special security measures are employed to prevent unauthorized entry. Air surface zone; controlled firing area; restricted areas (air).

Restricted areas (air):- Designated areas established by appropriate authority over which flight of aircraft is restricted. They are shown on aeronautical charts, published in notices to airmen, and provided in publications of aids to air navigation.

Restricted dangerous air cargo: Cargo which does not belong to the highly dangerous category but which is hazardous and requires, for transport by cargo or passenger aircraft, extra precautions in packing and handling.

Restricted items list: A document listing those logistic goods and services for which nations must coordinate any contracting activity with a commander's centralized contracting organization.

Restricted operations area: Airspace of defined dimensions, designated by the airspace control authority, in response to specific operational situations/ requirements within which the operation of one or more airspace users is restricted. ROA.

Restricted target list: A list of restricted targets nominated by elements of the joint force and approved by the joint force commander. This list also includes restricted targets directed by higher authorities. RTL.

Restricted target: A valid target that has specific restrictions placed on the actions authorized against it due to operational considerations.

Restrictive fire line: A line established between converging friendly surface forces that prohibits fires or their effects across that line. RFL.

Restrictive fire plan: A safety measure for friendly aircraft which establishes airspace that is reasonably safe from friendly surface delivered non-nuclear fires.

Resupply: The act of replenishing stocks in order to maintain required levels of supply.

Resuscitative care: Advanced emergency medical treatment required to prevent immediate loss of life or limb and to attain stabilization to ensure the patient could tolerate evacuation.

Reticle: A mark such as a cross or a system of lines lying in the image plane of a viewing apparatus. It may be used singly as a reference mark on certain types of monocular instruments or as one of a pair to form a floating mark as in certain types of stereoscopes.

Retirement: An operation in which a force out of contact moves away from the enemy.

Retrofit action: Action taken to modify in service equipment.

Retrograde cargo: Cargo evacuated from a theater.

Retrograde movement: Any movement of a command to the rear, or away from the enemy. It may be forced by the enemy or may be made voluntarily. Such movements may be classified as withdrawal, retirement, or delaying action.

Retrograde operation: Retrograde movement.

Retrograde personnel: Personnel evacuated from a theater who may include medical patients, noncombatants, and civilians.

Returned to military control: The status of a person whose casualty status of "duty status - whereabouts unknown" or "missing" has been changed due to the person's return or recovery by US military authority. RMC.

Returnee: A displaced person who has returned voluntarily to his or her former place of residence.

Return load: Personnel and/or cargo to be transported by a returning carrier.

Return to base: An order to proceed to the point indicated by the displayed information or by verbal communication. This point is being used to return the aircraft to a place at which the aircraft can land. Command heading, speed, and altitude may be used, if desired. RTB.

Riot control agent: Any chemical, not listed in a schedule of the Convention on the Prohibition of the Development, Production, Stockpiling and Use of Chemical Weapons and on their Destruction which can produce rapidly in humans sensory irritation or disabling physical effects which disappear within a short time following termination of exposure. RCA.

Riot control operations: The employment of riot control agents and/or special tactics, formations, and equipment in the control of violent disorders.

Rising mine: In naval mine warfare, a mine having positive buoyancy which is released from a sinker by a ship influence or by a timing device. The mine may fire by contact, hydrostatic pressure, or other means.

Risk: 1. Probability and severity of loss linked to hazards. 2. See degree of risk. Hazard; risk management.

Risk assessment: The identification and assessment of hazards (first two steps of risk management process).

Risk management: The process of identifying, assessing, and controlling risks arising from operational factors and making decisions that balance risk cost with mission benefits. RM. Risk.

Riverine area: An inland or coastal area comprising both land and water, characterized by limited land lines of communication, with extensive water surface and/or inland waterways that provide natural routes for surface transportation and communications.

Road block: A barrier or obstacle used to block or limit the movement of hostile vehicles along a route.

Road capacity: The maximum traffic flow obtainable on a given roadway using all available lanes; usually expressed in vehicles per hour or vehicles per day.

Road clearance time: The total time a column requires to travel over and clear a section of the road.

Road hazard sign: A sign used to indicate traffic hazards. Military hazard signs should be used in a communications zone area only in accordance with existing agreements with national authorities.

Road net: The system of roads available within a particular locality or area.

Road space: The length of roadway allocated to and/or actually occupied by a column on a route, expressed in miles or kilometers.

Roentgen: A unit of exposure dose of gamma radiation. In field Dosimetry, one roentgen is essentially equal to one rad.

Role number: In the medical field, the classification of treatment facilities according to their different capabilities.

Role specialist nation: A nation that has agreed to assume responsibility for providing a particular class of supply or service for all or part of the multinational force. RSN.

Roll back: The process of progressive destruction and/or neutralization of the opposing defenses, starting at the periphery and working inward, to permit deeper penetration of succeeding defense positions.

Roll-in-point: The point at which aircraft enter the final leg of the attack, e.g., dive, glide.

Roll-up: The process for orderly dismantling of facilities no longer required in support of operations and available for transfer to other areas.

Romper: A ship which has moved more than 10 nautical miles ahead of its convoy, and is unable to rejoin it. Straggler.

Rope: An element of chaff consisting of a long roll of metallic foil or wire which is designed for broad, low-frequency responses. Chaff.

Rough terrain container handler: A piece of materials handling equipment used to pick up and move containers. RTCH. Materials handling equipment.

Route: The prescribed course to be traveled from a specific point of origin to a specific destination. Axial route; controlled route; dispatch route; lateral route; reserved route; signed route; supervised route.

Route capacity: 1. The maximum traffic flow of vehicles in one direction at the most restricted point on the route. 2. The maximum number of metric tons which can be moved in one direction over a particular route in one hour. It is the product of the maximum traffic flow and the average payload of the vehicles using the route. See also railway line capacity.

Route classification: Classification assigned to a route using factors of minimum width, worst route type, least bridge, raft, or culvert military load classification, and obstructions to traffic flow.

Route lanes: A series of parallel tracks for the routing of independently sailed ships.

Routine message: A category of precedence to be used for all types of messages that justify transmission by rapid means unless of sufficient urgency to require a higher precedence. Precedence.

Routine supplies: Those items delivered as a result of normal requisitioning procedures to replace expended supplies or to build up reserve stocks. Follow-up supplies; supplies.

Routing indicator: A group of letters assigned to indicate: a. the geographic location of a station; b. a fixed headquarters of a command, activity, or unit at a geographic location; and c. the general location of a tape relay or tributary station to facilitate the routing of traffic over the tape relay networks.

Row marker: In land mine warfare, a natural, artificial, or specially installed marker, located at the start or finish of a mine row where mines are laid by individual rows. Marker.

Rules for the use of force: Directives issued to guide United States forces on the use of force during various operations. These directives may take the form of execute orders, deployment orders, memoranda of agreement, or plans. RUF.

Rules of engagement: Directives issued by competent military authority that delineate the circumstances and limitations under which United States forces will initiate and/or continue combat engagement with other forces encountered. ROE.

Run: 1. That part of a flight of one photographic reconnaissance aircraft during which photographs are taken. 2. The transit of a sweeper-sweep combination or of a mine-hunter operating its equipment through a lap. This term may also be applied to a transit of any formation of sweepers.

Runway visual range: The maximum distance in the direction of takeoff or landing at which the runway, or specified lights or markers delineating it, can be seen from a position above a specified point on its center line at a height corresponding to the average eye level of pilots at touch-down.

Rupture zone: The region immediately adjacent to the crater boundary in which the stresses produced by the explosion have exceeded the ultimate strength of the medium. It is characterized by the appearance of numerous radial cracks of various sizes. Plastic zone.

Ruse: In military deception, a trick of war designed to deceive the adversary, usually involving the deliberate exposure of false information to the adversary's intelligence collection system.

S

Sabotage: An act or acts with intent to injure, interfere with, or obstruct the national defense of a country by willfully injuring or destroying, or attempting to injure or destroy, any national defense or war materiel, premises, or utilities, to include human and natural resources.

Safe anchorage: An anchorage considered safe from enemy attack to which merchant ships may be ordered to proceed when the shipping movement policy is implemented. Refuge area.

Safe area: A designated area in hostile territory that offers the evader or escapee a reasonable chance of avoiding capture and of surviving until he or she can be evacuated.

Safe burst height: The height of burst at or above which the level of fallout or damage to ground installations is at a predetermined level acceptable to the military commander.

Safe current: In naval mine warfare, the maximum current that can be supplied to a sweep in a given waveform and pulse cycle which does not produce a danger area with respect to the mines being swept for.

Safe depth: In naval mine warfare, the shallowest depth of water in which a ship will not actuate a bottom mine of the type under consideration. Safe depth is usually quoted for conditions of ship upright, calm sea, and a given speed.

Safe distance: In naval mine warfare, the horizontal range from the edge of the explosion damage area to the center of the sweeper.

Safe house: An innocent-appearing house or premises established by an organization for the purpose of conducting clandestine or covert activity in relative security.

Safe separation distance: -The minimum distance between the delivery system and the weapon beyond which the hazards associated with functioning are acceptable.

Safety and arming mechanism: A dual function device which prevents the unintended activation of a main charge or propulsion unit prior to arming, but allows activation thereafter upon receipt of the appropriate stimuli.

Safety device : A device which prevents unintentional functioning.

Safety distance: In road transport, the distance between vehicles traveling in column specified by the command in light of safety requirements.

Safety fuze: A pyrotechnic contained in a flexible and weatherproof sheath burning at a timed and constant rate; used to transmit a flame to the detonator.

Safety lane: Specified sea lane designated for use in transit by submarine and surface ships to prevent attack by friendly forces.

Safety level of supply: The quantity of materiel, in addition to the operating level of supply, required to be on hand to permit continuous operations in the event of minor interruption of normal replenishment or unpredictable fluctuations in demand.

Safety line: In land mine warfare, demarcation line for trip wire or wire-actuated mines in a minefield. It serves to protect the laying personnel. After the minefield is laid, this line is neither marked on the ground nor plotted on the minefield record.

Safety wire: A cable, wire, or lanyard attached to the aircraft and routed to an expendable aircraft store to prevent arming initiation prior to store release.

Safety zone: An area reserved for noncombat operations of friendly aircraft, surface ships, submarines, or ground forces.

Safing: As applied to weapons and ammunition, the changing from a state of readiness for initiation to a safe condition. Dearming.

Salvage: 1. Property that has some value in excess of its basic material content but is in such condition that it has no reasonable prospect of use for any purpose as a unit and its repair or rehabilitation for use as a unit is clearly impractical. 2. The saving or rescuing of condemned, discarded, or abandoned property, and of materials contained therein for reuse, refabrication, or scrapping.

Salvage operation: 1. The recovery, evacuation, and reclamation of damaged, discarded, condemned, or abandoned allied or enemy materiel, ships, craft, and floating equipment for reuse, repair, refabrication, or scrapping. 2. Naval salvage operations include harbor and channel clearance, diving, hazardous towing and rescue tug services, and the recovery of materiel, ships, craft, and floating equipment sunk offshore or elsewhere stranded.

Sanction enforcement: Operations that employ coercive measures to interdict the movement of certain types of designated items into or out of a nation or specified area.

Sanctuary: A nation or area near or contiguous to the combat area that, by tacit agreement between the warring powers, is exempt from attack and therefore serves as a refuge for staging, logistic, or other activities of the combatant powers.

Sanitize: To revise a report or other document in such a fashion as to prevent identification of sources, or of the actual persons and places with which it is concerned, or of the means by which it was acquired. Usually involves deletion or substitution of names and other key details.

Satellite and missile surveillance: The systematic observation of aerospace for the purpose of detecting, tracking, and characterizing objects, events, and phenomena associated with satellites and in-flight missiles, friendly and enemy.

Scale: The ratio or fraction between the distance on a map, chart, or photograph and the corresponding distance on the surface of the Earth. Conversion scale; graphic scale; photographic scale; principal scale.

Scaling law: A mathematical relationship which permits the effects of a nuclear explosion of given energy yield to be determined as a function of distance from the explosion provided the corresponding effect is known as a function of distance for a reference explosion, e.g., of 1-kiloton energy yield.

Scan: 1. The path periodically followed by a radiation beam. 2. In electronic intelligence, the motion of an electronic beam through space looking for a target. Scanning is produced by the motion of the antenna or by lobe switching.

Scan line: The line produced on a recording medium frame by a single sweep of a scanner.

Scan period: The period taken by a radar, sonar, etc., to complete a scan pattern and return to a starting point.

Scan rate: The rate at which individual scans are recorded.

Scan type: The path made in space by a point on the radar beam; for example, circular, helical, conical, spiral, or sector.

Scatterable mine: In land mine warfare, a mine laid without regard to classical pattern and which is designed to be delivered by aircraft, artillery, missile, ground dispenser, or by hand. Once laid, it normally has a limited life.

Scene of action commander: In antisubmarine warfare, the commander at the scene of contact. The commander is usually in a ship, or may be in a fixed-wing aircraft, helicopter, or submarine.

Scheduled arrival date: The projected arrival date of a specified movement requirement at a specified location.

Scheduled fire: A type of prearranged fire executed at a predetermined time.

Scheduled maintenance: Periodic prescribed inspection and/or servicing of equipment accomplished on a calendar, mileage, or hours of operation basis. organizational maintenance.

Scheduled service (air transport): A routine air transport service operated in accordance with a timetable.

Scheduled speed: The planned sustained speed of a convoy through the water which determines the speed classification of that convoy.

Scheduled target: Planned target upon which fires or other actions are scheduled for prosecution at a specified time. Planned target; target.

Schedule of fire: Groups of fires or series of fires fired in a definite sequence according to a definite program. The time of starting the schedule may be ON CALL. For identification purposes, schedules may be referred to by a code name or other designation.

Schedule of targets: In artillery, mortar, and naval gunfire support, individual targets, groups, or series of targets to be fired on, in a definite sequence according to a definite program.

Scheduling and movement capability: The capability required by Joint Operation Planning and Execution System planners and operators to allow for review and update of scheduling and movement data before and during implementation of a deployment operation.

Scheme of maneuver: Description of how arrayed forces will accomplish the commander's intent. It is the central expression of the commander's concept for operations and governs the design of supporting plans or annexes.

Screening group: In amphibious operations, a task organization of ships that furnishes protection to the task force en route to the objective area and during operations in the objective area.

Scribing: In cartography, a method of preparing a map or chart by cutting the lines into a prepared coating.

S-curve distortion: The distortion in the image produced by a scanning sensor which results from the forward displacement of the sensor during the time of lateral scan.

Sea-air-land team: US Navy forces organized, trained, and equipped to conduct special operations in maritime, littoral, and riverine environments. SEAL.

Sea areas: Areas in the amphibious objective area designated for the stationing of amphibious task force ships. Sea areas include inner transport area, sea echelon area, fire support area, etc. Amphibious objective area; fire support area; inner transport area; sea echelon area.

Sea barge: A type of barge-ship that can carry up to 38 loaded barges. It may also carry tugs, stacked causeway sections, various watercraft, or heavy lift equipment to better support joint logistics over-the-shore operations.

Sea basing: In amphibious operations, a technique of basing certain landing force support functions aboard ship which decreases shore-based presence.

Sea echelon: A portion of the assault shipping which withdraws from or remains out of the transport area during an amphibious landing and operates in designated areas to seaward in an on-call or unscheduled status.

Sea echelon area: In amphibious operations, an area to seaward of a transport area from which assault shipping is phased into the transport area, and to which assault shipping withdraws from the transport area.

Sea echelon plan: In amphibious operations, the distribution plan for amphibious shipping in the transport area to minimize losses due to enemy attack by weapons of mass destruction and to reduce the area to be swept of mines.

Sea frontier: The naval command of a coastal frontier, including the coastal zone in addition to the land area of the coastal frontier and the adjacent sea areas.

Sealed cabin: The occupied space of an aircraft characterized by walls which do not allow any gaseous exchange between the ambient atmosphere and the inside atmosphere and containing its own ways of regenerating the inside atmosphere.

Sealift Readiness Program: A standby contractual agreement between Military Sealift Command and US ship operators for voluntary provision of private ships for defense use. Call-up of ships may be authorized by joint approval of the Secretary of Defense and the Secretary of Transportation. SRP.

Seaport: A land facility designated for reception of personnel or materiel moved by sea, and that serves as an authorized port of entrance into or departure from the country in which located. Port of debarkation; port of embarkation.

Search: 1. An operation to locate an enemy force known or believed to be at sea. 2. A systematic reconnaissance of a defined area, so that all parts of the area have passed within visibility. 3. To distribute gunfire over an area in depth by successive changes in gun elevation.

Search and rescue: The use of aircraft, surface craft, submarines, and specialized rescue teams and equipment to search for and rescue distressed persons on land or at sea in a permissive environment. SAR.

Search and rescue alert notice: An alerting message used for United States domestic flights. It corresponds to the declaration of the alert phase. ALNOT.

Search and rescue region: Inland search and rescue region; maritime search and rescue region; overseas search and rescue region.

Search attack unit: The designation given to one or more ships and/or aircraft separately organized or detached from a formation as a tactical unit to search for and destroy submarines. SAU.

Searched channel: In naval mine warfare, the whole or part of a route or a path which has been searched, swept, or hunted, the width of the channel being specified.

Searching fire: Fire distributed in depth by successive changes in the elevation of a gun.

Search mission: In air operations, an air reconnaissance by one or more aircraft dispatched to locate an object or objects known or suspected to be in a specific area.

Search radius: In search and rescue operations, a radius centered on a datum point having a length equal to the total probable error plus an additional safety length to ensure a greater than 50 percent probability that the target is in the search area.

Search sweeping: In naval mine warfare, the operation of sweeping a sample of route or area to determine whether poised mines are present.

Seashed: A temporary deck in container ships for transport of large military vehicles and outsized break-bulk cargo that will not fit into containers.

Sea state: A scale that categorizes the force of progressively higher seas by wave height. This scale is mathematically co-related to the Pierson-Moskowitz scale and the relationship of wind to waves. See also Pierson-Moskowitz scale.

Sea surveillance system: A system for collecting, reporting, correlating, and presenting information supporting and derived from the task of sea surveillance.

Seaward launch point: A designated point off the coast from which special operations forces will launch to proceed to the beach to conduct operations. SLP.

Seaward recovery point: A designated point off the coast to which special operations forces will proceed for recovery by submarine or other means of recovery. SRP.

Secondary loads: Unit equipment, supplies, and major end items that are transported in the beds of organic vehicles.

Secondary port: A port with one or more berths, normally at quays, which can accommodate ocean-going ships for discharge.

Secondary rescue facilities: Local airbase-ready aircraft, crash boats, and other air, surface, subsurface, and ground elements suitable for rescue missions, including government and privately operated units and facilities.

Secondary road: A road supplementing a main road, usually wide enough and suitable for two-way, all-weather traffic at moderate or slow speeds.

Secondary wave breaker system: A series of waves superimposed on another series and differing in height, period, or angle of approach to the beach.

Second strike: The first counterblow of a war.

Secretary of a Military Department: The Secretary of the Air Force, Army, or Navy. SECRET Internet Protocol Router Network — The worldwide SECRET-level packet switch network that uses high-speed internet protocol routers and high-capacity Defense Information Systems Network circuitry. SIPRNET.

Section: 1. As applied to ships or naval aircraft, a tactical subdivision of a division. It is normally one-half of a division in the case of ships, and two aircraft in the case of aircraft. 2. A subdivision of an office, installation, territory, works, or organization; especially a major subdivision of a staff. 3. A tactical unit of the Army and Marine Corps. A section is smaller than a platoon and larger than a squad. In some organizations the section, rather than the squad, is the basic tactical unit. 4. An area in a warehouse extending from one wall to the next; usually the largest subdivision of one floor.

Sector: 1. An area designated by boundaries within which a unit operates, and for which it is responsible. 2. One of the subdivisions of a coastal frontier. Area of influence; zone of action.

Sector air defense commander: Commander subordinate to an area/regional air defense commander and responsible for air and missile defenses in the assigned sector. Exercises authorities delegated by the area/regional air defense commander. SADC.

Sector of fire: A defined area which is required to be covered by the fire of individual or crew served weapons or the weapons of a unit.

Sector scan: Scan in which the antenna oscillates through a selected angle.

Secure: In an operational context, to gain possession of a position or terrain feature, with or without force, and to make such disposition as will prevent, as far as possible, its destruction or loss by enemy action. See also denial measure.

Security: 1. Measures taken by a military unit, activity, or installation to protect itself against all acts designed to, or which may, impair its effectiveness. 2. A condition that results from the establishment and maintenance of protective measures that ensure a state of inviolability from hostile acts or influences. 3. With respect to classified matter, the condition that prevents unauthorized persons from having access to official information that is safeguarded in the interests of national security.

Security alert team: Two or more security force members who form the initial reinforcing element responding to security alarms, emergencies, or irregularities. SAT.

Security certification: A certification issued by competent authority to indicate that a person has been investigated and is eligible for access to classified matter to the extent stated in the certification.

Security clearance: An administrative determination by competent authority that an individual is eligible, from a security stand-point, for access to classified information.

Security cooperation: All Department of Defense interactions with foreign defense establishments to build defense relationships that promote specific US security interests, develop allied and friendly military capabilities for self-defense and multinational operations, and provide US forces with peacetime and contingency access to a host nation. See also security assistance; security assistance organization.

Security cooperation activity: Military activity that involves other nations and is intended to shape the operational environment in peacetime. Activities include programs and exercises that the US military conducts with other nations to improve mutual understanding and improve interoperability with treaty partners or potential coalition partners. They are designed to support a combatant commander's theater strategy as articulated in the theater security cooperation plan.

Security cooperation planning: The subset of joint strategic planning conducted to support the Department of Defense's security cooperation program. This planning supports a combatant commander's theater strategy.

Security countermeasures: Those protective activities required to prevent espionage, sabotage, theft, or unauthorized use of classified or controlled information, systems, or material of the Department of Defense. Counterintelligence.

Security intelligence: Intelligence on the identity, capabilities, and intentions of hostile organizations or individuals who are or may be engaged in espionage, sabotage, subversion, or terrorism. Counterintelligence; intelligence; security.

Sedition: Willfully advocating or teaching the duty or necessity of overthrowing the US government or any political subdivision by force or violence.

Segregation: In detainee operations, the removal of a detainee from other detainees and their environment for legitimate purposes unrelated to interrogation, such as when necessary for the movement, health, safety, and/or security of the detainee, the detention facility, or its personnel.

Seize: To employ combat forces to occupy physically and to control a designated area. See also combat forces.

Seizures: In counterdrug operations, includes drugs and conveyances seized by law enforcement authorities and drug-related assets confiscated based on evidence that they have been derived from or used in illegal narcotics activities. Counterdrug operations; law enforcement agency.

Selected Reserve strength: The total number of guardsmen and reservists in the Selected Reserve who are subject to the 200K Presidential recall or mobilization under declaration of war or national emergency.

Selective identification feature: A capability that, when added to the basic identification friend or foe system, provides the means to transmit, receive, and display selected coded replies.

Selective loading: The arrangement and stowage of equipment and supplies aboard ship in a manner designed to facilitate issues to units.

Selective release process: The process involving requesting, analyzing, and obtaining approval for release of weapons to obtain specific, limited damage on selected targets.

Selenodesy: That branch of applied mathematics that determines, by observation and measurement, the exact positions of points and the figures and areas of large portions of the moon's surface, or the shape and size of the moon.

Self-defense: A commander has the authority and obligation to use all necessary means available and to take all appropriate action to defend that commander's unit and other US forces in the vicinity from a hostile act or hostile intent. Force used should not exceed that which is necessary to decisively counter the hostile act or intent and ensure the continued safety of US forces or other persons and property they are ordered to protect. US forces may employ such force in self-defense only so long as the hostile force continues to present an imminent threat.

Self-destroying fuze: A fuze designed to burst a projectile before the end of its flight.

Self-protection depth: The depth of water where the aggregate danger width relative to mines affected by a minesweeping technique is zero. Safe depth is a particular self-protection depth.

Self-sustaining containership: A containership with shipboard-installed cranes capable of loading and off-loading containers without assistance of port crane service. Containership.

Semi-active homing guidance: A system of homing guidance wherein the receiver in the missile utilizes radiations from the target which has been illuminated by an outside source.

Semi-controlled mosaic: A mosaic composed of corrected or uncorrected prints laid so that major ground features match their geographical coordinates.

Semi permanent joint task force: A joint task force that has been assigned an expanded or follow-on mission and will continue to conduct these operations in a specified area for an undetermined period of time. Joint task force; mission; operation.

Senior contracting official: The lead Service or joint command designated contracting official who has direct managerial responsibility over theater support contracting. SCO.

Sensitive: Requiring special protection from disclosure that could cause embarrassment, compromise, or threat to the security of the sponsoring power. May be applied to an agency, installation, person, position, document, material, or activity.

Sensitive compartmented information: All information and materials bearing special community controls indicating restricted handling within present and future community intelligence collection programs and their end products for which community systems of Compartmentation have been or will be formally established.

Sensitive site exploitation: A related series of activities inside a captured sensitive site to exploit personnel documents, electronic data, and material captured at the site, while neutralizing any threat posed by the site or its contents. SSE.

Separation zone: An area between two adjacent horizontal or vertical areas into which units are not to proceed unless certain safety measures can be fulfilled.

Sequel: In a campaign, a major operation that follows the current major operation. In a single major operation, a sequel is the next phase. Plans for a sequel are based on the possible outcomes associated with the current operation.

Sequence circuit: In mine warfare, a circuit which requires actuation by a predetermined sequence of influences of predetermined magnitudes.

Serial: 1. An element or a group of elements within a series which is given a numerical or alphabetical designation for convenience in planning, scheduling, and control. 2. A serial can be a group of people, vehicles, equipment, or supplies and is used in airborne, air assault, amphibious operations, and convoys.

Seriously ill or injured: The casualty status of a person whose illness or injury is classified by medical authority to be of such severity that there is cause for immediate concern, but there is not imminent danger to life. SII.

Seriously wounded: A casualty whose injuries or illness are of such severity that the patient is rendered unable to walk or sit, thereby requiring a litter for movement and evacuation.

Service ammunition: Ammunition intended for combat rather than for training purposes.

Service environment: All external conditions, whether natural or induced, to which items of materiel are likely to be subjected throughout their life cycle.

Service force module: A hypothetical force module built per Service doctrine composed of combat, combat support, and combat service support forces and sustainment for an estimated period, e.g., 30 days.

Service group: A major naval administration and/or tactical organization, consisting of the commander and the staff, designed to exercise operational and administrative control of assigned squadrons and units in executing their tasks of providing logistic support of fleet operations.

Service mine: A mine capable of a destructive explosion.

Service squadron: An administrative and/or tactical subdivision of a naval service force or service group, consisting of the commander and the staff and organized to exercise operational and administrative control of assigned units in providing logistic support of fleet units as directed.

Service test: A test of an item, system of materiel, or technique conducted under simulated or actual operational conditions to determine whether the specified military requirements or characteristics are satisfied. Troop test.

Service troops: Those units designed to render supply, maintenance, transportation, evacuation, hospitalization, and other services required by air and ground combat units to carry out effectively their mission in combat. Combat service support elements; troops.

Service-unique container: Any 20- or 40-foot International Organization for Standardization container procured or leased by a Service to meet Service-unique requirements. Component-owned container. Common-use container; component-owned container.

Servicing: Common servicing; cross-servicing; joint servicing. Inter-Service support.

Shadowing: To observe and maintain contact (not necessarily continuously) with a unit or force.

Shallow fording: The ability of a self-propelled gun or ground vehicle equipped with built-in waterproofing, with its wheels or tracks in contact with the ground, to negotiate a water obstacle without the use of a special waterproofing kit. Flotation.

Shaped charge: A charge shaped so as to concentrate its explosive force in a particular direction.

Shear link assembly: A device designed to break at a specified mechanical load.

Sheet explosive: Plastic explosive provided in a sheet form.

Sheet lines: Those lines defining the geographic limits of the map or chart detail.

Shelf life: The length of time during which an item of supply, subject to deterioration or having a limited life which cannot be renewed, is considered serviceable while stored.

Shell (specify): A command or request indicating the type of projectile to be used.

Shelter: An International Organization for Standardization container outfitted with live or work-in capability. International Organization for Standardization.

Shielding: 1. Material of suitable thickness and physical characteristics used to protect personnel from radiation during the manufacture, handling, and transportation of fissionable and radioactive materials. 2. Obstructions which tend to protect personnel or materials from the effects of a nuclear explosion.

Shifting fire: Fire delivered at constant range at varying deflections; used to cover the width of a target that is too great to be covered by an open sheaf.

Ship counter: In naval mine warfare, a device in a mine which prevents the mine from detonating until a preset number of actuations has taken place.

Ship influence: In naval mine warfare, the magnetic, acoustic, and pressure effects of a ship, or a mine sweep simulating a ship, which is detectable by a mine or other sensing devices.

Shipping configuration: The manner in which an item is prepared for shipment.

Shipping control: Naval control of shipping.

Shipping designator: A code word assigned to a particular overseas base, port, or area for specific use as an address on shipments to the overseas location concerned. The code word is usually four letters and may be followed by a number to indicate a particular addressee.

Shipping lane: A term used to indicate the general flow of merchant shipping between two eparture/terminal areas.

Shipping time: The time elapsing between the shipment of materiel by the supplying activity and receipt of materiel by the requiring activity. Order and shipping time.

Ship-to-shore movement: That portion of the assault phase of an amphibious operation which includes the deployment of the landing force from the assault shipping to designated landing areas.

Shoal: A sandbank or bar that makes water shoal; i.e., a sandbank that is not rocky and on which there is a water depth of 6 fathoms or less.

Shock front: The boundary between the pressure disturbance created by an explosion (in air, water, or earth) and the ambient atmosphere, water, or earth.

Shore fire control party: A specially trained unit for control of naval gunfire in support of troops ashore. It consists of a spotting team to adjust fire and a naval gunfire liaison team to perform liaison functions for the supported battalion commander. SFCP.

Shore party: A task organization of the landing force, formed for the purpose of facilitating the landing and movement off the beaches of troops, equipment, and supplies; for the evacuation.

T

Table of allowance: An equipment allowance document that prescribes basic allowances of organizational equipment, and provides the control to develop, revise, or change equipment authorization inventory data. TOA.

TABOO frequencies: Any friendly frequency of such importance that it must never be deliberately jammed or interfered with by friendly forces. Normally, these frequencies include international distress, CEASE BUZZER, safety, and controller frequencies. These frequencies are generally long standing. However, they may be time-oriented in that, as the combat or exercise situation changes, the restrictions may be removed. Electronic warfare.

Tacit arms control agreement: An arms control course of action in which two or more nations participate without any formal agreement having been made.

Tactical Aeromedical evacuation: That phase of evacuation which provides airlift for patients from the combat zone to points outside the combat zone, and between points within the communications zone.

Tactical air commander (ashore): The officer (aviator) responsible to the landing force commander for control and coordination of air operations within the landing force commander's area of operations when control of these operations is passed ashore.

Tactical air control center: The principal air operations installation (ship-based) from which all aircraft and air warning functions of tactical air operations are controlled. Navy TACC.

Tactical air control party: A subordinate operational component of a tactical air control system designed to provide air liaison to land forces and for the control of aircraft. TACP.

Tactical air coordinator (airborne): An officer who coordinates, from an aircraft, the actions of other aircraft engaged in air support of ground or sea forces. TAC(A).

Tactical air direction center: An air operations installation under the overall control of the Navy tactical air control center (afloat)/Marine Corps tactical air command center, from which aircraft and air warning service functions of tactical air operations in support of amphibious operations are directed. TADC.

Tactical airfield fuel dispensing system: A tactical aircraft refueling system deployed by a Marine air-ground task force in support of air operations at an expeditionary airfield or a forward arming and refueling point. TAFDS.

Tactical air groups (shore-based): Task organizations of tactical air units assigned to the amphibious task force that are to be land-based within, or sufficiently close to, the objective area to provide tactical air support to the amphibious task force.

Tactical air operations center: The principal air control agency of the US Marine air command and control system responsible for airspace control and management. It provides real-time surveillance, direction, positive control, and navigational assistance for friendly aircraft. It performs real-time direction and control of all anti air warfare operations, to include manned interceptors and surface-to-air weapons. It is subordinate to the tactical air command center. TAOC.

Tactical air support: Air operations carried out in coordination with surface forces and which directly assist land or maritime operations. Air support.

Tactical air support element: An element of a US Army division, corps, or field army tactical operations center consisting of Army component intelligence staff officer and Army component operations staff officer air personnel who coordinate and integrate tactical air support with current tactical ground operations.

Tactical air transport operations: The carriage of passengers and cargo within a

theater by means of: a. airborne operations: (1) parachute assault, (2) helicopter borne assault, (3) air landing; b. air logistic support; c. special missions; d. aero medical evacuation missions.

Tactical assembly area: An area that is generally out of the reach of light artillery and the location where units make final preparations and rest, prior to moving to the line of departure. Assembly area; line of departure.

Tactical call sign: A call sign which identifies a tactical command or tactical communication facility.

Tactical combat force: A combat unit, with appropriate combat support and combat service support assets, that is assigned the mission of defeating Level III threats. TCF.

Tactical concept: A statement, in broad outline, which provides a common basis for future development of tactical doctrine.

Tactical deception group: A task organization that conducts deception operations against the enemy, including electronic, communication, visual, and other methods designed to misinform and confuse the enemy.

Tactical digital information link: A Joint Staff-approved, standardized communication link suitable for transmission of digital information. Tactical digital information links interface two or more command and control or weapons systems via a single or multiple network architecture and multiple communication media for exchange of tactical information. TADIL.

Tactical exploitation of national capabilities: Congressionally mandated program to improve the combat effectiveness of the Services through more effective military use of national programs. TENCAP.

Tactical intelligence: Intelligence required for the planning and conduct of tactical operations. Intelligence.

Tactical intelligence and related activities: Those activities outside the National Foreign Intelligence Program that accomplish the following: a. respond to operational commanders' tasking for time-sensitive information on foreign entities; b. respond to national intelligence community tasking of systems whose primary mission is support to operating forces; c. train personnel for intelligence duties; d. provide an intelligence reserve; or e. are devoted to research and development of intelligence or related capabilities. Specifically excluded are programs that are so closely integrated with a weapon system that their primary function is to provide immediate-use targeting data. TIARA.

Tactical level of war: The level of war at which battles and engagements are planned and executed to achieve military objectives assigned to tactical units or task forces. Activities at this level focus on the ordered arrangement and maneuver of combat elements in relation to each other and to the enemy to achieve combat objectives.

Tactical loading: Combat loading; unit loading.

Tactical locality: An area of terrain which, because of its location or features, possesses a tactical significance in the particular circumstances existing at a particular time.

Tactical-logistical group: Representatives designated by troop commanders to assist Navy control officers aboard control ships in the ship-to-shore movement of troops, equipment, and supplies. TACLOG group.

Tactical map: A large-scale map used for tactical and administrative purposes.

Tactical minefield: A minefield that is employed to directly attack enemy maneuver as part of a formation obstacle plan and is laid to delay, channel, or break up an enemy advance, giving the defending element a positional advantage over the attacker.

Tactical mining: In naval mine warfare, mining designed to influence a specific operation or to counter a known or presumed tactical aim of the enemy. Implicit in tactical mining is a limited period of effectiveness of the minefield.

Tactical nuclear weapon employment: The use of nuclear weapons by land, sea, or air forces against opposing forces, supporting installations or facilities, in support of operations that contribute to the accomplishment of a military mission of limited scope, or in support of the military commander's scheme of maneuver, usually limited to the area of military operations.

Tactical obstacles: Those obstacles employed to disrupt enemy formations, to turn them into a desired area, to fix them in position under direct and indirect fires, and to block enemy penetrations.

Tactical operations center: A physical groupment of those elements of a general and special staff concerned with the current tactical operations and the tactical support thereof. TOC.

Tactical questioning: Direct questioning by any Department of Defense personnel of a captured or detained person to obtain time-sensitive tactical intelligence information, at or near the point of capture or detention and consistent with applicable law. TQ.

Tactical range: A range in which realistic targets are in use and a certain freedom of maneuver is allowed.

Tactical recovery of aircraft and personnel: A Marine Corps mission performed by an assigned and briefed aircrew for the specific purpose of the recovery of personnel, equipment, and/or aircraft when the tactical situation precludes search and rescue assets from responding and when survivors and their location have been confirmed. TRAP.

Tactical reserve: A part of a force held under the control of the commander as a maneuvering force to influence future action.

Tactical security: In operations, the measures necessary to deny information to the enemy and to ensure that a force retains its freedom of action and is warned or protected against an unexpected encounter with the enemy or an attack.

Tactical sub-concept: A statement, in broad outline, for a specific field of military capability within a tactical concept which provides a common basis both for equipment and weapon system development and for future development of tactical doctrine.

Tactical transport aircraft: Aircraft designed primarily for the carriage of personnel and/or cargo over short or medium distances.

Tactical troops: Combat troops, together with any service troops required for their direct support, who are organized under one commander to operate as a unit and engage the enemy in combat.

Tactical unit: An organization of troops, aircraft, or ships that is intended to serve as a single unit in combat. It may include service units required for its direct support.

Tactical warning and attack assessment: A composite term. See separate definitions for tactical warning and for attack assessment. TW/AA.

Tactics: The employment and ordered arrangement of forces in relation to each other. Procedures; techniques.

Tagline: A line attached to a draft of cargo or container to provide control and minimize pendulation of cargo during lifting operations.

Tanker Airlift Control Center: The Air Mobility Command direct reporting unit responsible for tasking and controlling operational missions for all activities involving forces supporting US Transportation Command's global air mobility mission. The Tanker Airlift Control Center is comprised of the following functions: current operations, command and control, logistic operations, aerial port operations, aero medical evacuation, flight planning, diplomatic clearances, and weather. TACC.

Tanker airlift control element: A mobile command and control organization deployed to support inter theater and intratheater air mobility operations at fixed, en route, and deployed locations where air mobility operational support is nonexistent or insufficient. The tanker airlift control element (TALCE) provides onsite management of air mobility airfield operations to include command and control, communications, aerial port services, maintenance, security, transportation, weather, intelligence, and other support functions, as necessary. The TALCE is composed of mission support elements from various units and deploys in support of peacetime, contingency, and emergency relief operations on both planned and "no notice" basis. TALCE.

Tare weight: The weight of a container deducted from gross weight to obtain net weight or the weight of an empty container.

Target: 1. An entity or object considered for possible engagement or other action. 2. In intelligence usage, a country, area, installation, agency, or person against which intelligence operations are directed. 3. An area designated and numbered for future firing. 4. In gunfire support usage, an impact burst that hits the target.

Target analysis: An examination of potential targets to determine military importance, priority of attack, and weapons required to obtain a desired level of damage or casualties.

Target approach point: In air transport operations, a navigational check point over which the final turn into the drop zone/landing zone is made.

Target area survey base: A base line used for the locating of targets or other points by the intersection of observations from two stations located at opposite ends on the line.

Target array: A graphic representation of enemy forces, personnel, and facilities in a specific situation, accompanied by a target analysis.

Target audience: An individual or group selected for influence. TA.

Target base line: A line connecting prime targets along the periphery of a geographic area.

Target bearing: 1. true – The true compass bearing of a target from a firing ship. 2. relative – The bearing of a target measured in the horizontal from the bow of one's own ship clockwise from 0 degrees to 360 degrees, or from the nose of one's own aircraft in hours of the clock.

Target classification: A grouping of targets in accordance with their threat to the amphibious task force and its component elements: targets not to be fired upon prior to D-day and targets not to be destroyed except on direct orders.

Target complex: A geographically integrated series of target concentrations.

Target component: A set of targets within a target system performing a similar function. Target; target critical damage point.

Target concentration: A grouping of geographically proximate targets. Target; target complex.

Target critical damage point: The part of a target component that is most vital. Critical node. Target; target component.

Target data inventory: A basic targeting program that provides a standardized target data in support of the requirements of the Joint Chiefs of Staff, Military Departments, and unified and specified commands for target planning coordination and weapons application. TDI.

Target date: The date on which it is desired that an action be accomplished or initiated.

Target development: The systematic examination of potential target systems - and their components, individual targets, and even elements of targets - to determine the necessary type and duration of the action that must be exerted on each target to create an effect that is consistent with the commander's specific objectives.

Target discrimination: The ability of a surveillance or guidance system to identify or engage any one target when multiple targets are present.

Target dossier: A file of assembled target intelligence about a specific geographic area.

Target folder: A folder, hardcopy or electronic, containing target intelligence and related materials prepared for planning and executing action against a specific target.

Target information center: The agency or activity responsible for collecting, displaying, evaluating, and disseminating information pertaining to potential targets.

Targeting: The process of selecting and prioritizing targets and matching the appropriate response to them, considering operational requirements and capabilities.

Target intelligence: Intelligence that portrays and locates the components of a target or target complex and indicates its vulnerability and relative importance.

Target materials: Graphic, textual, tabular, digital, video, or other presentations of target intelligence, primarily designed to support operations against designated targets by one or more weapon(s) systems. Target materials are suitable for training, planning, executing, and evaluating military operations.

Target nomination list: A target-consolidated list of targets made up of the multiple candidate target lists. A prioritized list of targets drawn from the joint target list and nominated by component commanders, appropriate agencies, or the joint force commander's staff for inclusion on the joint integrated prioritized target list. TNL.

Target overlay: A transparent sheet which, when superimposed on a particular chart, map, drawing, tracing or other representation, depicts target locations and designations. The target overlay may also show boundaries between maneuver elements, objectives and friendly forward dispositions.

Target pattern: The flight path of aircraft during the attack phase.

Target priority: A grouping of targets with the indicated sequence of attack.

Target response (nuclear): The effect on men, material, and equipment of blast, heat, light, and nuclear radiation resulting from the explosion of a nuclear weapon.

Target signature: 1. The characteristic pattern of a target displayed by detection and identification equipment. 2. In naval mine warfare, the variation in the influence field produced by the passage of a ship or sweep.

Target stress point: The weakest point (most vulnerable to damage) on the critical damage point. Vulnerable node. target critical damage point.

Target system analysis: An all-source examination of potential target systems to determine relevance to stated objectives, military importance, and priority of attack. It is an open-ended analytic process produced through the intelligence production process using national and theater validated requirements as a foundation. TSA.

Target system assessment: The broad assessment of the overall impact and effectiveness of the full spectrum of military force applied against the operation of an enemy target system or total combat effectiveness relative to the operational objectives established.

Target system component: A set of targets belonging to one or more groups of industries and basic utilities required to produce component parts of an end product, or one type of a series of interrelated commodities.

Task component: A subdivision of a fleet, task force, task group, or task unit, organized by the respective commander or by higher authority for the accomplishment of specific tasks.

Task element: A component of a naval task unit organized by the commander of a task unit or higher authority.

Task force: 1. A temporary grouping of units, under one commander, formed for the purpose of carrying out a specific operation or mission. 2. A semi-permanent organization of units, under one commander, formed for the purpose of carrying out a continuing specific task. 3. A component of a fleet organized by the commander of a task fleet or higher authority for the accomplishment of a specific task or tasks. TF.

Task group: A component of a naval task force organized by the commander of a task force or higher authority. TG.

Tasking order: A method used to task and to disseminate to components, subordinate units, and command and control agencies projected targets and specific missions. In addition, the tasking order provides specific instructions concerning the mission planning agent, targets, and other control agencies, as well as general instructions for accomplishment of the mission. TASKORD.

Task order: Order for services placed against an established contract. Civil augmentation program; cost-plus award fee contract.

Task organization: 1. In the Navy, an organization which assigns to responsible commanders the means with which to accomplish their assigned tasks in any planned action. 2. An organization table pertaining to a specific naval directive.

Task-organizing: The act of designing an operating force, support staff, or logistic package of specific size and composition to meet a unique task or mission. Characteristics to examine when task-organizing the force include, but are not limited to: training, experience, equipage, sustainability, operating environment, enemy threat, and mobility.

Task unit: A component of a naval task group organized by the commander of a task group or higher authority.

Taxiway: A specially prepared or designated path on an airfield for the use of taxiing aircraft.

Tear line: A physical line on an intelligence message or document separating categories of information that have been approved for foreign disclosure and release. Normally, the intelligence below the tear line is that which has been previously cleared for disclosure or release.

Technical analysis: In imagery interpretation, the precise description of details appearing on imagery.

Technical architecture: A minimal set of rules governing the arrangement, interaction, and interdependence of the parts or elements whose purpose is to ensure that a conformant system satisfies a specified set of requirements. technical assistance — The providing of advice, assistance, and training pertaining to the installation, operation, and maintenance of equipment.

Technical characteristics: Those characteristics of equipment that pertain primarily to the engineering principles involved in producing equipment possessing desired military characteristics; e.g., for electronic equipment, technical characteristics include such items as circuitry as well as types and arrangement of components.

Technical escort: An individual technically qualified and properly equipped to accompany designated material requiring a high degree of safety or security during shipment.

Technical evaluation: The study and investigations by a developing agency to determine the technical suitability of material, equipment, or a system for use in the Military Services. Operational evaluation.

Technical information: Information, including scientific information, that relates to research, development, engineering, test, evaluation, production, operation, use, and maintenance of munitions and other military supplies and equipment.

Technical intelligence: Intelligence derived from the collection, processing, analysis, and exploitation of data and information pertaining to foreign equipment and materiel for the purposes of preventing technological surprise, assessing foreign scientific and technical capabilities, and developing countermeasures designed to neutralize an adversary's technological advantages. TECHINT.

Technical review authority: The organization tasked to provide specialized technical or administrative expertise to the primary review authority or coordinating review authority for joint publications. TRA.

Technical specification: A detailed description of technical requirements, usually with specific acceptance criteria, stated in terms suitable to form the basis for the actual design development and production processes of an item having the qualities specified in the operational characteristics.

Technical supply operations: Operations performed by supply units or technical supply elements of supply and maintenance units in acquiring, accounting for, storing, and issuing Class II and IV items needed by supported units and maintenance activities.

Technical survey: A complete electronic and physical inspection to ascertain that offices, conference rooms, war rooms, and other similar locations where classified information is discussed are free of monitoring systems.

Techniques: Non-prescriptive ways or methods used to perform missions, functions, or tasks.

Telecommunication: Any transmission, emission, or reception of signs, signals, writings, images, sounds, or information of any nature by wire, radio, visual, or other electromagnetic systems.

Telecommunications center: A facility, normally serving more than one organization or terminal, responsible for transmission, receipt, acceptance, processing, and distribution of incoming and outgoing messages.

Teleconference: A conference between persons remote from one another but linked by a telecommunications system.

Telemedicine: Rapid access to shared and remote medical expertise by means of telecommunications and information technologies to deliver health services and exchange health information for the purpose of improving patient care.

Teleprocessing: The combining of telecommunications and computer operations interacting in the automatic processing, reception, and transmission of data and/or information.

Television imagery: Imagery acquired by a television camera and recorded or transmitted electronically.

Temperature Gradient: At sea, a temperature gradient is the change of temperature with depth; a positive gradient is a temperature increase with an increase in depth, and a negative gradient is a temperature decrease with an increase in depth.

Tempest: An unclassified term referring to technical investigations for compromising emanations from electrically operated information processing equipment; these investigations are conducted in support of emanations and emissions security. Counterintelligence.

Temporary interment: A site for the purpose of: a. the interment of the remains if the circumstances permit; or b. the reburial of remains exhumed from an emergency interment. See also emergency interment; mortuary affairs.

Terminal: A facility designed to transfer cargo from one means of conveyance to another. (Conveyance is the piece of equipment used to transport cargo; i.e., railcar to truck or truck to truck. This is as opposed to mode, which is the type of equipment; i.e., ship to rail, rail to truck.

Terminal attack control: The authority to control the maneuver of and grant weapons release clearance to attacking aircraft. Joint terminal attack controller.

Terminal clearance capacity: The amount of cargo or personnel that can be moved through and out of a terminal on a daily basis.

Terminal control: 1. The authority to direct aircraft to maneuver into a position to deliver ordnance, passengers, or cargo to a specific location or target. Terminal control is a type of air control. 2. Any electronic, mechanical, or visual control given to aircraft to facilitate target acquisition and resolution.

Terminal control area: A control area or portion thereof normally situated at the confluence of air traffic service routes in the vicinity of one or more major airfields. See also control area; controlled airspace; control zone.

Terminal guidance: 1. The guidance applied to a guided missile between midcourse guidance and arrival in the vicinity of the target. 2. Electronic, mechanical, visual, or other assistance given an aircraft pilot to facilitate arrival at, operation within or over, landing upon, or departure from an air landing or airdrop facility.

Terminal guidance operations: Those actions that provide electronic, mechanical, voice or visual communications that provide approaching aircraft and/or weapons additional information regarding a specific target location. TGO.

Terminal operations: The reception, processing, and staging of passengers; the receipt, transit, storage, and marshalling of cargo; the loading and unloading of modes of transport conveyances; and the manifesting and forwarding of cargo and passengers to destination.

Terminal phase: That portion of the flight of a ballistic missile that begins when the warhead or payload reenters the atmosphere and ends when the warhead or payload detonates or impacts. For ballistic missiles that do not exit the atmosphere, terminal phase begins when the warhead or payload reaches apogee and ends when the warhead or payload detonates or impacts.

Terminal velocity: 1. Hypothetical maximum speed a body could attain along a specified flight path under given conditions of weight and thrust if diving through an unlimited distance in air of specified uniform density. 2. Remaining speed of a projectile at the point in its downward path where it is level with the muzzle of the weapon.

Termination criteria: The specified standards approved by the President and/or the Secretary of Defense that must be met before a joint operation can be concluded.

Terms of reference: 1. A mutual agreement under which a command, element, or unit exercises authority or undertakes specific missions or tasks relative to another command, element, or unit. 2. The directive providing the legitimacy and authority to undertake a mission, task, or endeavor. TORs.

Terrain analysis: The collection, analysis, evaluation, and interpretation of geographic information on the natural and manmade features of the terrain, combined with other relevant factors, to predict the effect of the terrain on military operations.

Terrain avoidance system: A system which provides the pilot or navigator of an aircraft with a situation display of the ground or obstacles which project above either a horizontal plane through the aircraft or a plane parallel to it, so that the pilot can maneuver the aircraft to avoid the obstruction.

Terrain clearance system: A system which provides the pilot, or autopilot, of an aircraft with climb or dive signals such that the aircraft will maintain a selected height over flat ground and clear the peaks of undulating ground within the selected height in a vertical plane through the flight vector. This system differs from terrain following in that the aircraft need not descend into a valley to follow the ground contour.

Terrain exercise: An exercise in which a stated military situation is solved on the ground, the troops being imaginary and the solution usually being in writing.

Terrain flight: Flight close to the Earth's surface during which airspeed, height, and/or altitude are adapted to the contours and cover of the ground in order to avoid enemy detection and fire. TERF.

Terrain following system: A system which provides the pilot or autopilot of an aircraft with climb or dive signals such that the aircraft will maintain as closely as possible a selected height above a ground contour in a vertical plane through the flight vector.

Terrain intelligence: Intelligence on the military significance of natural and manmade characteristics of an area.

Terrain study: An analysis and interpretation of natural and manmade features of an area, their effects on military operations, and the effect of weather and climate on these features.

Terrestrial environment: The Earth's land area, including its man-made and natural surface and sub-surface features, and its interfaces and interactions with the atmosphere and the oceans.

Terrestrial reference guidance: The technique of providing intelligence to a missile from certain characteristics of the surface over which the missile is flown, thereby achieving flight along a predetermined path.

Territorial airspace: Airspace above land territory, internal waters, archipelagic waters, and territorial seas.

Territorial sea: A belt of ocean space adjacent to and measured from the coastal state's baseline to a maximum width of 12 nm. Throughout the vertical and horizontal planes of the territorial sea, the coastal state exercises sovereign jurisdiction, subject to the right of innocent passage of vessels on the surface and the right of transit passage in, under, and over international straits. Territorial sea areas that are a continuation of sea lanes through archipelagoes are subject to archipelagic sea lane passage, with the same transit rights as those that apply to international straits.

Terrorist: An individual who commits an act or acts of violence or threatens violence in pursuit of political, religious, or ideological objectives.

Terrorist group: Any number of terrorists who assemble together, have a unifying relationship, or are organized for the purpose of committing an act or acts of violenceor threatens violence in pursuit of their political, religious, or ideological objectives.

Test depth: The depth to which the submarine is tested by actual or simulated submergence. Maximum operating depth.

Theater: The geographical area for which a commander of a geographic combatant command has been assigned responsibility.

Theater-assigned transportation assets: Transportation assets that are assigned under the combatant command of a geographic combatant commander. Combatant command; single manager for transportation.

Theater detainee reporting center: The field operating agency of the national detainee reporting center. It is the central tracing agency within the theater, responsible for maintaining information on all detainees and their personal property within a theater of operations or assigned area of operations. TDRC.

Theater distribution: The flow of personnel, equipment, and materiel within theater to meet the geographic combatant commander's missions. Distribution; theater; theater distribution system.

Theater distribution management: The function of optimizing the distribution networks to achieve the effective and efficient flow of personnel, equipment, and materiel to meet the combatant commander's requirements. See also distribution; theater; theater distribution.

Theater distribution system: A distribution system comprised of four independent and mutually supported networks within theater to meet the geographic combatant commander's requirements: the physical network; the financial network; the information network; and the communications network. Distribution; distribution plan; distribution system; theater; theater distribution.

Theater event system: Architecture for reporting theater ballistic missile events, composed of three independent processing and reporting elements: the joint tactical ground stations, tactical detection and reporting, and the space-based infrared system mission control station. TES.

Theater missile: A missile, which may be a ballistic missile, a cruise missile, or an air-to surface missile (not including short-range, non-nuclear, direct fire missiles, bombs, or rockets such as Maverick or wire-guided missiles), whose target is within a given theater of operation. TM.

Theater of operations: An operational area defined by the geographic combatant commander for the conduct or support of specific military operations. Multiple theaters of operations normally will be geographically separate and focused on different missions. Theaters of operations are usually of significant size, allowing for operations in depth and over extended periods of time. TO.

Theater patient movement requirements center: The activity responsible for intratheater patient movement management (medical regulating and aero medical evacuation scheduling), the development of theater-level patient movement plans and schedules, the monitoring and execution in concert with the Global Patient Movement Requirements Center. TPMRC.

Theater special operations command: A subordinate unified or other joint command established by a joint force commander to plan, coordinate, conduct, and support joint special operations within the joint force commander's assigned operational area. TSOC.

Theater strategy: Concepts and courses of action directed toward securing the objectives of national and multinational policies and strategies through the synchronized and integrated employment of military forces and other instruments of national power.

Theater support contract: A type of contingency contract that is awarded by contracting officers in the operational area serving under the direct contracting authority of the Service component, special operations force command, or designated joint head of contracting activity for the designated contingency operation. External support contract; systems support contract.

Thermal crossover: The natural phenomenon that normally occurs twice daily when temperature conditions are such that there is a loss of contrast between two adjacent objects on infrared imagery.

Thermal energy: The energy emitted from the fireball as thermal radiation. The total amount of thermal energy received per unit area at a specified distance from a nuclear explosion is generally expressed in terms of calories per square centimeter.

Thermal exposure: The total normal component of thermal radiation striking a given surface throughout the course of a detonation; expressed in calories per square centimeter or mega joules per square meter.

Thermal imagery: Imagery produced by sensing and recording the thermal energy emitted or reflected from the objects which are imaged.

Thermal pulse: The radiant power versus time pulse from a nuclear weapon detonation.

Thermal radiation: 1. The heat and light produced by a nuclear explosion. 2. Electromagnetic radiations emitted from a heat or light source as a consequence of its temperature; it consists essentially of ultraviolet, visible, and infrared radiations.

Thermal shadow: The tone contrast difference of infrared linescan imagery which is caused by a thermal gradient which persists as a result of a shadow of an object which has been moved.

Thermal X-rays: The electromagnetic radiation, mainly in the soft X-ray region, emitted by the debris of a nuclear weapon by virtue of its extremely high temperature.

Thermonuclear: An adjective referring to the process in which very high temperatures are used to bring about the fusion of light nuclei with the accompanying release of energy.

Thermonuclear weapon: A weapon in which very high temperatures are used to bring about the fusion of light nuclei such as those of hydrogen isotopes with the accompanying release of energy. The high temperatures required are obtained by means of fission.

Thorough decontamination: Decontamination carried out by a unit, with or without external support, to reduce contamination on personnel, equipment, materiel, and/or working areas equal to natural background or to the lowest possible levels, to permit the partial or total removal of individual protective equipment and to maintain operations with minimum degradation. This may include terrain decontamination beyond the scope of operational decontamination. Immediate decontamination; operational decontamination.

Threat and vulnerability assessment: In antiterrorism, the pairing of a facility's threat analysis and vulnerability analysis.

Threat identification and assessment: The Joint Operation Planning and Execution System function that provides: timely warning of potential threats to US interests; intelligence collection requirements; the effects of environmental, physical, and health hazards, and cultural factors on friendly and enemy operations; and determines the enemy military posture and possible intentions.

Threat-oriented munitions: In stockpile planning, munitions intended to neutralize a finite assessed threat and for which the total requirement is determined by an agreed mathematical model. Level-of-effort munitions.

Threat warning: The urgent communication and acknowledgement of time-critical information essential for the preservation of life and/or vital resources.

Threshold: The beginning of that portion of the runway usable for landing.

Tie down diagram: A drawing indicating the prescribed method of securing a particular item of cargo within a specific type of vehicle.

Tie down point: An attachment point provided on or within a vehicle for securing cargo.

Tie down point pattern: The pattern of tie down points within a vehicle.

Tilt angle: The angle between the optical axis of an air camera and the vertical at the time of exposure.

Time-definite delivery: The consistent delivery of requested logistic support at a time and destination specified by the receiving activity.

Time fuze: A fuze which contains a graduated time element to regulate the time interval after which the fuze will function.

Time interval: Duration of a segment of time without reference to when the time interval begins or ends. Time intervals may be given in seconds of time or fractions thereof.

Time of attack: The hour at which the attack is to be launched. If a line of departure is prescribed, it is the hour at which the line is to be crossed by the leading elements of the attack.

Time of delivery: The time at which the addressee or responsible relay agency receipts for a message.

Time of flight: In artillery, mortar, and naval gunfire support, the time in seconds from the instant a weapon is fired, launched, or released from the delivery vehicle or weapons system to the instant it strikes or detonates.

Time of origin: The time at which a message is released for transmission.

Time of receipt: The time at which a receiving station completes reception of a message.

Time on target : 1. Time at which aircraft are scheduled to attack/photograph the target. 2. The actual time at which aircraft attack/photograph the target. 3. The time at which a nuclear detonation as planned at a specified desired ground zero. TOT.

Time over target conflict: A situation wherein two or more delivery vehicles are scheduled such that their proximity violates the established separation criteria for yield, time, distance, or all three.

Time-phased force and deployment data: The Joint Operation Planning and Execution System database portion of an operation plan; it contains time-phased force data, non unit-related cargo and personnel data, and movement data for the operation plan, including the following: a. In-place units; b. Units to be deployed to support the operation plan with a priority indicating the desired sequence for their arrival at the port of debarkation; c. Routing of forces to be deployed; d. Movement data associated with deploying forces; e. Estimates of non-unit-related cargo and personnel movements to be conducted concurrently with the deployment of forces; and f. Estimate of transportation requirements that must be fulfilled by common-user lift resources as well as those requirements that can be fulfilled by assigned or attached transportation resources. TPFDD. Time-phased force and deployment data maintenance; time-phased force and deployment data refinement; time-phased force and deployment list.

Time-phased force and deployment list: Appendix 1 to Annex A of the operation plan. It identifies types and/or actual units required to support the operation plan and indicates origin and ports of debarkation or ocean area. It may also be generated as a computer listing from the time-phased force and deployment data. Joint Operation Planning and Execution System; time-phased force and deployment data; time-phased force and deployment data maintenance; time-phased force and deployment data refinement.

Times: (C-, D-, M-days end at 2400 hours Universal Time (Zulu time) and are assumed to be 24 hours long for planning.) The Chairman of the Joint Chiefs of Staff normally coordinates the proposed date with the commanders of the appropriate unified and specified commands, as well as any recommended changes to C-day. L-hour will be established per plan, crisis, or theater of operations and will apply to both air and surface movements. Normally, L-hour will be established to allow C-day to be a 24-hour day. a. C-day. The unnamed day on which a deployment operation commences or is to commence. The deployment may be movement of troops, cargo, weapon systems, or a combination of these elements using any or all types of transport. The letter "C" will be the only one used to denote the above. The highest command or headquarters responsible for coordinating the planning will specify the exact meaning of C-day within the aforementioned definition. The command or headquarters directly responsible for the execution of the operation, if other than the one coordinating the planning, will do so in light of the meaning specified by the highest command or headquarters coordinating the planning. b. D-day. The unnamed day on which a particular operation commences or is to commence. c. F-hour. The effective time of announcement by the Secretary of Defense to the Military Departments of a decision to mobilize Reserve units. d. H-hour. The specific hour on D-day at which a particular operation commences. e. H-hour (amphibious operations). For amphibious operations, the time the first assault elements are scheduled to touch down on the beach, or a landing zone, and in some cases the commencement of countermine breaching operations. f. L-hour. The specific hour on C-day at which a deployment operation commences or is to commence. g. L-hour (amphibious operations). In amphibious operations, the time at which the first helicopter of the helicopter-borne assault wave touches down in the landing zone. h. M-day. The term used to designate the unnamed day on which full mobilization commences or is due to commence. i. N day. The unnamed day an active duty unit is notified for deployment or redeployment. j. R-day. Redeployment day. The day on which redeployment of major combat, combat support, and combat service support forces begins in an operation. k. S-day. The day the President authorizes Selective Reserve call up (not more than 200,000). l. T-day. The effective day coincident with Presidential declaration of national emergency and authorization of partial mobilization (not more than 1,000,000 personnel exclusive of the 200,000 call up). m. W-day. Declared by the President, W day is associated with an adversary decision to prepare for war.

Time-sensitive target: A joint force commander designated target requiring immediate response because it is a highly lucrative, fleeting target of opportunity or it poses (or will soon pose) a danger to friendly forces.

Time slot: Period of time during which certain activities are governed by specific regulations.

Time to target: The number of minutes and seconds to elapse before aircraft ordnance impacts on target.

TNT equivalent: A measure of the energy released from the detonation of a nuclear weapon, or from the explosion of a given quantity of fissionable material, in terms of the amount of TNT (trinitrotoluene) which could release the same amount of energy when exploded.

Tolerance dose: The amount of radiation that may be received by an individual within a specified period with negligible results.

Top handler: A device specially designed to permit the lifting and handling of containers from the top with rough terrain container handlers.

Topographic map: A map that presents the vertical position of features in measurable form as well as their horizontal positions.

Topography: The configuration of the ground to include its relief and all features. Topography addresses both dry land and the sea floor.

Toss bombing: A method of bombing where an aircraft flies on a line towards the target, pulls up in a vertical plane, releasing the bomb at an angle that will compensate for the effect of gravity drop on the bomb. Similar to loft bombing; unrestricted as to altitude.

Total active aircraft authorization: The sum of the primary and backup aircraft authorizations.

Total active aircraft inventory: The sum of the primary and backup aircraft assigned to meet the total active aircraft authorization.

Total dosage attack: A chemical operation which does not involve a time limit within which to produce the required toxic level.

Total materiel assets: The total quantity of an item available in the military system worldwide and all funded procurement of the item with adjustments to provide for transfers out of or into the inventory through the appropriation and procurement lead-time periods. It includes peacetime force materiel assets and war reserve stock.

Total materiel requirement: The sum of the peacetime force material requirement and the war reserve material requirement.

Total overall aircraft inventory: The sum of the total active aircraft inventory and the inactive aircraft inventory.

Total pressure: The sum of dynamic and static pressures.

Touchdown zone: 1. For fixed wing aircraft — The first 3,000 feet or 1,000 meters of runway beginning at the threshold. 2. For rotary wings and vectored thrust aircraft— That portion of the helicopter landing area or runway used for landing.

Toxic chemical, biological, or radiological attack: An attack directed at personnel, animals, or crops, using injurious agents of chemical, biological, or radiological origin.

Toxic industrial biological: Any biological material manufactured, used, transported, or stored by industrial, medical, or commercial processes which could pose an infectious or toxic threat.

Toxic industrial chemical: A chemical developed or manufactured for use in industrial operations or research by industry, government, or academia. For example: pesticides, petrochemicals, fertilizers, corrosives, poisons, etc. These chemicals are not primarily manufactured for the specific purpose of producing human casualties or rendering equipment, facilities, or areas dangerous for human use. Hydrogen cyanide, cyanogens chloride, phosgene, and chloropicrin are industrial chemicals that also can be military chemical agents.

Toxic industrial material: A generic term for toxic or radioactive substances in solid, liquid, aerosolized, or gaseous form that may be used, or stored for use, for industrial, commercial, medical, military, or domestic purposes. Toxic industrial material may be chemical, biological, or radioactive and described as toxic industrial chemical, toxic industrial biological, or toxic industrial radiological.

Toxic industrial radiological: Any radiological material manufactured, used, transported, or stored by industrial, medical, or commercial processes. For example: spent fuel rods, medical sources, etc.

Track correlation: Correlating track information for identification purposes using all available data. tracking. Precise and continuous position-finding of targets by radar, optical, or other means.

Track management: Defined set of procedures whereby the commander ensures accurate friendly and enemy unit and/or platform locations, and a dissemination procedure for filtering, combining, and passing that information to higher, adjacent, and subordinate commanders.

Track of interest: In counterdrug operations, contacts that meet the initial sorting criteria applicable in the area where the contacts are detected. TOI.

Track production area: An area in which tracks are produced by one radar station.

Track symbology: Symbols used to display tracks on a data display console or other display device.

Track telling: The process of communicating air surveillance and tactical data information between command and control systems or between facilities within the systems. Telling may be classified into the following types: back tell; cross tell; forward tell; lateral tell; overlap tell; and relater tell.

Trafficability: Capability of terrain to bear traffic. It refers to the extent to which the terrain will permit continued movement of any or all types of traffic.

Traffic circulation map: A map showing traffic routes and the measures for traffic regulation. It indicates the roads for use of certain classes of traffic, the location of traffic control stations, and the directions in which traffic may move.

Traffic control police: Any persons ordered by a military commander and/or by national authorities to facilitate the movement of traffic and to prevent and/or report any breach of road traffic regulations.

Traffic density: The average number of vehicles that occupy one mile or one kilometer of road space, expressed in vehicles per mile or per kilometer.

Traffic flow: The total number of vehicles passing a given point in a given time. Traffic flow is expressed as vehicles per hour.

Traffic flow security: The protection resulting from features, inherent in some crypto equipment, that conceal the presence of valid messages on a communications circuit, normally achieved by causing the circuit to appear busy at all times.

Traffic information (radar): Information issued to alert an aircraft to any radar targets observed on the radar display that may be in such proximity to its position or intended route of flight to warrant its attention.

Traffic management: The direction, control, and supervision of all functions incident to the procurement and use of freight and passenger transportation services.

Traffic pattern: The traffic flow that is prescribed for aircraft landing at, taxiing on, and taking off from an airport. The usual components of a traffic pattern are upwind leg, crosswind leg, downwind leg, base leg, and final approach.

Train: 1. A service force or group of service elements that provides logistic support, e.g., an organization of naval auxiliary ships or merchant ships or merchant ships attached to a fleet for this purpose; similarly, the vehicles and operating personnel that furnish supply, evacuation, and maintenance services to a land unit. 2. Bombs dropped in short intervals or sequence.

Trained strength in units: Those reservists assigned to units who have completed initial active duty for training of 12 weeks or its equivalent and are eligible for deployment overseas on land when mobilized under proper authority. Excludes personnel in non-deployable accounts or a training pipeline.

Train headway: The interval of time between two trains boarded by the same unit at the same point.

Training aids: Any item developed or procured with the primary intent that it shall assist in training and the process of learning.

Training and retirement category: The category identifying a reservist's training or retirement status in a reserve component category and Reserve Component.

Training-pay category: A designation identifying the number of days of training and pay required for members of Reserve Components.

Training period: An authorized and scheduled regular inactive duty training period. A training period must be at least two hours for retirement point credit and four hours for pay. Previously used interchangeably with other common terms such as drills, drill period, assemblies, periods of instruction, etc.

Training pipeline: A Reserve Component category designation that identifies untrained officer and enlisted personnel who have not completed initial active duty for training of 12 weeks or its equivalent. Non deployable account.

Training unit: A unit established to provide military training to individual reservists or to Reserve Component units.

Train path: In railway terminology, the timing of a possible movement of a train along a given route. All the train paths on a given route constitute a timetable.

Trans attack period: 1. In nuclear warfare, the period from the initiation of the attack to its termination. 2. As applied to the Single Integrated Operational Plan, the period that extends from execution to termination of the Single Integrated Operational Plan.

Transfer loader: A wheeled or tracked vehicle with a platform capable of vertical and horizontal adjustment used in the loading and unloading of aircraft, ships, or other vehicles.

Transient: 1. Personnel, ships, or craft stopping temporarily at a post, station, or port to which they are not assigned or attached, and having destination elsewhere. 2. An independent merchant ship calling at a port and sailing within 12 hours, and for which routing instructions to a further port have been promulgated. 3. An individual awaiting orders, transport, etc., at a post or station to which he or she is not attached or assigned.

Transient forces: Forces that pass or stage through, or base temporarily within, the operational area of another command but are not under its operational control. Force; transient.

Transit bearing: A bearing determined by noting the time at which two features on the

Earth's surface have the same relative bearing.

Transition altitude: The altitude at or below which the vertical position of an aircraft is controlled by reference to true altitude.

Transition layer: The airspace between the transition altitude and the transition level.

Transition level: The lowest flight level available for use above the transition altitude. Altitude; transition altitude.

Transit passage: The non-suspendable right of continuous and expeditious navigation and/or over flight in the normal mode through an international strait linking one part of the high seas with another.

Transit route: A sea route which crosses open waters normally joining two coastal routes.

Transit zone: The path taken by either airborne or seaborne smugglers. Zone can include transfer operations to another carrier.

Transmission factor (nuclear): The ratio of the dose inside the shielding material to the outside dose. Transmission factor is used to calculate the dose received through the shielding material.

Transmission security: The component of communications security that results from all measures designed to protect transmissions from interception and exploitation by means other than cryptanalysis. Communications security.

Transonic: Of or pertaining to the speed of a body in a surrounding fluid when the relative speed of the fluid is subsonic in some places and supersonic in others. This is encountered when passing from subsonic to supersonic speed and vice versa.

Transponder: A receiver-transmitter which will generate a reply signal, upon proper interrogation.

Transportability: The capability of material to be moved by towing, self-propulsion, or carrier via any means, such as railways, highways, waterways, pipelines, oceans, and airways.

Transport area: In amphibious operations, an area assigned to a transport organization for the purpose of debarking troops and equipment.

Transportation closure: The actual arrival date of a specified movement requirement at port of debarkation.

Transportation emergency: A situation created by a shortage of normal transportation capability and of a magnitude sufficient to frustrate military movement requirements, and which requires extraordinary action by the President or other designated authority to ensure continued movement of essential Department of Defense traffic.

Transportation movement requirement: The need for transport of units, personnel, or materiel from a specified origin to a specified destination within a specified timeframe.

Transportation operating agencies: Those Federal agencies having responsibilities under national emergency conditions for the operational direction of one or more forms of transportation. Federal modal agencies; federal transport agencies.

Transportation priorities: Indicators assigned to eligible traffic that establish its movement precedence. Appropriate priority systems apply to the movement of traffic by sea and air. In times of emergency, priorities may be applicable to continental United States movements by land, water, or air.

Transportation system: All the land, water, and air routes and transportation assets engaged in the movement of US forces and their supplies across the range of military operations, involving both mature and immature theaters and at the strategic, operational, and tactical levels of war.

Transport control center (air transport): The operations center through which the air transport force commander exercises control over the air transport system.

Transport group: An element that directly deploys and supports the landing of the landing force (LF), and is functionally designated as a transport group in the amphibious task force organization. A transport group provides for the embarkation, movement to the objective, landing, and logistic support of the LF. Transport groups comprise all sealift and airlift in which the LF is embarked. They are categorized as follows: a. airlifted groups; b. Navy amphibious ship transport groups; and c. strategic sealift shipping groups.

Transporting (ordnance): The movement or repositioning of ordnance or explosive devices along established explosive routes.

Transshipment point: A location where material is transferred between vehicles.

Traverse: 1. To turn a weapon to the right or left on its mount. 2. A method of surveying in which lengths and directions of lines between points on the earth are obtained by or from field measurements, and used in determining positions of the points

Traverse level: That vertical displacement above low-level air defense systems, expressed both as a height and altitude, at which aircraft can cross the area.

Traverse racking test load value: Externally applied force in pounds or kilograms at the top-corner fitting that will strain or stretch end structures of the container sideways.

Treason: -Violation of the allegiance owed to one's sovereign or state; betrayal of one's country.

Trend : The straying of the fall of shot, such as might be caused by incorrect speed settings of the fire support ship.

Triangulation station: A point on the Earth, the position of which is determined by triangulation. Trig point.

Tri-camera photography: Photography obtained by simultaneous exposure of three cameras systematically disposed in the air vehicle at fixed overlapping angles relative to each other in order to cover a wide field.

Trig list : A list published by certain Army units that includes essential information of accurately located survey points.

Trim: The difference in draft at the bow and stern of a vessel or the manner in which a vessel floats in the water based on the distribution of cargo, stores and ballast aboard the vessel. Draft; watercraft.

Triple point: The intersection of the incident, reflected, and fused (or Mach) shock fronts accompanying an air burst. The height of the triple point above the surface, i.e., the height of the Mach stem, increases with increasing distance from a given explosion.

Troop basis: An approved list of those military units and individuals (including civilians) required for the performance of a particular mission by numbers, organization and equipment and, in the case of larger commands, by deployment.

Troops: A collective term for uniformed military personnel. Airborne troops; combat service support elements; combat support troops; service troops; tactical troops.

Troop safety (nuclear): An element that defines a distance from the proposed burst location beyond which personnel meeting the criteria described under degree of risk will be safe to the degree prescribed. It is expressed as a combination of a degree of risk and vulnerability category. Emergency risk (nuclear); negligible risk (nuclear); unwarned exposed; warned protected.

Troop space cargo: Cargo such as sea or barracks bags, bedding rolls or hammocks, locker trunks, and office equipment, normally stowed in an accessible place. This cargo will also include normal hand-carried combat equipment and weapons to be carried ashore by the assault troops.

Troop test: A test conducted in the field for the purpose of evaluating operational or organizational concepts, doctrine, tactics, and techniques, or to gain further information on material.

Tropical storm: A tropical cyclone in which the surface wind speed is at least 34, but not more than 63 knots.

Tropopause: The transition zone between the stratosphere and the troposphere. The tropopause normally occurs at an altitude of about 25,000 to 45,000 feet (8 to 15 kilometers) in polar and temperate zones, and at 55,000 feet (20 kilometers) in the tropics.

True airspeed indicator: An instrument which displays the speed of the aircraft relative to the ambient air.

True altitude: The height of an aircraft as measured from mean sea level.

True bearing: The direction to an object from a point; expressed as a horizontal angle measured clockwise from true north.

True convergence : The angle at which one meridian is inclined to another on the surface of the Earth.

True horizon: 1. The boundary of a horizontal plane passing through a point of vision. 2. In photogrammetric, the boundary of a horizontal plane passing through the perspective center of a lens system.

True north: The direction from an observer's position to the geographic North Pole. The north direction of any geographic meridian.

Turbojet: A jet engine whose air is supplied by a turbine-driven compressor, the turbine being activated by exhaust gases.

Turnaround: The length of time between arriving at a point and being ready to depart from that point. It is used in this sense for the loading, unloading, re-fueling, and re-arming, where appropriate, of vehicles, aircraft, and ships.

Turnaround cycle: A term used in conjunction with vehicles, ships, and aircraft, and comprising the following: loading time at departure point; time to and from destination; unloading and loading time at destination; unloading time at returning point; planned maintenance time; and, where applicable, time awaiting facilities.

Turning movement: A variation of the envelopment in which the attacking force passes around or over the enemy's principal defensive positions to secure objectives deep in the enemy's rear to force the enemy to abandon his position or divert major forces to meet the threat.

Turning point: In land mine warfare, a point on the centerline of a mine strip or row where it changes direction.

Turn-off guidance: Information which enables the pilot of a landing aircraft to select and follow the correct taxiway from the time the aircraft leaves the runway until it may safely be brought to a halt clear of the active runway.

Two-person control: The continuous surveillance and control of positive control material at all times by a minimum of two authorized individuals, each capable of detecting incorrect or unauthorized procedures with respect to the task being performed and each familiar with established security requirements.

Two-person rule: A system designed to prohibit access by an individual to nuclear weapons and certain designated components by requiring the presence at all times of at least two authorized persons, each capable of detecting incorrect or unauthorized procedures with respect to the task to be performed.

Types of burst: Airburst; fallout safe height of burst; height of burst; high airburst; high altitude burst; low airburst; nuclear airburst; nuclear exoatmospheric burst; nuclear contact-surface burst; nuclear proximity-surface burst; nuclear underground burst; nuclear underwater burst; optimum height of burst; safe burst height.

Type unit: A type of organizational or functional entity established within the Armed Forces and uniquely identified by a five-character, alphanumeric code called a unit type code.

Type unit data file: A file that provides standard planning data and movement characteristics for personnel, cargo, and accompanying supplies associated with type units.

U

Ultraviolet imagery: That imagery produced as a result of sensing ultraviolet radiations reflected from a given target surface.

Unaccounted for: An inclusive term (not a casualty status) applicable to personnel whose person or remains are not recovered or otherwise accounted for following hostile action. Commonly used when referring to personnel who are killed in action and whose bodies are not recovered. See also casualty; casualty category; casualty status; casualty type.

Unanticipated target: A target of opportunity that was unknown or not expected to exist in the operational environment. Target of opportunity.

Unauthorized commitment: An agreement that is not binding solely because the United States Government representative who made it lacked the authority to enter into that agreement on behalf of the Unites States Government. Ratification.

Uncertain environment: Operational environment in which host government forces, whether opposed to or receptive to operations that a unit intends to conduct, do not have totally effective control of the territory and population in the intended operational area.

Uncharged demolition target: A demolition target for which charges have been calculated, prepared, and stored in a safe place, and for which execution procedures have been established. See also demolition target.

Unclassified matter: Official matter which does not require the application of security safeguards, but the disclosure of which may be subject to control for other reasons. Classified matter.

Unconventional assisted recovery: Nonconventional assisted recovery conducted by special operations forces. Authenticate; evader; recovery.

Unconventional assisted recovery coordination cell: A compartmented special operations forces facility, established by the joint force special operations component commander, staffed on a continuous basis by supervisory personnel and tactical planners to coordinate, synchronize, and de-conflict nonconventional assisted recovery operations within the operational area assigned to the joint force commander. Joint operations center; joint personnel recovery center; special operations forces; unconventional assisted recovery.

Unconventional assisted recovery mechanism: A recovery mechanism developed and managed by special operations forces. Unconventional assisted recovery.

Unconventional assisted recovery team: A designated special operations forces unconventional warfare ground or maritime force capable of conducting unconventional assisted recovery with indigenous or surrogate forces.

Unconventional warfare: A broad spectrum of military and paramilitary operations, normally of long duration, predominantly conducted through, with, or by indigenous or surrogate forces who are organized, trained, equipped, supported, and directed in varying degrees by an external source. It includes, but is not limited to, guerrilla warfare, subversion, sabotage, intelligence activities, and unconventional assisted recovery.

Unconventional warfare forces: US forces having an existing unconventional warfare capability.

Undersea warfare: Operations conducted to establish and maintain control of the underwater environment by denying an opposing force the effective use of underwater systems and weapons. It includes offensive and defensive submarine, antisubmarine, and mine warfare operations. Antisubmarine warfare; mine warfare.

Underwater demolition: The destruction or neutralization of underwater obstacles; this is normally accomplished by underwater demolition teams. Under stowed cargo.

Underwater demolition team: A group of officers and enlisted specially trained and equipped for making hydrographic reconnaissance of approaches to prospective landing beaches; for effecting demolition of obstacles and clearing mines in certain areas; locating, improving, and marking of useable channels; channel and harbor clearance; acquisition of pertinent data during pre-assault operations, including military information; observing the hinterland to gain information useful to the landing force; and for performing miscellaneous underwater and surface tasks within their capabilities.

Underway replenishment force: A task force of fleet auxiliaries adequately protected by escorts furnished by the responsible operational commander. The function of this force is to provide underway logistic support for naval forces. Underway replenishment.

Underway replenishment group: A task group configured to provide logistic replenishment of ships underway by transfer-at-sea methods.

Unexploded explosive ordnance: Explosive ordnance which has been primed, fused, armed or otherwise prepared for action, and which has been fired, dropped, launched, projected, or placed in such a manner as to constitute a hazard to operations, installations, personnel, or material and remains unexploded either by malfunction or design or for any other cause. also explosive ordnance.

Unified action: The synchronization, coordination, and/or integration of the activities of governmental and nongovernmental entities with military operations to achieve unity of effort.

Unified Command Plan: The document, approved by the President, that sets forth basic guidance to all unified combatant commanders; establishes their missions, responsibilities, and force structure; delineates the general geographical area of responsibility for geographic combatant commanders; and specifies functional responsibilities for functional combatant commanders. Combatant command; combatant commander.

Uniformed services : The Army, Navy, Air Force, Marine Corps, Coast Guard, National Oceanic and Atmospheric Administration, and Public Health Services. Military Department; Military Service.

Unilateral arms control measure: An arms control course of action taken by a nation without any compensating concession being required of other nations.

Unintentional radiation exploitation: Exploitation for operational purposes of non information-bearing elements of electromagnetic energy unintentionally emanated by targets of interest.

Unintentional radiation intelligence: Intelligence derived from the collection and analysis of non information-bearing elements extracted from the electromagnetic energy unintentionally emanated by foreign devices, equipment, and systems, excluding those generated by the detonation of nuclear weapons. .

Uni-Service command: A command comprised of forces of a single Service.

Unit: 1. Any military element whose structure is prescribed by competent authority, such as a table of organization and equipment; specifically, part of an organization. 2. An organization title of a subdivision of a group in a task force. 3. A standard or basic quantity into which an item of supply is divided, issued, or used. In this meaning, also called unit of issue. 4. With regard to Reserve Components of the Armed Forces, denotes a Selected Reserve unit organized, equipped, and trained for mobilization to serve on active duty as a unit or to augment or be augmented by another unit. Headquarters and support functions without wartime missions are not considered units.

Unit aircraft: Those aircraft provided an aircraft unit for the performance of a flying mission.

Unit commitment status: The degree of commitment of any unit designated and categorized as a force allocated to NATO.

Unit designation list: A list of actual units by unit identification code designated to fulfill requirements of a force list.

United States: Includes the land area, internal waters, territorial sea, and airspace of the United States, including the following: a. US territories, possessions, and commonwealths; and b. Other areas over which the US Government has complete jurisdiction and control or has exclusive authority or defense responsibility.

United States Armed Forces: Used to denote collectively only the regular components of the Army, Navy, Air Force, Marine Corps, and Coast Guard. Armed Forces of the United States.

United States Civilian Internee Information Center: The national center of information in the United States for enemy and US civilian internees.

United States controlled shipping: That shipping under US flag and selected ships under foreign flag considered to be under "effective US control," i.e., that can reasonably be expected to be made available to the United States in time of national emergency.

United States Military Service-funded foreign training: Training that is provided to foreign nationals in United States Military Service schools and installations under authority other than the Foreign Assistance Act of 1961.

United States Naval Ship: A public vessel of the United States that is in the custody of the Navy and is: a. Operated by the Military Sealift Command and manned by a civil service crew; or b. Operated by a commercial company under contract to the Military Sealift Command and manned by a merchant marine crew. Military Sealift Command.

United States Prisoner of War Information Center: The national center of information in the United States for enemy and US prisoners of war.

United States Signals Intelligence System: The unified organization of signals intelligence activities under the direction of the Director, National Security

Agency/Chief, Central Security Service. It consists of the National Security Agency/Central Security Service, the components of the Military Services authorized to conduct signals intelligence, and such other entities (other than the Federal Bureau of Investigation) authorized by the National Security Council or the Secretary of Defense to conduct signals intelligence activities. Counterintelligence.

United States Transportation Command: The unified command with the mission to provide strategic air, land, and sea transportation and common-user port management for the Department of Defense across the range of military operations. Global transportation network; single port manager; transportation component command; unified command.

Unit identification code: A six-character, alphanumeric code that uniquely identifies each Active, Reserve, and National Guard unit of the Armed Forces.

Unitized load: A single item or a number of items packaged, packed, or arranged in a specified manner and capable of being handled as a unit. Unitization may be accomplished by placing the item or items in a container or by banding them securely together. Palletized unit load.

Unit line number: A seven-character alphanumeric code that describes a unique increment of a unit deployment, i.e., advance party, main body, equipment by sea and air, reception team, or trail party, in a Joint Operation Planning and Execution System time-phased force and deployment data.

Unit loading: The loading of troop units with their equipment and supplies in the same vessels, aircraft, or land vehicles.

Unit movement control center: A temporary organization activated by major subordinate commands and subordinate units during deployment to control and manage marshalling and movement. Deployment; marshaling; unit.

Unit of issue: In its special storage meaning, refers to the quantity of an item; as each number, dozen, gallon, pair, pound, ream, set, yard. Usually termed unit of issue to distinguish from "unit price."

Unit movement data: A unit equipment and/or supply listing containing corresponding transportability data. Tailored unit movement data has been modified to reflect a specific movement requirement.

Unit personnel and tonnage table: A table included in the loading plan of a combat loaded ship as a recapitulation of totals of personnel and cargo by type, listing cubic measurements and weight.

Unit price: The cost or price of an item of supply based on the unit of issue.

Unit-related equipment and supplies: All equipment and supplies that are assigned to a specific unit or that are designated as accompanying supplies. The logistic dimensions of these items are contained in the type unit characteristics file standard.

Unit reserves: Prescribed quantities of supplies carried by a unit as a reserve to cover emergencies. Reserve supplies.

Unit training assembly: An authorized and scheduled period of unit inactive duty training of a prescribed length of time.

Unit type code: A Joint Chiefs of Staff developed and assigned code, consisting of five characters that uniquely identify a "type unit."

Unity of effort: Coordination and cooperation toward common objectives, even if the participants are not necessarily part of the same command or organization - the product of successful unified action.

Universal Joint Task List: A menu of capabilities that may be selected by a joint force commander to accomplish the assigned mission. Once identified as essential to mission accomplishment, the tasks are reflected within the command joint mission essential task list.

Universal polar stereographic grid: A military grid prescribed for joint use in operations in limited areas and used for operations requiring precise position reporting. It covers areas between the 80 degree parallels and the poles.

Universal Postal Union: A worldwide postal organization to which the United States and most other countries are members. The exchange of mail, except parcel post, between the United States and other nations is governed by the provisions of the Universal Postal Union convention.

Universal transverse Mercator grid: A grid coordinate system based on the transverse Mercator projection, applied to maps of the Earth's surface extending to 84 degrees N and 80 degrees S latitudes. .

Unknown: 1. A code meaning "information not available." 2. An unidentified target. An aircraft or ship that has not been determined to be hostile, friendly, or neutral using identification friend or foe and other techniques, but that must be tracked by air defense or naval engagement systems. 3. An identity applied to an evaluated track that has not been identified. Assumed friend; friend; hostile; neutral; suspect.

Unmanned aircraft: An aircraft or balloon that does not carry a human operator and is capable of flight under remote control or autonomous programming.

Unmanned aircraft system: That system whose components include the necessary equipment, network, and personnel to control an unmanned aircraft. UAS.

Unmanned aerial vehicle: A powered, aerial vehicle that does not carry a human operator, uses aerodynamic forces to provide vehicle lift, can fly autonomously or be piloted remotely, can be expendable or recoverable, and can carry a lethal or nonlethal payload. Ballistic or semi ballistic vehicles, cruise missiles, and artillery projectiles are not considered unmanned aerial vehicles.

Unplanned target: A target of opportunity that is known to exist in the operational environment. Operational area; target; target of opportunity.

Unscheduled convoy phase: The period in the early days of war when convoys are instituted on an ad hoc basis before the introduction of convoy schedules in the regular convoy phase.

Unstable patient: A patient whose physiological status is in fluctuation. Emergent, treatment and/or surgical intervention are anticipated during the evacuation. An unstable patient's rapidly changing status and requirements are beyond the standard en route care capability and requires medical/surgical augmentation.

Unstuffing: The removal of cargo from a container. Also called stripping.

Unwanted cargo: A cargo loaded in peacetime which is not required by the consignee country in wartime.

Unwarned exposed: The vulnerability of friendly forces to nuclear weapon effects. In this condition, personnel are assumed to be standing in the open at burst time, but have dropped to a prone position by the time the blast wave arrives. They are expected to have areas of bare skin exposed to direct thermal radiation, and some personnel may suffer dazzle. Warned exposed; warned protected.

Urban triad : The three distinguishing characteristics of urban areas: complex manmade physical terrain, a population of significant size and density, and an infrastructure upon which the area depends. Infrastructure; joint urban operations.

Urgent mining: In naval mine warfare, the laying of mines with correct spacing but not in the ordered or planned positions. The mines may be laid either inside or outside the allowed area in such positions that they will hamper the movements of the enemy more than those of our own forces.

Urgent priority: A category of immediate mission request that is lower than emergency priority but takes precedence over ordinary priority; e.g., enemy artillery or mortar fire that is falling on friendly troops and causing casualties or enemy troops or mechanized units moving up in such force as to threaten a breakthrough. See also immediate mission request; priority of immediate mission requests.

US commercial assets: US commercial aircraft, spacecraft, flag shipping, offshore, and land based assets located landward of the outer limit of the continental shelf of the United States, its territories, and possessions, and excluding those privately owned oil rigs operating under foreign license in disputed offshore areas.

Use of force policy: Policy guidance issued by the Commandant, US Coast Guard, on the use of force and weapons.

US Defense Representative: A senior US officer in a foreign country representing the Secretary of Defense, the Chairman of the Joint Chiefs of Staff, and the commander of the unified command that coordinates the security matters regarding in-country, non As combat Department of Defense elements of personnel and organizations under the command of a combatant commander but not assigned to, or attached to, the combatant commander.

US forces: All Armed Forces of the United States, any person in the Armed Forces of the United States, and all equipment of any description that either belongs to the US Armed Forces or is being used (including Type I and II Military Sealift Command vessels), escorted, or conveyed by the US Armed Forces.

US national: US citizen and US permanent and temporary legal resident aliens.

US person: For intelligence purposes, a US person is defined as one of the following: (1) a US citizen; (2) an alien known by the intelligence agency concerned to be a permanent resident alien; (3) an unincorporated association substantially composed of US citizens or permanent resident aliens; or (4) a corporation incorporated in the United States, except for those directed and controlled by a foreign government or governments.

US Transportation Command coordinating instructions: Instructions of the US Transportation Command that establish suspense dates for selected members of the joint planning and execution community to complete updates to the operation plan database. Instructions will ensure that the target date movement requirements will be validated and available for scheduling.

V

Validate: Execution procedure used by combatant command components, supporting combatant commanders, and providing organizations to confirm to the supported commander and US Transportation Command that all the information records in a time-phased force and deployment data not only are error-free for automation purposes, but also accurately reflect the current status, attributes, and availability of units and requirements. Unit readiness, movement dates, passengers, and cargo details should be confirmed with the unit before validation occurs.

Valuable cargo: Cargo which may be of value during a later stage of the war.

Value engineering: An organized effort directed at analyzing the function of Department of Defense systems, equipment, facilities, procedures, and supplies for the purpose of achieving the required function at the lowest total cost of effective ownership, consistent with requirements for performance, reliability, quality, and maintainability.

Variability: The manner in which the probability of damage to a specific target decreases with the distance from ground zero; or, in damage assessment, a mathematical factor introduced to average the effects of orientation, minor shielding, and uncertainty of target response to the effects considered.

variable safety level — safety level of supply.

Variant: 1. One of two or more cipher or code symbols that have the same plain text equivalent. 2. One of several plain text meanings that are represented by a single code group. This is also called alternative.

Variation: The angular difference between true and magnetic north.

Vehicle-borne improvised explosive device: A device placed or fabricated in an improvised manner on a vehicle incorporating destructive, lethal, noxious, pyrotechnic, or incendiary chemicals and designed to destroy, incapacitate, harass, or distract. Otherwise known as a car bomb.

Vehicle cargo: Wheeled or tracked equipment, including weapons, that require certain deck space, head room, and other definite clearance.

Vehicle distance: The clearance between vehicles in a column which is measured from the rear of one vehicle to the front of the following vehicle.

Vehicle summary and priority table: A table listing all vehicles by priority of debarkation from a combat-loaded ship. It includes the nomenclature, dimensions, square feet, cubic feet, weight, and stowage location of each vehicle; the cargo loaded in each vehicle; and the name of the unit to which the vehicle belongs.

Verification: 1. In arms control, any action, including inspection, detection, and identification, taken to ascertain compliance with agreed measures. 2. In computer modeling and simulation, the process of determining that a model or simulation implementation accurately represents the developer's conceptual description and specifications. Configuration management; independent review; validation.

Verify: To ensure that the meaning and phraseology of the transmitted message conveys the exact intention of the originator.

Vertex: In artillery and naval gunfire support, the highest point in the trajectory of a projectile.

Vertical air photograph: An air photograph taken with the optical axis of the camera perpendicular to the surface of the Earth.

Vertical and/or short takeoff and landing: Vertical and/or short takeoff and landing capability for aircraft.

Vertical envelopment: A tactical maneuver in which troops, either air-dropped or air-landed, attack the rear and flanks of a force, in effect cutting off or encircling the force.

Vertical interval: Difference in altitude between two specified points or locations, e.g., the battery or firing ship and the target; observer location and the target; location of previously fired target and new target; observer and a height of burst; and battery or firing ship and a height of burst, etc.

Vertical landing zone: A specified ground area for landing vertical takeoff and landing aircraft to embark or disembark troops and/or cargo. A landing zone may contain one or more landing sites. Landing zone; vertical takeoff and landing aircraft.

Vertical loading: A type of loading whereby items of like character are vertically tiered throughout the holds of a ship so that selected items are available at any stage of the unloading. loading.

Vertical probable error: The product of the range probable error and the slope of fall.

Vertical replenishment: The use of a helicopter for the transfer of materiel to or from a ship.

Vertical separation: Separation between aircraft expressed in units of vertical distance.

Vertical strip: A single flight line of overlapping photos. Photography of this type is normally taken of long, narrow targets such as beaches or roads.

Vertical takeoff and landing aircraft: Fixed-wing aircraft and helicopters capable of taking off or landing vertically. Vertical landing zone; vertical takeoff and landing aircraft transport area.

Vertical takeoff and landing aircraft transport area: Area to the seaward and on the flanks of the outer transport and landing ship areas, but preferably inside the area screen, for launching and/or recovering vertical takeoff and landing aircraft. Aircraft transport area. Vertical takeoff and landing aircraft.

Very seriously ill or injured: The casualty status of a person whose illness or injury is classified by medical authority to be of such severity that life is imminently endangered.

Very small aperture terminal: Refers to a fixed satellite terminal whose antenna diameter typically does not exceed two meters.

Vetting: A part of target development that assesses the accuracy of the supporting intelligence to targeting.

Vignetting: A method of producing a band of color or tone on a map or chart, the density of which is reduced uniformly from edge to edge.

Visibility range: The horizontal distance (in kilometers or miles) at which a large dark object can just be seen against the horizon sky in daylight.

Visual call sign: A call sign provided primarily for visual signaling.

Visual information: Use of one or more of the various visual media with or without sound. Generally, visual information includes still photography, motion picture photography, video or audio recording, graphic arts, visual aids, models, display, visual presentation services, and the support processes.

Visual information documentation: Motion media, still photography, and audio recording of technical and nontechnical events while they occur, usually not controlled by the recording crew. Visual information documentation encompasses Combat Camera, operational documentation, and technical documentation. VIDOC. Combat camera; operational documentation; technical documentation.

Visual meteorological conditions: Weather conditions in which visual flight rules apply; expressed in terms of visibility, ceiling height, and aircraft clearance from clouds along the path of flight. When these criteria do not exist, instrument meteorological conditions prevail and instrument flight rules must be complied with.

Visual mine firing indicator: A device used with exercise mines to indicate that the mine would have detonated had it been poised.

Vital area: A designated area or installation to be defended by air defence units.

Vital ground: Ground of such importance that it must be retained or controlled for the success of the mission.

Voice call sign: A call sign provided primarily for voice communication.

Voluntary Intermodal Sealift Agreement: An agreement that provides the Department of Defense with assured access to US flag assets, both vessel capacity and intermodal systems, to meet Department of Defense contingency requirements. Carriers contractually commit specified portions of their fleet to meet time-phased Department of Defense contingency requirements. VISA.

Voluntary tanker agreement: An agreement established by the Maritime Administration to provide for US commercial tanker owners and operators to voluntarily make their vessels available to satisfy the Department of Defense needs. It is designed to meet contingency or war requirements for point-to-point petroleum, oils, and lubricants movements, and not to deal with capacity shortages in resupply operations.

Voluntary training unit: A unit formed by volunteers to provide Reserve Component training in a non-pay status for Individual Ready Reservists and active status Standby Reservists attached under competent orders and participating in such units for retirement points. Reinforcement training unit.

VOR: An air navigational radio aid which uses phase comparison of a ground transmitted signal to determine bearing. This term is derived from the words "very high frequency omnidirectional radio range."

Vulnerability: 1. The susceptibility of a nation or military force to any action by any means through which its war potential or combat effectiveness may be reduced or its will to fight diminished. 2. The characteristics of a system that cause it to suffer a definite degradation (incapability to perform the designated mission) as a result of having been subjected to a certain level of effects in an unnatural (man-made) hostile environment. 3. In information operations, a weakness in information system security design, procedures, implementation, or internal controls that could be exploited to gain unauthorized access to information or an information system. Information; information operations; information system.

Vulnerability assessment: A Department of Defense, command, or unit-level evaluation (assessment) to determine the vulnerability of a terrorist attack against an installation, unit, exercise, port, ship, residence, facility, or other site. Identifies areas of improvement to withstand, mitigate, or deter acts of violence or terrorism.

Vulnerability program: A program to determine the degree of any existing susceptibility of nuclear weapon systems to enemy countermeasures, accidental fire, and accidental shock and to remedy these weaknesses insofar as possible.

Vulnerability study: An analysis of the capabilities and limitations of a force in a specific situation to determine vulnerabilities capable of exploitation by an opposing force.

W

Wading crossing: Deep fording capability; shallow fording.

Walking patient: A patient whose injuries and/or illness are relatively minor, permitting the patient to walk and not require a litter.

Wanted cargo: In naval control of shipping, a cargo which is not immediately required by the consignee country but will be needed later.

Warble: In naval mine warfare, the process of varying the frequency of sound produced by a narrow band noisemaker to ensure that the frequency to which the mine will respond is covered.

Warden system: An informal method of communication used to pass information to US citizens during emergencies.

War game: A simulation, by whatever means, of a military operation involving two or more opposing forces using rules, data, and procedures designed to depict an actual or assumed real life situation.

Warhead: That part of a missile, projectile, torpedo, rocket, or other munitions which contains either the nuclear or thermonuclear system, high explosive system, chemical or biological agents, or inert materials intended to inflict damage.

Warhead mating: The act of attaching a warhead section to a rocket or missile body, torpedo, airframe, motor, or guidance section.

Warhead section: A completely assembled warhead, including appropriate skin sections and related components.

War materiel procurement capability: The quantity of an item that can be acquired by orders placed on or after the day an operation commences from industry or from any other available source during the period prescribed for war materiel procurement planning purposes.

War materiel requirement: The quantity of an item required to equip and support the approved forces specified in the current Secretary of Defense guidance through the period prescribed for war materiel planning purposes.

Warned exposed: The vulnerability of friendly forces to nuclear weapon effects. In this condition, personnel are assumed to be prone with all skin covered and with thermal protection at least that provided by a two-layer summer uniform.

Warned protected: The vulnerability of friendly forces to nuclear weapon effects. In this condition, personnel are assumed to have some protection against heat, blast, and radiation such as that afforded in closed armored vehicles or crouched in fox holes with improvised overhead shielding.

Warning: 1. A communication and acknowledgment of dangers implicit in a wide spectrum of activities by potential opponents ranging from routine defense measures to substantial increases in readiness and force preparedness and to acts of terrorism or political, economic, or military provocation. 2. Operating procedures, practices, or conditions that may result in injury or death if not carefully observed or followed.

Warning net: A communication system established for the purpose of disseminating warning information of enemy movement or action to all interested commands.

Warning of attack: A warning to national policymakers that an adversary is not only preparing its armed forces for war, but intends to launch an attack in the near future. Tactical warning; warning; warning of war.

Warning of war: A warning to national policymakers that a state or alliance intends war, or is on a course that substantially increases the risks of war and is taking steps to prepare for war. Strategic warning; warning; warning of attack.

Warning red: Air defense warning conditions. Warning Yellow/ Warning White.

Warning shots: The firing of shots or delivery of ordnance by personnel or weapons systems in the vicinity of a person, vessel, or aircraft as a signal to immediately cease activity. Warning shots are one measure to convince a potentially hostile force to withdraw or cease its threatening actions.

Warp: To haul a ship ahead by line or anchor.

War reserve materiel requirement: That portion of the war materiel requirement required to be on hand on D-day. This level consists of the war materiel requirement less the sum of the peacetime assets assumed to be available on D-day and the war materiel procurement capability.

War reserve materiel requirement, balance: That portion of the war reserve materiel requirement that has not been acquired or funded. This level consists of the war reserve materiel requirement less the war reserve materiel requirement, protectable.

War reserve materiel requirement, protectable: That portion of the war reserve materiel requirement that is either on hand and/or previously funded that shall be protected; if issued for peacetime use, it shall be promptly reconstituted. This level consists of the pre-positioned war reserve materiel requirement, protectable, and the other war reserve materiel requirement, protectable.

War reserve (nuclear): Nuclear weapons materiel stockpiled in the custody of the Department of Energy or transferred to the custody of the Department of Defense and intended for employment in the event of war.

War reserves: Stocks of materiel amassed in peacetime to meet the increase in military requirements consequent upon an outbreak of war. War reserves are intended to provide the interim support essential to sustain operations until resupply can be effected.

War reserve stock: That portion of total materiel assets designated to satisfy the war reserve materiel requirement.

War reserve stocks for allies: A Department of Defense program to have the Services procure or retain in their inventories those minimum stockpiles of materiel such as munitions, equipment, and combat-essential consumables to ensure support for selected allied forces in time of war until future in-country production and external resupply can meet the estimated combat consumption.

Wartime load : The maximum quantity of supplies of all kinds which a ship can carry. The composition of the load is prescribed by proper authority.

Wartime manpower planning system: A standardized Department of Defense DOD)-wide procedure, structure, and database for computing, compiling, projecting, and portraying the time-phased wartime manpower requirements, demand, and supply of the DOD components.

Washington Liaison Group: An interagency committee and/or joint monitoring body, chaired by the Department of State with representation from the Department of Defense, established to coordinate the preparation and implementation of plans for evacuation of United States citizens abroad in emergencies.

Watching mine: In naval mine warfare, a mine secured to its mooring but showing on the surface, possibly only in certain tidal conditions.

Watercraft: Any vessel or craft designed specifically and only for movement on the surface of the water.

Water space management: The allocation of water space in terms of antisubmarine warfare attack procedures to permit the rapid and effective engagement of hostile submarines while preventing inadvertent attacks on friendly submarines.

Water terminal: A facility for berthing ships simultaneously at piers, quays, and/or working anchorages, normally located within sheltered coastal waters adjacent to rail, highway, air, and/or inland water transportation networks.

Wave: 1. A formation of forces, landing ships, craft, amphibious vehicles or aircraft, required to beach or land about the same time. Can be classified as to type, function or order as shown: a. assault wave; b. boat wave; c. helicopter wave; d. numbered wave; e. on-call wave; f. scheduled wave. 2. An undulation of water caused by the progressive movement of energy from point to point along the surface of the water.

Wave crest: The highest part of a wave.

Wave height: The vertical distance between trough and crest, usually expressed in feet.

Wave length: The horizontal distance between successive wave crests measured perpendicular to the crest, usually expressed in feet.

Wave period: The time it takes for two successive wave crests to pass a given point.

Wave trough: The lowest part of the wave between crests.

Wave velocity: The speed at which a wave form advances across the sea, usually expressed in knots.

Way point: 1. In air operations, a point or a series of points in space to which an aircraft, ship, or cruise missile may be vectored. 2. A designated point or series of points loaded and stored in a global positioning system or other electronic navigational aid system to facilitate movement.

Weapon and payload identification: 1. The determination of the type of weapon being used in an attack. 2. The discrimination of a re-entry vehicle from penetration aids being utilized with the re-entry vehicle.

Weapon debris (nuclear): The residue of a nuclear weapon after it has exploded; that is, materials used for the casing and other components of the weapon, plus unexpended plutonium or uranium, together with fission products.

Weaponeering: The process of determining the quantity of a specific type of lethal or nonlethal weapons required to achieve a specific level of damage to a given target, considering target vulnerability, weapons characteristics and effects, and delivery parameters.

Weapons assignment: In air defense, the process by which weapons are assigned to individual air weapons controllers for use in accomplishing an assigned mission.

Weapons free zone: An air defense zone established for the protection of key assets or facilities, other than air bases, where weapon systems may be fired at any target not positively recognized as friendly.

Weapons of mass destruction: Weapons that are capable of a high order of destruction and/or of being used in such a manner as to destroy large numbers of people. Weapons of mass destruction can be high-yield explosives or nuclear, biological, chemical, or radiological weapons, but exclude the means of transporting or propelling the weapon where such means is a separable and divisible part of the weapon.

Weapons recommendation sheet: A sheet or chart which defines the intention of the attack, and recommends the nature of weapons, and resulting damage expected, tonnage, fuzing, spacing, desired mean points of impact, and intervals of reattack.

Weapon(s) system: A combination of one or more weapons with all related equipment, materials, services, personnel, and means of delivery and deployment (if applicable) required for self-sufficiency.

Weapon system employment concept: A description in broad terms, based on established outline characteristics, of the application of a particular equipment or weapon system within the framework of tactical concept and future doctrines.

Weapon-target line: An imaginary straight line from a weapon to a target.

Weather deck: A deck having no overhead protection; uppermost deck.

Weight and balance sheet: A sheet which records the distribution of weight in an aircraft and shows the center of gravity of an aircraft at takeoff and landing.

Wellness: Force health protection program that consolidates and incorporates physical and mental fitness, health promotion, and environmental and occupational health.

Wharf: A structure built of open rather than solid construction along a shore or a bank that provides cargo-handling facilities. A similar facility of solid construction is called a key.

Wheel load capacity: The capacity of airfield runways, taxiways, parking areas, or roadways to bear the pressures exerted by aircraft or vehicles in a gross weight static configuration.

White cap: A small wave breaking offshore as a result of the action of strong winds.

Whiteout: Loss of orientation with respect to the horizon caused by sun reflecting on snow and overcast sky.

White propaganda: Propaganda disseminated and acknowledged by the sponsor or by an accredited agency thereof.

Winch: A hoisting machine used for loading and discharging cargo and stores or for hauling in lines.

Wind shear: A change of wind direction and magnitude.

Wingman: An aviator subordinate to and in support of the designated section leader; also, the aircraft flown in this role

Withdrawal operation: A planned retrograde operation in which a force in contact disengages from an enemy force and moves in a direction away from the enemy.

Withhold (nuclear): The limiting of authority to employ nuclear weapons by denying their use within specified geographical areas or certain countries.

Working anchorage: An anchorage where ships lie to discharge cargoes over-side to coasters or lighters.

Working capital fund: A revolving fund established to finance inventories of supplies and other stores, or to provide working capital for industrial-type activities.

Working group: An enduring or ad hoc organization within a joint force commander's headquarters formed around a specific function whose purpose is to provide analysis to users. The working group consists of a core functional group and other staff and component representatives.

Work order: A specific or blanket authorization to perform certain work — usually broader in scope than a job order. It is sometimes used synonymously with job order. world geographic reference system.

Worldwide Port System: Automated information system to provide cargo management and accountability to water port and regional commanders while providing in-transit visibility to the Global Transportation Network.

Wreckage locator chart: A chart indicates the geographic location of all known aircraft wreckage sites and all known vessel wrecks that show above low water or can be seen from the air. It consists of a visual plot of wreckage, numbered in chronological order, and cross referenced with a wreckage locator file containing all pertinent data concerning the wreckage.

Y

Yaw: 1. This is the rotation of an aircraft, ship, or missile about its vertical axis so as to cause the longitudinal axis of the aircraft, ship, or missile to deviate from the flight line or heading in its horizontal plane. 2. Angle between the longitudinal axis of a projectile at any moment and the tangent to the trajectory in the corresponding point of flight of the projectile.

Z

Zero-length launching: A technique in which the first motion of the missile or aircraft removes it from the launcher.

Zero point: The location of the center of a burst of a nuclear weapon at the instant of detonation. The zero point may be in the air, or on or beneath the surface of land or water, depending upon the type of burst, and it is thus to be distinguished from ground zero.

Zone I (nuclear): A circular area determined by using minimum safe distance one as the radius and the desired ground zero as the center from which all armed forces are evacuated. If evacuation is not possible or if a commander elects a higher degree of risk, maximum protective measures will be required.

Zone II (nuclear): A circular area (less zone I) determined by using minimum safe distance II as the radius and the desired ground zero as the center in which all personnel require maximum protection. Maximum protection denotes that armed forces personnel are in "buttoned up" tanks or crouched in foxholes with improvised overhead shielding.

Zone III (nuclear): A circular area (less zones I and II) determined by using minimum safe distance III as the radius and the desired ground zero as the center in which all personnel require minimum protection. Minimum protection denotes that armed forces personnel are prone on open ground with all skin areas covered and with an overall thermal protection at least equal to that provided by a two-layer uniform.

Zone of action: A tactical subdivision of a larger area, the responsibility for which is assigned to a tactical unit; generally applied to offensive action.

Zone of fire: - An area into which a designated ground unit or fire support ship delivers, or is prepared to deliver, fire support. Fire may or may not be observed.